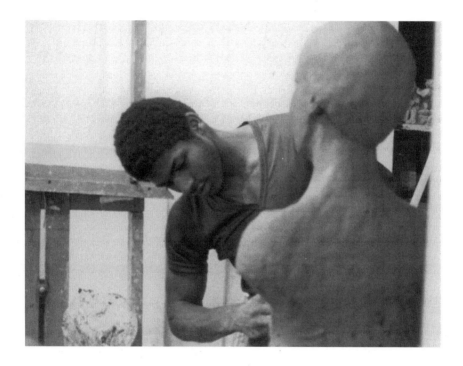

Frontispiece Joaquin worked for over ten years with art therapist Edith Kramer. Despite multiple handicaps, his evolving technical skills at self-portraiture point to the longevity potential of creative response activity.

Creative Response Activities for Children on the Spectrum

Creative Response Activities for Children on the Spectrum is a clear, comprehensive and intuitive guide that offers a wide selection of hands-on interventions to be used in any therapeutic or educational setting with children who are 'on the spectrum'. From drawing and writing poetry to skiing and skateboarding, this book describes these and many other creative activities geared towards children with autistic features, attention deficits, hyperactivity, paediatric bipolar disorder and other related conditions. This new resource provides an innovative blend of theory and illustrative case examples designed to help therapists and educators assess children's needs, formulate therapeutic and aesthetic interventions, and analyze creative outcomes.

David R. Henley, PhD, ATR, is a nationally recognized authority on child art therapy, a professor and the former chair of the creative arts therapy programs at the Art Institute of Chicago and Long Island University. He is the author of *Exceptional Children, Exceptional Art* and *Clayworks in Art Therapy*. During his career as an art therapist and educator, he has lectured, taught and written extensively on many aspects of art therapy. David is also a ceramicist and a mixed-media artist.

Creative Response Activities for Children on the Spectrum

A Therapeutic and Educational Memoir

David R. Henley

Routledge
Taylor & Francis Group
NEW YORK AND LONDON

First edition published 2018
by Routledge
711 Third Avenue, New York, NY 10017

and by Routledge
2 Park Square, Milton Park, Abingdon, Oxon, OX14 4RN

Routledge is an imprint of the Taylor & Francis Group, an informa business

Library of Congress Cataloging-in-Publication Data
Names: Henley, David (David R.), author.
Title: Creative response activities for children on the spectrum : a therapeutic
and educational memoir / David R. Henley.
Description: First edition. | New York, NY : Routledge, 2017.
| Includes bibliographical references.
Identifiers: LCCN 2017007044| ISBN 9781138686601 (hardcover : alk. paper)
| ISBN 9781138686618 (pbk. : alk. paper) | ISBN 9781315542621 (e-book)
Subjects: | MESH: Child Development Disorders, Pervasive--therapy
| Sensory Art Therapies | Personal Narratives
Classification: LCC RJ506.A9 | NLM WS 350.8.P4 | DDC 618.92/85882--
dc23LC record available at https://lccn.loc.gov/2017007044

ISBN: 978-1-138-68660-1 (hbk)
ISBN: 978-1-138-68661-8 (pbk)
ISBN: 978-1-315-54262-1 (ebk)

Typeset in Minion Pro
by Servis Filmsetting Ltd, Stockport, Cheshire

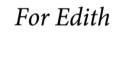

For Edith

Table of Contents

Acknowledgements

The author would like to thank first and foremost the parents of the children and the teens of age for consenting to write their stories and illustrate their many superb works of creativity. Their permission to publish images and text took great courage, and they have my deepest gratitude. My editors at Routledge should be commended for taking creative risks and allowing a work that departs from standard clinical formats.

I would like to acknowledge the work of my wife and collaborator, Dawn Henley, otherwise known by her students as 'Ms. Dawn'. Her ability to tame and elicit art from the wildest child was always magical to behold. To my son and 'action sports' provider, Kyle Henley, of PROGRESH, who in recent years has introduced me to new children and teens on the spectrum after my clinical years had ended. Without his outstanding work with many children with special needs, my case material would be woefully dated. To my daughter, Kimberly Henley Malito, whose professional and personal experiences with children on the spectrum have provided insights not otherwise possible to learn in the clinical setting. And to my grandchildren, Lia and Ronin Malito, whose artistic activities continue to teach me amazing lessons about child creative development.

To my teachers, of whom there were many, who are my heroes. Edith Kramer, to whom this book is dedicated, was a mentor, my toughest critic and dear friend. George Hecht, MD, supervisor and friend, who believed in me enough to become a primary therapist and whose premature loss is immeasurable. Roger Cardinal, tutor and friend, helped initiate me into the world of outsider art. David Jones, my ceramics instructor and sage mentor who taught me, among other things, to quit counting my pots. Judy Rubin, whose work led to my passion for working with deaf and blind children. Pearl Greenberg, who recognized I could never make it in a conventional classroom and assisted me in obtaining my first art therapy under-graduate clinical internship, when very few existed. Ellen Dissanayake, whose critical eye has improved my research and who remains a colleague and friend. Pat Allen, who helped me survive the initial culture shock of higher education and academia. Jim Pruznick, collaborator, who assisted me with the early medium of video performance. He documented our projects together for over thirty years. And to my indefatigable graduate assistants and senior counsellors, who often 'checked' my own work, especially Michele Amendolari, Carrin Honeycutt, Jee Hyun Kim, Shannon Pearce, Frances Smokowski and Stephen Dickens, all of whom have become superb professionals.

I

The Creative Response

Introduction

Why Creative Response Activities

The Journey into the Shaman's Cave

All of life's experiences are ephemeral; they are mostly fleeting memories unless preserved in some concrete or virtual form which captures the moment's resonance. Like the proverbial stone tossed into the pool, the expanding ripples reverberate into experiences that may otherwise be evanescent. Without 'fixing them in time and space' this energy eventually dissipates, losing its expansive power. Since time immemorial, humankind has responded to ephemerality by devising creative responses that attempt to record, reflect or commemorate experience through the arts and other activities. Thirty thousand years ago, shamans from the Aurignacian epoch crept deeply within the caves at Chauvet to draw and paint images of the animals with which they coexisted. Most of these monumental friezes focused on animals being hunted, and others seemed to magically ward off dangerous predators. Some subjects, however, appear created out of awe-inspiration, such as the two famous duelling woolly rhinoceroses, their enormous horns locked in a dramatic mating display. Others mix animal and human forms, a handprint which might enter the spirit to become one with the horse, the deer or the ox. What is most fantastic is how each image is drawn with an intrinsic understanding of the animal's behaviour, elegant and expressive, with lines and shading as masterful as any art in history. The artists, having crawled with great difficulty into the deepest recesses of the cave, must have imbued the drawings with magical, cultural and personal *weight*. The italicized term 'weight' alludes to the gravity of many of the works described in this volume—of how imperative they were. Shamanic paintings were not 'casual', but rather part of solemn rituals which were meant to ensure survival—the success of the hunt, feeding the clan, and protection from harm required beckoning the totem spirits.

In *The Mind in the Cave*, Lewis-Williams (2002) theorizes that the artists chosen for these cavernous journeys were probably atypical or somehow specialized tribal members. He muses that they perhaps not only possessed determination and artistic prowess, but were endowed with 'differentness', including altered states of consciousness which they harnessed to give powerful form to their creative responses. One of the last healing shamans, the revered Oglala

Sioux, Black Elk, described his own journey of being 'chosen' in childhood—when, during a prolonged fever, he was swept up and called upon to become an iconic healer (Neihardt, 1932, 2008). He experienced vividly realistic visions which elders prompted him to paint on his spirit shield—an expression of the fantastic, of being the chosen one. He reminds us that one seldom chooses to be 'different'. This is the analogy by which we start *this* journey—of the creative thoughts, actions and visions of those who are different. The works that will be illustrated and described portray creative responses of children whose own psyches are as much a burden as they are a sacred gift.

The metaphor of the cave may appear contrived or dramatic, but as the case material will bear out, the analogy is fitting. Many of the children described hole up or dwell in various inner states or lairs and the reasons vary: to feel comforted within their own world, to block out unwanted stimulation of our culture's constant avalanche of media, to work in secrecy or isolation to avoid judgement, or to commune with sensations or experiences unseen—which may be unfathomable to others. The children described are often beset by a world that is experienced with strangeness and intensity. Often, it is their otherworldly sensitivities that run contrary to established norms, placing them in conflict or out of place. Often, they are prompted into compliance by school, home or peers, leading to resistance and fight-or-flight reactions. Expressions may be reactions to these states of being—of seeing, hearing, feeling too much. Decoding what others want may become akin to learning a foreign language. Expressing sensations through alternative means often becomes a necessity, with drawing, writing, or the aesthetics of action or physical sport becoming their preferred means of communication. Being an artist and poet myself, and long suspected as displaying attention deficits, I am most comfortable with visual learning and expressing. I was once an athlete, and my body memories are as fresh as the first time I was on a wrestling mat or drawing a bow, with their choreographed movements an art form as much as any other.

Children on the spectrum have long captured my curiosity and fascination. They sparked an empathy and desire to assist them in their bid to creatively communicate the richness and struggles of their journeys. This book explores their expressions beyond those considered pathological and instead attempts to enter their world, on their terms. Creative activities hope to assist children to maximize their own gifts while coming to terms with this world and its demands. Engaging creativity gives form to dreams, fears, conflicts, anger or withdrawal, everything that comes with radical adjustment and change. Through their expressions, we may also be permitted a glimpse into another way of being and thus become richer for it.

The Scope of the Spectrum Child

Children on the spectrum, as described by Lorna Wing (1988), reflect Leo Kanner's (1943) early criteria of autistic disturbances of affective contact, which impairs social interaction and communication with stereotypical patterns of behaviour. Since Wing's research and experiences in the 1970s as a mother of a child with special needs, the spectrum has expanded beyond autism, to include children whose symptoms are more diverse. There is a range of children whose neurological makeup makes them hyperkinetic, manic, withdrawn, sensory deprived or vigilant, with attention differences as well as stereotypic behaviour. Being special also includes idiosyncratic giftedness, especially regarding technology or creativity. Most of these children are thus 'neuro-diverse', which is now described in a more normalizing tone as being members of their own 'neurotribe'—a kind of misunderstood culture which has long been a naturally occurring form of cognitive and emotional difference. Neurodiversity, or atypicality, as described by Silberman (2015) who views the spectrum children as a minority group, one that has been overly pathologized. He gives an encyclopaedic account of the condition, including the energetic political activism that now asserts full societal inclusion of these special individuals.

Jaarsma and Wellin (2012) maintain that spectrum disorders are not a single disease but a range of natural human variations that are not something to be cured. Those on the spectrum present as a 'curious form of human specificity' (pg. 23), involving alternative ways of socializing, communicating and taking in stimuli, —and that these differences should be accommodated. Yet unlike many cultural minorities which might be oppressed or marginalized, it cannot be overlooked that individuals on the spectrum have suffered brain-connectivity and synaptic dysfunction. When these 'wiring' problems interact with the demands of the environment, the result is often varied degrees of hyper- or hyposensory sensitivity, idiosyncratic beliefs and troubled emotions. Yet in returning to the analogy to the shaman, these individuals of such rare anomalies may contribute fresh, even visionary, expressions that enrich the often-dreary normality of mainstream culture. Hans Asperger, one of the heroes of recognizing the potential of these children, seconded this observation when he described the idea of 'autistic intelligence', that for success in art a necessary ingredient may be the ability to turn away from the everydayness to rethink a subject with originality and create in untrodden ways (Asperger, as cited in Silberman, 2015).

Broadening the Spectrum

Throughout my career as a creative arts therapist and educator, I have worked with hundreds of children who displayed shades of difference. Because of their variability, I have tried to avoid easy categorizations and diagnoses, preferring instead to conceive of the spectrum child as being on a broad curve. On this arc are those on the autism continuum, as well as children with varying combinations of hyperactivity, attention deficits, sensory integration problems, tics, mood disorders, and emotional and relational involvements. Baker and Steuernagel (2016) see each condition as a different narrative, where markers can be codified into meta-narratives, to the extent that they can even impact federal policies. This broader approach to neurodiversity explores the child's unique reactions to the environment, those behaviours and expressions that may be manifested in any number of atypical ways and combinations. Their narrative was one of the first to disregard the spectrum as some disease or wholly unacceptable condition but rather to see it as something fundamental to one's personhood.

The overarching issue of the spectrum is children's modulating hyper- or hypo-reactions to incoming sensory stimulation—as the onrush of confusing messages, demands and reactions constantly come at them. Delicato's *The Ultimate Stranger* (1974) was my introduction to understanding the sensory systems of children on the autistic end of the spectrum. Their task, as Delicato writes, is to 'modulate and filter', to resist over-reacting to what is perceived as intrusive stimulation. Discriminating as to which stimuli are relevant was the task facing a young Temple Grandin (1986). This self-described autistic and celebrity author wrote of her early life that learning to filter meaningful incoming stimuli was her greatest task. Anxiety reactions to noxious or difficult stimuli resulted in obsessive repetition. Perseverating with constant questioning became a means of self-soothing, and thus reassuring answers were received with comfort and pleasure—like any child hearing his favourite story read over and over. Obsessive questioning was also a means of decoding and adapting. By third grade the budding genius was already self-treating, envisioning a 'comfort machine'. This, she writes, would require crawling into a coffin-type space, in which she would then 'inflate the lining', thus applying a gentle embrace of proprioceptive pressure—the equivalent of the autistic hug (1986, pg. 34). Little did she know that this form of self-comforting would lead to her profession—of designing animal-handling systems which would provide the contact comfort when the animals were under duress. This system revolutionized the management of cattle and other animals with an empathic regard which had never occurred to professionals in the field. It took envisioning the problem from a fresh perspective, to approach non-verbal animals (and humans) with alternative means of regulating stimuli that were perceived as frightening or incomprehensible—an obvious metaphor analogous to her own way of being.

There are social implications when attempts to read the seemingly inexplicable emotions or intentions of others that may be utterly confusing. For Grandin, the nuances of communication were difficult to absorb, resulting in having to be defended. Trying to 'let go' of off-kilter responses, of faux pas, even after the interaction was long forgotten by the other, resulted in rumination. For many individuals along this arc, inner thoughts become a constant loop, as obsession becomes a critical defence and means of compensation. Without their fragile defences, I have observed many children resorting to withdrawing into their inner worlds. Some become 'refuseniks' when disturbed—meaning *everything* offered by parents or teachers may be distrusted or outright rejected. Other reactions to stimuli may include approach/avoidance conflicts—where engaging a person or activity is perceived as meaningless, strange or even a dangerous undertaking. The child attempts to decode and assess the dangers inherent in even the ministrations of well-meaning others. Yet the challenge also comes with unique positives. The creative responses explored vividly illustrate a worldview that is radically different than the norm—one that may be beguiling and deserving of dignity and respect. While these children's paths are often painful and difficult, contemporary culture has finally raised an awareness of emotional, learning and 'being' differences, with increased tolerance and inclusiveness for what these individuals endure and can create (Grandin & Panek, 2013).

The Creative Response

This is where the creative response activity enters the equation—that whatever is felt or perceived can become a fuel for creativity, regardless of how unfocused, hyperactive or even delusional the behaviour. With the provision of a secure maternal and familial base, therapeutic support and creative outlets can reframe a child's deficits to translate them into positives. Arousal levels, intrusive thoughts or difficulty with personal interrelations can all be creatively transformed into expressions, which Kramer (1971) has termed 'symbolic equivalents'. She has written that the process of creative exploration is seen as being intrinsically therapeutic. Because demands for behavioural and social compliance pose as constant stressors for many children, creative outlets remain a conduit for self-expression, where there is no wrong answer. While creative endeavour also requires much fortitude and mindfulness, children often succeed when they find their *own* interests on *their* terms—not just as a defence or escape. Creative work becomes a basis for expansion, a point of departure where the creative response enhances social, relational and functional problem solving. Idiosyncratic artistic, athletic or recreational activity becomes a kind of rebuttal to the so-called norm—a reshuffling of the narrative that meets the child's needs regardless of societal expectation. To have a taste of acceptance, along with creative freedom, has lasting emotional and intellectual effects. I have met and worked with many individuals who are on the spectrum, some of whom are now young adults, with three of them still corresponding with me after twenty years. There is a consensus that their formative experiences of searching out their creative selves still resonate deeply within them—paving the way for achievements that are remarkable considering their struggles.

The Spectrum Range

Spectrum issues are commonly first encountered during childhood, blossoming further through latency and early adolescence. Increasingly, one may also encounter individuals who have adapted sufficiently during adolescence to utilize their often-latent intelligence at university level. With early intervention initiatives has come greater access to support services, such as psychotherapy, behaviour training and socialization programs, leading to more young people on the spectrum being college bound. These young people are often identifiable despite their identities being confidential. It has been fascinating to witness how their issues were muted, given years of behavioural therapy and psychotherapy. Many displayed the mildest of symptoms until encountering obstacles that are typical among those on the spectrum: issues with social interactions, difficulties with low-reward activities, and chronic time management and organizational problems. Many who were behaviourally trained by rote or conditioned found it difficult to think critically and assimilate ideas which did not require a concrete 'correct answer'. In my classes on the creative arts, many struggled to build an argument—of why something is felt or thought. Beyond my at-risk university freshmen, some individuals on the spectrum also began applying to the undergraduate programs in fine arts and clinical art therapy training programs, both of which I have directed in Chicago and New York. Individuals were sometimes referred to as 'wounded healers', as individuals may gravitate to the helping professions to assist others. Personal experiences with trauma, spectrum issues or other challenges could be reframed and lent to others with great empathy.

While young people of all ages on the spectrum have shared commonalities, almost all of them have far-ranging differences in their capacity to adapt and function. Though the issues may be similar, the source of their spectrum issues can unexpectedly be linked to any number of causations or aetiologies: genetic predispositions, being prenatally exposed to infections or viruses, being relationally deprived and neglected, or possessing a neurochemical imbalance. Many remain anonymously or idiopathically on the spectrum. The conditions remain a mystery—that countless neurochemical, genetic or environmental factors intermingle, to present with identical diagnoses—a fact that is simply astounding. It is perhaps a lesson to move beyond nature/nurture multiple causations and deal phenomenologically with the person in front of us.

The Artist Self-Absorbed

One such individual, shown on the frontispiece, is Joaquin, a young man who is intensely working alone in the studio. He was treated for over a decade by the pioneering art therapist, Edith Kramer, to whom this book is dedicated. She began working with Joaquin during his tumultuous childhood when he was at times uncontrollable. Joaquin dealt with multiple, devastating markers—a degenerating visual impairment; autistic-like and hyperactive behaviours; and intense, sometimes uncontrollable, anger. His home life was complicated by parental abandonment and socio-economic deprivation of being raised in a dangerous inner city neighbourhood. This full complement of aggravating and complicating factors yielded a child with a feeling of isolation and sensory fragmentation. Despite his challenges, his decade of claywork therapy assisted him in his journey of integration and transformation. Beginning as a child making crude figures, over the course of eight more years he excelled as a sculptor. As he matured and received Kramer's technical assistance his work became increasingly realistic, with greater complexity and scale. As the frontispiece attests, he was finally able to sculpt life-size ceramic figurative sculptures, many of which were evocative self-portraits. These works were always done in Kramer's presence, as she provided the needed technical support, but more importantly, the nurturance. When pieces cracked, facial features became distorted, or the figure's identity became confused, she was there for him as an important ally.

Joaquin struggled with a barrage of symptoms, with severe fixations, perceptual difficulty and relational communication problems. He had difficulty describing emotions beyond anger, perhaps due to 'blindisms', which are akin to autistic behaviours. His art became a substitutive form of communication, his preferred *lingua franca*. As a compensation for verbal disarticulation, feeling states, ideas and perceptions were conveyed almost completely through his art. Articulating ineffable sensory and emotional states, Joaquin concretized these abstractions so that they became almost 'real', through their ever-enlarging forms and personalized content. As people took notice of his achievements, Joaquin was eventually able to bridge the divide between his isolative, distrusting self to eventually accept and appreciate the positive recognition. Unlike many on the autistic end of the spectrum, Joaquin used his art to connect with others, as he sought to *join* the people around him—something which set him apart from those with autistic markers. While setbacks were frequent and came as storms of anger and frustration, his passion to create often overcame these obstacles. As the next seventy-plus cases will bear out, these contradictory 'mixed states' are all part of this spectrum child's profile. Positive outcomes are *expected* to coincide with negatives.

Why Creative Responses

The following case examples provide a resounding 'why' of the importance of 'creative response activities'. For those on different shades of the spectrum, the creative arts became a critical outlet and preferred personal voice—one that is critical for meaningful self-expression and communication with the outer world. The common ground was finding a means to bypass a dependence on verbal expression with others and to directly translate their perceptions through visual or other sensorial means. Created among approving others, a dialogue begins—even if it is one way. Such is the creative potential of nonverbal expression that provides an alternative, equalizing force of communication.

Visual dialoguing is not unusual for those on the arc of the spectrum. Temple Grandin famously declared that from an early age she also 'thought in pictures'. In a world where jumbles of words mix with white noise ambient sounds, her mind was like an 'open microphone', the intensity of which led to constant problems of decoding and sensory overloads. Being neurologically wired in this way required high-level compensations. Grandin constantly translated the world's cacophony into what she terms inner-formed 'technicolor movies' (Grandin & Panek, 2013). These defences were a means of early survival, though eventually her powers of visualization evolved as creative compensations. She translated her sensations and relations, particularly with animals who were therapeutic surrogates, into forms of scientific and humanistic expression. While not every child on the spectrum explored in this book possesses Grandin's autistic-savant capacities, there are many examples where creativity is transformative.

Lorna Wing also posited the all-important why of creative response activity. Though a cognitivist and curiously uninterested in the creative potential of these children, Wing wrote that when children on the spectrum have alternative means of expression they become 'unencumbered', without having to exclusively focus on verbal means of expression. Without the typical cognitive clutter which many 'typicals' endure, Wing (1988) writes that the unfettered and direct communication of those on the spectrum can be surprisingly fresh and inventive. Bypassing conventional language, life experiences can be processed via alternative senses. Visual art, music, reading, kinaesthetic movement and computer-facilitated communication may be modalities preferred to the spoken word. I believe creative writing to be essential too, even though most of the children I have worked with often avoid the written word. Yet many illustrations are full of text, word or thought balloons that articulate their expressions. With ever more sophisticated technology, integrated with therapeutic assistance, digital means may facilitate communication. While tapping out text bypasses the need for face-to-face relating, it becomes a critical link to the outside. As with many typical individuals who now prefer to text or email, written communication remains a vital, expressive technique. Writing and reading as a creative response allows time for reflection as opposed to reactive responses. It allows one to *compose* one's thoughts, which then may add to their own 'composure'. Combined with imagery, the child has a potent tool to reach out to a world which may otherwise be overwhelmingly anxiety provoking.

The Vicissitudes of Seeing *Batman Returns*

The spectrum child often struggles to overcome the hyper-arousal that comes with everyday incoming stimuli. Decoding and assimilating stimuli require effective filtering—the process by which these children could defend against and eventually desensitize themselves to different sensations. While a stimulus may be repellent to a child, this same stimulus may also hold a powerful 'attraction'. Such contradictory responses are common in typical individuals as well, as a roller coaster or horror house may be terrifying yet attract crowds of enthusiastic participants. The difference for the child on the spectrum is that *every* house may be filled with untold horrors; any ride may be a plunge into oblivion. Hyper-arousal or -sensitivity, as Grandin stated, becomes a fact of everyday life with which to be reckoned.

For a thirteen-year-old Filipino boy, Evan, filtering was a constant struggle. Despite being bright and personable, his hyper-sensitivity and obsessiveness placed him on the autistic end of the spectrum continuum. It prohibited him from enjoying his most passionate interest—to go to the movies. Enabling Evan to better handle such activities fell to me and another art therapy graduate intern, Frances Smokowski, to work with him to achieve social parity. With this co-therapist arrangement, Evan was fortunate to have a 'mother-and-father' duo which formed a productive balance of personas. The initial task was to prepare him to see the latest Batman film. He was socially aware enough to realize that every seventh-grader considered it a 'must see', yet to break this new ground required months of therapeutic support. We assessed that if he could handle the film's supersonic onrush of stimulation, he would acclimate to almost any sensory experience. After successfully sitting through the whole film, he later lectured us about how Batman was a 'master of detection, a superhero that protects the powerless populace'—qualities that contrasted with his own fragile sense of self, but to which he aspired.

For most children, seeing a blockbuster film like *Batman Returns* should have simply been an exciting experience. Every one of his peers probably took pleasure escaping into the fantastic powers of this iconic superhero and his extraordinary redoubt, the Batcave. Yet for this child on the spectrum, the film presented a significant emotional risk. The gravity and the stimulation overload of the experience perhaps carried an emotional weight, analogous, we might surmise, to that of a shamanic journey. Both had braved the blackness of the cave to illuminate a sacred symbol. Jung considered the cave to be a powerful archetype, with multiple symbolism that is hardwired in our collective unconsciousness through eons of human evolution (Biederman et al., 1997). Such an experience might not have been too far removed from the shamanic 'films' put on by the cave painters who utilized the formations of rock to project their figures into space. By oil lamp, the animals would flicker, thus animating them with 'special effects'. For Evan, this experience was also a journey to which he later gave creative form.

On Taking Nothing for Granted

To enter the darkened theatre, this child required careful preparation to anticipate dealing with the crowds, of having to queue up amongst the jostling and equally excited moviegoers. It also meant tolerating the stress over finding the 'right' seat. Late entry allowed Evan to avoid much of the crowd commotion, but it would then be impossible to find a seat which gave him enough personal space, or what Hall termed 'proxemics' (as cited in Moore, Hickson, & Stacks, 2009). Public proxemics are a central, sensitive issue for many spectrum children (Altman, 1975). Seating is serious business for many. For Evan, it also entailed choosing an aisle seat for quick getaways and being isolated. His parents also adapted the experience by bringing him on a weekday to minimize long queues and boisterous crowds.

When the film finally begins, the tidal wave of stimulation comes—the blazing colour and sound, with the system's thunderous subwoofer bass being particularly bothersome. The child reported feeling its vibrations in his *chest*. It may have been so intense that the everydayness of the suburban screen might have rivalled anything imagined in the darkness, echoes and other sensations of a Palaeolithic cave. That Batman himself dwells in a cave, which coincides with the blackness of the theatre setting, is a double dose of stimuli. Once Bruce Wayne shape-shifts into his alter ego, he propels like a rocket into the city via a fantastic Batmobile. His body is no longer of the 'every day' but is encased like a seal in smooth, black rubber. The transformation is complete—we are in the 'other world'.

The Creative Response

During the post-film therapy session, Evan immediately began a response drawing, though the image was hardly a typical child's recap of the plot with the usual

Figure I.1 In response to Tim Burton's film *Batman Returns* (1992), Evan recounts his harrowing journey into the darkened cave of the supernatural. He focused most, however, on the theatre's facilities, accommodations and safety features.

superhero and action sequences. Instead, the narrative began by mapping out the 'essentials'—which were the challenges presented by the environment. Figure I.1 displays what Kramer terms a 'pictograph', with an inventory of critical images and text; particularly drawn are the theatre itself and the proxemics of the projectionist, carefully noting each emergency exit, the fire extinguishers and the gender-specific restrooms.

More schematically rendered are the stick-figure crowds, stacked in rows, which he reported 'stunk of popcorn', indicative of his olfactory sensitivities. Each skilfully drawn element is given a thoughtful compositional consideration. Each element must carefully be put into place before the goal of enjoying the film and his iconic hero could be enjoyed and symbolized. The emphasis on reiterating his quest for a secure environment perhaps helped lower Evan's threshold of discomfort enough that he could begin to enjoy his activity. Once the environment was rendered, he relaxed enough to draw the crowning element: the illuminated 'Batman Needed!' logo, projected upon the night skies of Gotham.

Handling Batman was to Evan not just an enjoyable creative activity; it was perhaps analogous to a shaman's journey: a personal and social *imperative*. Every life experience for children on the spectrum is a journey into the unsuspecting unknown. The need for pre-screening preparation—of describing the 'things that will happen' and the processing which occurs during the post-creative response activity go together. Assisting these children in handling each life experience also requires an enlightened public and community. Currently, many museum, movie and drama theatres now set aside special 'low-stimulation' days for children with spectrum issues. Growing awareness of these special needs promises a more fully inclusive future and cultural awareness for these individuals. While not every child is able to respond with such richness and elaboration, this book describes many children's attempts at venturing out into a hyper-stimulating, threatening and unpredictable world. Like the shaman, they take emotional risks to enter what Winnicott (1971) termed 'transitional space'.

Creative Responses in 'Transitional Space'

Aside from dealing with personal distance and proxemics, during the Batman film, Evan entered a different kind of space, a psychic space where reality was blended with fantasy. For the sensitive spectrum child, this space was full of what Winnicott (1971) termed 'potential space', where one enters an alternative world in which he is aroused, flabbergasted, terrified and even nauseated. Leaving the realm of home and comfort required a courageous leap into this unknown, intermediary space somewhere between the realm of the magical and everyday reality. Engaging both faculties within Winnicott's 'space in-between', references cohabitation within both inner and outer reality, which we 'typical' individuals may experience on any occasion. Within the realm of everydayness, we may recount a vivid dream, become enraptured at a concert or lose ourselves gazing at the night skies during a meteor shower—all normative, enriching experiences. For Evan, it meant becoming transported to another world—one that had intense emotional weight. Winnicott envisioned transitional space as a kind of 'controlled regression', a surrendering of our everyday defences to a state of openness to the possibilities of something magical. Artists routinely lose themselves when creating, hence the constant stories of their working through long, exhaustive periods lost in time, hyper-focused without rest or other daily needs.

Winnicott also considered transitional space as a portal to the creative self, a zone of potential transformation. For Evan, the entire film transported him (and back) from the fantastic. While we remain consciously rooted in reality, such imaginary excursions are what enrich life beyond the doldrums of the everyday. For many children on the spectrum, such as Evan, handling a powerful archetype required him to suspend belief in the real and 'dip' into the world of magic—and then return to gripping reality. Like any shamanic experience, one begins the journey of entering the darkness of his respective theatres with guidance and support. For the shaman, it may have been an animal totem or a clan ritual—for the spectrum child, it required the empathy and skill of experienced therapists. Creativity requires some shift into the maelstrom of what was once termed Freud's 'primary process' and now is termed 'primordial feelings' by Damasio (2010). For the experience to be transformative and creative, one's ego must re-emerge from the magical intact and not succumb to regression into more primitive states. Winnicott proposes that if the ego is well supported and fortified, we can temporarily dwell in the imaginal realm and re-emerge from whatever cave with a strengthened sense of self.

With a successful regression for clients, such as occurred in the cases of Joaquin and Evan, may come the strengthening of ego, with increased self-awareness to objectify and reflect upon their journeys, using the language of creativity. In many instances, the clients' expressions had the sense of being somewhat foreign, requiring that we try our best to 'translate' them, which Sacks (1995) wrote was akin to being 'An Anthropologist on Mars'. One requires accommodating an ontological shift away from the everyday, to attempt to reframe meaning and being. Such reframing requires an openness and receptivity beyond our own well-aligned frameworks towards those that glimpse at new paradigms and therapeutic prospects. One may witness movement from the client's being resistant or terrified of change to embracing his explorations, to even finding humour in his experience, after having reflected upon his journeys.

In fact, many of the children described throughout this book managed, in their response activities, not just to struggle, but to find their own brand of absurdist humour. Evan's oeuvre demonstrated how two years of work with Smokowski enabled him to habituate more often to his outer world, which evolved to ever more sophisticated levels. For instance, in one quirky drawing, his wry sense of social commentary is evident in his making a riff on the commercial promoting 'superglue'. As many on the autistic end of the spectrum may focus on commercial media, such as advertisements and jingles, content may further be elaborated via a creative response. The ad in question features a construction worker demonstrating the strength of superglue by adhering himself to an I-beam (Figure I.2). He is shown dangling perilously, all goggle-eyed and kicking away.

The work is again contradictory—while it is perhaps a work of tongue in cheek, it may simultaneously indicate trouble suspending belief. Such an occurrence of being glued to an I-beam might possibly occur ... why not? Thus, the double-edged image carries unusual sensory, emotional and cognitive weight. To assure us of what we are witnessing, Evan added text to the drawing, proclaiming 'AS SEEN ON TV'. Perhaps Evan, as many of the children in this book, attempted to distance himself from the stimulus. Writing a caption may reassure us, as well as himself, that it was not 'he' who could become glued, that he had come up with such an absurdity—it's our culture, stupid! The drawing's multilayered meanings may also indicate that our media have become a theatre of the absurd.

Evan also adds at the bottom how it is all 'OUT OF SERVICE | OUT OF ORDER'—an apt observation! Perhaps, this text reminds us of the fragility of a world that could easily become unhinged—that nothing again can be taken for granted—not a movie theatre, not a commercial—that countless things in this world remain inexplicably possible. One must remain vigilant. It points to the tenuousness of spectrum children's existence in this odd world while absorbing and neutralizing 'reality' to the best of their abilities. Again, this is most often a slow, difficult process, with halting, erratic increments. For those on the spectrum, these phenomena are

Figure I.2 Two years later, Evan created a visual pun, with a construction worker being superglued to an I-beam. Appropriating media is not unusual for those on the spectrum.

never taken lightly. Transitional space as explored in Smokowski's master's thesis (1993) alludes to a path to creativity and growth. Assisted by his art therapist as an auxiliary ego, he was helped in his own ego function to separate what is relevant, and thus he could thin the detritus of our culture—much of which should be laughed off if it weren't so pathetic. In this case, the process came by way of a pithy drawing.

In the following narratives, I hope to convey the insights and teachings which so many children have afforded me over thirty years of devotion to their creative endeavours: that to enter a cave of darkness where the journey may be long and frightful may eventually lead to the light at the end of the tunnel. It is up to us, as educators, therapists, parents and the community at large, to recognize each strength, whether it be just an inkling of interest or the oddest of passions, and expand it until creative response activities become integral to the child's life—in whatever form they may take. This process begins by providing the child with a therapeutic presence and companion, where a stimulating environment of psychological safety may encourage the taking of creative risks based upon trust and empathy. I have experienced this process personally. The following account, along with other formative experiences, sets the stage for the next thirty years of intensive clinical and educational work—based upon first-hand experience.

One

Beginnings

The Therapeutic Companion and Stolen Tongue Depressors

I began as a patient and an artist, identities which persist to this day. At seventeen, while a freshman art student, I was struck down with the autoimmune disorder Guillain-Barré syndrome, which took a year from me and ravaged my body into total quadriplegia. During the time I spent in recovery at a rehab centre, I was just another patient, one among a hundred other children as young as two: those with broken necks from diving accidents, hydrocephalics, those with spina bifida, brain-damaged car-crash victims and those afflicted with other terrifying conditions. As a former wrestler, losing my hard-won musculature was a blow— one moment breaking into the varsity team as a college freshman and the next unable even to close my eyelids. Then, there was the complete atrophy—I felt like I was slowly being erased. My mind was pumped with poisonous, but lifesaving, steroids. From the daily injections of cortisone came the hallucinations of seeing waltzing cats on the ceiling or a wall thick with butterflies, their wings slowly flapping, open then closed, open then closed—almost ceaselessly. I dared not say a word to anyone, assuming they were lysergic acid flashbacks from the psychedelic years. These visitations with psychosis were to prove useful in the years to come as a means of empathizing with others who involuntarily suffered or dwelled in radically alternative realities. In the hospital there were children all around me much worse off, but I didn't care. I laid there with marked indifference, watching the walls, refusing any therapy.

Roused from Self-Pity

After a month of sulking and fuming, an irritatingly upbeat, very British activity therapist entered my room and declared 'enough is enough'. She was reed thin, fashionable and fit, with a mischievous smile and spiky grey hair. She announced that not only was I going to participate, but I was to be her assistant. 'Assistant! I am a lifeless lump. What am I going to assist?' 'No matter', she said as she whisked me away through the halls, humming brightly, annoyingly so. I was finally wheeled to a stop and parked next to the bed of a quiet eleven-year-old boy named Christian, who tragically had collapsed on the soccer field with a brain lesion that left him paraplegic for life. He regarded me with undisguised disdain: 'You can't move nothin'', he said. 'So?' I shot back. Then I countered: 'I'm an artist though, and you're gluing together tongue depressors stolen from the nurse's station. Maybe I can help'. 'Hmm, stolen? That's cool', he said as he began gluing them end to end in a zigzag form, which finally grew too long for his lap table. I said, almost to myself, 'Maybe start a new one', which surprisingly he did.

He made a total of three, and as they laid flat, the glue drying, we just stared at them in silence, wondering what to do next with three wacky lines of wood. I then suggested, 'Maybe they could stand up'. He asked, 'How could they do that?' and I answered, 'Perhaps Ms. Activity Therapist there can mix some plaster, and we can stick them in something to support them'. She was, of course, closely monitoring our discussion, and before we realized, she had glided over and began mixing a batch of plaster of Paris. She said in a mockingly stern voice, 'You'll have very little time to decide how to form them up, so start planning now, you two!' So we thought, and I sat there, being useless, but studying the design problem. Finally, Christian exclaimed, 'Let's make a pyramid!' I agreed: 'A tripod might work'. He exclaimed, 'We'll stand them up and bring them together to a point!' I now was also excited: 'When she brings over the plaster, stick them in and have her tie them together at the top'.

What she brought, gliding stylishly in waiter style, was a pie tin full of the creamiest batch of plaster I have ever seen. It seemed almost edible. Christian had to move quickly, carefully positioning each 'leg' in a three-point stance. Then, upon his command, she deftly tied the intersecting apex with some yarn. We then waited for a seeming eternity for the plaster to harden. Ten minutes later, she ceremoniously removed the yarn, and out of the greased tin came, voilà, a wobbly, freestanding sculpture. Three rickety legs converged together, firmly grounded but swaying slightly, clacking together at their top point. 'They're standing up so tall', he marvelled. To us 'bed bounders' they did seem *towering ... everything did*. Sheepishly, we both smiled. 'A fine sculpture', I pronounced. Christian looked down and mumbled, 'You helped'. 'Me? I can't even move!' He regarded me with just the hint of a smirky smile. Again ... it was the 'glue' that bound us together.

Reanimated

Though I preferred to ply the depths of self-pity and helplessness, I had finally awakened and was even animated. This expert therapist had manoeuvred, stimulated and finally empowered me so that my art-school sensibility had finally kicked in. I unwittingly became a therapeutic presence and companion, one who was obviously of little physical help, but someone who had contributed enough to the process to form an uneasy, yet working, partnership. We were collaborators, creating an art object that 'stood tall', which neither of us obviously could. Looking back, the metaphor would be so transparent to anyone that it would qualify as cliché. But at the time, it escaped us both. After all, we were patients, just children still in trauma, but the metaphor operated unconsciously. My own spirits began to brighten enough to follow her yet more days and become more involved as I slowly, painfully regained the use of my arms and hands. The nursing staff recognized the change immediately—the depression lifted some, and I was more cooperative. I had refound myself, through her effective, sophisticated intervention. Years later, that experience prompted me to write a commemorative poem about her. To this day, I have never again felt the power of being a therapeutic companion as much as I did then. My presence had helped facilitate a lovely, creative response, with this shrewd therapist invisibly setting the stage and pulling the strings.

Rejoining the Zeitgeist of the 1960s

After a year of inpatient rehab, my nerve synapses finally began to fire again—enough so that I could begin to move. Now at home, I was no longer situated in a protective hospital, but became just a fragile being, whose psyche was not prepared to deal with life 'outside' my hospital bed. To allay my anxieties, I worked out almost compulsively, with physical therapy that began by trying to smile, flicker my eyelids and crush a paper cup. Nine months later, I had regained enough function to return to art school. Though still partially paralyzed, as I would be for life, and traumatized by the experience, I was determined to resume my work as an artist and aspiring art educator. I found myself amongst many young 'artistes' and New York–based professors coming out of the 1960s and early 1970s zeitgeist.

Given my own curious condition, I was drawn to working with other unusual persons, especially those who were also damaged and functioning outside the norm. In fact, 'normality' as a cultural and psychic construct was out of vogue in 1970. I found that my own weakened movements, which culminated in artworks produced on the most minute scale, were accepted as sufficiently odd that they were considered fashionably 'neuro-diverse'. My portfolio included paintings that were created using a pen taped to my mouth. For a year, I had 'pecked' and 'head daubed' away; few of my peers could match the odd-shaped pointillistic marks made by a semi-paralyzed mouth. One memorable professor intoned, 'No great art can arise from the norm'—a stance I heartily embraced. I revelled in the great heroes, including Blake, Goya, van Gogh, Lautrec and, most importantly, Frida Kahlo, with whom I still most closely identify; each suffered in his or her brand of condition marked by brilliance.

I had many other pioneering influences who continued to guide my path towards making creative response activities with other 'atypical' individuals, whose raw and untutored imagery struck a chord. It was a watershed time when art and creativity were in flux. Artist Jean Dubuffet was one of many pushing the limits of modern art, channelling the raw and untutored art of children, the mentally ill and other eccentrics working outside traditional artistic style. This stylistic influence may be seen in Figure 1.1, where I have placed two lively, scribbly images side by side. Which is the child's and which the professional's?

Figure 1.1 The reader is invited to decide which figure is the work of the professional modernist, J. Dubuffet, and a child with multiple spectrum involvements. Their 'outsider art' styles are strikingly similar.
Used with permission of Fondation Dubuffet and Artists Rights Society.

Their styles are almost identical, though their 'intentionality' may differ, with each coming from a vastly different mind-set. Unlike the professional Dubuffet, whose work is self-consciously 'primitive', the child with special needs is not influenced by anyone. Locked in his autism, he worked in isolation creating images from another world. This is the crux of art brut, or the 'outsider art', conundrum. The term *outsider art* was coined by my mentor, art critic Roger Cardinal (1972, 2004), and described in his lyric prose, "the outsider's rawness and energy coexisting with" a marked disinterest in conveying meaning for the viewer's benefit.

Along with the influence of Dubuffet and Cardinal's outsider art came a watershed exhibit at the Museum of Modern Art of the photographs of Diane Arbus (1972), a show opened to great fanfare soon after she took her life. In this influential collection, I was most struck by her also being drawn to those living on the margins—which critics consider central to her own alienation and depression. Her last works, titled the 'untitled collection 1-7' (1970–1971), centred upon portraits of intellectually handicapped people with Down syndrome, with the patients dressed up for Halloween, no less. These people were not unlike those where I was to begin my own career. The concept of 'total immersion', of cohabiting with individuals with severe involvements, was exemplified by Arbus's formally beautiful, yet unflinching, portraits. Yet she poses an aesthetic/ethical problem for us, as to her intent: the aesthetic power of her work is based upon the exploitation of her subjects. By exploring the borders of mental difference and venturing into these hitherto forbidden places, she became a celebrity artist. From my standpoint, being a 'helper' first and foremost, then an aesthete, hopefully mitigates the passion I bring to my subjects—one that sometimes borders on hyperbole. In any event, Arbus eventually became lost in her demons. Perhaps these late works, with their polarizing issues, formed symbolic equivalents to her own creative and mental demise.

This was also the time avant-garde filmmaker Francois Truffaut starred in and directed the film *The Wild Child* (1970) about the eighteenth-century case of treating a feral child who roamed the forests of France. The story shed renewed light on the nature/nurture debate and progressive education that dated back to the Enlightenment. In his anti-psychology stance, R. D. Laing (1965) was challenging the concept of insanity itself, positioning it as an alternative form of normality while Alan Watts was confusing Western psychoanalysts by applying the principles of Zen Buddhism (1961). Frederick Wiseman (1967) had released his extraordinary documentary of film vérité, shot and unedited within an insane asylum, depicting an unflinching account of the patients' lives. Reality itself was questioned by the enigmatic Carlos Castaneda (1968), who explored the possibility of 'brujos' and their induced, altered states while neurologist Oliver Sacks (2012) experimented with psychedelic mind expansion. He later applied these experiences to insights into the role hallucination plays within the art process. In child psychoanalysis, D. W. Winnicott had just published *Playing and Reality* (1971) and expanded upon the crucial concept of 'transitional space', previously described as a potential portal to the creative unconscious. Collaborators Dr. Anni Bergman and art therapy pioneer Edith Kramer were breaking new ground in the emerging field of treating disturbed and autistic children. Their joint therapeutic effort lasted for almost twenty years—a case that remains the standard of object relations analysis with a child with classic autistic features (Bergmann, 1999).

Into the Asylum

In my own formative and naive way, I sought to become part of this burgeoning psychological aesthetic and counterculture. In 1972, I convinced my mentor and pioneering art educator, Dr. Pearl Greenberg, to permit me to intern in the relatively new field of 'creative arts therapy'. I was to work with long-term psychiatric patients who were hospitalized, not so much from diagnosed conditions,—but seemingly from old-fashioned insanity and sheer madness. It was a world in which Arbus would have found the grail, as I witnessed and made art with those of tormented visions, inner voices and memories, which often gained graphic form in their unique personas and artistic creations. I found myself entering through the basement of this old 'madhouse', whose enormous blackened stones hailed from the Civil War era. Using the six-inch skeleton keys I was issued, which still fit into the ancient iron locks, was like travelling back in time. It was also an era when many patients were hospitalized for years, even decades. The homeless were admitted to sleep in the cellars. I was told by others that their presence was not even official. They existed in Winnicott's 'space-in-between', moving about in the shadows in the bleak, stone-walled basement with seemingly no supervision.

While I was in residency came the sensational account of the institution called *Willowbrook*. In 1972, a young, unknown New York investigative reporter named Geraldo Rivera and his videographer stole a key and infiltrated the horrific institution and filmed its forlorned inhabitants. Rivera's 'guerrilla' form of investigative reporting singlehandedly created a new genre of journalism. Almost overnight, the scandal led the New York state legislature to pass laws that ushered in the still-existing standard of 'deinstitutionalization' and community mental health care. It was, again, a time when patients were still vividly insane, ranting, hallucinating, and even posing hand in cloak, à la Napoleon. With few receiving modern psychotropic medications and their dulling side effects, these patients' illnesses were still startlingly unadulterated. Thus, I could experience mental health treatment still frozen in time, but just prior to an era when psychiatry would soon change forever.

On Romanticizing

It was and still is difficult not to become swept up in the romanticism of that time and place, as the cultural shifts of the 1960s were remaking the future, just as the Enlightenment, Belle Epoch and hedonism of the Weimar had before, each era rehashing the ideas and concepts from those earlier generations. Though fascinated by the 'tortured artist' paradigm in which creativity and madness are inextricably linked, I tried not to embrace foolishly its self-destructive aspects—as many of our cultural heroes had perished so prematurely (MacGregor, 1992). Kay Redfield Jamison, a brilliant, self-proclaimed manic, wrote *Touched with Fire* (1993), describing many other figures of the Romantic era—Goya, Lord Byron, Coleridge and Shelley, all of whom would die for their art. Lao Tzu wrote eons ago that the 'flame that burns twice burns half as long', which held true, though at a cost of lives being so dramatically short. In her biography, Jamison takes great pains to temper the Romantic notion of mania as a creative panacea. I have personally dealt with mania in my own family, which sobered my perspective of the artist's 'burning-out brightly' syndrome. Also, having suffered my own near death experience while I was becoming increasingly paralyzed, a certain pragmatism held my impulses in check—that one can stand in awe, but not pay the ultimate sacrifice just for one's art. Writing up these case studies for some thirty years still has me grappling with the 'Arbus conundrum'. Again, I am writing about those who are the most vulnerable, pointing out deficits, symptoms, even disturbed behaviour. In some instances, fictionalizing the cases is essential to maintaining anonymity. In other cases, the parents who gave consent considered their children's stories as a form of advocacy and not exploitation.

Two

First Clients and Creative Outcomes

On the Complexity of Gaining Trust

After a month of acclimating as a new art therapy intern, I had gained sufficient poise and nerve to accept my first client. I preserved my early process notations and eventually reworked them into a series of clinical poems. The protocol of the notations required that I include pertinent dialogue which brought to life the nuances of this formative and unforgettable journey. Wordsworth wrote in 'My Heart Leaps Up' (1901) that 'the child is the father of the man', an idiom which can be interpreted as meaning that the earliest childhood formative experiences are later re-enacted by the adult, or 'father'. In adults who are greatly disturbed, childhood traumas may be simmering just below the conscious psyche where early trauma may be awakened by an event. Such was the situation with my first case, a man named Bexley, who, as a twenty-year-old pilot, went to war and then met his enemy face-to-face … a German fighter pilot even younger than himself. During WWII, the air corps were the last vestige of fighting chivalry—a sensibility long lost by infantry slogging through the battlefield. There was still a *code,* which for the most part was followed by their airmen. Bexley's memories of the younger pilot would come vividly and hauntingly out of the past when I engaged in my first attempt at facilitating a creative response activity.

Bexley was then a long-term psychiatric patient in his fifties who had served during the waning days of WWII. Slight but still wiry, his British-inflected speech, sharp good looks and thin moustache gave him an air of the once young and dashing aviator. I soon realized he seemed frozen in time within this persona. I later learned that Bexley never recovered from wartime, suffering psychotic bouts of delusion—what were then termed 'shell shock'. During one session, we worked together on what I thought was a rather tame project—creating a batik to decorate the pulpit for Easter service. Its design involved two white doves rising amongst green and blue foliage. With experience and sureness, he layered the dyes over coats of molten wax, with no hint that anything was amiss. Suddenly, amidst brushing on some wax, he drew quiet and his eyes became distant.

In a faraway voice, he began talking about the war, a rarity for men of his 'silent generation'. Reaching back in memory more than forty years, he described, in an alarmingly changed and diabolical voice, how easily they had downed the young German pilots, virtually boys whom the Luftwaffe sent up in the last desperate months of the war. 'They were no match for us', he said, referring to the squadrons of his own well-trained airmen, flying in their storied Mustangs. He continued almost as in a dream: 'It was a shooting gallery, really, downing those little Nazis; we rather *enjoyed* it you know, after they half destroyed the world'. This disdainful tone soon softened after he recalled one encounter that had changed his life.

> But there was one little ME-109, fast and agile as a mosquito they were, but not in the hands of these *children,* the so-called Hitler Youth. He was taking hits everywhere and his crate caught fire. Amidst the strafing, the whirling turns, gunning him down, time seemed in slow motion despite the frenzy of tracers and cannon. Though his cockpit was filling with smoke I clearly made out his face; it was pale white, like transparent porcelain. He had the clearest blue eyes; they stared up, frozen in fear. This boy would not go down! So I swung around for another go; I fired again, again … his ship was shredded and finally he spiralled down in flames.

I was mesmerized by his tale until I realized I was feeling ill at ease with such charged memories and his disturbingly changed demeanour. I was not quali-fied to respond to such a deeply felt and dramatic reminiscence. Then, the trust unravelled: 'Yes, this blue-eyed boy, I shot him to pieces, you know, but that face … so young. It was like … yours! Come back to haunt me from the wreckage, have you?'

He was becoming increasingly agitated, flooded by this delusion. He reached across and clutched desperately at my hands. I hung on to his, alarmed but keep-ing my composure. By now, his panic had raised a general alarm in the studio and pandemonium reigned. Other patients started crying out and wailing. Attendants, big men in their infamous white coats, quickly entered and gently led them all away. Still weak legged and handicapped myself, I had fallen, insult to injury, beneath the upturned table and was lying amongst the ruins of our project. Being led away, he looked back amongst *our* wreckage and said coldly, 'It *was* you'.

My supervisor, hearing the commotion, ran into the studio. Surveying the upturned chairs, spilled dye, splattered wax, and the banner mangled on the floor, she put her arm around me and whispered, with a touch of irony, 'You run some kind of session, don't you?' Unwittingly, as a naive twenty-year-old, I had come face-to-face with the depth and power of the damaged human psyche and the perils of transitional space. The trauma was unleashed in that moment upon this war hero—the 'man had returned to the child'. His young pilot was a phantom, coming alive in his delusions and voiced in lamentations. How can the past rise so vividly, I wondered? How can the shock and trauma be relived as though it were only yesterday and not 'let go' after some forty years? I thought we'd made a nice connection, creating together a simple banner for the upcom-ing church service. How then could his creative response trigger a regression so sweeping? I had unwittingly become the subject of a terrifying transference that led to his post-traumatic psychotic episode. I was *that* young German airman he had destroyed. The issue of 'who am I now' is a recurrent theme in Connelly's (2015) art therapy work with traumatized, brain-injured clients, who struggle to find an identity after a traumatizing event. This was the case of Bexley, whose repressed identity as an airman from a world war long over was thrust into the present with frightening ferocity. It was crystallized in this singular moment, when our eyes became deeply locked together. Bexley's frightful gaze seemed to go *beyond* in some uncharted vision, all the while he was holding onto my hands, seemingly for dear life. His fearful, pleading expression is an image that has never left me, after forty years of practice.

Transitional Space and the Creative Response Activity

In my undergraduate classes in psychology, I had been studying Winnicott's (1971) concept of transitional space from his book *Playing and Reality*. However, reading about someone regressing to an alternative state of consciousness and then *experiencing* it first-hand with Bexley was shockingly different. I was ill prepared for the power of transitional and transference phenomenon, which it seemed I had precipitated by creating a banner for Easter.

Bexley's inner and outer worlds were never reconciled and remained only tenuously separated. The post-traumatic memory triggers were frequent and severe enough that psychotic regressions kept him intermittently hospitalized for decades. Unbeknownst to me, just the act of boiling wax and seeing its molten state perhaps triggered long-buried memories of a child trapped in a burning aircraft. Creating a banner in honour of Christ's return perhaps represented a resurrection that was at once redemptive and terrifying. This enemy pilot, thought to be destroyed some forty years earlier, now inexplicably appeared before him. My ghostly presence and art process seemed to link up with the holiest of holidays, creating the perfect storm—one that rendered Bexley delusional and the session in mayhem.

For me, it was all too much, far too complex a case. After all, I was just an immature artist, recently traumatized myself—it was too much for me to bear. Having experienced my own steroid psychosis, I understood Bexley's thoughts, how they could morph from the real into deep pathology. Were our regressions a reasonable, sane response, I wondered? This was the sixties, when it was not unusual for a professor to question 'is reality a cultural construct?' Whatever the case, our little creative activity had triggered a powerful 'transference', which left him in restraints and me with my aspirations utterly humbled. Since I was as yet 'unanalyzed', not knowing the nature of transference left me with my own bereft feelings, which slowly welled up. I dealt with yet another new sensation, that of 'countertransference'. Edwards (2014) indicates this effect does not necessarily intrude upon the therapist's process or a distorted perception. Awareness of this powerful dynamic may lead one to understand the psyche's many layerings, of how patient and therapist are relating to one another. In any event, I left the asylum's grounds that drizzly, grey early spring day, unsettled and teary. I found

myself flooded by remembrances of my own dad, who, as another young lieuten-
ant, trudged his way through Italy, fighting for his life against fanatical resistance.
Once again, it became all too much. But while I was confused and shaken, I also
had the realization, the exhilaration, that I had found my medium and my profession. Leaving my internship and all the beloved characters of the hospital was a
great loss—something most interns experience after their short, yet often intense,
bonding with their patients. I missed the old dark-stoned edifice, its dim corridors
filled with fascinating madmen.

Entering the Profession

When I graduated in 1973, I found that paid positions in this new and specialized field of creative arts therapies were scarce. Working with the most severely
brain-damaged children were the only openings available, as working with this
population, with its limited possibilities, was often the entry level into the field.
The position I took was in a state facility that was progressive enough to have
a creative arts department. There, I was faced with the most profoundly handicapped children, many of whom were considered not to have a measurable IQ,
some even lacking consciousness. Undeterred, I devised strategies to stimulate
these children, using whatever faculties and sensory abilities they possessed, and
to enrich their lives through creative response activities. These were the days
when artist Joseph Beuys, himself a traumatized war veteran, proclaimed 'anyone
is an artist!' He began the Fluxus Movement, which gave us license to paint our
faces, blow bubbles, dress up like fools and put on skits. We often bundled these
bed-bound patients into their gurneys and wheeled them outside, where we threw
around the autumn leaves and covered them in debris, giving the caregiver aides
fits, as the patients came back covered in red and orange maple leaves. We then
rolled ink upon the leaves and block printed them on bedsheets, art paper and
shirts. We did dramatic, almost random, readings; once we did Hamlet, and we
read the poems of Blake and, always, the stories of Dr. Seuss. Content at that
level was immaterial; not a single child understood a word. There was also much
banging on drums and showing eight-millimetre films on the ceilings. What was
important was the animating of the space, to stimulate some form of *response.*

The Inseparable Child

I eventually was entrusted with a caseload. I became aware of an eleven-year-old
child named Joey, who was so notorious within the institution that few were
permitted access to him. He suffered the most profound autistic symptoms of
self-injurious behaviour. He was so hypersensitive to interpersonal, intimate
proxemics that if he were separated for even an instant from being physically
held and coddled by his preferred caretaker, he would bang his head so violently
in protest that he would have to be completely restrained. Yet, conversely, this
profoundly disturbed sensory involvement coexisted with equally intense *hyposensitivity* to his self-administered pain, demonstrating a seemingly impossible

disconnect between sensations. Joey's rare condition was aptly described by Mahler (1969) as 'symbiotic psychosis', where attachment became arrested to the extent that the child could not conceive of nor tolerate any separation from the mother figure.

As conceived by Mahler and her researchers, the function of a symbiotic attachment in normal infancy is based on the maternal figure's being one with the infant (normal symbiosis), providing crucial contact comfort. Failure to separate can lead to an arrested state of symbiosis, which can occur in many guises. In the case of Joey, autism was the result of his being exposed to the rubella virus, which the mother had incurred during the first trimester of pregnancy. A history of family schizophrenia and his institutionalization from early childhood undoubtedly contributed to his severe manifestation of this rarest of conditions. This multiply handicapped child was so dangerous that he was off limits to the casual teaching specialist. Several staff members and a teacher had been hospitalized by his throwing objects and attacking. My goal was to gain access to him and become accepted as one of his few caregivers. Eventually, his experienced teacher-behaviourist, Lou Johnson, and then assistant, James Pruznick, permitted me to observe and then to visit regularly, and thus I became part of the landscape of his classroom setting. With his teacher's reassuring presence, Joey's self-abuse was minimized enough that I could interact with him without an outburst. Still, there were several near misses from thrown objects when he would lash out in fear, panic or rage, the emotion being too primitive to fathom. How could a child in a constant state of panic, with an IQ of eighteen, throw objects with such a high velocity and precision at an intended target? No one knew or seemed to care to know why or how; there it was the norm.

Over the course of months, a tenuous trust was built between us, enough that he could tolerate playing with me a few feet from his teachers. I introduced a pre-art activity, claywork with rolling clay coils, patting them flat and throwing them against the walls. To everyone's surprise, he would clap and flap his hands excitedly as the clay stuck to the walls. Perhaps at last he had found his own transitional object—if he wanted to whip bits of clay at walls to make them magically go away, then this was his opportunity. To his delight, they would reappear as I peeled the bits off the wall and presented the still moist material to him, ready to be used again. Joey had finally begun to link the clay to play in a way not unlike a toddler who throws toys outside his playpen, awaiting the mother to retrieve them—a 'give-and-take' game which could go on indefinitely.

By the fourth month, we had a regular regimen. He had learned to roll his own clay coils and with assistance build a simple pot around a form; yet even then, he was reluctant to disengage his hands from me. Figure 2.1 shows us *tête-à-tête* in a kind of hand combat while working on our clay project. The ritual began by his refusal to separate from my hand. His strength allowed him to cling to mine even as I twisted and turned it to try to disengage. My efforts would then escalate his panic, which forced me to return to holding him. This process was repeated over and over. By the sixteenth session, his clinging had diminished enough that both

Figure 2.1 Joey could not tolerate being separated from his trusted caregivers. During a ceramics project, he would sometimes lapse into self-injurious behaviour at the thought of being 'disconnected'.
Video still by the author.

his hands could remain on the vessel (Henley, 1983). I was now one of the few people to enjoy a symbiotic relationship with him from which we could work on disengagement and separation. For the time being, it was sufficient to have him *endure* me and my activities.

We eventually began a ritual together that his teachers had begun: when our work was done, I would signal that fun time could begin. He would latch himself to my lap, and we would take joyrides down the hall in my rolling chair. Though he was non-verbal, his pleasure was unmistakable; he chirped, giggled and smiled widely, all the while clutching on to me for dear life as we glided effortlessly along the terrazzo floors of the long halls. Even after thirty-five years of therapeutic and educational practice, those rides were the purest moments of bliss I have ever witnessed. Our ritual, however, was only a temporary respite from a hellish exist-ence. There were times that all our connection would inexplicably vanish, with regressions so violent that he would require surgery and hospitalization. After his release, we would begin *again*, at the beginning.

Professional Territoriality

On-site, I was introduced to contradictory paradigms. My work was required to be strictly behavioural, with my reports written using the operant condition-ing terminology of Ivar Lovaas. According to Lovaas, one 'shaped' behaviour by instituting a regimen of reward and punitive measures. This means of behavioural operant conditioning required that I record each instance of Joey's self-injurious behaviour, counting the number of self-inflicted 'hits' at fifteen-minute intervals. This charting was intended to corroborate evidence of progression or regression in Joey's claywork. This methodology was a dramatic departure from my university teachings from my Neo-Freudian Professor Kramer. I was determined to switch hats when necessary, to attempt serious research, while learning to adapt and live with competing theories. I made the most of this quantitative training, trying to demonstrate 'by the numbers' that Joey's symptoms of self-injurious behaviour had abated and eventually went into remission for three months. This outcome would have been impossible to achieve if it were not for the fact that the activity was continued and reinforced within the classroom with Johnson and Pruznick. Without this carry-over, the work would have been a case of 'scatter-shooting'. Such was the need for day-long, reinforced practice to the point of its becoming part of the daily ritual.

My on-site behaviourist supervisor remained sceptical that any 'soft' art education could affect behavioural change—to her it was merely playtime. Only after handing over forty hours of my raw video footage did she acknowledge that the interventions and Joey's creative responses correlated to my data as a slow, incremental diminishing of symptoms. When viewing the identical video as part of my master's thesis, Kramer, however, frowned upon my interrupting the flow of the session to chart these 'endless numerical notations' and scoffed at the intrusive 'behavioural prompts'. It was the out-take footage, the times 'when all bets were off', that interested her most. She pointed at the monitor, indicating how free and wonderful our after-session rituals were—when we raced down the hallways on my rolling chair. *This* play, she insisted, was evidence of developmental and maturational progress. To her mind, bonding with Joey was immeasurably more therapeutic and developmentally progressive than any skill or behavioural development. Regardless of these conflicting approaches, the work progressed, and I learned to adapt—a skill not so easily learned in professions where professional territoriality remains to this day. Within the psychological sciences are seemingly countless, disconnected theories, fragmenting both theory and practice. Barkow, Cosmides and Tooby (1995) regard the social sciences as 'adrift', with half-digested observations and a 'contradictory stew'. Within this mire one plows ahead, making use of any paradigm which holds promise.

Research initiatives aside, what endures is the memory of our rides together, which Kramer found so profound. For once, Joey was in quiescence, his need to hurt himself at least temporarily abated. Racing down the hall, bumping against the walls and spinning around the corridors was hilarious fun. Past the nervous secretaries and my supervisor's frowns, we boisterously breezed along while he clung to me, trilling in delight; we had formed an unforgettable *bond*.

The Feral Child

After two years of working with Joey and other autistic-like and brain-injured children in the institution, I was confident I could handle even the most challenging

child. Upon being transferred to a residential school for the deaf, I found inval-
uable my prior readings from Judy Rubin, one of the first art therapists to work
with the deaf. Her text *Child Art Therapy* (1978) guided my initial therapeutic arts
programming. I immediately sought out those deaf children who were identified
as 'disturbed' or otherwise neuro-atypical. Aware of my master's degree research
with Joey, school officials allowed me access to a 'special' boy, who I learned was
so uncontrollable that he spent half his time at the nearby state mental institution.
Although he had a hearing impairment, he wasn't considered a deaf student per
se, but could 'visit' the school briefly on his 'good' days. This fourteen-year-old
boy, whom we'll refer to as Ebie, had been born of a Central American family who
could not deal with his bizarre, probably autistic behaviours. He would eat off the
floor and relieve himself wherever; most revoltingly, he was a biter. Case notes
indicated that considering the parents' cultural mores and religious practices,
they saw him as a 'curse from God'. Truffaut's film, *The Wild Child,* now struck
a chord.

This child was not unlike the wild boy of Aveyron, who was the feral child roam-
ing the forests of France in the 1800s, also eating on all fours, inured to cold and
pain, and bruised and filthy. He too was eventually brought to a school, the Deaf
Institute in Paris. There, a young physician and progressive teacher named Jean
Itard took on the challenge of 'L'Enfant Sauvage' (Itard, 1962). For years, Itard
attempted to bond with the boy, whom he named Victor, to earn his trust so he
would permit Itard to teach him language and the customs of the day. Itard was
indeed an enlightened practitioner, introducing many varied, enriching experiences. In one of Truffaut's scenes in the movie, Victor is mesmerized while staring
into a simple candle flame as though it is something unearthly and miraculous—
which in a way it is. It illustrates how many on the continuum perceive natural
phenomena, without context, as magical constructs either feared or fascinating. In
another memorable scene, Itard permitted Victor some free play outside, only to
have him strip naked from his Fauntleroy clothes and go wild during a snowstorm.
Dancing, laughing and tossing the snow, he was finally unfettered by the demands
placed upon him; in his joy at being in *his* element, like Joey, he too was taking his
own 'blissful ride'. In Itard's real-life account of Victor, the parallels between Joey
and Ebie were striking, as all three cases posed questions about the eternal debate
over nature and nurture as manifested on the severest end of the spectrum.

As was the feral child of Victor's, Ebie's neglect resulted in animalistic behaviours that were barely controllable. Given the superstitions over his untamable
wildness, Ebie's parents decided to lock him in the cellar during daylight hours,
in this case for *five years*. He was allowed out only at night, like some animal, to
roam the city streets. The city became his forest of Aveyron, and he developed a
feral sense of survival, dodging the night's city dangers and for years evading the
authorities. Without language and seemingly deaf, he somehow flourished in the
anonymity of the urban landscape. Lithe and quick, he nimbly moved through
the alleyways and junk heaps without detection.

His feral existence rivalled that of Polly Samuel (aka Donna Williams), a
world-renowned 'recovered' woman with autism who as a child 'went feral' due to

parental neglect. This brilliant writer, artist and advocate escaped to the Australian streets at age three to avoid the domestic violence at home. She would navigate the parks surrounding her home, without language and toilet training, and dance under the stars in her nightgown. On her website, she writes, 'I was fascinated by my playground that was the wilderness of the streets. It was a feral childhood with all its fortune and its horror …. [I]t made me a natural anthropologist, watching from the sidelines' (Samuel, 2016).

Williams was eventually caught and returned to the chaos of her household. For nurturance, she would seek out her grandparents, who lived in a shed on the property, finding shelter and their kindly faces to avoid her parents' roughneck violence and drug abuse in their bleak life in the Australian inner city. During this long, incredible journey, Williams describes her struggles at piecing her world together. She eventually overcame many of her autistic behaviours. As an adult, she earned a master's degree in linguistics and became an art teacher, a lecturer and an author. Williams became one of the foremost autism advocates and an exceptional artist of evocative, hope-filled paintings; she is nothing less than a miracle (Williams, 1992).

While Williams was surviving the streets as a feral child half a world away, Ebie was returning every daybreak to his lair, his basement home, accompanied by all manner of junk. He preferred electrical appliances, including broken blenders, old lamps and other discarded appliances. In my article, 'Artistic Giftedness in the Multiply Handicapped Child' (Henley, 1989a), I describe how he possessed the ability to transform his beloved electric bric-a-brac into new and operable objects. This rare form of giftedness among those with autism and others on the spectrum is described as possessing 'islands of ability'. Despite being debilitated in most other ways, Ebie showed off his savant-like talent for taking apart and rearranging and then operating the most complex jumble of electrical components. His electrical ability outstripped my own, so I called upon an 'expert consultant', our gruff, yet kindly, school *electrician,* who helped sort out what we had and further guided my interventions. Unbeknownst to our electrician, he had unwittingly taken on the role of a substitute mother, with his electronics becoming transitional objects. Ebie seemed to anticipate our tech's arrival each week, by storing up his treasures of meters, vacuum tubes, wiring diagrams and motors. Ebie continued his fixated relationship with inanimate objects, which is a characteristic of children on the autistic spectrum. Bettelheim (1959) worked with his famed, autistic-like 'mechanical boy', who related to everything, including himself, as though it were an electrical phenomenon. Like Bettelheim's mechanically obsessed artist client, Ebie's electronics did not remain dormant; they sprang to life after his collaborative efforts with his electrician companion. The strength of this improbable bond was remarkable to everyone involved particularly since the 'electric man', as Ebie would sign to me, was clearly endearing to and had a profound calming effect upon him.

I then found his savant capabilities were not limited to electronics; Ebie was also a gifted draftsman. He began to draw the components around him with startling realism. Staring into space, he seemed to need first to visualize his drawing

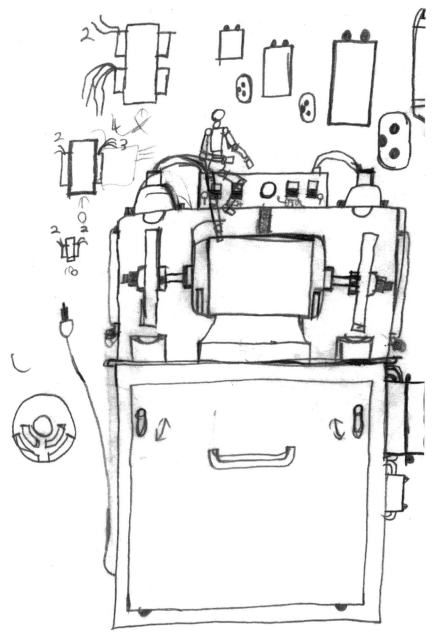

Figure 2.2   As a former 'feral' child who rejected all human contact. During four years of creative arts and attachment therapy Ebie worked exclusively with mechanical objects and was found to be a superb draftsman.

in mid-air. As his behaviour improved, I provided him with the paper to draw out his electronica. I staged tableaus of objects, which were placed on the various machines. I then snuck a mannequin onto the tableau to see whether he would draw this quasi-human figure. Surprisingly he did, which gave some relief to the mechanicals and enlivened his still lifes. Figure 2.2 is one of his many brilliant drawings, but this one was made special by the mannequin, which seems just as animated as the machinery.

This would be the first step towards creating a human form, which was still months away. His creative response activities eventually crossed media and disciplines, and he began to work in clay and mixed media, which blossomed under the care of a new art therapy intern. Their relationship and the extraordinary work that came of it will be continued in Chapter Seven, dealing with the maternal bond and attachment dynamics.

Early Research

Given my research interest into artistic giftedness I began a dialogue with Dr. Sacks whose fascination with savantism was mutual. With his encouragement I received a year's grant to study in Britain where I read aesthetics with Roger Cardinal at the University of Kent. I researched the vast collection of Victorian outsider art at Bethlem (Bedlam) Royal Hospital, London, and then began my field work visiting children with extraordinary abilities—such as Stephen Wiltshire, who would eventually accompany Sacks on a world tour drawing wondrous architectural vistas. I visited him as a sixth grader in the specialized Windmill School in Brixton and found this quiet yet amiable boy able to draw panoramic landscapes without visual aides. I also gained access to Nadia Chomyn, who at age five, astounded the psychological community with her gift at hyper-realistic drawing. I visited with Nadia as a young woman, ten years after her prodigious abilities had mysteriously evaportated. Observing both of these individuals became a point of departure from which to study the genesis of artistic ability.

On Nadia

In the 1970s, the autistic savant Nadia gave an extraordinary drawing demonstration for CBS's Walter Cronkite, such was her world renown among researchers and the public alike. A decade later, I found myself in her home, in a working-class neighbourhood in Nottingham, England. Now twenty years old, she resided in the Autism East Midlands group home during the workweek. I gauged the current state of her artistic abilities well after her capacity to draw had famously regressed. Her case had been chronicled in 1977 by Lorna Selfe, an educational psychologist whose book showed Nadia, at age five, drawing on the technical level of a young Michelangelo or Daumier. Meanwhile, her self-help skills, such as tying her shoelaces, were seemingly unattainable. I began by employing methods used in observing very shy primates, an ethological approach of being quiet, yet friendly, and unobtrusively mirroring her movements. I began by mirroring her father's actions of pruning the roses while she had ample oppor-tunity to observe me through the window that looked out on the garden. As she became habituated to me, I began drawing in the house while she entered and exited the room.

In Selfe's (1977) book, she describes presenting Nadia with simple children's book illustrations, such as those from a story about farmyard animals. From these simple illustrations erupted Nadia's own startlingly original drawings, which seemed inexplicable for a child so severely involved. A spectacular example is shown in Figure 2.3, in which Nadia, with unbridled intensity, redefined the 'copied' rooster.

Emerging from amongst a frenzy of random scratchings and sketches of zoo-morphic forms came a fully realized rooster, which majestically dominates the pictorial field. Unlike the saccharine book illustration, the bird seems to be squawk-ing in panic, its beak agape in some incomprehensible alarm. The bird's bulbous eyes stare past you—belying fear, confusion, indifference?—We shall never know which. Nadia's pictures were friezes, with many overlaid animals and abstracted contour line work, which I found reminiscent of the shaman's cave drawings. For whatever reason, generations of images were often superimposed many times over. Perhaps their closest contemporary correlates are the masks used by many indigenous peoples. In some cultures, intricately carved masks used during danc-ing are afterwards discarded; their magic dispersed, they are now useless husks. Nadia may have also intended for her many scribbled or fragmentary images to be throwaways, used as a prelude before the dominant image was unleashed.

Selfe's book presents Nadia's work in terms that are inadequate and misinter-preted. As an educational psychologist, she was not conversant with the dynam-ics of the art process, and thus, she simply cropped out those images which she deemed made no sense. In meeting with Selfe, she also stated that the cropping simplified illustrating for publication, as the multiple layering might have con-fused the already awestruck audience. Yet only by studying these compositions in their entirety is the viewer able to appreciate idiosyncratic Nadia's creative pro-cess. Free-associated montages, with the iconic, decipherable images, coexisted with random marks, infantile scribbles and undeveloped forms. From this chaos comes monumentality; the dominant figurative image emerges. Nadia's creative response—of transposing child-styled farmyard animals into a fireworks display of creatures with the rawest affect—puts the notion to rest that the individual with autistic savantism is devoid of emotionality. On the contrary, it simmers within, emerging only on the individual's own terms (Henley, 1989b).

Why her gift had evaporated by the age of eight remains a mystery. Selfe has revisited the issue and still contends that the intensive speech therapy Nadia received caused a neurological shift, opening a new channel of communication, to the detriment of the other. Selfe asserted that Nadia's laser-like fidelity drawing style was thus displaced by age eleven, when her copying became more in line with the normal development of dawning realism. Judging by her reworking of Toulouse-Lautrec's 'The Jockey', which she did from *memory*, reimagining the horse and rider, Nadia was able to work with greater realism but with markedly

Figure 2.3 Five-year-old Nadia was revisited when I journeyed to Britain to work with this most extraordinary of autistic-savants when in her teens. After age six, she mysteriously lost her artistic gifts.

Photograph by the Author.

less emotionality (Selfe, 2011). It is certainly no coincidence that during this critical period of regression, when Nadia was at her artistic height, her mother was succumbing to cancer, perhaps helping to extinguish Nadia's creative urge. All theories are open to suggestion. Whatever the reasons behind her regression, her case remains one of the great mysteries where neurology intersected directly with the inexplicability of art. It was hoped to become a kind of Rosetta Stone for researchers, to attempt to tease apart the nature and nurture dynamics of creativity on the spectrum.

Depending upon the motivational stimulus, the creative response activity sometimes takes on unseen powers. This was evidenced not just by Nadia's 'copies' of farmyard roosters but also with other stimuli, such as my unwittingly being swept up in the psychotic transference of a post-traumatic veteran. While Bexley's regression during our banner making might have ultimately had a therapeutic outcome, caution and awareness of providing a stimulus are a critical part of undertaking any creative response activity. Finding the joy and mastery in the creative act forms the basis of becoming what Winnicott called 'the authentic self'. Not somebody else's expectation of self, but one's *own* self is necessary whether someone presents with the severest of autistic symptoms, attention deficits, mood involvements or roaring mania. Creative response activities were shown to elicit strong participatory responses, reaching these most challenging individuals despite their condition. As Kanner finally admitted, let us put all the labels aside and celebrate the extraordinary potential of these children for the way they are. I was humbled by these individuals, with their enormous resilience to struggle, odd worldview, and learning and emotional differences; they laid down the methods of what was essential for me to know, that an empathic caregiver who can form a bond and earn their trust may be rewarded with the same, that providing a secure and magical space allows them to follow their own sparks of interest, which in turn can lead to an extraordinary chain of ideas and creative expressions. Inherent in each of these interventions is the promise for emotional and intellectual growth for all children on the *spectrum*.

Three

Mapping the Spectrum

As defined in this text, the spectrum must not be confused with categories in the *Diagnostic and Statistical Manual of Mental Disorders*, or DSM-5 (American Psychiatric Association, 2013). That manual sets diagnostic guidelines by the American Psychological Association (APA) and continues to revise categorizations, such as Autistic Spectrum Disorders, multiple times, such that they are hotly debated to this day. It is most useful as a diagnostic manual to ensure insurance reimbursement and secure specialized educational placement and as a general physician's reference. Departing from the APA's orthodoxy, I have already described how the spectrum is conceived as a broad continuum, which I visualize as an arc, a rainbow configuration, where colours of the spectrum are visibly saturated but then blended, forming secondary colours. For the purposes of visualizing the curve or a loose arc, the spectrum can be conceived as having different points, or *markers,* which demarcate where symptoms of any given involvement can be pinpointed and identified. The previous case accounts of Joey, Ebie and Nadia were among the most severely involved children and are thus conceived as being on the furthest extreme of the continuum.

The varying degrees of involvements in this wide-ranging spectrum combine and overlap with markers of autism, bipolar, mood disorders, attention deficits, Tourette's syndrome and learning and sensory integration problems, as well as others yet undesignated that make up the broad arc of a continuum. This arc ends on the mildest end of the curve, such as an eccentric artist who may function creatively and professionally in daily life but still display definitive markers. These individuals have now been recognized beyond the eccentric as being on the 'sub-threshold' on this continuum (Ratey & Johnson, 1997). Though not debilitated with severe neurological involvements, their problems may be considered *handicapping* mild conditions which could benefit from accommodations to allow some to function at a high level. These individuals may still deal with adjustment problems, interpersonal relation conflict, educational under-achievement or self-regulatory problems. During times of stress, transition or developmental changes, they may benefit from therapeutic support whether in therapy or in the educational sphere. While bordering upon the typical, a challenging environment may render them increasingly vulnerable.

From Typical to Atypical

Autism researcher and pioneer Lorna Wing (1988) also conceived the spectrum as being a 'broad curve', which individuals with differing markers occupy at different points on the continuum. As we reach the 'neurotypical' end of the spectrum, where we encounter the so-called 'norm'—whatever that is—it is commonplace that even these individuals may occupy markers on the spectrum, as everyone has their sensitivities, anxieties and neuroses—and can even display signs of stereotypical behaviour under certain circumstances.

To gauge when neurotypical behaviour becomes mildly symptomatic, I tried out a modest experiment on my willing and creative graduate students, who were subjected to my hour-long lectures. With my graduate assistant taking notes, I noted when the students began engaging in self-stimulatory behaviour—given these 'sensory-deprived' conditions. No fewer than five could be found mildly self-stimulating. One was twirling her hair and another biting a pencil; one kept fussing with her fingernails, and several displayed nervous, jumpy knees. One was quietly talking to herself. Several camouflaged their need to stay still and attentive by simply 'checking out' by surreptitiously gazing into the blue glow of their phones. These barely noticeable actions mimicked those of spectrum individuals, and though they were transitory and environmentally induced, the behaviours were still *there*—they exist within us all. These 'nervous' proclivities may be accompanied by the highest level of intellect, artistic giftedness or superb research abilities, suggesting how strength can stand alongside weakness, with each compensating for the other. It is perhaps this mosaic of capacities that renders us all fascinating creatures.

The Package Deal

Whether neurotypical or placed somewhere on the spectrum, everyone possesses different capacities for self-regulation during exacerbated arousal situations. We all have our strengths and weaknesses, and thus we are a 'package deal'. This term is one of the focal points mapping the spectrum, that as we undergo life's demands we marshal our inner resources to meet the environment's expectations. We may be stressed, exhausted or ill—each will deplete our abilities to combat that which is aversive. Throughout my university teaching the students' ebbing of inner resources always resulted in 'uneven' performance, while the opposite also held true; when healthy and less stressed, students did work that was more invigorated and stable. We might apply, and even generalize, the package deal to neurotypical children and adults alike, whose personality traits may demonstrate many of the deficits displayed by children on the spectrum, albeit on a lesser scale. Barkley and Newcorn (2009) term many of these traits of procrastination, indifference and selectively poor performance as products of 'low-reward motivation', meaning almost everyone lags when interest levels are low; thus we are all a study in contradiction. Jane Flax (1990) discusses how the postmodern era dictates subjectivity when considering personal norms and cultural and sexual differences as strengths which can coexist despite the disparity between behaviours. This package deal is tolerated (up to a point) as our culture becomes more diverse and tolerant towards an increasing range of 'differences'. The concepts of increased cognitive subjectivity, gender ambiguity and contradiction of opinion have gained traction in this age of inclusiveness. The cut-off line, if there is such a thing, between the 'typical and atypical' is a postmodern construct that requires an ongoing conversation. As social mores evolve, the lines of demarcation blur between typicality on the arc of the spectrum. It is worth keeping in mind that Grandin's work in the gentle handling of livestock has resulted in *millions* of animals being treated with empathy and compassion—this coming from an individual who still can barely read the intentions or expressions of a colleague.

Frequency and Severity

In addressing these 'differences' we recognize the element of subjectivity of our own perceptions as we attempt to discern the peculiarities of self and others. All of us occupy the spectrum, even imperceptibly, and carry with us feelings and ideas which shape our adjustment to typical life. They comprise intrapsychic strengths that include, inescapably, our neuroses. Yet the tipping point between the typical neurotic and the spectrum child may be considered when symptoms develop with sufficient *frequency and severity*—that the individual can no longer compensate adequately. The package deal may begin to tilt toward the negative as demands from the real world—school, friendships, family and leisure-time programs—all begin to wear and weigh the children down. Continual decline in a child's functionality often forces the parental or educational decision as to whether to accommodate and try to coexist with one's dysfunction. Another course of action is to reach out to address debilitating symptoms through professional treatment.

A common variable in mapping the spectrum, however, is that the postmodern construct of 'reality' and 'meaning' dictates differing perceptions of a given individual. Perceptions differ in one's own reality, of one's parents, extended families, teachers and community, all of which may have diverse standards of conduct. Different cultures and demographics may be tolerant towards eccentric behaviours, or those which are at odds with a norm. In our clinical practice, we have seen religiously schooled children be suspended for incidents which would go unnoticed in an inner-city school. I have encountered wealthy or entitled parents who expect a quick fix to problems whose existence they often play down or even deny. There are ultra-liberal, progressive households who can be permissive, who may not set limits on hyper- or other egocentric behaviours—to the chagrin of everyone, from educators to those in the grocery checkout line. Others are 'helicopter' parents, those micromanaging taskmasters who can be unreasonably demanding when engaging their child's school personnel, as well as this therapist. They may be puritanically strict and expect 'perfect conduct', while others are obsessed with increasing 'enrichment'. These examples are commonplace within both typical and neurotypical populations. Parenting styles are always subjective and easily second-guessed. For the spectrum child, the severity and frequency of challenging behaviours exacerbate parenting dynamics exponentially as the child enters the cultural or family fray. To remain aware empathically of how difficult it is for spectrum children to continually measure up to life's demands—which even typical adults often find stressful—remains one of the great challenges of parenting this population.

Finding a Label

While everyone possesses a complex range of pluses and minuses in their ability to function, children designated as being on the spectrum have already reached the threshold of severity and frequency of symptoms. I have pointed out that these symptoms may be so interwoven with varying degrees that it may prove useless to refer to the spectrum child with any homogeneous designation. Every child I have encountered has displayed, to some degree, comorbid 'mixed states'. Hyperactivity, social conflict and academic underachievement may accompany the predominant mood lability of bipolar clients. A child identified as attention deficited may entail central sensory processing disorders or Asperger's syndrome. Attachment disorders which present as being anxious separators from parents may be linked to underlying learning problems, especially when placed in regular academic settings. Severe autistic behaviour may be mistaken for mental retardation. Aggression or its opposite, emotional inhibition, may stem from posttraumatic stress or even a traumatic fall off a horse. Markers may imitate, overlap and mask each other, which challenges the most experienced diagnostic team to tease apart the multiplicity of symptoms. Labelling is an ongoing Sisyphean task matched by an imperfect taxonomic system (Wing, 1964).

We are a culture seemingly obsessed with classifications. Everyone and everything seems to demand a designation—a moniker that groups individuals, cultures, religions and disorders—that leads to broad generalizations. Semantics play a large part. Shifting political and cultural mores dictate changing labels. Consider that the words *idiot* and *moron* persisted into the twentieth century and the deaf were referred to until the 1970s as 'deaf and dumb'; another moniker, 'deaf mute', persists. Advocates for the deaf have cried out 'we are just deaf—!'

The reader may have already noticed that I have struck the term 'disability' from my nomenclature, in favor of a more descriptive labelling process. It is a word which, despite its political correctness and official standing, is to me an offensive pejorative. As someone who has overcome a condition, I have been *able* to accomplish many feats with proper accommodations. By 'dissing' anyone— whether it be disregarding, disrespecting or disenfranchising—is to negate one's potential and self-worth. Instead, I have returned to the more neutral term 'handicap', which implies a levelling of the playing field. As a partially paralyzed golfer, I could play against the best in the world, and since my physical handicap is figured into the match play, I could feasibly beat that champion—this is the spirit of the term. My usage has prompted catcalls from disability-advocate audiences and chagrin from editors. But perhaps it comes as another reform of advocacy and re-examination as postmodernism dictates. Labelling hinges on society's ability to shed its prejudices and move past stigmatization—that the label is not so much a problem within a person, but a lack of 'fit' between capacities and the demands of the environment. This sentiment echoes R. D. Laing's formulations in the early 1960s that it is the environment which often defines the individual's place within the community of those who are 'like-minded'.

Describe, Don't Call

In this book, labelling or referring to a child on the spectrum is not a 'people-first' designation. With the almost infinite shades of involvements which may comprise the handicapping condition, I resist 'naming' someone within a generalized category. Moreover, I do not denote children as autistic or 'having' ADHD, as though they are suffering from a common cold or a broken leg. For this reason, I refer to children on the spectrum as 'displaying autistic features' or 'presenting with sensory-motor problems'—and note their varying degrees of severity or mildness on the continuum. All this might entail extra verbiage, which to some readers may be burdensome—but I find it worth the inconvenience. It is by principle that I refer to descriptors rather than diagnostic terms. Referring to someone's condition as a descriptor, rather than a noun, avoids being defined by one's involvement and pushes back against what I contend is a pejorative tone. Defining the child by his handicapping condition may result in a label which might stick for life. Describing the child's behaviours and issues rather than *naming* acknowledges the infinite intricacies of the child's makeup of mind, body and spirit.

Our culture is currently experiencing a rise in autism labelling; everyone, from a quiet or friendless child to da Vinci and Lincoln, has been linked to the autistic spectrum. There are strident activists who have politicized handicapping conditions to improve services and acceptance into the greater community. Taking the cue from the deaf and the blind, many vocal advocates have reframed their identities, not as handicapping conditions, but rather as 'oppressed minorities'. The removal of the word *infantile* from autism in DSM-III-R was another attempt to reframe the disorder as a lifelong condition—away from the early work of Bettelheim and Kanner (Silberman, 2015). Attempting to remain 'culturally correct' and acknowledge cultural ownership is an ongoing task. Often, diagnoses are culturally determined generalizations; a prime example is the wastebasket term 'emotional disturbance'. What does this profile entail—delinquent, violent, antisocial behaviour? The term has vastly different connotations when applied to children in poor inner-city environments as opposed to upscale bedroom communities. Under certain circumstances, traits, such as aggression, serve as survival mechanisms when living in hostile, dangerous environments. Building a narrative that is constantly open to revision is essential if we are to do justice to the complexity and uniqueness inherent in all people, no matter what their profile.

I am not undermining the importance of finding the cause of the child's suffering, even if it resorts to labelling. It is often reassuring to parents to finally home in on the 'name' of the condition from which their child suffers. Finding a label can be a great consolation to parents who for months or years have been running to endless clinics, doctors and clinicians, sometimes in a maddening circle. This is part of the heartbreak and frustration of dealing with not just obviously symptomatic children but also the many subthreshold, mixed types whose changing symptoms are subject to environmental stressors or maturational development. In the hands of an experienced psychiatrist or psychologist diagnostician, a diagnosis may objectify atypical symptoms that have eluded other less experienced professionals and deprived children of needed services. It must be pointed out that insurance companies require the diagnostic code if they are to reimburse for services. For the purposes of educational placement, a label can enable a child to gain access to needed services. For the educational staff, a label may mark a shift in empathic understanding, to view spectrum behaviours as a neurological condition rather than 'deficits of character'. Labelling may raise the professional's awareness that it is the handicapping condition that complicates learning, behaving and socializing. Such greater attunement may ensure accommodations, which in turn may ease the child's struggles while in the often-harrowing school setting.

Variations and Profiling within Populations

Plotting the markers on the spectrum may be present in varying degrees even within identifiable populations. For instance, when I began working with the deaf, I assumed, as many do, that it was a homogeneous population. Yet my experience eventually bore out that the opposite was true. Countless variables and mixed-spectrum conditions abounded within *one* school: autistic behaviours, impulsivity, aggression, hyperactivity, sensory distortion, interpersonal relating, and language and learning difficulties. Immaturity was almost the rule—hence they are given educational services until age twenty-one. This is just the variability of one population. This myriad of issues expands exponentially when combined with limited auditory input, thus requiring a unique approach to each child.

During my four years with the school for the deaf, and another five at a psychiatric hospital specializing in the deaf, I gained an appreciation of not just the different involvements but also the diverse forms of education and therapeutic services required to serve them. I was able to work with preschool children in Montessori training. Many middle-schoolers were at the height of hormonal changes that impacted impulse control. The programs for deaf/blind and other multiply handicapped children required tactile and other sensory-stimulation activities. At the high school level, I taught resistant vocational students to make art while being trained in auto repair or upholstery shops. The teens in the academic high school were often taking my fine art courses as part of advanced placement classes before being college bound. Others, who were hospitalized, suffered delusions and hallucinations that were specific to their population. Within this one population was an entire spectrum arc—with each student requiring flexible, adaptive creative response approaches.

The Environment as Emotional Disturbance

As professor and clinical supervisor of art therapy and art education at the Art Institute of Chicago, one of my responsibilities was to observe interns and student teachers. During these forays, I often entered the grim Near West Side of Chicago, where spectrum markers were camouflaged by the weight of socio-economic duress. I appreciated how young student teachers and interns courageously elected to venture into neighbourhoods that were virtual war zones. These areas were entrenched by generations of poverty and gang life which permeated the projects where many children were trapped and victimized. The children attending these programs were living in crime-ridden, toxin-ridden communities and were exponentially at risk for spectrum and behavioural issues—a view fully acknowledged and shared by Autism Speaks (Environmental Factors in Autism Initiative). I visited one student teacher in a school that serviced Chicago's most notorious low-income project complexes. Being located just blocks from the city's premier 'gold coast', the transition was shocking. Upon arrival, I surveyed the surrounding community of broken pavement, with well-kempt bungalows coexisting with partially torn-down houses.

I was formally met and escorted into the school by a bona fide Chicago policeman. From there I was met by a class of loud but unusually polite third-graders who had responded to a strong and maternal role-modelled teacher. This commanding woman in dreadlocks and an African kaftan was a powerful and yet empathic presence. It was clear she fulfilled the multiple roles of maternal caregiver, disciplinarian and general dispenser of 'tough love'. She explained that the noise level and almost hyperactive atmosphere was due to the children's culture and, for some, their hypervigilance. Gang violence plagued their lives and had become the norm—a stunning admission which put into perspective that within this country, such third-world conditions persist. She explained that many children had learned which streets to cross and where the gang's territorial borders could and sometimes did invite the sniper's bullet. This statement is not hyperbole, as Dumke's (2012) report on the level of shootings bears out. Despite its partial demolition in 2011, the West Side remains a troubled reminder of a city's failure of community building in this and its other urban areas—a task which a young local community organizer named Barack Obama was devoted to during his formative years of public service.

My student teacher, Megan, echoed her mentor's approach, working *within* this comparatively disruptive climate (if she was to survive). It was perhaps the most valuable lesson that prepared her for professional teaching. She had adapted superbly to this atmosphere where shouting, pushing and laughing loudly were the norm. Yet several children stood out with severe pathologies. I was told that these children were pulled for special education but were mainstreamed along with their typical peers for 'specials', such as art class.

Weaponizing Art

Megan took it upon herself to work one to one with one of these children, eight-year-old Tonya. My observation of this child was one of constant agitation, boundary transgressions and aggression towards others. My student teacher bravely requested this child despite its not being a therapeutic venue. Her creative responses were unelaborated and impoverished, with only rudimentary stick figures being elicited. I timed my visit after the students had been given a workshop by an African sculptor, who conducted a group project of creating painted 'talking staffs', which were indigenous to his ancestral 'tribe'. They were to be used to signify that they held the right to speak—that they commanded the floor. Comprising pre-cut and sanded wooden canes, the children were to elaborate on them, adding bangles, feathers and other elements while painting the top in bands of colour. When Tonya chose her paints, they were at first unremarkable until the head teacher informed my student that they were in fact her neighbourhood gang colours. Things regressed further when she jabbed another girl in the ribs with the stick when she was thought to have spoken out of turn. Her project had now become weaponized. When reprimanded Tonya remarked, 'I'll do the talking—she won't mess with me no more'.

As an intervention, Megan embarked on a program where creative activities were *functionalized,* meaning they addressed not aesthetic issues so much as those which brought a modicum of safety and personal ownership to the process. Projects such as making a tie-dyed canvas handbag helped to organize her things. A ceramic mug was created, which she drank from each morning during the class breakfast club. These objects stayed within the classroom to remain intact and not be destroyed or stolen. Unless fully functional, aesthetic-minded response activities were senseless since her basic needs were not met. Maslow's (1954) tenet, that art is not made unless basic needs for survival are met, is almost universal. Tonya's spectrum issues were an adaptive response to a violent world. The hypervigilance and aggression virtually required this fragile eight-year-old to survive the poverty and violence that were part of her daily life (Perry, 2001).

The Therapeutic School

In 1994, I left the Art Institute of Chicago and found I needed to take a break from university teaching. I found work with children in an alternative school, on a full-time basis, which would test my abilities to help such a challenging group of underserved children. I realized I was no longer the passive observer and ivory towered supervisor, but now had to practise what I had been teaching. Since most children had not even tolerated a self-contained special education setting, they required individualized therapeutic and behavioural programming. They were classified as 'emotionally disturbed', which did describe many antisocial behaviours. They were referred due to school expulsion, substance abuse or rehabilitation, or were recently released from jail. Here again, the diversity was far-ranging, but all held in common an incapacity to handle authority. The silver lining was that these 'last-chance' students were being placed in such an innovative therapeutic school. Emotional disturbance aside, each of these twelve- to eighteen-year-olds presented with various mixed spectrum symptoms. Half of my class of ten displayed hard neurological signs, such as dyslexia, hyperactivity, hypervigilance, clinical depression or mania, with almost all having predilections towards aggressive behaviour. As was the case in Chicago, it is unclear as to which came first: disturbances from the neglectful environment or genetic predispositions to disturbances, which then were exacerbated by the environment. This nature/nurture–chicken/egg debate is ongoing, but the consensus is that the endless variables involved are always an intricately woven combination. As the scientists finally proved the obvious, the issue became functionally moot. I was dealing with neurological, hormonal, genetic, parental and environmental factors, all of which were kept just barely under control.

Behavioural challenges with their overlapping and complex markers contributed to the teens' diminished capacities for academic work. Creative response activities were the preferred modality, as they required the most minimal participation where there was no wrong answer. One needed to 'go to where the child was' and entailed positively oriented rap sessions, vigorous drumming and poetry sessions. Despite these innovative attempts at reaching these teens, negative mixed outcomes were the norm, and my daytime impact upon them was at best palliative. Students went home to their variously toxic environments and undid all the gains made the previous day or week. All behavioural programs using tokens, privileges and punitive measures proved weak and ineffective. I came away realizing that there could be no easy fixes, and there were to be no Hollywood endings—just grinding out one tough moment to the next. Yet this intensive year of *immersion* helped me regain a much-needed perspective of how much these young people had endured, what they had to overcome, especially when factoring in the environmental circumstances.

It is a common statistic that children on the hyperactivity and mood disordered end of the continuum are more susceptible to substance abuse (Biederman et al., 1997). A common misconception had also been proven—that it was not only inner-city minority children at risk, but also my students, suburban middle class teens who had begun using hard drugs. Heroin, prescription opiates, speed and inhalants eventually reached epidemic levels in this affluent community—as well as many other bucolic and rural states. Stimulant medications to address spectrum markers were crushed and sniffed. Whipped cream canisters, right from market shelves, were inhaled before class. Despite our best efforts at providing an atmosphere of 'corrective caretaking', the day's progress would often regress the next morning after a night of getting high. It underlined the need for extended school days, yet this was often impossible, as the students could not handle another minute of organized programming—even if offered as leisure-time activities. Despite an empathic school atmosphere, a legion of social workers and safety net programs, the teens were caught in a self-reinforcing web that seemed intractable to change.

The Clinical Group

After a year with the alternative school, I was appointed chair of the Art Therapy Program at Long Island University. I also accepted a part-time position of creative arts activity therapy coordinator in a private practice where I could continue my clinical work while teaching—striking a productive balance. The Hecht Group was led by its namesake, noted psychiatrist and analyst George Hecht, who specialized in children with spectrum disorders. As my approach was non-verbally oriented, many of those referred to my caseload were on the autistic or defensive spectrum, yet also possessed creative dispositions. My program involvement was to provide individual creative response activity therapy and develop a clinical summer camp and afterschool programs. Most referrals were children with social impairments and limited self-regulation. Even within a stable socio-economic demographic, almost every child came with mixed or comorbid involvements, which placed them on multiple points on the spectrum. Much of their prognosis was based upon whether they were supported by intact and supportive families who committed to long-term care of at least a year. Some brief examples come from actual cases (though certain details have been changed) to demonstrate the *range and complexity* of involvements which these children presented: out-of-control, almost feral, behaviour; children locked in with autistic withdrawal; hyperkinetic children, some born with foetal alcohol syndrome; 'little professors' who were experts on WWII battleships; and adopted children from Eastern Europe who suffered institutionalization syndrome; all mixed with milder types of inattentive children who were underachieving due to any number of mixed involvements.

One of the hallmarks of this practice was that with early intervention, real marked change could be evidenced especially if the child received both psychiatric treatment *and* therapy. With the therapeutic team as a collective resource, almost any issue could be handled, with many children being seen for two to six years. Such long-term work is rare in this contemporary climate of managed care and socialized medicine. The key was to offer a comprehensive program that touched almost every element of the children's lives: medical, psychiatric, social work, educational consultation and group work as well as individual therapy. Throughout this text, the reader will encounter their stories as gleaned from detailed process notations that provide a narrative about their struggles and creative outcomes.

The Spectrum at the University

In my university teachings, I increasingly encountered teens who had special needs and required extra support and empathic instructors. Many of them were clearly on the spectrum and had obviously benefitted from early intervention, ongoing therapy and educational inclusion services that enabled them to make it to university. I was excited to expand my work beyond young or latency children and teach especially the at-risk freshmen who were on a probationary status. Their special status necessitated acclimating to dorm life, to having to study 'low-reward' subjects, and to curtail the pitfalls of excessive party life and all its temptations. Many acclimated through extra counselling, tutoring, testing accommodations and enrichment opportunities. Although some of these freshmen were on the spectrum, all were legally adults protected by confidentiality, which left professors uninformed about diagnosis, such that even I was occasionally taken by surprise for the need for individualized intervention. There were students with learning differences, autistic features, Tourette's syndrome and attention deficits, and those who were disadvantaged from inner-city environments. Despite their anonymity, many students displayed 'mixed-type' features with comorbid learning and psychological issues. This population allowed me a 'snapshot' of long-term outcomes—of how the grade-school children, who had received years of accommodations, support and therapy, had 'turned out'. I was able to develop a creative response curriculum that engaged both academic and emotional intelligences, which mapped the specific challenges that late adolescents encountered once gaining access on an advanced education level. Adaptive strategies that were sensory-specific, or required demonstrative teaching, or pairing specific individuals for group work, are just a few accommodations made that went beyond just teaching a course—but were therapeutic minded.

Issues Related to the Spectrum

The problems that are endemic to these and other individuals on the spectrum are too numerous, and presenting them would be exhaustive to detail. However, some major issues, many of which have been touched upon in the introductory case material, require further definition with case examples. Most are framed as psychodynamic constructs but will also have correlates to the latest cognitive and behavioural interventions which have proved their efficacy. These presenting issues are a general frame of reference, which the practitioner will encounter along the entire continuum, again, in varying degrees of frequency and severity.

Arousal and the Stimulus Barrier

A major construct described throughout this work is the issue of hyper- and hypoarousal; children on the spectrum modulate incoming stimuli in decidedly different ways than typical children. However, all people have their sensitivities to sound and tactile sensation, frustrating circumstances, family problems, somatic complaints or setbacks. I have identified filtering of incoming stimuli as a major constituent in dealing with the environment. The term correlates to the work done by Spitz (Spitz & Cobliner, 1966), who termed the filtering apparatus the 'stimulus barrier'. This is the capacity to self-protect by responding selectively and adapting to incoming stimuli—known in the vernacular as developing a 'thick skin'. The construct was first conceived as a natural developmental defence mechanism. It is an inborn, invisible membrane in infancy when the sensorium shuts down when stimulation rises to intolerable levels (Spitz, 1961). This is a physiological barrier, one whose resilience varies from individual to individual and continues to evolve through the lifespan. Individuals are subject to variations in their ability to control arousal levels depending upon their predispositions or traumas in their environment.

Thus, for those on the spectrum, the stimulus barrier defends against noxious stimuli for those who may be particularly fragile and variable, such as Evan, who dealt with different thresholds whereby the volume, content and frequency of stimuli can result in the stimulus barrier's being breached or supported. Spitz's early psychodynamic use of the term correlates to the current theory of hyper-arousal, that when neural systems are overwhelmed, they disconnect with an increase in anxiety and an exaggerated startle reflex, such as conditions often associated with post-traumatic stress. Being barraged by constant stimulation pushes the threshold for fight-or-flight reactions to noticeably higher levels of anxiety and sensory over-responsivity (Green & Ben-Sasson, 2010). Personal space also enters into the equation, as the child may be extra-sensitive to the proximity of others. The 'proxemics' between intimate, casual, public and even cyber social space are constant variables which affect the child's stimulus barrier. As a defensive gesture, I have noticed many spectrum children retire to their comfort zones, such as bedrooms or other safe spaces. 'Bed tents' are popular with spectrum children for creating their own personal spaces and a secondary stimulus barrier, acting like a darkened womb-like membrane that is comforting and filters out unwanted stimuli. Weighted blankets, hypoallergenic pillows, or velour or jersey pyjamas, accompanied by an ocean soundtrack, may all be included in a simple bedding proposition.

On 'Not Letting Go'

Defences in children with spectrum markers are often weak and must be therapeutically bolstered if the children are to withstand intrusive or invasive thoughts. To assist the child to also *let go* of that which is disturbing or traumatic is often an ongoing issue of the weak stimulus barrier. Everyone has difficulty letting go, as one cannot get over a condition if it persists. Hence, *everyone* to some degree ruminates in his mind or loses sleep about an ongoing issue—or perseverates aloud, usually to a trusted figure. Ideas and emotions, such as regrets, recrimination, retaliation and guilt, were routinely encountered over my years with this practice, with both parents and children. Many children suffered repetitive, even persecutory, thoughts that were played in their minds as an endless tape loop, like a song that one cannot get out of one's head. Any stimulus can bring on invasive thoughts, making the weakened stimulus barrier even more vulnerable. Several of these children retreated to their rooms to play computer games to block out or just avoid the fray.

In one instance, a high school freshman, Lyle, had just begun to emerge from months ensconced in the dark cave that was his game room. After months of therapeutic work, he began to integrate slowly into the family's routines, displaying more relatedness and willingness to let go of addictive gaming. This included his joining the ritual of watching family-oriented shows after supper—a switch that certainly qualified initially as a positive outcome. Lyle's parents were counselled by Dr. Hecht to limit his exposure even to neutral content. They chose the BBC program *Nature,* a seemingly innocuous enough show, but then, one finds it often adds a 'doomsday' element forewarning of extinctions and calamities. One program focused on climate change and the shrinking ice pack in the Arctic. The piece showed footage of a starving polar bear stranded on land, unable to hunt seals on the ice flow. It came as a blow—this magnificent animal shown emaciated, probably near death. Lyle could not get the image out of his head (nor could I). He described it repeatedly, but neither of us could find a creative solution to address this issue. It pointed to problems of being too 'mindful' about a certain stimulus. I responded by adapting the creative activity as a means of supporting healthy denial—to making pots and other concrete craft-like activities as in occupational therapy. By making things by hand that were utilitarian and of gift quality, he could put mankind's cruelty to animals out of his mind until such time his ego was able to desensitize disturbing realities. It is a testament to how the stimulus barrier, once aroused, struggles to defend—in this case against the stark realities that all children face—that of a new epoch called the Anthropocene, part of the 'Sixth Extinction'.

Object Constancy

Another issue that presents, particularly among the severe end of the spectrum, is that of 'object constancy' (Mahler, Pine, & Bergman, 1975). This developmental process is an offshoot of Piaget's construct that is well known for the cognitive capacity to understand that objects continue to exist when they cannot be observed—an issue that arose in many instances with the blind and the deaf and others with neurohandicaps. One visually-impaired, autistic-like boy would feel around the edges of the door frame before entering any room. Even when the door was clearly open, he had to decide whether and when it was 'safe' to enter, as doors are unpredictable entities—they slam, they're closed, they crack open. Their actions were not taken for granted, and thus a ritual needed to be performed. Many typicals also suffer object permanence issues, as we cannot always anticipate whether life's 'door' is a portal that is welcoming or dangerous.

In normal development, toddlers eventually realize that an object unseen still exists. Object constancy is asserted in response to the mother's presence and absence. Mahler (1969) indicates that the infant holds an internalized image of the mother as a separate entity who provides comfort and care. During periods of separation, the infant learns to mentally picture and retain an image of being loved and cared for by the maternal caregiver. In adulthood, 'separation anxiety', jealousy and trust issues find their root in object constancy. Trusting that love persists despite distance and periods of time, without anxiety or insecurity, is, like other object relation constructs, a lifelong developmental task. Internalization of Winnicott's (1965) 'good-enough mother' is often the litmus test for the durability of a relationship. Having the maternal caregiver's love fully assimilated sets the stage in later adult relationships to separate with a degree of confidence; enjoy personal independence without neediness; and explore life, seek out novel experiences and take creative risks. With the secure attachment as the 'anchoring object', one is self-assured enough to enter the 'space-in-between', or transitional space, where, again, reality and the magical are blurred and creative potential can flourish.

Approach-Avoidance Conflict

As early as 1890, the philosopher-psychologist William James asserted that motivational ambivalence is a state basic to human nature. It is an evolutionary imperative that organisms 'do what helps them survive'. Motivation is key to the decision whether to engage with a stimulus or shun it, for the dangers of risk-taking can be a life-and-death decision. Approach-avoidance is a dynamic which reaches across the domains of biology, evolutionary psychology, ethology and cognition. Each of these systems engages as the cost-benefit analysis of whether the gamble to explore, or 'approach', something new and inviting will outweigh the risks. Avoiding a perceived danger may be life preserving, yet it may also stifle forward movement and thus personality growth. As an example of how universal this dynamic is, we might return to the Pleistocene—to a scene where ice-age hunters are deciding whether to attack a mastodon, with its rich rewards of food for a winter, or whether half of the hunting party could be lost. The few moments taken to process this cost-benefit ratio is a marvel of high-level cognitive reasoning. It combines overcoming intense emotionality to rationally sort out and study the problem. Enormous trust was needed to follow the orders of their leader or reach a group consensus, or the community would suffer dire consequences. Such choices, on an individual or a national level, begin with the need to approach cautiously and explore the new, or 'uncharted', without putting self or others in harm's way.

For children on the spectrum, decisions to approach or avoid a stimulus, whether it be playing with a newly introduced toy, engaging with a stranger or joining a social group, may carry additional emotional weight. With their different cognition and emotional confusion and inconsistent support behind them, spectrum children are handicapped in their capacity to weigh such decisions. For children with impulsive hyperactivity, approach-risk behaviour may become an afterthought, sometimes with disastrous consequences. For children on the autistic end of the continuum, risk aversion and avoidance may be the predominating response—yet if there is sufficient decision-making agency, there will always be a degree of 'what if'. Will it be worth the anxiety to venture into the dark theatre despite the crowds, the booming noise, having to weigh the exit strategies, all to gain the prize? The key may lie in the method.

Luring

The therapeutic method of 'luring' a child to overcome approach-avoidant reactions was applied through an unlikely source, the ethologist and animal behaviourist Nikko Tinbergen (Tinbergen & Tinbergen, 1983), who recognized that every evolved creature possesses an innate curiosity. Although usually shy, many of the animals he studied overcome their inhibitions by being presented with the 'carrot'—a bait, something irresistible. The theory holds that if one can find an intrinsic motivator, even the most severe child on the spectrum might overcome his shyness and interact or participate. Adapted by Tinbergen's experiences with his grandchild who presented with autistic behaviours, it is the creative media, activities or actions which play a pivotal role throughout this text. It may be anything that might lure children beyond their shell, but the rewards to taste the richness of the outer world and those individuals within it may be worth the risk.

Part of overcoming over-cautiousness is the issue of personal space previously described in the case of Evan. It seems everyone modulates the critical distance between others. For instance, intimacy proxemics come into play when individuals engage in a greeting ritual: Do we shake hands, or do we succumb to our culture's propensity to hug another (the act is often awkward for the most typical adults)? Years ago, this ubiquitous behaviour would be too 'familiar' but is now the new norm. In therapy, both Evan and Ebie were acutely sensitive to the physical distance. It is critical, then, that with shy or new clients, I am careful to be seated across a table, in my own space, between which lies an array of curiously interesting art media or other materials which buffer our proximity. I try not to loom large or stand above children especially while they work, as hovering over a child's shoulder (or anyone's shoulder) almost always gives rise to discomfort. Often if hand-over-hand assistance is required, I will kneel for the entire hour, to be level with the height of the child.

For a therapy-resistant teenaged girl, the issue of personal distance was immediately apparent given her introverted behaviour. At the first session, Eileen, an accomplished photographer, took one look at the studio's small size (used for individual sessions) and would not even enter the space; she wordlessly left the building. With her mother's permission, I followed her to the door and reassured her that we could continue the session outside, perhaps for a field shoot. In this proxemics intervention, I could give her the needed personal space for therapy— to roam the nearby riverside and investigate our small field and the town streets. Interestingly, she spent much of the session around the dumpster, where, ever the artist, she began a sequence of cropped, abstracted forms that were entangled within the dumpster (Figure 3.1).

The image's forms are geometric, clean and somewhat remote—not at all the mess I expected with her dumpster diving. Their metallic, perforated forms were spotless, and the highly formalized designs might refer to the cool relations between us—one can never know. It took several sessions for her to invite me to view the images, which required that I share a space on a park bench. Seemingly still aware of our personal space, she handed me the camera to scroll through, to which I responded with phrases such as 'let me see that one again' or just 'hmm'. These vocalizations were carefully non-critical, as I did not seek to judge or praise, but rather to display a mild, benign interest. This sensitive teen elected to attend six more sessions despite her initial resistance. However, she, like

Figure 3.1 Sensitive to close proximity, teen photographer Eileen departed the studio to work en plein air. This montaged series explores the insides of dumpsters and how we 'worked beside' without invading her space.

other therapy-averse children, reiterated she attended for 'artistic reasons' and not therapy. Although inherently therapeutic, with aesthetic, relational and self-expressive goals fully engaged, she could relax and participate, as 'all bets were off'.

Autistic Avoidance

For more 'locked-in' children or for those who find direct interaction traumatic, complete avoidance is obviously difficult to overcome. One such child was Patricia, who attempted to join our therapeutic summer camp (Henley, 1999). She suffered acute approach-avoidance conflict due to PTSD, to the degree that she outright refused to enter the summer camp cottage. Since the mother drove a spacious van, I suggested bringing projects outside to her. Standing in the parking lot facing the van's open sliding door, I stood outside, materials in hand, eventually laying them onto the van's carpeted floor. After two days of 'standing beside' for twenty minutes while being completely ignored, she finally overcame her inhibition (or stubbornness) and began to interact with the interesting materials I made available. After a week of this necessary indulgence, our therapeutic team advised that it was time to have the mother lead her to the cottage, where, at creating her own proximal distance, she could observe the children with various activities under way. With some muted protests, she eventually overcame her resistance and joined an age-appropriate group. She had achieved a modest therapeutic victory just by accepting human interaction. It was perhaps again my perseverance that allowed her to realize 'I meant no harm but I was also not going away'—that I would 'wait her out'. Since the activities were fun, she eventually relented. To overcome this form of resistance requires a promise that there must be a high-reward benefit to make it worth their while to take such a risk. For many children on the spectrum, this is takes a leap of faith; whether to approach a potential friend; put their hands in soft, wet clay; or join a fun-filled group is a cognitive involvement termed 'mindblindness'.

Mindblindness

Perhaps the most debilitating marker spectrum children suffer is the phenomenon termed 'mindblindness'. Mindblindness was described by Frith as the child lacking 'introspection'. She framed the condition as a lack of intuition available to one's mind that allows the imagining of another's wishes, beliefs and thoughts (Frith, 2001). Taking the lead from his mentor, Simon Baron-Cohen (1995) experimented with this extreme form of self-consciousness, linking it to the 'Theory of Mind'. Baron-Cohen described his experiments which demonstrated that those on the spectrum may suffer from the incapacity to 'mentalize' the intentions or feeling states of others. It is the incapacity of the spectrum child to fully 'self-observe' the social dynamics which are transpiring. Unable to read the situation, the individual remains functionally 'blind'; thus, the leap of trusting others helps guide their interactions.

The concept of mindblindness was lifted from earlier primate studies by Premack and Woodruff (1978), whose chimpanzee, Sarah, demonstrated she could mentalize the goals, intentions and even the empathic perceptions of others. She was also able to demonstrate beliefs, doubts, guesses and even pretending—all states that are challenges for certain spectrum children. Building upon these experiments, Baron-Cohen's experiments indicated that children on the autistic continuum cannot integrate incoming information as a cohesive whole. In typical attachment development, empathy develops after four years of age, as children can comprehend the feelings of others and the impact their own behaviour has upon them. Immaturity and self-centeredness persist despite the most persistent and well-executed therapeutic and behaviour interventions. Egocentric interpretations of the world that revolve around these children's needs and perspectives dictate behaviours. These behaviours may not just take the form of mild social awkwardness or autistic-like behaviour, but can also occur as hyperactivity, where the children may be unaware of bodily boundaries or their risk-taking behaviour. The concept of mindblindness is not limited to children on the autistic end of the spectrum but occurs again, on a loose arc of variation, through to typical individuals. For instance, it is virtually the norm for seventh-graders to be egocentric and not empathetic. Tuning into the wishes of others when it is not in their interests to do so is the norm, indicating a personality with developmentally immature self-awareness. In typical children, the incapacity for empathy is a transitory, normal state. In children on the spectrum, this issue may be prolonged or become arrested throughout their lifespans.

Mindblindness may manifest as the child's incapacity to attend to discrete 'details' of a stimulus rather than the overall gestalt. Grandin (Grandin & Panek, 2013) reports that her 'detailed' visual orientation often misses the big picture. In a complex social interaction with several participants, when side discussions or extraneous information are interjected, the gist of the content discussed may be missed altogether. For instance, in the classroom, a child must attend to a teacher instructing sometimes boring or complex concepts. Meanwhile, she may be a distraction herself, with different clothing, a hairstyle change or an irritating voice intonation, all requiring coping measures. Facial expressions and verbal commands may require constant decoding. Factor in the unpredictability of active peers who are also sending out complex social information and expecting in return coherent responses, and integration can often remain chaotic or incomplete, resulting in either shutting down or responding with off-kilter responses.

However, egocentricity happens to be in line with the temperament and self-absorption of the artistic persona. As the remarkable art in this book will attest,—creativity is not arrested by mindblindness. I agree with Evans and Dubowski (2001) that the spectrum imagination is simply 'different', along with the rest of the child's behaviours. This difference includes the child's use of symbolism, humour and even appropriation of culture. It is again the conspicuous omission of humans which sets children on the autistic continuum apart, which again is indicative of their worldview. Researcher Donna Betts (2003) has considered this incapacity by developing a projective drawing test stimulus that explores facial portrait drawings for those on the autistic continuum. To address facial blindness, she sought to build, from the ground up, increased facial recognition and memory. Later Richard, More and Joy (2015) introduced an intervention that is like the 'potato-head' projects that were countlessly created in group or camp. Their approach involved building a face using a three-dimensional model where the children could manipulate their own facial structures. While this work lends some insight as to how children build their schemas, the exercises are all cognitive in nature rather than tapping root issues. For others with attentional, hyperactivity, obsessive compulsive or bipolar features, the creative act can also remain an egocentric process, with little awareness of the traits of others. Many children seem untouched by the necessity for empathy or socialization even when working figuratively.

It should be said, however, that artists throughout history have been self-centred, socially difficult, even notorious in their aversion to others. They can be generalized as characters with easily bruised egos with irreverent single-minded vision. Although the artist's persona is romanticized, creating is essentially a solitary act, whether it be an artist in front of his easel or a batter facing a blazing fast-ball. The solitary creator works through her own unique lens, facing her joys and demons—whatever the outcome. Translating this into cooperative group or social action projects poses a challenge, but can be effective and rewarding if facilitated by experienced practitioners. In that case, raising the child's social awareness requires cognitive strategies and a paradigm shift, which is a completely different process than individual creation.

The cognitive-behaviour response to mindblindness attempts to help the child focus upon reading the needs of others, such as Betts's early research or the 'build-a-face' intervention. Teasing apart what is relevant information in the social sphere, as well as the world at large, is often a struggle. The spectrum child may be confused by the multiplicity of stimuli, which is immaterial, and will often respond to the 'extraneous' rather than the matter at hand. Off-point responses impact the child's capacity to functionally relate on many fronts. Mindblindness may entail being 'hearing blind'—often lacking in listening and auditory discrimination skills or talking over or through others. Others may be 'face blind', with an incapacity to recognize even familiar faces, especially when out of their usual context. 'Boundary blind' refers to the inappropriate personal spacing to others. Emerging is the condition of 'cyber blindness'—the inability to recognize when social media or the Internet is misleading, predatory or otherwise detrimental. Being able to self-monitor, tune in, pause, inquire and truly recognize the concerns or topics of others has a direct bearing on the capacity for self-observation and regulation.

During creative response therapy, one of our core cognitive interventions to address mindblindness is to have the children 'restate' that which has just occurred—whether it be narrating back to me the content of a picture or, in a social context, processing what they feel just occurred between peers. Inconsistent retrieval of relevant information is an indication that mindblindness remains an ongoing goal in therapy. Having the creative act assist in articulating memories, actions and reactions of others may mitigate the children's handicaps and raise their level of functioning—in familial, academic, social and generalized settings. Both our individual and group sessions, even on the university level, often end with the participants reiterating the content of their outcomes and recalling the responses of others. In this way, they may be better prepared to respond coherently and productively post-session and to keep the conversation going.

Literal Mindedness

Literal mindedness as a form of mindblindness presents yet another therapeutic challenge especially during social interactions. In group and individual work, figures of speech and particularly idioms were used in creative response activities with latency age children as a thematic structure in the social group setting. Sayings were chosen for their relevance to the spectrum and the propensity towards literal mindedness. Idioms drew upon figures of speech, describing familiar behaviours, such as 'going overboard' or being 'over the top'. Idiomatic expression was often practised in session, using drawings and collages, which help reinforce and provide a forum to discuss the meaning. One idiom, feeling like a 'fish out of water', was explored in literal and social terms of feeling socially estranged. After much discussion of its figurative meaning, we happened to transition to releasing the fish we had caught from our camp's aquarium. While this ritual was always done at the end of each day, in this instance it was special. While the fish were being netted for release, a small bass wriggled out of the net and flew in the air. As it flopped around on the floor, everyone scurried to catch the interloper. One bright, autistic-like boy, named Devin, proclaimed 'fish out of water!' Everyone laughed and finally 'got the joke'. Later he created a drawing response—a variation on the idiom. As he had just literally turned the idiomatic expression back on its head, that the figurative can become the literal, with a healthy dose of absurdity and irony—so could a pictorial image. On page 181, he is shown dropping a fishbowl, with the glass crashing to the floor—yet inexplicably the water and fish retain their shape! This unusual humour and intelligence indicated he had internalized its many contexts and allowed him to poke fun at the exercise, indeed even at us professionals.

Manipulative Behaviour

Everyone hopes that the person they are relating to is being authentic in their interactions. Neurotypical or not, this is unfortunately rarely the case. Consciously or unconsciously, everyone is out to ensure their goals and needs are met, and if it takes some disingenuousness, so be it—a bit of 'manipulative behaviour' is called for. What constitutes a conniving manipulation and what remains a marker of the spectrum (which should be defined as a medical symptom that simply cannot be helped) is an ongoing, ageless question. Behavioural manipulation can be foremost a compensatory mechanism, not just for the spectrum child, but for anyone who attempts to further their agenda; from a child who shirks their chores to an adult who plays politics to attain a promotion, manipulation is by far the most effective tool in the ego's arsenal. Manipulation may even be construed as a positive trait, as it indicates a level of savviness that the individual can successfully 'work' the system, whether through charm, playing one against the other, being ingratiating, or even through threatening behaviour. In positions of power, manipulation may be skilfully employed without repercussion, to reap whatever reward is desired.

Spectrum children actively employ this defence, usually in negative situations that result in less than favourable outcomes. Especially in those with high intelligence, manipulative behaviour may be the unconscious defence of choice. Power struggles are a constant, ongoing issue, as low-reward responsibilities are avoided or when impulses are not immediately gratified. Splitting or triangulation is perhaps the most egregious, as one parent or friend may be played against the other, to gain permission or some other power. The 'weak-link' parent is often the most common dynamic, as the child asks the one parent permission after the stronger of the two has already given their decisive 'no!'. Remaining consistent and fair in one's behavioural expectations regarding consequences can confound the most experienced professional or parent.

Manipulation may even occur in children with minimal intelligence. I recall early in my career working with a child with multiple sensory involvements and arrested intelligence. Before indulging in fun-oriented creative activities, we would make our way to the studio by way of climbing a short stairwell, which to this mobility-impaired child meant *work*. However, it was a necessary part of our therapy if the child was to have her fun at the sand table (see Henley, 1992). Despite her resistance and struggles, she became fully adept at climbing the six stairs to claim her prize—the clean white sand with all its playful treasures. However, after going on holiday with her temporary foster parents, she returned and was literally being carried in the arms of her volunteer father. Had she been injured? 'No, she just can't walk'. The child had given them the impression she was immobile; thus, she had enjoyed being carried around like a queen for the entire holiday break! I think I detected the slimmest of smile from this child as she was handed back to me—in the stairwell.

This balancing act reminds us once again that *everyone* constantly bids to have their needs met with the least expenditure of effort. We all try to manipulate to ease the challenges in our lives. This child was no different despite possessing severe symptoms and a diminished IQ. Discerning when we become unwilling partners in a power struggle or succumb and lapse into enablers or accommodators—or when we finally to decide to play the enforcer and set limits—is an ongoing task of assessment. Parents, and multiple professions, including those in our society, must constantly confront manipulation, which remains an intractable, ever-present challenge.

Four

Socialization Challenges

One of the foremost aspects of mapping out the spectrum continuum is these children's challenges and impairments in social relations. Who feels like being sociable especially when their self-awareness is just functional enough to realize they face peer rejection? A fitting example is Devin, who was a prolific artist, expert at capturing the alienation and defeatism facing these children. He depicts his mother banging on his door, harping on him to come out of his room and 'be social'—a mantra heard by many of the children and teens featured in the case material (Figure 4.1).

Figure 4.1 Few additional comments, beyond this boy's superb articulation of his existential state, are needed to convey this image of social dislocation.

If we assume the creature inside sitting on the bed is a self-representation, he conceives of himself as having morphed into a worm-like creature. It underlines the reality that even he understands that worm creature would be an undesirable playmate. He responds like most of us who are unmotivated to overcome inertia in many guises with a laconic, 'Maybe later'. For a boy firmly on the autistic end of the continuum, Devin was an art star for his capacity not just to convey his existential quandary but also to elaborate it with comical yet darkly Kafkaesque precision. When someone's issues are actively symptomatic, how can it be possible to relate to others without betraying their problems?

In social milieu, Baron-Cohen theorized that social mindblindness is slanted towards the male gender—that the propensity to 'systematize', or attend to the parts of stimuli, are a male brain phenomenon. Indeed, many boys in the practice were strikingly limited when attending to discrete objects of interest, without taking in the gestalt (Baron-Cohen, 2002). While its causes are unknown, this debilitating cognitive faculty may prevent the spectrum child from critical self-observation and monitoring while socially interacting. There may be little awareness of what the others are feeling, expecting or preferring—thus, the safe bet is to remain socially withdrawn, a defence that provides self-protection. For other, more outgoing children, their narrow bandwidth of high-fidelity, 'detailed' attention surmounts the 'give and take' required of social discourse. Those who do attempt often do so 'blindingly'. In schoolyard settings, I have observed children, especially girls, trying to mimic certain clique styles, show off the latest accessories and attempt to fit in, while remaining slightly behind the curve in comprehending social mores. In the most serious form, the child may present with social disinhibition.

Social Disinhibition

Mindblindness is often most prominent when children actively seek out peer acceptance, which is deeply longed for. They may not be able to modulate seeking out others, as engaging almost anyone can become indiscriminate or otherwise disinhibited. This includes the most serious form of disinhibition, reactive attachment disorder, where children exhibit poor relational boundaries and selectivity in their search for caring others. Disinhibition is described by Rutter et al. (2007) regarding the institutionally deprived who were poorly attached to caregivers. Approaching the wrong person, at the wrong time or in the wrong situation may end disastrously. If or when they are tolerated, it is often by children younger than themselves, whom they can dominate and often relish, for it is a power position of status that they rarely occupy. Conversely, many children gravitate to and find acceptance from more empathically minded adults. Adults are predictable and more tolerant than cruel middle-school peers. However, approaching those older than themselves exposes children with mindblindness to those who may have bad intentions. The child may not be able to 'read' their intent and, being eager to please, they may consent to the wrong demands, revealing *too much* personal information or taking up dares—any of which can be posted on social media. Particularly with pubescent girls, as their body matures, disinhibition becomes a liability in terms of keeping them both psychologically and physically safe.

Play Revisited

A generation ago, almost every child was expected to go out and play on their own, with just a few objects of amusement: a mitt, a bike, a hula hoop, a doll set. Even in the most impoverished environments, children had a rubber ball, with which any number of games could be played, whether bounced off a stoop or batted in a busy street. There was little of the intense social programming that we see in today's middle class parenting—children just 'went out to play'. Our present play dynamics have become much more formalized, with structured play dates that complement often over-programmed social activities. Children on the spectrum are particularly at a loss to amuse themselves. Parents often compensate for the infrequency of friendly relationships by providing material amusements, from the latest video games, to automatic pitching machines. Eventually, however, some form of engagement beyond self- or sibling relating becomes a necessity—children need to go public. It then becomes a complex venture when attempting to introduce even a like-minded peer into the mix.

The Play Date

Play is the antecedent to eliciting creative behaviours. Having a pair of special needs children play together can become a form of social engineering—a process that the parents must structure, monitor, adapt and, at times, referee. Socializing 'on demand' is an artificial experience for anyone; one may witness adults at a social gathering, dinner or party—alcohol or other substances are a necessary social lubricant to pave the way for recreative social interaction. Even then, adult-version mindedness, including faux pas, boorish behaviour or overly talking about one's self, is frequent and processed 'after the fact'. Yet we expect children, including those on the spectrum, to accomplish this feat while 'straight', without being offensive or awkward. It is a hypocritical injustice.

Parents with special needs children often facilitate socialization by orchestrating the play date, beginning with choosing a suitable or receptive child and then carefully setting up the logistics of the social situation. Parents must try to create a relaxed, natural play session where both children are able to share interests and activities with minimal conflict. In some cases, this means the play is in parallel with one another. It is common to witness two children engaged in two completely different activities, complete with dialogue and sound effects. Overcoming egocentric or self-preoccupation requires the capacity to inquire about the interests of others. It is the first step towards establishing a *mutual* relationship. Concurrently, parents or social organizations must be proactive to anticipate issues before they result in a failed experience. Such engineering then also possesses relational *weight*. An experience with even one disastrous date, as can happen in any typical or even adult situation, may result in few second chances. Structuring the social event takes away from awkwardness and artificiality. A media or destination event, such as a movie or museum, assists everyone— whether typical adults or children—to find a common stimulus. A structured activity may provide just enough limited downtime for children to discuss the favourite aspects of the zoo animals or sleigh ride. It may seed conversations and stimulate mutual dialogue.

Destination activities should not, however, be conceived by adult standards. The two children may not be able to sit through even the most coveted animated film or the greatest pizza slice with any degree of social synchronicity. Witness the hyperactive child who wolfs down their food in minutes and then becomes rambunctious—what to do while the others are eating at a typical pace? Any downtime may result in awkward silence or conflicts. Parents must be attuned to the restlessness and disruptive inattentiveness and gauge when to bail, to ensure the time spent is about quality rather than quantity.

When more independent free play does begin, it is advisable to closely monitor interactions, as at any minute conflict might strike. Sharing may become an issue, different games are insisted upon, rambunctiousness turns physical—each scenario requires well-attuned parents to intervene, armed with alternative, more structured activities. There will always be conflicts during play, which is a necessity for social learning. Yet the frequency and intensity of these social conflicts guide our interventions as to how closely the children are monitored and whether interventions are warranted. In a perfect world, the children will have learned to compromise and work things out between themselves—though this is often beyond the ability of the spectrum children. As the child's inner resources ebb and flow, changes in tolerance can be expected. What worked on a weekend may be disastrous at school—there is no straight-line, upwards trajectory of an evolving relationship.

On school grounds, some children may lack the capacity to join in play activity. I have observed many hours of playground behaviour as a means of learning about children in their naturalized environment. Some children were often observed hugging the perimeter of the playground fence, marginalized and unnoticed by school aides. A disinhibited child was teased when she over-compensated, doubling her efforts at acceptance and then meeting with even greater derision and rejection. One child still could not 'take the hint' until she was literally pushed away. One group of boys played dodgeball, striking one victimized child in particular. A playground aide remained oblivious. More than once, I have lobbied schools to have a teacher oversee play activities at recess. During these times of low or transitional supervision, children on the spectrum suffer the most, changing classes, the social free-for-all of recess, the under-supervised school bus—just walking home can invite predatory behaviour. The school must be held accountable for such instances. Social conflict issues should become a measurable goal when formulating 'Independent Educational Plans' (IEPs), where social objectives are identified and given equal weight with academics. Therapeutic intervention can then complement social goals and objectives, coordinating socialization and play initiatives. It may help, however, if like-minded individuals are sought out to have a more forgiving atmosphere to try out socializing behaviours.

Equals in Social Awkwardness

We return to eleven-year-old Devin, who refuses his mother's pleading to come outside (Figure 4.1, pg. 58). Eventually, he relented and joined our summer camp. Although on the autistic end of the continuum, he was initially resistant and withdrawn and then became passive when with others; he began depicting images of the other equally autistic-like boys. His preference was the storyboard format with image and text. The image (see Figure 4.2) is amiable except for how he portrays the duo. As in his earlier work, when his self-image is a forlorn, worm-like

Figure 4.2 This same artist, Devin, created a zoomorphic dolphin friend as a symbolic equivalent for a companion, though 'who is who' remained transitional, protean and thus uninterpreted.

creature, he again treats the human form as a zoomorph; the pair are posed as *dolphins*.

Dolphins were almost certainly an aquarium favourite for Devin. They are renowned for their relatedness to each other as well as to humans, in both captivity and the wild. Being social and playful, wild specimens routinely come close to shore to swim amongst human beings. Thus, it was a positive identification, with the pictorial content depicting an easy-going, friendly spirit. The form remains consistent with the inclination for those on the autistic end to avoid fully human pictorialization. One might consider the response as an expression of artistic license—the boy knew he was not a marine mammal; thus it may be an example of rare and fascinating autistic humour. Utilizing an alternative but kindred species perhaps lessened the anticipatory anxiety that accompanies dates even between established friends (though again, such social anxiety is not unusual even by newly introduced, well-adjusted typical individuals). His method of problem solving, while ingenious, still indicates inhabitation within the autistic realm. With a social engagement looming and transitional space interfacing with the real, such intimacy aroused a curious form of depersonalization. Though the characterization is eccentric, it is ingeniously humorous and benign—qualities indicative of this bright and mild-mannered child.

Social Fragility

Finding two children who are relatively equal on the social scale is a worthy goal, as evidenced by the previous vignette, yet it cannot be overstated that such relationships are still fraught with fragility. Another social-response drawing bears this out when a sixth-grade girl we'll name Imelda had a play date with a close and like-minded friend. Together, they played with their pets and dressed up and put on skits, only to have Imelda react to some slight, which she depicted in her drawing as being so upsetting that she laid face down in the grass, sobbing inconsolably (Figure 4.3).

Meanwhile, her mate seems dismayed and surprised, one moment playing with a party hat and then shown with a confused expression. While the process notes are incomplete on this work, its narrative is clear: during the play activity, something was done or said which set the child off, resulting in her being devastated. Despite the melodramatic reaction, Imelda could recreate the incident with almost perfect realism. There is no distortion or other elements of emotional upheaval that impacted the finished drawing—even her friend's upsetting expression is faithfully recorded, indicating that the child possessed sufficient ego strength in some mental compartment, which allowed the narrative to be reported with exacting realism. Being a non-verbal child, however, she made few verbal comments which explained the events of what had occurred. The drawing, then, is received at face value, with limited capacity for further analysis.

A major issue with spectrum children is 'recovering' from such a setback—which appears to be the case in this captured moment. Once the offence has been

Figure 4.3 Imelda's play date is sensitively and skilfully rendered with a clear representation of the hurt and suffering. Identities were also fluid and shifting as to which child was scorned.

committed, whether warranted, too subtle to notice or a major conflict, I have stated the damage may already be done, with the play date in ruins. As to who was responsible, oversensitive or insensitive, all remains moot. The session is over— with the hopes that there is a next time. Interestingly, however, many children with mindblind issues may counterintuitively forget about the event even if in the recent past and can start afresh after a cooling-down period. It is possible that the mindblindness regarding the social dynamics in play may prevent the child from recalling the whys and hows of the conflict. I have witnessed this many times— how a child may resume a relationship without residual feelings. However, if mindblindness is the culprit, it may also prevent the child's verbalizing or creating about the incident, and it goes unprocessed. Probing the child about the drawing, even with its dramatically realistic form and content, is not necessarily the path for resolution. One can only trust the process—that Imelda's drawing was cathartic, releasing pent-up emotions, giving them a positive avenue of release. The creative response hopefully distanced herself from the event rather than feeding the flames further, which in turn could result in perseveration, or failure to 'let go' of the conflicts. In any case, it is not known which way the stimulus played out. Despite Imelda's articulate skilled hand as an artist, her narrative gives vague form to the social problem at hand, with solutions which have not yet been cognitively or emotionally worked out.

After-School Programming

The Hecht Group organized an after-school socialization program which addressed those social issues that could not be resolved through independent play or extracurricular activity (Henley, 1998). Issues were addressed in dyads, triads or group sessions according to age and functioning level, or organized amongst neighbourhood friends, whose parents had banded together their spectrum children for therapeutically supervised social sessions. Issues were identified and group activities tailored to fit interventions with creative materials and processes. An example of the 'friend-conflict model' addressed one of the more poisonous social dynamics, that of the triad, where the adage 'three's a crowd' still holds.

Triangulation conflicts occur when a trio of friends are without one of their partners, which may lead to speaking ill of the absent, talking behind each other's backs or ganging up (Simon, 2008). Particularly among those with immature personalities, one unconsciously 'splits' individuals into negative and positive parts, creating what Simon describes as 'opposing realities', with one child's being over-idealized one moment and then being devalued the next. These oscillations between idealization and degradation were a fluid, ever-changing dynamic that was at its height during the triadic relationship, with the key element of one child missing.

Triangulation and splitting were seen in three 'tween' age girls, who were given several sessions by their parents as a means of 'clearing the air' and trying to reset these children's relationships. They volunteered enthusiastically; however, since all three were present, it obscured the issue of triangulation, and thus there was no antisocial acting out generated. But the issue was brought up at the session's beginning, with non-confrontational discussion that did not require verbal processing. But they clearly knew what issue I was alluding to and that the session's focus was to work on awareness of playing one against the other—that no one deserves to be spoken about behind their back. By keeping the verbal element emphatic, but not harped on, defences remained open for our group drawing activity. The three skilled artist children worked together on a piece which gave a glimpse of the triad dynamic at play. The resulting creative arts outcome was a complex image depicting them in fanciful and realistic play.

All three in the group remained in good spirits and interacted pleasantly and, at times, even affectionately. There was no conflict over dominating the picture, dictating components, or anything else—these were indeed three close friends. One began by drawing butterflies, a glaring sun, a huge rainbow and other well-crafted elements which enliven the composition (Plate 1).

It was a highly stimulating, even hyperactive, narrative, with two sets of characters. There were the seemingly 'live' figures who coexisted with those who were barely 'there'. These latter figures are transparently drawn ciphers who display facial expressions that are variously blank or scratched out, while others display emotional expressions—some amused and others distressed. Meanwhile, 'their real selves', as the children termed them, are drawn in action, full force. They are displayed in a flurry of colourful activity, watering flowers and picking fruit, hugging trees, or letting a frog go while cavorting around a fountain. This quantity of narrative activity was matched by the energy brought to the project. With multiple activities depicted in full swing, with each girl actively engaged, behaviourally, there was no hint of triangulated conflict.

The fact that all three were present again prevented triadic splitting—the issue could not be tapped. The parents suggested perhaps holding a two-child session, leaving one of the children out; yet this arrangement might have artificially induced splitting and was considered a 'setup' by my supervisor, Dr. Hecht. He counselled that I decline the parent's well-meaning suggestion but use the session to gently remind the girls 'how they were partners', to remember 'how one feels when left out' or how gossip is destructive to all. At the end of this drawing free-for-all, the girls' parting image was to draw a kite to fly aloft above their rainbow. Was it a call for unity? A celebration of an otherwise fragile friendship? If so, perhaps the group image graphically indicated the limitations of triad relationships. For three girls with mixed spectrum issues, or for any 'tween' for that matter, it is only natural to gossip or play one against the other when only two are present. The solution was for the parents to socially engineer their play dates to avoid twosomes. By keeping the children together as a social unit during play or creative activity, splitting and other destructive dynamics could be minimized. Adults too could benefit from this social lesson.

Ganging Up and Mixed Loyalties

Children gang up; it is an undeniable tenet of childhood. Yet the dynamics can be as complicated as any social interaction. When a group includes one or more children on the spectrum, the dynamic is further complicated. In one scenario, my sixth-grade client, Kenneth, and his brother, Richard, shared a sibling session that was complex and difficult to recount. Both boys came in conflict while engaged in a pickup hockey game during recess. The teams included their friend, James, who was a child outside of our practice but well-known as probably ADHD with aggression and impulsivity. In the session following the game, Kenneth drew the vignette, which illustrated the conflict over 'who would play the team's goalie'. Kenneth's other teammate, Thomas, vied for the position and was 'backed up' by older brother, Richard. However, Kenneth's 'hot-tempered' friend, James, became infuriated and subsequently tried to 'whack' Thomas with his stick.

The resulting narrative image (Figure 4.4) is a dramatic re-enactment, which for a child with attentional deficits was no easy task. Having two boys interpret the incident required an extended session, which I could accommodate. For these boys to sort out issues of team and sibling loyalty while keeping tempers from flaring in the heat of the moment proved almost impossible. Further still, juggling these demands occurred while playing a tough contact sport without adult supervision. Without a referee's structure, boys on the hyperactive and aggressive end

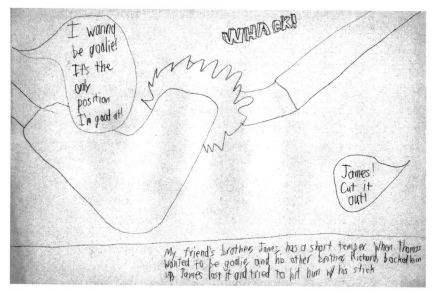

Figure 4.4 Another complicated social interaction depicting a pickup hockey game, which required extensive drawing, text and therapeutic conversation to unravel the social dynamic.

of the spectrum are liable to display unsportsmanlike behaviour. Articulating this complex dynamic required two boys to create an action image and text to convey the unfolding dramatic events.

The creative response assisted Kenneth and his brother to communicate an entangled event by teasing apart the situation visually—to express their story in all its complexity. In the end, the session elucidated how unstructured social activity during contact sports or pickup games becomes complicated and amplified in terms of frequency and intensity of conflict when children on the spectrum enter the mix. Unless the children can explore issues related to their impulsivity and aggression through therapeutic activities, these incidents may not be professionally sorted out. Both brothers left with a sense of how the team dynamic shaped their games and when to anticipate when conflicts will arise.

The Socialization Group

The socialization group sought to create a naturalized environment where children of mixed spectrum types could interact, play and be creative together. The Hecht Group sessions were composed of four to eight children with two co-therapists and an aide. They were held for an hour and half, a long stretch, but one that went by quickly given their structure of different segments. The sessions were divided into four components, with the first segment being a destination activity that encouraged structured free play. The destination element changed over the months to renew the element of novelty and ranged from an electric train set and a realistic dinosaur diorama to a group of fish tanks with assorted creatures. Each of these elements drew the children immediately together, to gather around, allowing for free interactions yet structured by this novel interactive object. The second phase was a group circle, where children shared anything they wished about their week or free play. During this segment, the children knew they were 'working', meaning play was over and we were now engaged in discussions that were serious but framed in funny anecdotes, stories and even song. Thirdly, the group adjourned to the creative arts or action sport sessions, either of which constituted group therapy. For the final ten minutes, the therapists charted while an aide allowed the children time for unstructured, free play and readied them to transition back to their parents.

Interspersed throughout the hour and a half were ongoing discussions, demonstrations and mini-activities, which reminded the children and reinforced the rules of engagement. The children were not lectured about behaviour as though in school, but expectations were 'massaged' into their awareness, using encouragement or gentle prompts, or they were unobtrusively taken aside. Over weeks and months, the children came to know the sessions' ground rules and behavioural expectations, with their most important therapeutic tenet—that what was discussed or acted out 'stays within the group' (Safran, 2002). The latter element helps build trust, as well as providing for positive boundaries and limit setting.

Transitioning is a difficult concept for anyone with the merest anxiety. Coming from school, Scouts or homework club, the clients' anxiety, agitation and impulsive behaviour were usually at their highest when they first entered. As a distracting stimulus, the destination activity could absorb many of these transitioning behaviours, becoming the 'transitional object' in the process. It assisted the children in separating from their parents and became the focal point of socialization, rather than face-to-face interaction. With the object beckoning, children could immediately enter the realm of make-believe while still being cognizant of their social behaviours.

During one session, one ten-year-old, Raj, announced his presence by his distinctive footfall, skipping down the last three stair steps, tripping on his untied shoelaces and landing with a thump. Much effort was expended on keeping this hyperactive boy becalmed and focused during this after-school transition. The effects of his stimulant medication were in a 'rebound', or wearing-off mode, thus increasing his irritability. Good natured but oblivious, Raj immediately barged past everyone and took the controls of the destination stimulus—in this instance, a fully landscaped miniature HO train set. Built over the course of three months by the children and therapists, it was an imposing eight feet in length, taking up an entire nook of the studio. Its size permitted the group of children enough personal space to prevent over-crowding yet still encourage constant interaction. The train set consisted of two trains—a locomotive with different cargo cars and a caboose, and a diesel engine with passenger cars. The set had a controller, switches and other controls that invited participation and manipulation. It was realistically landscaped with a hollow mountain for the raised trestle and a plastic landscaped 'lake'. This was surrounded by a forest of trees, which became a novel stimulus. Children had to demonstrate sufficient self-composure to be permitted to wield the hot-glue gun, which attached each tree and shrub. There were green fields, which the lesser functioning children delighted in creating—sprinkling the green granules over glue painted onto the board, which magically stuck, creating a verdant field. There was a 1940s era town, which taught the children about a different time—of when America's lifestyles reflected a slower, more personable agrarian society. It had a quaint downtown of miniature storefronts, Victorian homes, old-fashioned cars and small figures—people out fishing, doing errands, unloading coal and operating a water tower. The activity permitted an immediate, stimulating interactive experience. However, given the miniature scale of the landscape and train set, levels of stimulation were finely tuned and relatively controlled. Everyone took turns as the engineer, which was usually punctuated by crack-ups and derailments—excellent metaphors for later use in group therapy. Others manned the video camera, animated characters, wrote screenplays or performed skits, with each child in speaking roles. They were often performed for parents when every few months there would be a mixed child-parent meeting.

Returning to our hyperkinetic Raj, aside from pronounced hyperactivity, his body in space was controlled chaos. He presented with poor boundaries, lacking even a beginner's sense of empathy towards the needs and feelings of others. He would immediately seize the controls, almost knocking us over as he drove the locomotive into high-speed crashes. Those on the inhibited or autistic end of the spectrum tended to shy away and avoid his instant commotions. Unobtrusive cues and prompts were required for him to maintain, including the use of timeouts—not as a punishment, but an alternative activity with the counsellor that was less rewarding. They angered the boy, which initially detracted from the efficacy of therapy.

To help Raj reframe the session in a more positive light, Dr. Hecht had me schedule a post-session for him, as a one-to-one time when I could reintegrate and gently revisit his behaviours during group. During this session, he took it upon himself to carefully reset the trains and props for the next incoming group. He was allowed to greet and assist the younger incoming boys with the diorama, even helping them navigate the controls with uncommon patience. He admonished the younger children 'not to go too fast or you'll crash'—which drew knowing smiles from the co-therapists. As with other children with hyperactive or similar issues, he thrived when in leadership positions especially with younger children. The therapeutic outcome was then salvaged after almost three hours of therapeutic work. This positive 'reset' helped him demonstrate his strengths, exercise empathy and derive a therapeutic benefit from his after-school program.

Evidence Base

Both the summer camp and after-school group activities were evidenced based, with charts using a variable checklist depending upon the program that included twenty or more objectives, including space for a narrative component (Table 4.1).

Table 4.1 Summer Camp and After-School Program Progress Worksheet

Summer Camp and After-School Program

Child: _____

Date: _____

Free Play / Socialization / Recreation: _____

Initiates or joins other in play	1	2	3	4	5

Comments: _____

Initiates conversation with peers	1	2	3	4	5
Ability to follow rules – safety	1	2	3	4	5
Ability to negotiate conflicts	1	2	3	4	5
Displays patience, tolerance	1	2	3	4	5
Ability to share toys/games	1	2	3	4	5
Quality of transition from play	1	2	3	4	5

Friendship Circle – Short Term Goal: _____

Able to recall and articulate goal	1	2	3	4	5

Comments: _____

Participates in discussion	1	2	3	4	5
Able to read intentions, facial cues of others	1	2	3	4	5
Quality of eye contact and voice modulation	1	2	3	4	5

Able to manage _____ minutes of group discussion/processing

Snack / Lunch / Hygiene: _____

Demonstrates washroom self-care	1	2	3	4	5

Comments: _____

Meal time manners	1	2	3	4	5
Socializes during meal time	1	2	3	4	5
Ability to relax during quiet times	1	2	3	4	5

Therapeutic Activity – Theme: _____

Ability to explore issues related to goal	1 2 3 4 5

Comments: _____

Degree of self-expression	1 2 3 4 5
Attention span /concentration	1 2 3 4 5
Uses materials appropriately /creatively	1 2 3 4 5
Ability to discuss and reflect upon therapeutic experience	1 2 3 4 5

Overall Behavior: _____

Self Awareness of impulse control	1 2 3 4 5

Comments: _____

Degree of arousal sensitivity	1 2 3 4 5
Awareness of body in relation to space and others	1 2 3 4 5
Awareness of voice and facial expression	1 2 3 4 5
Display of empathy or consideration for others	1 2 3 4 5
Ability to regain composure after setbacks or upsets	1 2 3 4 5
Displays of verbal and/or physical abuse	1 2 3 4 5
Transitions during arrival and departure	1 2 3 4 5

Narrative: Strengths and Weaknesses

Counselors: _____
_____
_____

Therapist: _____
_____
_____

Key: 1 – unresponsive to issues
2 – shows awareness of issues
3 – attempted solutions with cues and support
4 – self-control/self-expression with minimal support
5 – independent mastery of goals

These data needed to be quickly tabulated while the children ended their day with story time at the end of the programming day. Each counsellor or therapist checked off goals, made comments and added creative response work to their daily 'package'. The narrative component especially was critical to framing the child's performance and highlighting accomplishments and strengths while also making note of any unresolved issues still in process. This was by no means a static document, but was edited constantly as the child's and program's circumstances dictated. This material gave the parent, the social worker or Dr. Hecht a 'snapshot' of the child's day, available in their files for future reference. Without them the author's publications would be fiction. That such meticulous data were generated over the five years of this program's tenure, with thousands of notes recorded, also allowed schools and insurance companies to view the charts of the children's maturational development. With this evidence-based documentation, many insurance companies considered both Camp Friendship and 'The Treehouse Afterschool Program' to be high-level group psychotherapy. Their considerable cost for such individual attention was then reimbursable to parents—thus encouraging critical, long-term 'membership', which proved to have the maximum efficacy.

The Problem with Summer

The most intensive need for social programming occurs during summer, when the structure, rhythm and time frames of the child's day change overnight. Returning to The Hecht Group's programs, with a successful after-school program came a call for a summer camp. In this sense, the practice became a 'wrap-around' service, attempting to meet the needs of children year-round, as many children could not attend regular camp, join a competitive athletic team, or simply be part of the circle of friends within their local neighbourhoods. 'Camp Friendship' offered an adaptive, leisure-time creative response-oriented program as the locus of social and therapeutic treatment (Henley, 1999). For almost a decade, this was a family-run summer program, which was under the auspices of our psychiatrist, Dr. George Hecht. A camp director, head counsellor, myself as resident therapist and two college-level counsellors per every four or five children, including a floating aide, ensured the needed manpower. This program also used process notation documentation and thus also qualified as 'outpatient therapy' by major insurance companies.

The bucolic camp was housed in a stone cottage set by large, open space lawns, woods and a sizable lake, where wading, netting and fishing flourished, and it had a bird-watching blind for nature watching—all presented with accessible leisure-time activity. It also had enough macadam to accommodate bicycle and other black-top activities. Each morning, twenty children, ages five to twelve, with varying degrees of severity, separated with varying success from their parents. They eventually lined up with their fishing poles all awry, backpacks full of favoured stuffed toys, lunches and meds, their Xanax or Dexedrine at the ready, all set to try their best to productively make it through the seven-hour day. Handling transitioning from parents also occurred in reverse—'terminating' the camp day, when children had to again navigate the transition back to summer home life. The issue of transition remains a major thread that runs throughout this book, and it was in clear evidence in the first and last hours of the camp day, when children's and counsellors' nerves were frayed.

Creative Responses

Creative response activities were at the centre of establishing individual and group identities. The camp director, Ms. Dawn, would present a theme for each week, which laid out the conceptual elements, media and related activities that would be combined to produce a final, Friday group exhibition or performance. In this way, large-scale productions comprised many smaller elements. This kept themes and outcomes manageable, with each personal project leading up to group participation. Invariably, dramatic productions, child-made videos and songfests added up to an avalanche of stimulation—one that would take up all of Friday morning's production. During one week, the theme was conceptualized as a Renaissance Fair. Included in the projects was a session creating miniature clay figures that engaged in jousting tournaments, all decked out with armour, costumes and heraldic banners, and using plastic straws as jousts. The point was to knock the rider off the ceramic horse—which too was sculpted well armoured (Henley, 2002). Finally, the castle was erected, and the kings and squires, beak-headed jesters and ladies all assembled for the celebration and performance (Figure 4.5).

Figure 4.5 At the end of summer camp week, Ms. Dawn would combine all the expressive projects and integrate them into an afternoon's multimedia performance piece.

For four years of often gruelling but fruitful eight-week summer sessions, each week's theme produced a melange of cooperative art and project making. These dramatic enactments resulted in hundreds of hours of video documentation and still pics, along with over a thousand detailed process notations of each child's daily social and creative outcomes. These voluminous quantitative and qualitative data and photographed images permit me to report on case vignettes as though it were yesterday. The summer program would eventually morph into an after-school program held once each week in fall and spring terms, creating a continuous cycle of socialization programming.

Socialization on the University Level

For students training to become professional creative arts therapists, it is important to establish a positive group dynamic through interpersonal relations, in and outside of class. This often required experiencing psychotherapy first-hand. It was incumbent upon students who would eventually become healers to have their adolescent, even childhood, issues addressed before or during training. Students with unresolved issues often created disharmony and conflict among their peers. At times, it was displaying and commenting on their art expressions, which were obviously issue laden. If too severe or frequent in form or content, creations needed to be dissected during their own therapeutic work, and not publically in an academic setting. I can count many instances when the room quieted as a student shared material while oblivious to the issues being shared. The entire class dynamic was often affected. Thus, it was expected that students attend therapy themselves to manage their own neuroses. With the cumulative effect of 'everyone in therapy' came the potential for social harmony within the classroom.

However, among these students were those on the spectrum who required more services than their typical counterparts. Most presented with symptoms related to attention deficit disorder, Asperger's syndrome or bipolar disorder. During group discussions, some of these students interfered with the group dynamic by a range of means: dominating class discussions with long-winded, poorly articulated comments or questions, and others making faux pas regarding 'over-sharing' personal material. These issues eventually compromised relations with peers, making therapy an even more compelling requirement.

One particularly difficult student was taken aside in several instances of talking through others and displaying poor boundaries when discussing her creations. This student was eventually counselled out of the program until she could become medically stabilized. Amazingly, this student sought the needed services after taking a leave and then returned fully stabilized after a year's counselling and a new medication regimen. She had gone through a strict protocol for diagnosing the condition. To come away with a prescription required an exceedingly rigorous process of testing and a set of three extensive interviews. Having been diagnosed for the first time, this student found Adderall to have an almost immediately recognized therapeutic effect. It was observable in her classes as well, with previous issues of late submission of papers and social unpredictability being vastly improved. During socialization events, her relating was less awkward and more nuanced; she was even elected to take on a leadership position within the program's club. Comments during class discussion were also more organized, succinct and coherent. She revealed to me that, yes, she was diagnosed with attention deficits and other issues and the medication had now improved her life beyond her expectations.

However, stimulant medication, such as Ritalin or Adderall can be abused, especially on the university level. Just as past generations of university students had used amphetamines to pull all-night sessions of 'cramming', so too do contemporary students with or without medical conditions find their stimulant medications to 'enhance' performance (Schwartz, 2016). Another student with undisclosed attention deficit hyperactivity issues fell prey to such abuse. Finding that he had slid from his prescriptive doses to managing his 'own program', the medication took on a life of its own. It had slowly and insidiously become 'supernormal' in its effects, with side effects of sleep deprivation, mood lability, weight loss and deteriorated social relations. Researchers Kerley, Copes and Griffin (2015) contend that the stimulant misuse is in keeping with the 'culture of success' where elevating one's performance, especially among the middle class, is now a disturbing norm— as overachieving and drug use are part of mainstream culture.

This undergraduate art therapy student eventually sought out the university's psychiatrist to address his escalating problem. The doctor had him undergo a program for controlling what was now deemed an addiction. Withdrawal came with almost immediate, observable effects with agitation, restlessness, lethargy and decreased motivation. Addiction to stimulants had crept up on this student on the spectrum, whose limited self-awareness left him perhaps mindblind to self-increasing the dosages of this potentially dangerous drug. When Adderall is abused, the rush of dopamine increases arousal levels, resulting in feelings of euphoria. A permanent 'rebound effect' then takes effect, and the withdrawal becomes insufferable.

After an almost disastrous semester, his intake had fortunately resumed at safe, prescribed levels—but only after sinking into toxicity with volatile mood swings and depression. He confided to me that the psychiatrist had stated that he was now 'an addict in remission'. He would have to be permanently hypervigilant against the dangers of over-medicating. Once medically stabilized, he was again his outgoing, quirky 'normal self'—a splendid artist, sometimes a bit 'over exuberant' when relating to peers, but generally popular within the program. But this came with a price of having to increase his self-awareness and vigilance, perhaps in perpetuity.

Five

Approaches to Creative Activity

History

Creative response therapy takes its history from a long tradition of progressive artists, educators and therapists who can be traced to the turn of the twentieth century. After WWI, child-centred art education was imported to the United States by Europeans who had been traumatized and war torn. These emigres introduced a new pedagogical emphasis that was an empathy-based, 'child-centred' philosophy. Focus was on the individual needs of the child—a radical view when children of the poorer classes were previously viewed as no more than cheap labourers. John Dewey (1934), philosopher, educator and aesthete, recognized that through creative education one's personal potential can be realized, not through the dry acquisition of questionable facts or rote learning, but rather through creative experiential learning. In 1919, Margaret Naumburg founded the progressive Walden School in New York City, where she drew upon Dewey's ideas, with whom she studied at Columbia. Naumburg's educational philosophy also focused upon the 'individual transformation' of the child through creative response education. Her sister, Florence Cain, also gained notoriety as the school's innovative therapeutic art educator. At the same time, Rudolf Steiner and his Waldorf School was founded with a pedagogy that emphasized practical, hands-on activities integrated within the role of individual imagination. Each of these pioneers drew upon psychodynamic theory, which emphasized a productive harnessing of primary psychic forces, engaging the child at the deepest level within both education and creative expression. From Vienna came art educator Viktor Lowenfeld, who was among the first to write on the 'therapeutic aspects of art education'. He articulated how the child's creative outcomes span mental and physical disability (1957). His work with the handicapped helped 'level the creating-field', making child response activities accessible to all capabilities. He also was the first to discuss a 'stimulus', which provides the child with a modicum of structure by way of theme, sensory experience or conceptual idea. Also, in 1953, came psychoeducator Clark Moustakas, whose book, *Children in Play Therapy,* applied humanistic and existential psychology approaches to children's social and play dynamics. I was fortunate to study with this brilliant pioneer late in his career. He possessed the wisdom of a sage yet with childlike qualities that coloured his teachings.

After moving on from the Walden School, Naumburg applied her psycho-analytic approach to art therapy—the field she is credited with founding. She initially practised as an art therapist with traumatized children in New York City during the advent of WWII. There, she initiated creative response activities that built upon Lowenfeld's emphasis upon sensory experiences while working within a psychiatric inpatient setting. She emphasized free-associative, internally gener-ated images. Her seminal cases demonstrate how the therapist might elicit images from the depths of the unconscious in a bid to free up repressions and other defences that result in neuroses (Naumburg, 1947, 1973). The second founder of the field, Edith Kramer, was also a refugee from fascist-dominated Austria. She was an apprentice to mentor Friedl Dicker, who was eventually arrested by the Gestapo and interned, becoming the famed art teacher of the Nazi camp, Terezin. There, she somehow managed to elicit wondrous art from the doomed children in this camp. Eventually, in 1944, Dicker was transported to Auschwitz, where she eventually perished. Some of the art pieces elicited from the chil-dren by Dicker and others in the camps were miraculously preserved and still form a beacon of hope from terror, worldwide (Makarova, 2000). Influenced by Dicker's association with the Bauhaus, Kramer began analytically oriented teaching at the progressive Little Red School House in New York's Greenwich Village. Building on Naumburg's psychodynamic work, she eventually moved in 1953 to provide art therapy services to delinquent children at a residential school, The Wiltwyck School for Boys (Kramer, 1958). Her approach, branded as 'Art as Therapy' (1971, 2000), echoes the early founders' philosophies, that of the 'child as artist'. Working as an artist-teacher, she modelled the foundation of artistic self-expression and craftsmanship, which in her hands became inherently therapeutic and educational.

Integrating the Founders

Modernism flourished for almost half a century, enduring two world wars and rev-olutionizing once again the importance of individual expression as a creative force. As the 1970s approached, the era of postmodernism emerged, which asserted that 'originality' constituted an illusory impossibility, that the arts are rarely original but rather are usually revisited and reconstituted. Art forms that allude to mod-ernism can be found in the most ancient cave art, in the sleek Cycladic sculptures dating to 3000 BC, to the early seventeenth- to eighteenth-century African masks, whose forms Picasso borrowed in the primitivist painting *Les Demoiselles d'Avi-gnon*. Postmodernism dictates that all creativity is a 'rehashing' of art forms that preceded each succeeding contemporary era, which is especially obvious in archi-tecture, as almost every monumental building is a knock-off of classic Greek style. For millennia, the postmodern ethos was alive, with cycles of acceptance and per-secution of individuals with learning and emotional differences. Shamans, ecstat-ics and eccentrics in antiquity had been accepted, even prized for their unique visions and contributions to their respective cultures. They were also sometimes burned at the stake. Such are the vagaries of being 'different'—at times in history celebrated, the next moment, maligned—all in a great revolving circle.

Creative Development and Making Special

Creative response expressions often begin at the pre-symbolic level, when expressive capacities may be extremely limited in scope. With arrested cognition or deep autism, expressions may not culminate in an aesthetic product and are thus considered pre-art. Children may manipulate sand, water, cotton balls and blocks, but these activities are akin to play rather than endowing the activity with symbolism. The first stage towards symbolization is that of 'making special'. This sociobiological term was coined by the evolutionary oriented art critic Ellen Dissanayake (1988), who examines pre-aesthetic expressions of individuals across diverse cultures, including the cave or rock images of early man. She poses the questions about the 'original' creative impulse: What does mark-making or the pre-symbolic manipulation of materials tell us about the developing human mind? Cardinal also addresses the question when studying mark-making from graffiti to the ancient rock engravings of ancient man, which he characterized as the 'primitive scratch' (1989). He describes creative expression at its most basic— as minimal traces, seemingly mute, indigent, even paltry—which still may possess the power of eloquence. Marks or manipulations of even non-aesthetic material may be 'evidence of an unusual conjuncture of the crudest means and great creative density' (pg. 113). The individual at the pre-art stage may eventually mature sufficiently to also elaborate upon and formalize their own impulses in personalized terms. Almost any action may be endowed with 'specialness', whenever an object is imbued with meaning and thus decorated to enhance its appearance. My preschool grandson finds a piece of rose quartz and keeps it—it is his original creative impulse of making special. Some months later, walking by our river, he notices that others have balanced their stones atop other rocks. As a five-year-old, he 'gets' the idea and begins placing his own atop other cairns. While not quite symbolic art, it stands as a proto-creative response indicating the process of ushering in an aesthetic sensibility which is not far off. Being bright and artistic, he has since developed a sense of formalized aesthetic expression at age six. It is a process that perhaps began to define modern humans some thirty thousand years ago when the Upper Palaeolithic peoples began 'making special' their appearance by painting bodies or stringing together cowrie beads (White, 1993).

Enhancing the ordinary with unique and personalized attributes is the first step towards a creative response. With children on the more severe end of the spectrum whose development is arrested, the pre-art phase may be protracted for indefinite periods, even when long-term interventions are forthcoming. In Figure 5.1, Ms. Dawn is shown working with a deeply autistic boy who was inhibited and preferred to hang on the fringes of the camp's garden fence. She engaged him at his level and in his own proxemic territory, and invited him to elaborate the chain links with crepe paper streamers.

Figure 5.1 'Making special' is a concept coined by Dissanayake to confer personal or cultural elaboration of an object. Ms. Dawn is shown helping a boy make a chain-link fence 'special'.

By helping and encouraging him to hang multicoloured strips, which rustled in the breeze, she is stimulating and setting the stage for making special. While his response was passive, and cognitive awareness of the creation is open to question, the sensory stimulation afforded him seemed a pleasurable experience. It is the first step towards the leap from purely sensory and emotional experience to conceptual thinking, which is a tremendous feat for those with severe impairments. It is the transition from utilitarian to elaboration. Whether that boy ever succeeded in bridging that divide we shall never know, such was the intractability of his handicap. Yet it did not deter Ms. Dawn from modelling procreative behaviours, regardless of his functioning level.

The creative response activity, then, makes use of creative expression to help enhance and elaborate upon life activities. The range of making special is almost boundless, through art, music, literature, creative writing, movement, manipulating images or simply formalizing an action. Expressions may be elicited in the creative arts studio, at home following directions off the Internet, or done in complete secrecy and shown to no one, or emerge as part of a group project from school or work. Its emphasis is always centred upon a response to some stimuli so-far described. These may hopefully ignite children's inborn passions that express something of their inner and outer worlds (Henley, 2007). Miles Davis famously declared, it is not art until you have something to say. The creative response stimulus may assist in realizing or translating the children's ideas from their own perspective and transform their unique worldview into a creative response. They include the following tenets:

1 Possessions, expressions or experiences that are 'made special'—emanating from life attachments, which may evolve into therapeutic, educational or formed aesthetic quality.
2 Activities which maximize social discourse, interaction and cooperation through aesthetic outcomes.
3 Activities which are open ended, with a minimum of direction, with a stimulus which may gently guide and structure one's expressions.
4 Applications can be adapted to any setting, such as school, houses of worship, home, play, or social leisure-time activities, as well as in the therapeutic setting.
5 Interventions are discrete and ideally unnoticeable with 'camouflaging' when possible; the therapist is a facilitator, not the authority figure.
6 To tolerate outcomes which may not be totally appropriate but are productive for the individual's development. This stance requires a balance between empathic acceptance and limit setting according to the social mores of the setting.
7 To maintain and adjust behavioural expectations during activities, based upon what the child can *handle.*
8 Assist the child in developing healthy defences, of learning compensation, compartmentalization and sublimation via the creative response activity.
9 Methodologies are based upon observation and intervention, fostering development and not as purely research experimentation. They ideally translate into clear goals, objectives and outcomes which can be empirically notated.
10 Creative responses may ideally be generalized into the child's behavioural mainstream, with indicators that what has been worked on in the therapeutic program has been *internalized.*

These core values are flexible and dynamic. They are applicable to any number of settings and populations, from putting on a group art performance to stringing crepe paper in a chain-link fence. In reaching the most developmentally arrested child, professional orientations of the practitioner become secondary; any approach which evokes a creative response is welcomed. As the introductory case vignettes have already indicated, children on the spectrum evolve with surprising diversity, sometimes with a special brilliance. The cover image was created by a teen named Jeff, who was legally blind and deaf with autistic features—though he was atypically friendly with people. The image was spontaneous with no visual aids besides his photographic memory. The high-rise is drawn without a straight edge, with the monolithic projects looming over the street life in the city—one can even make out a tiny figure standing patiently at a bus-stop shelter. Outcomes such as Jeff's are rarely as spectacular, as most others are variously eccentric and bizarre, especially when influenced by current media, such as the super-glued guy in Figure I.2 (pg. 15). They may be elicited in accordance with school projects in which academic outcomes are the expectation, but somehow become infused with aesthetic sensibility. The creative response may not even take an artistic form. The 'activity' itself may be the out-come, such as an archer shooting a longbow—no further response or elaboration needed.

Mixed Outcomes

Almost all the creative responses described in the case material are 'mixed responses', meaning both positive and negative aspects exist simultane-ously within the expression. Bexley, the WWII fighter pilot from Chapter Two, and Tonya, the child from Chicago's Near West Side from Chapter Three, point out how spontaneous creative responses were unpredictably mixed. Bexley's breakdown from an otherwise sunny theme and Tonya's weaponized gang-inflected art demonstrate that art can be both destructive *and* cathartic. Again, in the spirit of postmodernism, outcomes can hold true, with both pos-itives and negatives coexisting without contradiction. They may reflect Jung's (1989) concept of the shadow side—the darkness embedded in everyone that requires one's inner resources to merge and assimilate it into the whole person, as descent struggles for ascendance. Often, creative outcomes recognize the ten-uous existential state of being of their creator. We welcome them, with some limitations, as authentic personal expressions that do not detract from their specialness.

Accommodating Extreme Outcomes

When working with any child on the severe or even mild end of the spectrum, extreme outcomes may be the first step towards productive expression, or remain a regression—temporary or intractably negative. Regressions may be loosened by any stimulus, which may strain already fragile defences, releasing the unfettered power of aggressive or libidinal drive energy. On one occasion I was swept up in such a regression while working with deaf children hospitalized with psychiatric issues. I was conducting an initial session with an intense, impulsive eight-year-old girl named Julie, a hyperactive child, unpredictable and often uncontrollable. My process notes indicate an utterly disastrous first session, as I failed to control the outcome of a 'simple' painting project. It transcended clinical prose, prompting me to adapt it to a poem in which the wild scene became far more visually alive than clinical descriptors, as it transpired in the child's own sign language:

RED!
Want-Paint-Red!
OK says helpful me, let's pour a little out….
Jar grabbed, turned over, slowly a wave of thick deep red
misses half the bucket—hands dive in,
No!
Elbow deep in red.
Paper picture obliterated, hand prints, wall, table, floor.
Window smeared murder red!
Wags her finger; 'OK, now must clean!'
'Need more water'; No, No, water multiplies red.
Splattered walls….everything now washed in Red.
The commotion draws supervisor.
Who cares about 'boss lady' she signs.
She stands back-lit, stern arms on hips, flashing signs *what is going on!*
'All over Red! Much Good Cleaning!'
Barked orders unheard, I'm slumped over the mop bucket
I mumble something weakly, *then,*
Julie signs 'Go Away!'
Her elongated slimmest of white hands sign in wild flurry.
Shielding dejected me…still hunched bum-like on a stained red mop,
Her signs cut the air:
'This is Private Here'.
'This Man is Tired Now…'.
'Leave Us!'……………

The poem paints a vivid picture of a session whose events had overtaken me and spun out of control. Powerful forces emanated from this little pixie of a child, whose creative response to 'red', the most emotional of colours, led to the wild breakdown. Protecting me from the supervisory reprimand, this child took a stand and spoke for me—declaring the sanctity of the therapeutic session would be preserved—*no matter what*. This child's almost maniacal creative response barely contained the powerful effects that overwhelmed us both. It was debatable whether this extreme outcome was therapeutic. Yet something special happened; a child rose up and, although deaf, found her *voice*.

In individual therapy like this, much more acting out is tolerated. Creative expressions which are not a threat to self or others have a right to exist and be expressed within the safety of the one-to-one setting. In this case, the authority in charge (supposedly me) perhaps needed to set more limits—yet the atmosphere would have shifted from therapy back to 'school'. Any trust earned would have evaporated. Julie's *lack* of control was expressed in what Kramer refers to as 'chaotic discharge', which is an understatement. Yet it is incumbent at times to trust the process, to take behavioural and aesthetic risks to mine therapeutic material which hopefully culminates in a productive outcome. Outside the private session, when other individuals or institutions are involved, whether an educator, a group art facilitator or even a gallery—all must curate which expressions or actions fit within their respective venue. In such cases, work created as therapeutic outcome must be kept private, as its consumption by others would be a breach of confidentiality. Some work is made for exhibition, but even within a classroom, expressions might need to be censored.

If work is to be exhibited in venues where viewed by the public or family, it is the audience which must dictate what is appropriate to be seen or watched. Case examples such as those found on pages 211, 249, and 251 could be construed as so offensive, it could be debated whether they should have even been included in this book. When too provocative, profane, explicit or hateful, expressions such as these may need to remain under 'house arrest'. If expressions born of the child's suffering cannot be consumed by a viewing public, they may need to be confiscated and kept 'safe' within the personal confines of the studio or classroom. For instance, Tonya's painted wooden staff eventually found a home within her teacher's locker, for 'security' purposes. As a potential weapon, it was now deemed a 'private' creative expression and was thus under protective custody. It was taken out only when it was her turn to 'speak' with stringent reminders: 'Can you *handle* safely holding this stick?' This puts the onus on the child, to rise to the occasion and control their impulses or have it taken away. On occasion, the child herself may become frightened by her own creations. Our little aggressive seven-year-old deaf girl eventually created works of graphic abuse from which her anger was ignited. Her rudimentary storyboards that depicted her abusive figures needed to be locked away, as they seemed to frighten or perhaps even re-traumatize her. With a bit of ceremony, she herself secured the work in the flat file, using a small padlock. It kept 'the ghosts in', she signed in a rough translation. She was permitted to keep the key. Whether a stick figure drenched in red, a ribbon on a fence or a speaking stick, creative expression of any form or content can be aesthetically or therapeutically analyzed. One set of aesthetic criteria has been set forth by Kramer (1971). Her criteria have proved immensely useful for examining the art of professional, historic artists to a young spectrum child. Its value lies not in criticizing or judging a child's self-expressions but as a means of plotting where the child is in their creative process and to measure the potential for further growth.

Aesthetics: Kramer's Formed Expression

Aesthetics is a philosophy which explores the boundaries of art and its merits, which has a place in analyzing client therapeutic work. The works in this text have been chosen for their aesthetic worth, as well as therapeutic outcome, from among hundreds of others. Many more works in my collection are impoverished, copied or stereotypic, while some of them are just bland. Curating the illustrations chosen was a matter of seeking 'balance' between beauty and saccharine sweetness or angry discharge and well-articulated indignation; if it was a borrowed image from the media, its intent needed to be deciphered. Is it meant to stay a 'ready-made', or instead, will it be transformed into something refreshed? Each of these is an aesthetic problem that has been debated since creative expression began. Kramer's system of aesthetics is useful for critiquing, yet it too exists along a continuum—of loosely defining what constitutes 'art in the truest sense of the word' (Kramer, 1971). Her benchmark concept, termed 'formed expression', has equivalents in other cultures and aesthetics. Neurologist V. S. Ramachandran (Ramachandran & Blakeslee, 1999) uses the word *rasa,* which in Sanskrit translates roughly as 'capturing the essence of', where creative activity enhances, transcends and even distorts reality in the service of abstraction or artistic license and 'other secrets of the mind'.

'Formed expression' is useful for gauging aesthetic rasa, whether it be 'high' art or the lowliest expression. This 'high-low art' continuum was explored by Kirk Varnedoe (1990) in a landmark exhibit at the Museum of Modern Art and the Art Institute of Chicago. Included within his exhibition analysis was the aesthetic 'place' of so-called primitivists, outsider artists and children, which Varnedoe also placed upon a loose arc mixed with modernist masters. Varnedoe placed Stan Lee's Marvel comics alongside Roy Lichtenstein's pop art: What exactly is the difference again? I posed the same aesthetic question in Dubuffet's image in Figure 1.1 (pg. 20): How does one discriminate between the two? Kramer also contributes to the high-low conundrum by defining expressions such as pictographs—for example, Evan's first piece (see Figure I.1, pg. 12), which are often communiques more than art—the aesthetic relied more on schematics than formed images. This model is not intended as a judgement per se. Evan's piece still fascinates. The analysis rests on simply describing, in everyday terms, 'where' the individual falls on the creative continuum (Kramer, 2000).

Form and Content Continuum

Formal expression indicates the child's use of elements of design; form describes their sense of line, colour, texture and perspective. Content is the narrative that runs through the expression. These ideas are the 'nouns' of the story the work tells: thoughts, memories, references and relationships. Both form and content can be discussed and analyzed either in concert or independently. For instance, a child may have profound ideas that are depicted in the content of a picture, but take the form of impoverished stick figures. Many pictographic 'storyboards' fit this format, as the artist's *intent* is to convey thoughts and actions with little interest in elaborating the figures or other elements. Again, they are visual communiques. However, even the most aesthetic 'looking' image may be devoid of narrative. Nadia's brilliant formal draftsmanship (see Chapter Two) was most likely *without* context and high-level ideation, but utilized high-fidelity visual translation. When there is integration between quality of form and content, there comes the potential for the most powerful and meaningful formed expressions, which become creative in the truest sense of the word. Analyzing form and content assists the therapist in establishing a baseline, of assessing where the child 'is' in the process and then indicating creative growth or regression. One might note expressions that are developmentally arrested, aesthetically impoverished or pathologically symptomatic. There are indications of successful compensations, hard-fought therapeutic victories and effortless artistic giftedness.

Symbolization and Sublimation

When form and content combine to create a symphonic aesthetic experience, it often serves self-expression *and* communication. Symbolization derives its power through the drives, but also via the partial neutralization of drive energy, whether it be libido or aggression. The degree of 'transformation' of drive energy may indicate whether a work or activity is fully realized as a sublimation—the highest 'quality' defence that Freud theorized. When there is a sublimation, both form and content transcend each other, unifying, strengthening and communicating at the highest level. Despite being rare instances, sublimations can occur in children who have never spoken a word or made eye contact, or whose anger knows no bounds. What distinguishes a work of sublimation is its ineffable rasa, that the child's 'essence' has been captured and communicated in an aesthetically powerful form. To employ these tenets in the analysis, they must be translatable into other modalities, from art to athletics, fishing to writing verse. As Kramer's formulation was described regarding artistic expression, it can be applied to almost any creative endeavour and is defined as thus:

- Kramer asserts that true art is always 'emotionally charged'—it arises from and evokes feeling. While these feelings may constitute a range of emotional states, even those difficult to understand, it does not detract from the individual's own subjective experience. Emotions can be as chaotic as pounding on clay to the most sophisticated painting; here again is a 'loose arc'.
- Secondly, creative responses ideally possess an 'economy of means'. The adage 'saying so much with so little' recognizes this as a universal construct. It means that in art, poetry or casting for a brook trout, no element 'need be added nor should it be taken away', whether it be in form, content or action. The strongest creations do not shout 'look at me', but are understated. Each attempt to strike an edgy balance between form and content makes it fully 'replete'. Repleteness is a useful term, as it indicates the relative weight of each element, how much of a figure, a tree or a cloud, and the colour red 'counts' in terms of aesthetic or thematic importance. By analyzing how 'economical' a creation is, one can infer a command over ideas and material.
- Lastly is the quality of 'inner consistency', which asks the question: Has the artist been true to himself? Many artists, athletes and musicians struggle between remaining true to their inner passion and the need for outside affirmation. When outside pressures exert force on a creator to submit to the demands of another's taste, whether it be an art teacher exhibiting in grade school or a band

playing to forty thousand fans in an arena, maintaining inner consistency takes enormous self-fortitude—especially for spectrum children, as they must juggle many demands to conform to mainstream expression.

Kramer's requirements of what constitutes art are again conceived with flexibility, sometimes as an unattainable ideal. As stated, few children on the spectrum can be expected to achieve a refined state of performance in either of the three categories. We witnessed the most primitive expression with Julie's chaotic discharge turned loose in my poetic treatment of the colour 'red'. Bexley's outcome was equally chaotic. These two sessions consisted of 'acting out', where the creative process was aborted before or after anything had even taken form. This discharge may not necessarily detract from therapeutic efficacy. Note Joey (see Chapter Two), the self-injurious child whose repetitive rolling and pounding clay served a crucial function, to redirect self-destructive impulses while remaining proximally close. Individuals on the severe end of the continuum, such as Tonya and Julie, may be caught in the uprush of previously repressed emotions during the creative act, especially when triggered by a powerful stimulus.

On the other extreme of emotionality is autistic inhibition. Returning once again to Evan's work (see Figure I.1, pg. 12), stereotypic defences ruled form and content. The creative response was expressed as an inventory of environmental variables of the theatre. After his survival needs had been met, he could turn his attention to highlighting the sky-lit beam of the Batman logo. Here, Kramer's criteria can be applied, as Evan's expression did arise from passions about his subject. He evoked feelings about the theatre and its accoutrements and for his superhero. He was obviously true to his artistic and autistic self—and as such, his work was inner consistent. Yet we might conclude that his art failed to reach fully formed expression, as his defensiveness left him faltering regarding an economy of means. His work was overladen with stereotyped elements of restrooms, fire exits and extinguishers, each of which was a marker of the child's obsessionality and anxiety. It was, however, endowed with personal possibility. After two years of work, Evan comes closer to a sublimation and formed expression, as his anxieties gave way to the sly, quirky sense of humour (Figure I.2, pg. 20). The super-glued construction worker dangling helplessly from his head gives more dynamic form to the deep-seated anxieties he will perhaps always feel. Yet by wryly channelling these emotions by appropriating and commenting on his culture via an absurd commercial, he indicated higher levels of self-observation. Kramer's categories indicate how the creative responses are coming along, whether related to artistic, social or developmental terms. Throughout the case material, the criteria will serve as a therapeutic and aesthetic guide which might assist therapists to be more precise in their process notations, whether giving a clinical impression or articulating evidence of change. It is a gentle form of art criticism. Analysis does not necessarily require an interpretation of the symbolism of the work per se. We cannot pretend to know what lies behind the artist's intent, as meaning is always multilayered with complex meaning.

On Interpretation

Analysis of an outcome is not necessarily an interpretation of 'covert' symbols. One may describe and attribute form or content to salient issues without ascribing symbolic connotation of some underlying issue. We may suggest there exists symbolism, but what an element actually *means* is most often impossible to say. The artist himself may be bereft of words. I discovered this early on in my career when a teacher brought one of her second-grader's paintings to me concerned that she always painted towards the bottom of the paper using muddy colours. Being conscientious, she had read up on the symbolism of children's art and found that some interpreters considered that location and muddy colouring to be indicative of low self-regard and self-esteem. I took the opportunity to observe the little girl as she painted at a floor easel rather than on a table. She could reach only the lower regions—thus, she painted only at the bottom of the paper! Moreover, the dull coloration came from dirty wastewater, as her propensity to 'play' in colour, mixing the whole palette together, formed a brown soup which deadened her colours. Closer observation of the child's process rather than psychological interpretation would have proved the obvious, that interpretation flourishes with the naturalistic method of observing the child in her environment to assess that which is readily observable and meaningful form and content.

This little girl's painting points out the pitfalls of psychologically overanalyzing. Restraining oneself from over-interpreting takes discipline and a self-awareness of one's training, orientation prejudices and the amount of experience the observer possesses—in whatever medium being used. The use of cautious interpretation of the creator's process and product is one that cannot easily be quantified. Some talented researchers have attempted to quantify, but most results have become formulaic and over-generalized (Hammer, 1968). The problem is that there are just too many variables to factor into the analysis to arrive at the 'correct' conclusion. Therefore, throughout the discussion of case material, most outcomes utilize disclaimers—that an outcome 'perhaps' alludes to this or that issue, spectrum marker, culture, developmental level, intellect or pathology. I have tried strenuously to avoid finding symbols where there are none, beyond what is manifest or readily observable. By being experienced and attuned to one's discipline, the practitioner can analyze manifest form and content without over-reaching.

Therefore, remaining phenomenological keeps practitioners grounded in the here and now of the children before them—in all their infinite complexity. My impressions are rarely based upon projective or psychological tests, such as the 'house-tree-person'. The way a child positions or elaborates on a house roof has never symbolized an overactive fantasy life, as Buck (1992) contends. Or that a closed window correlates to being a 'closed-minded individual'. Another well-worn example is the proverbial knots or holes drawn in the trunk of a tree. In my experience, holes in trees are almost synonymous with the whole of typical and spectrum child-art, and not as Buck suggests, indicative of a void of ego function (Buck, 1992). These types of interpretations attempt to objectify highly variable, protean states, both conscious and unconscious, in ways that are quantifiable.

I have previously cited a projective test designed by Betts who collected data on how children on the autistic continuum 'face-build' their schemas (2003). The research poses important questions and yielded some interesting outcomes. However, in my experience, the protean quality of the creative process defies easy categorization and objectification. One cannot hope to generalize the test's findings, as its design could not factor in every personal, developmental, cultural or other variable from this disparate population. With her modest samplings, one never knows 'which kind' of autism she is testing—as there is no one child with the same autistic features or causality. There are hundreds of kinds of autism. Then, there is showing a real face to such children as a stimulus. Its realism may be too daunting for them to engage. The schema was not adjusted to the child's developmental level—thus a realistic, stereotypic, white male image can be foreign and even repulsive and yield little useful information with which to generalize. Any interpretation about a creative response must come with disclaimers, or it can lead to dangerous generalizations. Even if testing hundreds or thousands of 'subjects', no one's aetiology, nature of neurodifferences, gender, socio-economic status, race or faith can ever be fully considered. For this reason, I remain dubious of the current trend in the creative arts therapies to aspire to become more evidence based with quantifiable research. The 'test reliability', 'mean changes' and other indecipherable statistics collected have yet to bridge, in my opinion, the gap to functionality. These data mean little when exhorting a refusenik child who holes up in the family van for days, before finally overcoming her avoidance and joining summer camp. Such data are intuitive and virtually unknowable unless analyzed on an individual basis.

Intentionality

One of the means of analyzing form and content of an aesthetic or action response attempts to understand children's *intent*, meaning whether their creations *overtly* correlate to their actions, emotions and behaviours. While many images operate on an unconscious level, intentionality may be gleaned by closely *seeing* what is actually *there*. Creative arts or action productions often convey their meanings, usually by the most obvious means. For instance, if the child with visual impairments with autistic features accentuates, distorts or omits a door repeatedly, we can reasonably assume there are issues around entering through this portal; it may have been slammed on the child in the past or be closed off or frightening once inside. Hence, a personal stereotype has been created to respond to a sensory, cognitive or emotional issue—the exact nature of which remains ambiguous. It is pretentious to suppose that we can truly know inner workings of children's inner symbolic life, but we can make connections with images that link cause and effect (Henley, 2012a).

This reluctance to interpret unconscious symbols does not preclude the child self-analyzing his own productions. Children of all stripes are capable of showing great insight of their own creations. Later in the text, we shall encounter an artist on the autistic continuum, named Max, who equates his colours as personal 'signposts' (Figure 19.2, pg. 289). Through colour choice he confers the differing hues as symbolic equivalents for his different affective states. The children are always invited to share their own interpretations, which are never discounted, but remain a part of our artistic camaraderie with unconditional empathic regard. Verbal associations remain a critical but still ambiguous piece of assembling the child puzzle. Presenting images along with the child's verbal associations has long proved a vital adjunct, one that assists the clinical team in arriving at the fullest clinical picture possible.

Multiple Expressive Modalities

Creative responses often flourish when individual projects are combined and culminate in a larger production. I have previously described the summer camp program where most of the projects were broken down into incremental activities, which then culminated in a 'big ruckus'. Each thematic camp project employed multiple, discrete elements. An example involved bibliotherapy, costume design, a dramatic performance and cooking a special breakfast. The first stimulus comprised reading the Dr. Seuss rhythmic tale 'Green Eggs and Ham'. While it's a childish story, many of the camp's twelve-year-olds enjoyed it and built up their self-esteem by reading it to the younger children. In Seuss's iconic story, Sam-I-Am is a pesky creature (a common social theme in camp) who harasses two little children who resist eating such an absurd meal. After the camp's children read the book, they broke up into their respective groups to further process its relevance to their own situations. For the next day, the camp director, Ms. Dawn, had prepared an 'action activity', where the older children prepared a performance to act out the story. Ms. Dawn first had costumes created and props organized. Then, the older children were chosen to read aloud from the story while dressed in character. They practised reciting sometimes just a single line, which they then spoke on their counsellor's cue. Everyone contributed depending upon their capabilities. In the finale, the older children cooked a batch of green food-coloured eggs, which the performers served the audience as a breakfast.

The culminating moment was particularly challenging, as the older children were charged with reciting, cooking and serving. The outlandish-looking dyed green eggs made the meal 'special'—a stimulating motivator that helped guide the participants through these demanding steps. A singular moment came when one particularly autistic-like boy, Liam, whose faint voice was rarely heard during the camp day, was entrusted with the story's end line. After much practice and preparation, Liam rose to the occasion and while dressed as top-hatted Sam, recited his one punchline audibly, with authority. As he and the older children served the coloured eggs and ham to the eagerly awaiting younger children, there was a discernible shift in the group dynamic. For a change, they became the caregivers rather than 'clients', taking responsibility for serving the food with humour yet with care and hygienic competency. Each facet built up the tableau. They began with a bibliotherapy experience, with the literary and poetic, and ended with the dramatics and cookery, which then assumed a social action function of serving and eating. All were important activities that, once integrated, formed a piece of therapeutic 'fluxus' or performance art.

Hot Zingers

Later, during individual therapy with Liam, who had spoken his final line with startling clarity, the thematic chain remained linked together. He decided to revisit his character and the morning's event. Perhaps Liam needed to further process his recital, particularly what he later felt was his creepy character—Sam-I-Am. He did not discuss his 'line' or success at cooking and serving, all of which he managed flawlessly. His creative response drawing registers the residual feelings of assuming the identity, of 'becoming' the pesky character Sam, who perhaps seemed to him somewhat menacing. Drawn by tracing the figure's outline and then filling it in with exacting realism, Liam then improvised.

Sam is drawn walking away, his back to the viewer, with a mixed expression—disdain, haughty, anxious, indifferent? Liam's only comment was that Sam would suffer 'three hot zingers', which referred to the small, flaming arrows shot into the character's back (Figure 5.2).

It is a work of much complexity especially when factoring in the other elements of his performance piece and his first dramatic recital to a live audience. To

Figure 5.2 After reading and performing Dr. Seuss's 'Green Eggs and Ham', Liam responded by creating the mischievous Sam, who is being shot with flaming arrows, or 'hot zingers'.

analyze its meaning is fruitless except to say that Liam illustrated how the creature sustained an attack from behind. His form is strong and sure, his facial expression open to many interpretations. Maybe the attacking references were based upon a post-performance adrenaline slump, which one can find in any drama setting. Attention might be drawn to the contradictory nature of this figure—he is a funny master joker but also an antagonist. His moods, intent and even ridiculous rhymes are hard for a child with severe but high-functioning autism to decipher—and are thus confounding or disturbing. His response reminds us that as these children venture beyond their comfort zones, there will be outcomes of ambivalence with creative expressions so over-layered that they cannot be teased fully apart and understood. Such is the fascinating complexity of the creative response.

Six

Stimulus-Based Interventions

History

Ms. Dawn's project utilized multiple elements beginning with a single powerful stimulus—Dr. Seuss's story. This deceptively simple children's book brought on powerful responses from devising a performance, to a child's assuming camp leadership, of self-empowerment mixed with feelings of vulnerability, and even victimization. Every stimulus possesses unseen power, which the therapist can anticipate but not fully control. Evoking emotional and ideational responses to everyday life, stimuli such as summer camp and personal memories are all filtered through the unconscious and executive psyche. Almost every creative response in this book emanated by some form of a stimulus. Lowenfeld (1957) coined the term from his work in art education as a directive to children, rather than giving the usual old-fashioned cutting 'snowflakes' and other art projects of the day. Lowenfeld was determined to overcome the technology of the 1950s and tap into the child's sensorium—their sight, hearing, proprioceptive and sense of smell to inject direct sensations into their art. Appropriating the culture of adults was a taboo for Lowenfeld. Having escaped Nazi fascism, where supposedly superior adults murdered a million children or more, he proclaimed that from then on children's expressions should be free of adult interference. The imaginational stimulus was his rebuke and a child's rights protest. Instead he relied exclusively on the child's perceptions to report them directly through the medium. Adding thematic or sensorial experience adds open-ended structure, where individual outcomes were most prized. Lowenfeld's famous directive, 'picture yourself picking an apple of the tree' (1957) exhorted children to embrace the apple as a universal construct. Apples were a subjective experience for children—depending upon their culture, rural or urban; their age group; gender and extent of their typicality. Outcomes ranged from orchard-picking experiences to trying to find an unbruised example at their local bodega.

Seonaid Robertson (1963), a noted British Jungian art educator, issued a more emotionally loaded stimulus when she asked children of Welsh coal miners 'Who wants to make a cave?' Needing no further encouragement, these children of the mines began stacking classroom chairs, blankets and flashlights;

they literally engaged the sub-theme of this book—that of the *cave journey*. Jung considered caves to be a major archetype of the collective unconscious, symbolizing the embracing, protective womb and the journey into the unknown. For Robertson's children, confronting the darkness of their own caves had to be daunting yet also playful. For children of men who plied possibly the world's most dangerous profession, this exercise had intense ramifications—facing their own well-reasoned fears of loss and survival. It being the impoverished and drab post-war time in Britain added another dimension, as many children were orphaned and relied on elders for support—who, returning home from a ferocious war, *still* had go down into the coalfields. The post-creative responses Robertson illustrated were many primary process-inflected images, of cavernous halls cloaked in darkness, some with distant points of light. Another includes an angelic figure seemingly of hope, while other images are lost in swirling maelstroms. Robertson's students took a psycho-physical journey, which Jung described as at once 'blissful and terrible'—another powerful portal into transitional space.

Edith Kramer describes her early teen years being exhorted by her then teacher Friedl Dicker to 'pretend you're a bamboo shoot growing upward and upward' as the students would mimic the movements in a gestalt way, as their images spiralled into abstraction (Kramer, 2006). Margaret Naumburg (1947, 1973) urged her multi-spectrum, eight-year-old patient, Frank, 'to choose something from his room looking down upon the East River' to redirect his anxiety and obsessions. Distraught with the attack on Pearl Harbour, he tended to perseverate upon themes of nationalism, such as stereotypic drawings of the American flag. Using sensory based interventions, outcomes became more expansive, such as chronicling river traffic that included an emphasized Statue of Liberty (a symbol which was not perhaps coincidental).

Self-Imagination

Being dependent upon different stimuli, the imagination is the wellspring of creativity. From our inner worlds come fantasies, memories, hopes and dreams. They inform not just artistic expression but our personalities—with libidinous passions and aggressive forces combining to create worlds which know no bounds. As a stimulus, the imagination perhaps shows itself most prominently in early childhood. It is not uncommon for a child to have a fantasy friend or become engrossed in a world of imagination. Before age five it is normal for a child to imbue their stuffed toys with names, personalities and feelings. E. H. Gombrich's brilliant essay in *Meditations on a Hobby Horse* (1963) gives a prime example; he pointed out the importance of economy in creative expression—that it is the viewing or interactive audience which supplies the images and symbols in an aesthetic response. He cited how children often play more fruitfully with a simple broomstick when playing 'horsey', than choosing an adult-conceived, realistically decorated toy. He pointed out that it is the child's imagination and the fictional world that it stimulates and thus adds the needed magic. It is a transformation from everyday inanimate object to a kinetic toy and symbol, *re-imagined*. Children often keep their imaginary 'friends' secret from adults. Even at a young age, self-aware children realize they may be ridiculed over an immature, imaginary construct. In the play of children with spectrum issues, they may carry with them their imaginary friends and worlds in secret, which are then allowed free rein in therapy (Gnaulati, 2008).

Popular Media as Stimulus

Appropriating media and culture can have a powerful impact upon the imagination and sensorium of young children. The impact of current video games or films can have a deadening effect upon one's inner visions, memories and thoughts, or to the contrary, seeing a film or other media piece may become a profound experience, opening immense horizons during one's formative years. While sometimes the attachment may become all-consuming for children on the spectrum, leading to obsessions and blending of realities, one should remain open to the effects that media play.

Fantasia as Stimulus

Few media events have captured the imaginations of so many generations of children as Disney's *Fantasia*. This ground-breaking film from 1940 was re-released on the 'big screen' in the late 1950s. As a seven-year-old, my parents ventured to a Times Square theatre—a rare hyperstimulating event. Expecting another *Bambi*, instead my parents and I were presented with a profound, experimental, psychedelic opus—far reaching in narrative scope and dazzling in special effects. I can recall sitting transfixed, as one memorable scene—the iconic 'Sorcerer's Apprentice'—captivated me, even to this day. The animated piece is a tale based on a poem by the great Romantic poet, Goethe. It was set to the musical score by the maestro Leopold Stokowski, who is conducting the Philadelphia Orchestra, shown live, in dramatic back-lit silhouette. The scene begins when America's cartoon idol, Mickey Mouse, is cast as the apprentice of sorcerer Yen Sid, who under his supervision, allows Mickey to try out his magical powers. However, as the master naps, Mickey dons the sorcerer's pointed hat and ill-advisedly tries it out. It occurs to him that, rather than doing his own chores, well, he'd use the magic! Commanding a straw broom to do the arduous task of lugging pails of water up the winding stone steps from the well, eventually, the magic spell spins out of his control. As he tries to rein in the broom, to Mickey's horror, the brooms multiply exponentially. Now, dozens of identical brooms mindlessly march one after the other, bringing countless pails, all splashing the frothy water into the cistern, all while Stokowski's score crashes and thunders. Eventually, the master awakens to the vast flood and breaks the spell while poor Mickey is chastised for misusing the magic. For me, it became nothing less than an archetypal cautionary tale for an impressionable seven-year-old. It stimulated transitional phenomena—of the bridge between realities that developed and informed my artist persona, for the artist does trade in illusions. The film also inspired almost every academic interest still alive with me today—in mythology, poetry, symphonic music, animation, creation myths, the march of geological time and even how music can take on visual form. I have used the film's segments as a stimulus in many experientials, both with clients and university students, with creative responses never falling short of being intense.

The film was put to work during one summer camp session, when the activity was devised to combine music, movement and art therapy. Working with a group of 'tween' boys, I showed segments of the film during a morning rain shower, only to have the sun shine through for an afternoon's outdoor activity. While outside, I played them Stravinsky's *Rite of Spring* and Tchaikovsky's *Nutcracker* as a stimulus to accompany a large-scale 'action' painting project. Some of these mixed-spectrum boys held a mental picture from the film to assist in structuring their creative responses—while others remained oblivious and painted non-objectively. Whether visualized or not, the music became a powerful group stimulus that encouraged vigorous movement, translating the powerful symphonic pieces into a visual painting project.

Movement

For many children in our program, movement therapy was a vital creative response activity. To those on the autistic continuum, bodily movement was often constricted and even robotic. Some were so inhibited that even a powerful stimulus rendered them frozen in stillness or self-stimulation. On the other end of the spectrum arc, those who were hyperkinetic, stimulated movements were often poorly coordinated and locomoted non-stop. The *Fantasia* activity, then, was an exercise in freeing up the body while translating *The Rights of Spring* with poetic vigour, while remaining aware of their bodily coordination, boundaries and brushwork. The counsellors helped by modelling different movements, creating a choreography of both exuberance *and* self-control. Swinging their arms, hopping into the air with loaded paintbrushes all sought to celebrate freedom of movement. Those children on the hyperactive end required little prompting to skip and hurtle themselves about, their sweeping and splattered brushwork being a kinetic record of their movement. One boy who was more autistic sat cross-legged with his personal aide, who exhorted him to swing his arms and paint in time to the music.

With a ten-foot roll of paper laid out on the lawn, the soundtrack booming, most of the children began to freely dance about, brushing on their paint in the manner of Pollock's action style. The video footage documenting the event follows the children as they responded to the symphonic score, translating these sensations into visual form. In the postmodern sense, they responded to something vintage—the classics that dwelled up from the past, standing the test of time, while they are refreshed into the present. Their ten-foot banner was proudly displayed, draped across the camp's cottage doorway.

Fantasia for University Students

A similar project was part of an art/music experiential given to graduate students in their art therapy training, in which they painted in the same large-scale manner using *Fantasia*'s piece by Mussorgsky, *Night on Bald Mountain*. As the night bell tolls, the craggy mountain morphs into a devilish creature. As he unfolds his bat-like wings, he also releases the souls of the dead—exhorting them to rise and fly into the night sky. Again, as a child I was transfixed as these transparent ghostly figures, some even on horseback, were liberated, until the coming of the dawn, when the sun's rays had them return to their places of rest. For those students who had seen the film, their paintings prompted more contextual narrative. Others who had not seen the film painted in a style that was more free, abstract and sensory related. Having these two groups was an effective little experiment. We separated them during the critique and pointed out that the visual stimulus prompts differing variations of elaborated moods and visual responses. *Fantasia* serves as a timeless, multi-sensory and narrative experience. It can elicit a range of individual interpretations, as the montage of stories, images, sound and movements spark the imagination—for children and adults alike.

Personal Attachments as Stimulus

Stimulation often includes the possessions and passions of the client. Children have brought everything to session as a stimulus, from their hamsters wheeling furiously in their cages, skateboards and new digital devices, to a teen cruising up in his first car. Each of these themes served as a means of increasing personal investment in the process. Permission to bring in prized objects helped cement our therapeutic bonds, as their excitement was 'mirrored'. The mirroring construct of Mahler's is based upon another infant milestone as the maternal caregiver makes exaggerated facial and auditory sounds to elicit excitement and joy from the baby as they engage a rattle or hug their bunny. As with most object relationships, this phase evolves throughout the lifespan. *Everyone* who is excited about their new job, a new love interest or a new toy *needs* to have their own excitement mirrored back. We have all felt a feeling of deflation or even rejection when there is no 'mutuality'—we never outgrow the need to have our passion mirrored. This is also a key construct in therapy—that mirroring should be as authentic as the therapist can muster—but I admit to what a strain it is to mirror excitement of stimuli that are foreign. It is not so easy to become revved about another new video game, electronic dancehall track or the tenth generation of the same digital device. Yet there are universal stimuli that seem to cross every cultural or typicality divide—which can prompt an immediate sense of both excitement and ownership of a product.

The Mandala as Stimulus

Circular configurations are a universal archetypal form. The circle is perhaps the first object of attachment encountered after birth as the neonate roots out the mother's breast and nipple, which is hardwired as a means of survival. Perhaps this deep-seated 'form of attachment' is the reason why circular motif comprises countless images throughout art history, from the three-year-old's first intentionally drawn circle, to the spirit shields of Native Americans, to Tibetan sand paintings, to Robert Motherwell's abstract, *Eulogy to the Spanish Republic*. The Japanese iconic form, 'Enso', a dashing calligraphic circle, has become a worldwide symbol and even logo for international companies and brands.

Jung considered the mandala part of the collective unconscious—again stemming from our earliest attachments to cross every culture and historical timeline (Jung, 1989). Jung himself became skilled with creating and using mandalas therapeutically—a technique still in use as the path to what he termed 'individuation'. He also explored his own unconscious, creating hundreds of meticulously painted mandalas. Many were included in the illuminated transcript known as the *Red Book: Liber Novus*—his confrontation with the unconscious. During the fifteen-year (1915–1930) project, Jung recorded his fantasies, visions, dreams and other stream-of-consciousness imagery using the circle as the structure that contained and composed his images (2009). He became remarkably adept at creating ornate text and images, reaching seven-hundred pages of spectacular gouache paintings and Gothic calligraphy.

Mandala as Therapy

For the young or children on the autistic end, one often faces a limited repertoire of self-stimulating or stereotypical expressions—but the circular form remains a constant. While practising with severely brain-injured children, Joey's work was a prime example—if it weren't for the spinning banding wheel (another circular experience), upon which his hand-built pots were built—his motivation to play and engage would have been assuredly diminished. To him, spinning the wheel *was* the creative response. I spent years with children who'd spin, scribble or create countless circles, which sometimes evolved into idiosyncratic figures. To intentionally close the circle required a great conceptual leap—one that made the figurative motif become possible—until then the scribble remained a purely kinaesthetic activity.

The Circle in Play Art

The autistic ability to spin is legendary—it can reach amazing levels of skill. Such was Jules, a boy of ten, who was adept at spinning almost anything almost acrobatically, from pens to dinner plates. Drawing on this capacity I introduced a 'drawing top', a gimmicky yet fun design-making toy which has a reservoir of ink. When spun it issues a fine corkscrewing or spiral line. I demonstrated the device as a third-hand intervention, working in parallel, with no expectation or pressure, for this ten-year-old to try out. In another instance of the ethological 'luring' method, I attempted to stimulate his innate but latent curiosity, such that he might overcome his tendency to avoid almost anything other than spinning objects. To overcome his refusals and initiate some approach behaviour, the stimulus needed to be novel and intriguing, yet not a threat. The goal was to open a new door to be creative and playful—all in keeping with his spinning repertoire. After three sessions of seemingly indifferent observation, he finally grasped the thing while still in motion and tried his hand. Judging by his excited hand flapping, it was a resounding success.

The Nest Builder

Circular configurations were also an object of obsession with a nine-year-old girl camper we'll name Helen, who came for three weeks with multiple-spectrum markers. Helen's main autistic marker was her propensity to make 'nests' while avoiding most interpersonal interaction. This was borne out by our first moments of summer camp. Before her things were even dropped off and sorted, she ignored everyone and disappeared, only to be found behind the camp cabin gathering up the dried weeds. Within moments she had formed a small depression of spiralled grass expertly woven together. Later, we would find perfectly round nest forms woven during diverse activities—a paper-weaving project, a grass nest hidden in the girls' bathroom—one was a thimble-sized nest formed amazingly from her own hair which was woven and kept on her forefinger. These were aesthetically lovely and expertly made as though by a bird. They fascinated us all yet were also symptomatic. While many artists are single minded in their style, Helen was *stuck* with her woven circles, and thus we encouraged her to move beyond this isolative activity. Art therapists Kaiser and Deaver have reviewed the use of the nest as a projective test as a means of assessing the quality of relational attachment in their subjects (2009). They cited research that an 'empty' nest—without birds or accompanying stories—indicated lack of attachment. This may or may not be the case for this child on the autistic end of the continuum, again, depending upon the extent of samplings involved. However, our goal was in line with their findings, to facilitate attachment by extending her frame of reference regarding the context of her mandala preferences—as Lowenfeld counselled (1957).

As much of the camp day allowed her many opportunities to make nests, Helen was also subject to our stimulating projects. One project was conducted while wading into the water and along its grassy shoreline. Helen revelled in her favoured medium. She was often redirected by her counsellor to divert her attention from weaving grasses to our claywork project, where the focus was pinching pots. Hoping the circular motif of the pinch pot would redirect her obsession, she eventually engaged the material and pinched a serviceable pot the first try. Then, wading into the lake-shore shallows with her pot, she seemed interested in the group working on transforming their pinched forms into a 'community' (Henley, 2002). These pinch-pot forms required a careful, rhythmic rotation, of slowly forming and thinning the mandala. Once hollowed we demonstrated to the children that when inverted, they became igloo-formed or tepee shelters, which were then tucked amongst the rocks and reeds along the shore, creating our little village. This stimulus was meant to bind the group of children together by making

Figure 6.1 Usually isolated, 'nest-builder' Helen was finally lured to join a group activity down at the lakeshore. She perched her clay 'tepee' on the rocks, embellished by a sprig of grass.

private yet neighbouring residences. In Helen's case the goal was to build upon her circular motif and extend it to a claywork project with social interaction. It was another form of making nests, but in a substitutive material. The familiarity of the form, the pinching rotating motion of 'making round', stimulated the child enough to participate. She still interacted with other children in parallel, nestling her tepee form into the rocky outcrop of the shore. She is shown elaborating her little rock-cliff shelter with a sprig of dried grasses (Figure 6.1).

Working amongst her community of fellow muckers, Helen increased her tolerance to others, as close a proximity as she could manage. We played amongst the shelters with little plastic figurines for the next two days—which reinforced the project's process and the social exposure, the stimuli of the rounded, architectural nesting form—with her peers who accompanied her along the shore. As a group, we all returned to our village using it as an object of play—another example of chain activities.

The Circle and Exquisite Corpse

As children develop a sense of self-control and boundaries, more challenging stimuli might be introduced. For a group of older children an activity again involved the circle. This project centred upon writing poetic verses. The novelty was to write on paper plates pinned to the backs of each other. Using washable crayon, the writing entailed penning a single line of verse; then using the line written previously by another peer, the poem would develop. It is a version of 'exquisite corpse'—assembling a collection of free verse that when collectively assembled becomes a playful, interactive creative response. Given its propensity to be over-stimulating, as touching the backs of their cohorts was in and of itself provocative, stringent rules were set to contain this highly stimulating activity.

To handle the boundary limitations, to stay focused and creatively respond to each line of verse in a poetic way, was of course a challenge. It was strategically introduced at the end of the camp week's program with a group of acclimated and well-socialized children. To be able to 'handle' touching the backs of others required impulse control to not become silly and over-stimulated. It required yet another lecture about the 'things that could happen' by my demonstrating as a role-model how we go about controlling ourselves while having fun (Figure 6.2). By clearly demonstrating appropriate behaviours, the aim was to raise self-awareness of how to switch partners with a minimum of commotion and how to respond to another's verse to prepare the children for this stimulating activity.

When the activity began in earnest, the group began calmly enough, with each person 'pausing to think', then writing a new verse, then changing partners, each playing off the last verse until there was a full poem. Eventually stimulation levels reached their limit and the activity was drawn to a close. The works were then collected and the poems read aloud to everyone's cheers and jeers. Again, this was yet another example of barely controlled chaos, of gloriously messy outcomes—of poems that did and didn't make sense, of the giggles of bumping and confusion as everyone switched partners. It is an example of when the therapist must take

Figure 6.2 Personal boundaries were tested when the author initiated a group poetry project. Each child wrote a line of verse in response to another—as the poems were tied to their backs!

ownership of the stimulus. A poor assessment might result in the children becoming 'set up' to be infringed upon, lose control or act out beyond their capacity to self-regulate. Sound assessments and interventions may curb over-heated emotional responses, allowing for measured outcomes that are both pro-creative and therapeutic.

Academics as Stimulus

When I accepted a position as classroom teacher at the alternative school for last-chance students, the mission was to *keep them in school*. To accomplish this, it was obvious that the process could be ugly, the outcomes messy. Stimuli would need to be strong and to some extent 'edgy'. Without meeting these students on their level, they would become truant or drop out altogether. I wrote a 'therapeutic curriculum', where alternative educational material was connected directly to various creative response activities (Henley, 2016). With almost no curriculum materials to work with (as these were still back-ordered), I had to adapt. Before school was in session I happened to be reading the Sunday *New York Times,* which featured an educational subscription. When I contacted the *Times* they were eager to act as our impromptu curriculum. The choice centred on the issue of form and content. All the provocative news stories which these jaded teens yearned for were right *there,* all the street killings, drug swindling, sports scandals, political gaffes, foreign wars, mob trials, dangerous weather, earthquakes, *ad nauseam*. Yet what separated the *New York Times* from other papers was their exquisite writing of *form*. Even the most horrendous story was written with even-handed, editorial élan. It was factual, matter of fact and included almost no gratuitous or exploited treatment of even the most gruesome story.

Each morning the newspaper graciously delivered twelve morning editions, from which the group help planned the day's activities. Their daily 'sections' would designate the subject areas under study:

- The Monday edition was devoted to *World Affairs,* with stories of global events and governmental affairs, and was somewhat dry. It was fortuitous that Monday's edition also included the week's main *Sports* segment.
- On Tuesdays, *The Science Times* covered breaking news about natural history, sciences, health and medical breakthroughs.
- On Wednesdays, the segment was on *Food*. After reading recipes and discussing their favourite processed fast foods, we decamped to the school kitchen, where we *cooked*.
- Thursday, we departed from our regimen to read our own local county newspaper to cover local current events within our community.
- Fridays were given over to analyzing video film segments in the mornings with writing response essays while afternoons were all-out 'drumming' sessions.

Many creative responses were born from these news stories, from history, to genetics, to sugar-free diets to the latest video release. Reading a paper yielded more than stories on lurid murders or the weather in Rio; it became a morning routine for teens who mostly had none. It was a time when our own dysfunctional 'family' gathered around with tea and hot chocolate to peruse the morning paper, as might any intact household—an atmosphere I intended to emulate. Yet how did one control or filter the content when the lead stories were unavoidably disturbing? Again, assessing and anticipating outcomes from the stimulus issue was constantly arising. This was the time of domestic and international terror, with our country at war. At many points in time the stimulus was pronounced a negative outcome, resulting in revoking the paper and resulting in a temporary news blackout. Surprisingly, when more conventional book learning took over, the students vigorously protested. I compromised, as they had been taught over and over that I would lift the ban when 'drone bombing' or other content returned to its 'normal' level of disturbance. Despite their motivation to engage in violence in the media, the choice was taken out of the students' hands—as the cardinal rule remained one of psychological safety. Despite these interventions, there were many fascinating yet expectedly mixed outcomes.

Visual Tactile Experiences

Attempting to educate this population in a therapeutic way avoided conventional teaching with verbal lectures, board work or worksheets and instead required visual and tactile experiences. Academics who did not have hands-on or other sensory learning were usually ignored. For instance when teaching a science unit on prehistory and Earth's beginnings, the highlight was dinosaurs and fossils, not memorizing geological strata. Dinosaurs hold almost universal appeal especially for the predominantly male makeup of the classroom. Even the most jaded learner couldn't pass up handling stone-like mastodon and camel teeth, or fish impressions fossilized in the Wyoming mud, which each teen examined and discussed. Several pieces of ancient mudstone had been donated so that the more-focused or patient students could unearth the fossil. Dremel mini-grinding tools and dental picks were used as a way of cutting away the matrix—these select teens appreciated that exposing fossil for the first time in a hundred million years was something special.

Clips of animated films were also screened when interest lagged, with exciting sequences of Tyrannosaurus battling Triceratops and other creatures. Books were read and short response pieces were written, which encouraged illustrating the fossil examples. One exceptional student, Will, revelled in handling these objects but then worked on his essay with typical indifference. Yet when allowed his free-drawing time, he illustrated virtually the whole of our lesson, plus some fanciful elements (Figure 6.3). His image is most interesting when considered a fantasy role-play. Shown with his back to the viewer, the engrossed scientist works studiously at the computer—supposedly on 'top secret' material.

Recreations of the dinosaur battle were drawn on the walls to add action to an otherwise quiet scientific 'laboratory' environment. Aside from being remarkably drawn without any use of copied visuals, it spoke perhaps of an unattainable ego ideal—one that identified with the excitement of a dinosaur-hunter persona. His

Figure 6.3 A response to a hands-on lesson in palaeontology, a gifted teen named Will visualizes a laboratory which was romanticized by the intrepid dinosaur hunter, Roy Chapman Andrews.

identification with an academic-type adult was a rarely positive expression of personal aspiration. Of course, archaeology is perhaps the most boring scientific discipline, requiring expert geological knowledge and endless walking through difficult terrain in extreme environments, sometimes searching decades before finding anything of value. But the romantic side of discovery captures the imagination of many children, teens and adults, who flock to natural history museums to view a most recent find.

One of the books Will had access to was on the intrepid Roy Chapman Andrews, the most famed and romanticized of the early fossil hunters of the 1920s. The model for *Indiana Jones,* when Chapman was not harpooning whales off the coast of Japan or playing polo near his villa in Beijing, he would be courting the Park Avenue elite for funding his next excursion. With his financiers' funding he became the first Western explorer to roam the red sands of Mongolia's Gobi Desert—one of the most remote regions on earth—searching for fossils. However fascinating, I did not expect Will or anyone to read at length about Chapman's exploits, which would just be too laborious. Instead, I would take up the book and read passages aloud to the class during their 'quiet time'. Ensconced in their beanbag chairs, many students revelled in the action sequences, such as when Andrews's caravan was attacked by nomadic brigands and ended with a classic but Mongolian shoot-out. In this way, I could both reinforce his interest level and keep the collective imagination alive. The mixed quality of the therapeutic outcome engaged the young man, whose art was a resounding, positive creative response—but perhaps it played into aspirations which were not realistic for this handicapped young man. But everyone deserves to dream.

Veiled Outcomes

The *Times* demonstrated on many occasions that even with a well-balanced story, an innocent, informative theme may invite negative outcomes—some of which were expertly camouflaged to escape censorship. For instance, on one afternoon, a boy discussed a self-generated assignment on some newly discovered, obscure Egyptian pharaoh and his burial artefacts. Some gathered around to admire pictures of their jewellery, particularly the animal motifs, such as Anubis and the scarab beetles—objects several voiced an interest to create, which was not a simple task. The stimulus was productive; we had gone from a lesson on Pharaonic history to the iconography of their cartouches and then embarked on learning the jewellery-making techniques of these ancient craftsmen.

Coincidently, I had previously set up a small light-metals shop, which we quickly adapted to the new Egyptian theme. The first step in making these small three-dimensional forms was to make a negative mould. By sketching the figure and then carving it into soft cuttlebone (the same material found in bird cages), the students created a negative mould into which molten pewter was poured. Several interesting Egyptian-styled small sculptures and jewellery were then cast. Much excitement arose when it was decided which students could best 'handle' the propane torch to melt the pewter, as any miscue could prove catastrophic. Finally, two trustworthy students were 'elected'. The metal was quickly melted and, using an iron ladle, was poured carefully—hopefully with a minimum of splashing that could burn through skin. I recall the principal pacing outside during this and other projects. He anxiously monitored the potentially dangerous process through the window in the door. Once the pour was completed, I noted how he quickly exited without comment.

One teen, who was probably bipolar with mania, was also a self-avowed white supremacist. An ex-convict on parole, Adam, worked surprisingly hard and unusually long on an intricate medallion. The *Times* had included in their piece bits on Egyptian mandalas. In the article the author wrote how they represented the seamless cosmos, of eternity and coming full circle, and were common forms in carved cartouches and jewellery. Seizing on the article, Adam brought the work home to finish, ostensibly to file and smooth the piece with steel wool. This was very unlike him—and I would soon understand his enthusiasm. The following day he proudly wore the piece to school, but to my dismay, overnight he had deviously sawed away several key interior elements of the circle. His piece now became a three-inch round swastika—an ingenious provocation, which I unceremoniously confiscated. With the administration and me already at odds over my 'playing with fire' and several other questionable outcomes, this piece did not advance my cause. Being an avid reader, Adam vigorously protested. He cited how we had already studied how swastikas were a universally revered mandala form until the Nazi's co-opted it as a symbol of hate. With the *Times* article backing his slick argument, he attempted to advance his cause. I was not moved by his rationale. He had already received what behaviourists term 'second-hand gain', as the other classmates had seen the piece before confiscation as he gloated over 'beating the system'. It was part of his 'jailhouse' mentality adopted during incarceration—'to get over on the man'. The gain, with its cleverness and shock value, had raised his status amongst his peers despite my best efforts to shut it down. The outcome was clearly negative, constituting egregious acting out, a stimulus which I had failed to anticipate.

When the Mind Travels at Ease

Thus, it is an expected part of working with teens that they push the limits whenever possible. Our last example is a cautionary tale, that a positive stimulus and object can turn ugly overnight. In another stimulus-based project, the teens were to choose collage elements which conveyed something positive. It began by choosing from a pile of text fragments which I had pre-cut from magazine ads or articles. The students were invited to incorporate whichever phrase caught their interest and then draw around the text to elaborate or associate as they wished. Our class artist, Will, who had created the previous laboratory scene, was a highly gifted artistic and musical young man who displayed multiple mixed markers, with attention deficits and probably early-onset mania. This sixteen-year-old could draw with startling realism and savage caricature, directly from imagination, a skill that far surpasses that of this writer's. Will carefully sifted through the folder of clippings choosing a text fragment that read 'When the body is comfortable, the mind travels at ease, too'. He stapled it to his paper and began to draw quietly for almost forty minutes, no small feat for this hyperactive, distracted teen. The outcome is a whimsical and skilled coloured pencil drawing with no pathological distortion—just a wily, cartoonish piece that evocatively spoke directly to the theme at hand (Figure 6.4).

However, Will's relaxation scheme implied going home and smoking some cannabis. While inappropriate in the group and school setting, the response to the text was in sync in keeping with his culture and refers to a relaxation method partaken by millions since prehistoric times. To Will's credit, the smoke was not presented in gratuitous terms, nor was it meant for secondary gain or to solicit the attention of his peers. The work was an authentic expression—a creative response which fit Kramer's criteria of 'inner consistency', meaning the artist 'was being true to himself' (1971). It also was spot-on true to the text fragment, as the drawing evoked a contemplative feeling with well-composed elements of economy. In short it was a 'fully formed' creative response.

Yet even fully formed artistic creation does not translate in school as an inalienable right. As a young man with current substance abuses, it was not an 'ideal' outcome. Though I valued the piece, any form of drug references were verboten in school. Yet it was his form of relaxation; the question had been

Figure 6.4 Will was invited to free associate on a fragment of text. Designated a 'mixed outcome', he interprets it by drawing himself peaceably high on cannabis.

asked and he answered. This puts the practitioner in a double bind. One asks for authenticity, for subtlety, aesthetic wit and elegance, and receives it, yet it is ultimately undesirable. In my keeping with the curatorship rules, the cannabis piece was deemed worthy—yet it needed a 'safe space' in the lockup. Being witty and savvy, Will aligned himself with Adam's confiscated Nazi medallion and shouted: 'CENSORSHIP!'—as many adult professional artists delight in doing. I found myself wearing a private smile at the sheer ingenuousness and charm of these incorrigibles.

Drumming, Music and Rhythm as Stimulus

'Somebody give me a beat!' I hollered, letting my hair down just a bit on 'Drumming Fridays'. After our week's academic work came to an end, most students were rewarded by a session of 'spontaneous percussion'. This art form engaged them in some of the most primal and intense sounds and beats that have gone unchanged from the dawn of history. The drum is among the most primitive and glorious art forms, which celebrate the creative response in many guises. It served as a means of keeping Fridays together, controlling yet expressing in one vigorous activity. Learning percussion could become an acceptable leisure-time activity—one that could be developed and integrated into band and academic settings.

For those who could 'handle' the frenzy of stimulation, we would decamp to the 'sound room', an area of the school whose walls were partitioned by a concrete wall, making it impervious to sounds that might disturb the rest of the classrooms. In this room was a donated drum kit and the all-important five-gallon buckets with cutoff broom handles that served as the main instrument. We listened to and played along with all forms of music—from Afro-pop rhythms, to hip-hop to jazz, the Beastie Boys to the big-band era of drumming, including the frenzied Gene Krupa, whom the class deemed 'was out of control', in 1943. It was another 'teachable moment' how someone so ancient could push expressive limits but still be acceptably creative. The beat was unfettered free expression, serving as a much-needed cathartic end to the work week.

A simple beat from a song or riff someone brought in offered some structure and avoided mayhem. As a stimulus, I used beat-heavy songs by Santana and Gato Barbieri. Playing along with this percussive Latin-styled song helped the group find a source, one that kept the rhythm at least somewhat coherent. The beat goes:

> Ba-ba-ba, Ba-ba-ba, Ba-ba-ba, Ba Ba!
> Ba-ba-ba, Ba-ba-ba, Ba-ba-ba, Ba Bam!

With this beat laid down came improvisations, embellishments and even rap lyrics. Various other songs accompanied by percussive instruments made in school or scrounged were brought into the mix: cowbells, drum pads and even a large metal garbage can and lid made up our 'drumming circle'. Eventually the students came up with their own beats and were permitted to 'teach' them to the group, providing they assumed a teacherly persona. Having them demonstrate while being patient with the numerous false starts and other mixed outcomes was an exercise in leadership. While drumming, everyone was free to switch off instruments, take a break or stop the tune altogether. It was a barely controlled, raucous stimulus, which invited vigorous and harmless participation regardless of skill level.

Paolo Knill (1994) was an early proponent of drumming as a therapeutic modality, which he writes allows individuals to draw upon their natural, perhaps inborn, capacity for rhythm and beat. Drawing upon other cultures beyond our Latin emphasis, Knill used African, Indonesian and Indian drumming as a stimulus. As an adjunctive activity, he emphasized researching these different cultures and their instruments. He termed it the 'quiet' side of this activity. We too included history and culture of the music into the curriculum, with some academic work 'earning' the class two hours of a percussive free-for-all.

Mindfulness and Relaxation Therapy

Knill also discusses the high/low sensory sensitivity levels of sound being tailored to different individuals as a key to successful implementation. Since two of my ten students were on the autism end of the spectrum, they required an alternative to the din of loud drumming. My aide or intern would conduct an alternative quiet-based 'sound therapy' as musical relaxation. Sitting in beanbag chairs, gazing out at our bird feeders, these two children *chose* their own sounds that would relax and entertain, from recorded nature sounds and Native American flute music to their own attempts at tapping out a beat. These sessions became the flip side of the drumming circle, replacing catharsis with relaxed mindfulness—both were welcomed elements of the curriculum.

Relaxation or contemplation, whether it be by drumming, sound therapy or other calming modalities, were often introduced as another core stimulus of the curriculum. As applied to creative work, Franklin (2017) has found contemplative practice amongst practitioners and clients alike to be an aid to awakening deeper insights into the self. However, if mindfulness and relaxation traditions were to guide one deeper into self, what might the individual find? A damaged, anxious, fragmented self? How can creativity be enhanced unless the relaxation or meditation possesses curative benefit? Neurologists have now documented how these modalities heal emotional and somatic duress through brain imaging and heart monitoring. Many modalities which were previously 'alternative' modalities are becoming increasingly accepted by venues, from cardiac wards to pre-schools (Rappaport, 2013).

The practice in the alt-school setting was meant to avoid any practice that was esoteric. It sought to remain uncomplicated, to start by lying down, progressively relaxing limb by limb, closing one's eyes, and visualizing something positive. I stressed 'loving-kindness thoughts', to help these boys try to quiet the mind—a problem which most of us suffer. Mindfulness and relaxation are meant as a warm-up to try, no matter how difficult, to free up body and mind together as a means of naturally combating hyper-, unfocused or impulsive action. Throughout our curriculum, the students were engaged in mindfulness exercises—often without their knowing it—from 'silence only' time during walks to the river, to gazing at geese flying in formation or shooting foul shots on the blacktop—with eyes closed. In each case the emphasis was upon fun activity that encouraged mind-body awareness, intensive focusing that sought to still these teens' constantly agitated minds.

Guided Imagery

Another relaxation stimulus employed is guided imagery. Simply described, I would canvas the students as to what stimuli they would envision as a means of finding some relaxation. After discarding responses such as a field of cannabis or abundant naked women, appropriate responses finally came, such as travelling to a deserted island or the peaks of the Himalayas. The group would be asked to choose one and then our experience would begin, to again close one's eyes and spend time envisioning such a scene, and by doing so, attempt to cleanse the mind of invasive thoughts. While my efforts were viewed as amateurish, the administration took advantage of a grant to bring guided imagery at a professional level into the program. A 'facilitator in residence' was engaged, an experienced woman who came with good intentions but with weak experience with such challenging adolescents.

I attempted to pre-service this well-meaning professional, both to avoid using formulaic activities that she found effective and to adapt her methodology to the immediate needs of this specialized population. I warned her that it would not be an easy audience. Listening attentively, she then proceeded to revert to her own approach and orientation. Most were false starts, with her being either ridiculed or ignored altogether. Several students responded by drawing images which clearly registered their discomfort, anger and alienation by such practice. One such image (Figure 11.2) is shown on page 207, where the outcome illustrates how such stimuli put the child in touch with his negative self-concept. Without close therapeutic follow-through to process the picture, guided imagery becomes a setup. Some students accessed deeply held emotional material, which was then glossed over by the facilitator through superficial discussion. These outcomes required 'debriefing', as I took it upon myself to conduct post-workshop interventions. By 'checking in' with the teens to gauge any residual effects in evidence, there came the opportunity to address unresolved thoughts or feelings. There is no one-size-fits-all idea of a calming, focusing image. Stimuli need to be carefully tailored to each population, and even then, the stimulus may backfire, with mixed or negative outcomes being an expectation.

When children on the spectrum are introduced to novel stimuli, such as guided imagery, we should not have the expectation that the expression will emerge on the so-called 'normal' hash mark. Often there may be an exaggerated response, where there is either 'surplus' or acting-out behaviour, or a retreat to 'deficient' or inner feeling states. By becoming in touch with raw emotional material, defences may become vigilantly activated to ward off either state. This may also be the case in student and professional adults, who may become surprisingly emotional when the wellspring of emotions is unexpectedly tapped. On one occasion a novel stimulus proved to be a powerful experience, even for a group of well-defended adults. As an in-service experiential, I introduced a stimulus to a group of mental health professionals, which prompted them to express surprisingly raw and unfiltered outcomes.

Turning the Tables

In the vignette cited earlier, on page 23, which explored Wordsworth's line, 'child is father to the man', I described how our 'inner child' (if it were not so clichéd) is a powerful construct. From our infancy to adolescence, formative experiences inform our upbringing and quality of relationships and affect us in later life. Childhood remains simmering just beneath the veneer of adulthood, especially when a stimulus intentionally precipitates an age regression. When working with a group of professional adults, the stimulus of 'age regression' is something I would *never attempt* with children. But this being a group of experienced adult clinicians, it was safe to assume they had been in therapy and could handle a stimulus in which regression was a possibility. It was also an opportunity for social workers and counsellors to recognize the potential for creative response activities.

During this in-service training, I elicited outcomes which surprised several of these seasoned professionals.

On this occasion, it was one of the toughest audiences I have encountered; one hundred counsellors from the New York City School System. I was to be the last presenter of two days of professional in-service trainings, not an enviable position. It was also scheduled post-luncheon—meaning I inherited a sluggish group trying to digest and endure one last in-service training on a Friday afternoon. Sensing their fatigue and resistance, I am an experienced enough presenter to know when it is time to abandon my agenda. I stood before this mostly minority, jaded audience who were required to suffer through yet one more 'expert' and then promptly threw out my notes. Thinking on my feet, I came up with an experiential; I asked them to picture in their mind's eye 'their worst social nightmare … ever'. This could be from early childhood, teenage and collegiate years or as recently as a faculty party. They were then asked to compare notes voluntarily with their sub-groups 'if they wished'. When the whole audience reconvened, many seemed surprised at hearing their usually tough colleagues' descriptions of feeling so vulnerable. I had encouraged them to make notes, verses or sketches. Perhaps because of the novel experience and diminished energies, their defences were more relaxed and susceptible to the age regression through creative responses.

Many outcomes were written in blurbs; others stick figured pictographs, and some even produced poetic material. Several volunteers began describing being punched on the school bus, isolated at lunch tables, the wallflower at year-end dances, booed after a blown play on the playing field. What was significant is how freshly reported these occurrences were as though they had happened yesterday. Each response seemed a still-lingering narcissistic injury—much like the failure to 'let go' that the spectrum children deal with on a constant basis. I asked if anyone would like to stand and describe their experience—which drew a nervously derisive laugh from the group. One woman, who admitted to being a 'closet poet' chose the vernacular of a nine-year-old child growing up in unforgiving 'Bed-Stuy', a copy of which I possess to this day. When she read it aloud, there was the expected hesitation, yet she recited it in a clear and forceful voice:

'Brand New Sneaks'
Was sooo proud to show 'em off.
But I wore 'em when I shouldn'a.
When I stepped in dog shit, it left me cryin.
Brand new clean sneakers, now shit stuck in them souls,
Kids jus threw'm up on to them street wires.
Hang there stinkin forever—for all I care,
Let the wind swing them sneaks of dog shit kid—
Moma said too bad, 'Now you don' get nuthin',

'No new Keds for you girl'.

This short poem seemed to suck all the air out of the room; many were nodding, even shouting 'uh huh' or 'go girl'—their empathy and perhaps own traumas overcoming their 'in-service fatigue'. The group was now enlivened. The experience brought this woman back to her hardened childhood, her humiliation finally outed, a picture of the tough luck, Mom's tough love, and poverty that could not replace her gym shoes. The experience suggests the power of the stimulus to ignite a controlled 'regression in the service of the ego', Ernst Kris's construct whereby regression is prompted through some intense memory, resulting in an evocative creative act (1952, 1999). Now visibly softened, they witnessed how a strong stimulus and equally strong woman confronted her childhood's long-buried memories. Who knows what may be dredged up—of all things, 'sneakers', prized and yet forbidden by her mother to be worn to school. When the rule was disobeyed and soiled, they were left to rot on a power line. Dipping into previously repressed and unresolved material may be painful as well as offering some degree of emotional closure. This woman had unwittingly entered unfamiliar territory—that of transitional space, where regression prompted creativity and catharsis. It was met by peer empathy, camaraderie and, especially, renewed energies which followed them out of the room on that last Friday in June. Lingering perhaps was her own longing for the tough-love mother now lost and tenderly recalled in transitional space—the portal to creative expression.

II

Towards a Theory of the Psyche

Seven
The Psyche and Competing Paradigms

In the last vignette, we saw how an experienced social worker found herself in a role reversal, in a vulnerably regressed state. Recalling a humiliating experience which centred upon her losing something precious given to her by her mother, and then her mother's refusal to replace her lost sneakers, was a moment of re-imagining her feelings in startling detail. Her mother's purchase came at a tremendous sacrifice. It is a rite that exists across many cultures and economic circumstances to start school with new gym shoes. But this gift had, with terrible swiftness, become immediately sullied. Ridiculed, they were immediately thrown up and away, the child in disgust, leaving the worn sneakers to the sneers of her peers—for whom a new pair of sneakers are a cultural necessity. The poetic writing alluded to the ambivalence with which almost all view our mothers or caretakers—they giveth and unfortunately also taketh away. This dynamic is alive throughout the lifespan, from the earliest moments of bonding with mother, through to our most mature adult relations with loved ones. It is the enduring quality of attachment, which, recalled during different moments in life, continues to colour our capacity for intimacy with all its caveats of love, partnership, abandonment, rapprochement and loss.

Attachment Theory

As one of the four instinctual drives conceived by Freud in the later nineteenth century, attachment theory is finding new veracity through the evolving field of neuroscience. New research methods such as fMRI are locating and redefining the drives in more contemporary terms, indicating that Freud's earliest constructs remain fundamentally unchanged (Peterson, 2005). The individual's quality of bonding with a maternal caregiver impacts upon maturation throughout one's life, being reflected throughout our relationships for better or worse. The concept of the mother as being the primary provider has also changed. One no longer speaks of just the biological mother, but of a 'maternal caregiver' who may be an aunt, a step-parent, a sibling or an extended family—even a village—who provide for the infant's physical and emotional survival.

Freud's early emphasis upon infantile attachment theory was built upon by many of his disciples, particularly his daughter, Anna, whose Hampstead Nursery

Clinic treated many children whose attachments were disrupted during mass relocations and casualties during wartime England (Midgely, 2013). She also worked with foreign child refugees who survived the Nazi camps, whose cases have endured as a testament to this enduring psychodynamic drive. Anna Freud and her collaborator, Sophie Dann, found that many of the children had survived by invisibly inhabiting an 'underground' world beneath the barracks, with little adult support (1951). There, they formed extended families who were often older children who had formed 'households' and cared for the young, giving sustenance and affection. Freud and her collaborators described twelve-year-olds filling the maternal vacuum under the direst circumstances imaginable. In treatment, they found that those children who could form an emotional bond with these extended families were less damaged, the effects of their neglect and terror less intractable and more responsive to therapy (Midgley, 2013).

Another of Anna Freud's collaborators was child psychoanalyst John Bowlby, who also worked with wartime evacuees and emphasized the critical role attachment plays from birth. His seminal observations expanded beyond human infants, examining the early relationships between other primate species as comparisons. He meticulously recorded how bonding and attachment are also critical in chimpanzees, monkeys and all the higher mammals (1969). In observing similar patterns of bonding, separating and becoming independent and dealing with loss, he recognized the universal need for early attachments for not just emotional safety but for the species' survival. This echoed Winnicott's contention that infants are biologically predisposed to attachment and the formation of a 'holding environment'. The mother provides the infant with a precise reflection of her own experience—of feeling cared for, protected, developing a sense of basic trust—one that is revisited through the empathic relationship with the therapist (1965).

As attachment theory has become a neurological construct, there are those within the scientific community who are validating the work of earlier psychodynamic analysts. Researchers are finding that well-attached toddlers have lower cortisol reactivity when stressed (Nachmias et al., 1996). Oxytocin is a neurochemical which is released during pair-bonding activities, such as hugging, and other forms of contact comfort (Macdonald & Macdonald, 2010). In latency, the bonded, well-secured child exhibits an enhanced self-concept, stronger peer relationships, and social problem solving (Jones et al., 2014). The emotional faculties of empathy and attunement to others and other requirements of interpersonal relationships are mapped out by the neural connections established during a developmental 'window' during the first few years of life. During this crucial period, a 'relational template' is formed which impacts upon the quality of relationships the child carries into future relational interactions (Schore & Schore, 2008). In the social milieu, the secure base becomes one more mediator of the child's capacity to cope with stress. Without the maternal 'anchoring' presence, the individual's development can be arrested if they are predisposed to spectrum issues. The process can be reversed if the individual possesses a strong predisposition to attachment, such as the case of Ebie (pg. 30)—yet the more severe the neglect, the greater the therapeutic challenge.

Attachment Realized

Beyond neurochemistry and genetic predispositions is the 'nurture' side of attachment. The evolving case of Ebie (pg. 30) is again a case in point, as his successes with eclectronica and drawing schematics was gaining the attention of many within the school, creating several opportunities for interpersonal encounters. While his drawings were special, his interactions with others remained limited. He was focused squarely upon the mechanical realm, with the conspicuous omission of human involvement. His relational self remained limited until the introduction of art therapy intern, Anne Thompson. Ebie at first just tolerated her presence, being another figure besides myself—a potential threat to his mechanicals and his important work of drafting and diagramming. Eventually, however, he began to respond to this therapist's benign interest and then her genuine warmth. With her low-key kindness, empathy and mutual interest in his 'things', she became a special 'fixture'. Perhaps her smiling face, with a smooth, rounded female form, might have contributed to reopening a missed tactile and visual developmental window. Her attributes might have the potential for the 'corrective mothering' described by Winnicott, to become an antidote to the neglect he had previously suffered. Perhaps he would progress towards her becoming a therapeutic companion or maternal-type object.

After a month of observation and co-led work in various activities, I suggested that Ebie's fascination with the potter's wheel might be a means by which Anne could become more intimate, by working with Ebie to throw pots. Teaching Ebie to throw was intended to capitalize on his fascination with this favourite of machines. Another example of the appeal of mandalas was that these forms became fully animated; Ebie always relished turning the wheel on, standing mesmerized as the two wheels (the top head and the flywheel) spun at dazzling speeds. He witnessed our electrician again working his magic as he'd visit and make a show of adjusting its bearings and truing the fly, or 'kick wheel'. Ebie checked on his 'patient' weekly, ensuring its electronics and mechanicals were still in fine form.

My intent for this coupling was to utilize the wheel as a transitional object—to meld the mechanical with the human, as the wheel and now the woman were becoming objects of libidinal passion that could lead to a working alliance. Since an instructor was indispensable to learning the skill of throwing, it was hoped Ebie would accept Anne's proximity. The child study team concurred that perhaps a change of gender might appeal to this young adolescent as less threatening and more comforting. Thus, the plan was implemented.

When teaching to centre or pull up the piece, it is best to work hand-over-hand so the student can 'feel' the pressure needed to centre. They need to feel this for extended periods, to learn in tactile terms what degree of pressure is exerted at what specific time (Henley, 2002). It would necessitate a degree of intimacy, requiring close physical contact, if he were to master this skill. Initially Ebie was approach avoidant. Bear in mind the wheel was not just his patient but was part of his 'territory'. He cared for it and defended it against anyone beyond the author's operation. Ebie's avoidance was overcome, however, given his motivation to learn how to use this kinetic machine, and now, especially from Anne. After several attempts, he permitted Anne to cup her hands around his, to centre the clay, joining them together and literally becoming a symbiotic pair. After six sessions, they were 'centring' together.

As a metaphor, centring was made famous by M. C. Richards (1964). This Zen-inspired potter and poet considered centring in almost cosmic terms; as the hands come together sensitively, yet firmly, to form the artistic object, they also connect with the humanity of it all, becoming a poetic dance in the process. She viewed the process as a singular mandala moment, even erotic in its pressing of flesh, piercing the spinning clay ball and then penetrating it to 'open' unto oneself. Ebie's excitement mounted as their lump of clay was raised into a wobbling pot—it became yet another 'machine', one that seemed to grow from his own hand, taking on a life of its own. He became proficient with small pieces with me at the helm, but always signed 'woman, woman' to begin any throwing session—clearly, he preferred her warm touch to mine.

Post-Response Activity

I encouraged Anne to follow each session with a drawing activity, which became a post-creative response activity—one that reinforced both the skills learned and the relationship made. The formative images were mostly of the wheel and its electrical intricacies, with Anne rendered as a cursory schema. As their relationship deepened, she emerged as a more equal presence. Ebie's figurative studies of Anne became increasingly naturalistic and sophisticated. His finale, where one could argue the autistic nature of his art had been transformed, was a sensitive portrait that possessed the most exacting realism he had ever given a human form (Figure 7.1). It is a life-drawn sketch that any gifted teen artist might create, far from his former feral self. Anne was now related to as a sentient being, drawn casually perched at rest on the wheel's bench, sitting poised, hands demurely clasped with a pleasant smile.

Her proportions, detailing and emotionality are spot on. Yet it is significant that the electronics of the potter's wheel are still given detail, almost equally loving attention, in keeping with the original object of attachment.

The wheel retains its vital presence, perhaps because it became Winnicott's 'potential space', a portal to transitional space, that through this machine and its wondrous process came his new-found relationship. Beyond its symbiotic ties, developmental progress is indicated in that the wheel is now well separated from her body. The bilateral division of the composition seems a reference to balancing the inner and outer reality of the experience. While the wheel's electrical world of being switched in 'on/off' positions is still given prominence, Anne is shown fully separate; it is an exquisite sublimation that is fully formed with the artist being true to his objects of attachment. Ebie inadvertently created a psychic map of his development—between both mechanical and maternal 'good objects'. Attachment had been achieved, albeit with this one momentous caretaker. It had

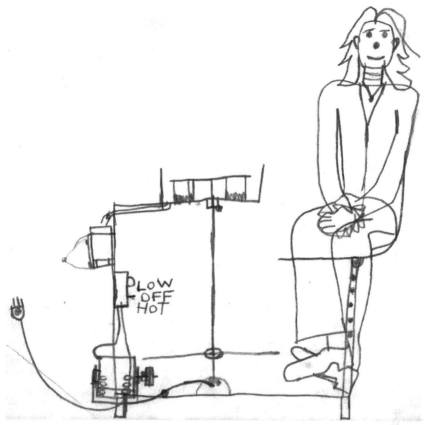

LOW
OFF
HOT

Figure 7.1 Attachment is realized as Ebie abandoned drawing mechanical objects. After bonding with his intern, he created this sensitive portrait of her relaxing on the wheel after their ceramic lesson.

yet to be generalized to others—such is the severity of developmental arrest at work. For this child and others like him, a therapeutic bond remains vulnerable, subject to deep reaction when interrupted or 'lost'.

Object Loss

The reverse dynamic of attachment is separation, and loss was experienced when Thompson eventually terminated her internship and therapeutic relationship with Ebie after four months. This 'object loss' as described by Bowlby (1969) precipitated a kind of mourning, where her disappearance and reaction to his abandonment was confounding—how could she just get up and leave their work together? It defied reason. Anticipating regression, Anne studiously instituted the typical termination strategies, each of which was ignored or rejected. Making a drawing portfolio and a photo-memory book was given cursory treatment. She inscribed the bottoms of pots with 'goodbye' words and cartoons, but this also fell short of preparing this child, who suffered such deep emotional mindblindness when faced with a new sensation of object loss.

During times of regression it is crucial to give the child his space—to reduce demands and structure. In this case, Ebie was permitted to wander restively around the studio with the goal being to head off serious behavioural regressions (Bowlby, 1960). The question remained whether the boy would be able to 'feed' off his attachment after his love object had disappeared—to visualize or feel her warm comforts despite their being no longer available. After Anne had terminated her internship, his attachment eventually began to naturally fade. His loss was observable; he regressed to drawing his former electrical schemas, even losing interest in pot making. This changed, however, when Ebie embarked upon a life-drawing study whose content appeared part of the journey for searching and re-imagining the lost object.

While his group was life drawing in the school's courtyard, he set upon studying a statue that had long ago been installed at the inception of the school. Ebie sat quietly and began drawing the human figure covered in moss with classic features—the first since her departure. He seemed to have superimposed Anne's likeness upon the allegorical statue. While the sketch is portrayed accurately as a piece of statuary, it is endowed with Anne's hair length and her recognizable, amiable facial expression (Figure 7.2). She stands seemingly in repose, perhaps imagined that she had now returned to him.

Perhaps as a tribute or a means of self-soothing, Ebie's statue is rendered with an abbreviated facial schema of Thompson's caring smile. The statue has lost its stone-hard texture and stiffness, instead projecting a softness and surprisingly a burgeoning sense of libidinal passion. Bearing in mind he was now eighteen, it is natural that her globular breast forms were clearly accentuated. Her hands seem accentuated, for it was through these strong and soft hands he felt perhaps his first caring touch. Surrounding her are a network of loosely drawn trees which seem to weave around and ensconce her. This projection seems another form of transitional space—as the statue had bridged the fantasy of Anne magically re-imagined. Yet Ebie had evolved cognitively in four years of our work, and he surely comprehended the statue was stone. It posed an impervious stimulus barrier itself, which is perhaps a reference to his growing sense of dealing with his loss.

This piece reflects both the cognitive and emotional maturation that enabled him to recall and reconstruct not just the physical but the emotional; Ebie's object relationships had come full circle. In the final stroke, Anne had been immortalized as many statues are intended. It perhaps symbolized that he had achieved a degree of 'object permanence', that Winnicott's 'holding mother' had been internalized and could be conjured in his mind or creativity as a means of comfort. Given this achievement, attachments could hopefully be generalized to others of importance—which they did, as Ebie attached to other teachers and one particular aide, albeit with less intensity as his first love. Few cases present such a remarkable glimpse at a developmental progression

Figure 7.2 Internships ultimately terminate. Once Anne had moved on, Ebie 'searched' for the lost object. He re-created her likeness by sketching a piece of stone statuary, where her features seem to come alive.

resulting in a powerful sublimation. The clarity of achieving this dynamic was such that it became the subject of Thompson's master's thesis, with detailed data that were qualitatively gathered but no less empirical than other, more scientific studies. Yet we never lost sight in the analysis of how the creative response first becomes an agent of healing. Our goal, then, is ultimately to follow these children through their development, to assist their creative response progress to perhaps become generalized into the child's behavioural mainstream. In this case, the data were not reduced to mere anecdote, but stood as a guidebook for other professionals to follow. Many educators on the child study team marvelled at the power of this couple's mutual libidinal energy—how it propelled the process further, with the ceramics work being the buffering agent and transitional object—elucidating the wonders of attachment theory and object relations work.

Twins as Maternal Objects

Attachment theory again presented itself when working with others who had been maternally deprived. At The Hecht Group, I was therapist to nine families over an eleven-year span who, unbeknownst to the parents, adopted children with cultural or post-institutionalized issues. These children ranged from those with mild adjustment issues to inhibited children and a few with deep autistic markers. Others were so disinhibited they seemed to attach indiscriminately to anyone with well-meaning intentions. One family adopted a pair of two-year-old Romanian twins whose medical records had also been falsified. Later testing indicated foetal alcohol syndrome and arrested developmental milestones due to their institutional deprivations. Over a two-year course of sibling therapy with these now seven-year-old boys, it became apparent they had survived their ordeal by bonding with each other. While typical twins often become symbiotically tied to each other, these boys were exclusively intertwined with attributes that bordered on maternal caretaking—an obvious adaptation in the relatively neglectful institutional environment. Despite their adoptive mother's genuine affection, she was not being accepted as the primary caregiver—hence their referral for therapy. In the attachment sense, the siblings had mutually imprinted upon each other, with each brother tending to the other while institutionalized, ensuring that their emotional and daily needs were met. Their neglect was severe enough that it impeded both intellectual and bonding capacities, but had not impaired their creative expression. Of the thirty images elicited in creative arts therapy, twenty-four featured the two siblings as the dominant theme—whether they were seen in session together or alone. Pictured doing an array of sibling activities, their portraits were most fully elaborated as relating figures. One stick-figure picture, which somehow survived, shows each boy's self-image as an intertwined mass of lines. Meanwhile, to the chagrin of the mother, if she was pictured at all, her stick figure was situated on the periphery.

On Dr. Hecht's advice, I instituted triadic sessions when the mother would join her sons. During a group collage, she was engaging and lively, trying to animate the boys and their enthusiasm level, which met with mixed results. Each added collage elements, stock pictures, fabric or found objects, but the investment level remained low. Most activities could be characterized as going-through-the-motion projects, which neither boy would verbally elaborate upon. After many such sessions, with different activities such as singing songs to a karaoke machine, to playing board games, the result was a triangulation; the mother was still extraneous. Returning to their sibling sessions, the process notes of the time indicate a resurgence in each boy's relatedness in their creative outcomes. The lack of discernible progress in attachment therapy created tension with the mother, who terminated our work after two months. Urged not to give up, this well-meaning but rejected mother was devastated by the boys' reliance upon each other as caretakers—for the developmental window for bonding had passed.

Attachment and object relationship expression have been presented as a major issue when addressing the needs of children on the spectrum, particularly on the autistic end of the continuum. The capacity to relate and bond impacts the capacity for fruitful relations throughout one's life. Neglect during critical periods damages the brain in ways that are still a mystery, yet the consequences range from developmental arrest to devastating incapacity. As many of these 'attachment children' are nonverbal, the creative response remains a window into their world—one that enables them to convey something of their unique relating.

The Instinctual Drives

As part of the psychodynamic model first proposed by Freud in 1923, infantile attachment was conceived as part of the psychic apparatus, governed largely by the instinctual drives. Despite Freud approaching the phenomenon as a nineteenth-century neurobiologist through the Victorian lens, his insights have proved prescient. Attachment theory was part of a triumvirate psychic apparatus, followed by three other main constructs Freud termed (in a poor English translation) the id, ego and superego. These constructs, which have long been dismissed, have sparked a new generation of 'neuropysychoanalysts'. These individuals are reconsidering Freud's formulations through neuroimaging, brain mapping or other hard scientific methodologies. Neuroresearchers Solms and Panksepp (2012) have turned their attention to 'primal consciousness perspectives', where lower brainstem phenomenal experiences provide the 'energy' for the development of higher-order cognitive consciousness. Carhart-Harris and Friston (2010) explore whether Freudian constructs, such as the primary process, are indicated during increased limbic discharge and temporal lobe activity, resulting in the 'non-ordinary' states examples which can be witnessed in the creative expressions in many of the children under review. Their reconceptualization focuses upon the evolution of primary process affective experience as a 'default mode network' (Raichle et al., 2001). This network of neural regions of internally driven thoughts is most active during unconscious states of mind wandering or fantasizing or during periods of introspection. The neuroimaging experiments bear out that 80 percent of our wakeful hours may be given over to functions of memory collection, self-reflection, processing different narratives, and understanding the emotions of self and others (Graner et al., 2013). Weak connectivity to the default mode network may result in many of the presenting problems in those on the spectrum. Despite advances in fMRI neuroimaging and other means of locating the brain's responses, the psyche remains a mysterious element of the mind. With this purposes in mind, I shall describe Freud's functional concepts of the psychic apparatus and then attempt to update his antiquated formulations as they pertain to children on the spectrum.

The Neuro-Id

A boy encounters a vision of a pharaoh while walking to school; another confesses to confusion over sleeping and waking states; one impulsively runs away from camp thinking he is under attack; a teen adopts an avatar which guides his relationships and decision making. These are some of the inexplicable behaviours described of children on the spectrum, for whom reality testing and self-regulation of impulses are a constant struggle. Creative responses may reflect a range of id-derived 'leakage' with images or behaviours that blur the boundary between real and altered states. They vary in intensity and frequency, but are reactions which are commonplace and sometimes intractable. The behaviour stems from what Damasio terms 'primordial impulses' (2010), an updated reference to Freud's id, now described as a phenomenon that is synonymous with the unconscious, which aims at drive discharge. These domains search out immediate gratification pleasures to avoid pain or frustration or to act out impulses, regardless of the dictates of reality. The primary processes harbour strong emotional reactions which can interfere with and disrupt cognitive processing (Solms & Panksepp, 2012). Many of the case examples demonstrate how children can react in extreme ways without having insight into, or even memory of, their aggressive behaviours. Goldberg in the *The Executive Brain* (2002) theorizes that slight structural differences in the brain's fragile frontal lobes and their pathways are indicated between typicals and those on the spectrum. As the umbrella term 'seat of judgement' suggests, it is theorized that dysfunction in the frontal lobes weakens executive control and permits primal impulses more opportunity to be acted out. While the two are not synonymous—as one *can* have executive function with damage to the frontal lobes, and vice versa—the correlation is acceptably generalized. Spectrum-based behaviours have their basis in the primitive portion of the brain's largely autonomic 'arousal centres' consisting of 'instinctual neural circuits' which lack the mediation capacities of higher-order cortical structures of the midbrain and forebrain (Gaskill & Perry, 2014). Any factors which increase the excitatory activity of the brain stem increase the dysregulation of the individual's neurochemistry. Freud himself stated that if he had the means of understanding the 'organic interior' of physiological and chemical dynamics, his direction would have been neuroscience, though he was bound by the constructs of his time. Had Freud been able to study levels of dopamine, serotonin and epinephrine as they surge and deplete, new theories of inhibiting self-control of libido and aggression and other aspects of drive regulation, he would have undoubtedly been a pioneer in neuroscience (Bartels & Zeki, 2004). Stress, pain or fear levels become overwhelming and serotonin levels drop, manifesting responses from hyperactivity to fiercely aggressive behaviour.

Thus, the child on the spectrum has difficulty maintaining self-control in the face of stimuli that result in excitatory arousal. Until the child can develop self-awareness over these impulsive defences, id-derived reactivity predisposes the individual to frustration, anger or aggressive behaviour. Thus, the newly conceptualized 'neuro-id' remains as powerful a construct today as Freud envisioned it over a century ago. Without the constraints of self-awareness, a child's reactions can often remain chaotic and hypervigilant, resulting in under-socialized behaviour. Despite thousands of experimental studies, fMRI and neuroimaging have led to an increased understanding of the neurobiological basis of aggression, yet have contributed little to its functional social expression. Experiments have yielded only limited insight to the complexity of feeling states that govern more complex, mixed expressions, such as hate, misogyny or prejudice. The experimental 'data' generalize that the brain, for whatever reason, has been over-*aroused*.

Aggression or Violence

One of the primordial instincts of the id-primary process is that of aggression—another inborn drive that is latent within all humans as well as most of the animal kingdom. It is a biological imperative that evolved as a means of ensuring the survival of the species. For severely brain-damaged children, such as Joey, aggression came in the form of head banging when separated from his caregiver. Tonya, an environmentally disadvantaged girl, without provocation violently jabbed her staff into the ribs of her peer. Factors putting children at risk of greater aggression include severe autistic symptoms, lower IQ, language deficits and impoverished surroundings, any of which can increase frustration leading to aggression and even violent episodes. Aggression is, however, communicative; it expresses profound frustration, anger and fear, conveying the emotional or biological needs of the child. Behaviours may be reflexive actions to noxious sensory stimulation or express biological conditions of pain or hunger—which to the nonverbal child may be incomprehensible and incommunicable. Every attempt must be made to understand the source of these feeling states and utilize every resource to keep the child and others safe. This sometimes requires restraining a child. I recall taking a pleasant walk with a multiply involved boy with autism, when we encountered the school's principal. Without warning the boy slammed his head against the corner of a brick wall. Together, we took the boy down and held him safely. For whatever reason, he exploded beyond control, endangering his safety and those around him. It is an intervention of the last resort, to avoid becoming punitive or abusive, while also ensuring that 'holding' may sometimes become, literally, a matter of restraint.

Aggression as Survival

Aggression does not necessarily entail violence. The drive has evolved as a positive life-sustaining evolutionary adaptation to securing one's basic needs (Lorenz, 1966). Aggression in the guise of evolutionary principles has a role to play in our inclusive fitness—in self-protection, constructive competition, self-assertion and other attributes which enable us to survive—whether it be a kitten struggling for a place at the nipple or a schoolchild asserting themself on the playground. In spectrum children, our goal is to express the aggressive drive through culturally acceptable means. This involves redirecting the impulse of aggression ideation or feeling via alternative behaviours, such as channelling through creative, athletic or other productive activities. This underlines the spectrum child's need for opportunities to learn to control the build-up of frustration, anger or aggressive ideation before it becomes physical.

This challenge is faced throughout the animal kingdom, as every higher-functioning individual is either programmed or taught to redirect aggression amongst peers. Lorenz devoted his Nobel Prize work on aggression by studying ritualized aggression, or 'display behaviour'. Moments after returning to this passage, I noticed a pair of flicker woodpeckers out my window, scuffling about beneath my feeder. They were 'facing off'—hopping at each other and spreading their wings to display their brilliantly orange plumage, which is otherwise hidden as mottled camouflage. For twenty minutes, they engaged in lively faux jousting with their long and powerful beaks. These animal conspecifics limited their aggression as a show of force, avoiding injury or worse—remaining alive to settle their score another day. Aggression via display behaviour indicates adaptive fitness whether protecting one's infants, attracting a mate or defending territory. In the case of juveniles, animals or children, play fighting with siblings or peers establishes pecking orders and prepares for adult competition. In sociobiological terms, human males also display via body posturing, developing muscular physiques or decreasing their proximal distance (read, 'getting in someone's face'). Each culture has its own display behaviours in which facial and body language, threat behaviours and even games that assert dominance require a finely tuned set of rules that govern aggression (Eibl-Eibesfeldt, 1989; Morris, 1967).

Fine-Tuning Aggression

These rules are evident in Western culture regarding contact sport. American and European football, wrestling and rugby are centred upon finely tuned, controlled aggression—wherein certain violent forms of contact are permitted—yet often the level of aggression spins out of control. Watching a hockey game and its brawling, I am sometimes struck by why players or 'enforcers', bent on hurting an opposing player, are not taken off the ice and arrested on the spot for aggravated assault. But these are cultural mores—that in certain conditions violence is accommodated and even enjoyed, more than a thousand years after the Romans enjoyed watching real battles in the Colosseum.

For children on the spectrum, such fine-tuning brings extra challenges. One boy, Owen, was treated for hyperactivity and impulse control issues. He had few constructive outlets for his frustration-anger cycle of hyperactive behaviour. He was an enthusiastic watcher of professional football and enjoyed playing neighbourhood pickup games. During his freshman year, Owen tried out for and made the freshman football team. One of his positions was defensive end; his task was to target the ball carrier or quarterback—an aggressive task he found quite satisfying. He was allowed to 'hit' an opposing player with impunity. It was a cathartic release—all within the parameters of culturally sanctioned violent action. Problems began when Owen found that he could be targeted as well and he took objection. He found he did not handle being blocked, taking it as a personal affront. After being knocked out of a play, he began to lose control, drawing fouls and resulting in being benched until he could compose himself—which only intensified his anger and resentment.

Dr. Hecht asked that I reach out to his coach, discussing the boy's ADHD and impulsivity issues. I explained that he was perhaps unable to modulate the finely tuned levels of the aggression necessary for this position, to which he agreed. Football for Owen posed a conundrum; it permitted him an outlet to express his aggression, often to violent levels. In school culture, it was not only sanctioned, but included garnering praise and status when he succeeded. Ideally, organized sport should have become a constructive means of displacement, one that provided discipline, skill building and social camaraderie.

Despite the latter benefits, everyone reached a consensus that now in his development, with increasing outbursts, he couldn't 'handle' the game. In session while exploring his options, he finally confided how he felt the chaos of violence was frightful—that with all the hitting, there was such confusion on the field. Not only did he need to modulate the force of his hitting and deal with being blocked, but also he could not follow the play calling. The constant comings and goings of players and the erratic time differential of having to stand around and then explode into motion and contact became too much for his attention deficits and hyperactivity to sort out. The increasing potential to sustain neurological trauma was also thus averted.

Owen's perception of the game's paradoxes was well illustrated when he created a fascinating portrait (Figure 7.3). He poses himself as the 'football devil' (the team had the nickname 'Devil' in it—an obviously outmoded, ill-advised choice). He is depicted in a disturbingly frightening manner—armed to the hilt, a dangerous creature with a trident and reptilian tail.

His slanted, malevolent eyes, bulging muscles and the numerals '666' pasted across his uniform fill out the devilish persona. The faceguard, which he complained often cut him, is configured like a harpoon-like offensive weapon rather than as a protective device. Each of these contradictory elements speaks to his

Figure 7.3 The ability to fine-tune aggression was beyond the capacity of a hyperactive boy trying to play freshman football. His self-portrait projects a sense of malevolence and self-defence.

aggressive impulses, while also alluding to concomitant fears. While our psychiatrist, Dr. Hecht, attempted to titrate his medications into a productive balance, Owen's adolescent brain chemistry proved an elusive target to stabilize. In psychodynamic terms, this self-image included 'identifying with the aggressor'. This primitive, often last-resort defence gave the boy a symbolic modicum of psychic protection. By unconsciously aligning himself with the ultimate in evil, his powers of aggression were dealt with through sympathetic magic. As the cave painters drew out their own aggressors invoking magical powers of dominance, so too did Owen project his feelings. Until he matured and learned greater self-control, the team counselled that his anger would be better served swimming the butterfly or smashing a forehand. These recommendations were brought to the child study team during Owen's Individual Education Plan meeting, which the coach was invited to attend. He concurred that the boy might wait out another year to discern whether maturation might catch up with his physical skills—an insight which everyone in attendance agreed on—one must always keep the door *open*.

Libido and Passion

As aggression can be a constructive force in everyone's life, so too is the case with libido. Too often, however, this instinctual drive is associated purely as a sexual connotation. Libido of course includes the sexual act as another evolutionary imperative which ensures the survival of the species. Sexual gratification is another Freudian construct which has been dismissed as a vestige of Victorian culture, with its hysterical women with sexual repressions and 'phallocentric' theories. Reframing sexuality in contemporary terms of libido widens the context by which we apply the drive to children on the spectrum.

In latency aged children, libido is most often displayed in the form of social attachments and passionate interests. For those on the autistic continuum, attachment and passion are ubiquitous—for example, Joey's symbiotic ties, Ebie's mechanicals, Helen's nests and little clay house, and even Will's seeking a euphoric moment through his use of cannabis may all be considered passionate attachments. Each possesses *cathexis,* or investment of psychic energy in a person, place or thing—one that motivates, invests, bonds, covets and urges one to seek out other interests and pleasures. Passions may also be tragic, devastating one emotionally, but be a fact of life that one's maturation brings to bear. In any case, attachments and passion make us feel alive. Without attachment and passion and a sense of love or intimacy, sex becomes purely a physical, or mechanical, means of drive discharge. Passion provides this critical element. A child can mature into asexuality, autosexuality or androgyny—these are alternative sexualities which are alive and well everywhere in this book—in love, in loss, in coveting, in singing, in art, in a run down the slopes.

Libido in Latency

For many latency aged children, especially those of the autistic continuum, creative response outcomes of overt sexuality are rarely depicted—yet these impulses are there. They are at the mercy of surging testosterone, oestrogen and oxytocin—hormones which excite arousal and fantasy. As the id dictates, sexual impulses may be immature and developmentally remain limited to crushes and other affections, yet they will be expressed in forms both problematic and productive. A deaf girl named Hilda was a draftsman with superb cartooning and realistic drawing skills which offset her special needs. Her saccharine-type images indicated appropriate stereotypes. Her works are still somewhat oblivious towards overt sexual activity though they indicate a growing interest in boys. Her art is a healthy outlet for her to process her feelings and awareness of herself as she matures.

Hilda's art productions are fascinating since they reveal a point in time when early adolescence straddles the last vestiges of childishness. She draws in a style Lowenfeld would term 'dawning-realism', when children abandon drawing conceptually—or what they know—and instead begin to depict their subjects as they visually appear (1957). Latency bridges childhood and adolescence, with expressive styles which become somewhat less creative, relying more on current fads or cultural or personal stereotypes. As a skilled cartoonist, Hilda drew profusely, though at the end of our two years her content extended to rendering herself with a boy she called Chris, on whom she had her first crush (Figure 7.4). She and her friend are shown creatively labelled using bubble letters as an added graphic element.

Figure 7.4 The social mores of latency are laid bare as a deaf 'tween' draws about her first crush. Her artistic giftedness gives a glimpse of her boyfriend, in the realms of both the ideal and the realistic.

They are shown sitting side by side together in class, broadly smiling, keenly attentive, each with their pencils at the ready—an obviously idealized scenario. It is a well-adjusted and innocent creative response which hints at the greater realism and gender relations to come. Secondary elements extend the narrative into present realities. The facial portraits shown below and left perhaps hint at deeper emotive and psychological complexity. Hilda depicts herself as half asleep, which was a realistic reference to her attention deficits. Chris is also shown heavy lidded, with an ambiguous expression that belies his earlier sunshine image. The two seated portraits are more stereotyped, displaying the ego ideals of well-conducted students—while the more intimate faces are perhaps truer to the situation but rendered coincidently. Each coexists with contradiction, without concern or confusion. What is especially evident is the ghostly little kitten shown top left—perhaps a punctuation marking the phasing out of Hilda's childhood attachments.

Hilda's learning disabilities and immature sociability have not interfered with her ability to depict complex developmental and social mores. She is still naive to the precocity of other peers who were more sexually advanced. Her innocence perhaps staved off sexual pressures from the amorous teenage deaf boys who were becoming sexually active. These characters' sexuality remains within latency, yet realism is close at hand. As a Latina, Hilda struggled with language acquisition that included learning to lip read Spanish, sign in American Sign, and then learn to write and read proper English as a second language. Articulating ideas and feelings required also that Hilda compensate for language deficits by learning body language. Chris's ambiguous expression in the head shot perhaps indicates Hilda's inability to read his emotions and intentions, which in any event are probably muddled. Perhaps too her whimsical little genie shown emerging from his lantern places her still within the magical realm. With more active libido, perhaps it cast a little spell between these two children on the cusp of active affection.

On the Disturbed Continuum

For disturbed children entering sexual development, libidinous impulses may find expression in any combination of androgynous, asexual, auto-aroused or fantasy-bound expressions. As in the previous case, attachments may also be directed to an 'unrealistic' person or persona. Sensations from media are seductive and may further exacerbate and stimulate obsessions. For twelve-year-old Lee, a boy with severe delusional symptoms, the onset of sexual feelings was disinhibited, with overtly sexualized figures drawn in the privacy of the individual session. His sexual yearnings were at their most primitive, with the intertwining of both libidinal and aggressive energy with little differentiation. He was a mild-mannered boy until age fifteen, when hormonal changes set in, expressed by bouts of manic fantasies that would interfere with his thought processes. Libidinous and aggressive thoughts twisted his art productions with graphic form and content. Such regressions were anticipated, and he was 'held' in the Winnicottian sense, until he could be medically stabilized. In Figure 7.5, Lee spontaneously drew what

Figure 7.5 Lee has a disturbed concept of sexual intimacy, confused by distorted media stereotypes which exaggerated his depictions of sexual characteristics with that of aggression.

he termed his 'dream girl', evoking sexually charged imagery with his immature and bizarre associations appropriated from mainstream media.

Lee was a devotee of the thankfully defunct television show *Baywatch*, a 1980s confection involving a team of uber-buxom California lifeguards acting out endless inane plots mixing heroism and sexism. During one session, he portrayed its 'star', who was drawn as a creature deformed by her most attractive attributes, an amazon of a woman, with super-charged bared breasts, California tanned and blond. As breasts seem to be rising like balloons, the paw of a black panther hovers menacingly. It is poised to do what? Seduce? Eviscerate? This mixture of sexual and violent ideation indicates significant confusion and ambivalence about sexual ideation. Fantasy and reality become blurred by internal pressure to express his sexuality, which was then filtered and distorted further by the media.

As television assumed obsessional proportions for this sensitive boy, he was subject to a 'media blackout'. All movies, television and other media were censored and supervised. Even the most innocent show of the two sexes interacting could morph into monstrous creatures. Libidinous figures could not be expressed as tender or intimate, but only as confused animal instincts. While Lee could express his burgeoning drives only within the safety of the therapeutic environment, there was little indication of drive neutralization. When in the throes of regression, his mentation was given over to near unadulterated id derivatives. He was barely able to achieve a degree of displacement, as he did not directly act out on his urges. He was not a predator, though the team was consulted whether this material could become so. With such charged imagery, the therapist must be cognizant not to over-stimulate these primitive impulses, to avoid encouraging further, potentially destructive negative outcomes.

Role of Creative Response Activities in Drive Neutralization

Our work in the creative response activities, then, must assist the child in developing more adaptive filtering and stronger defence mechanisms. The psychodynamic approach, when employed, becomes a vehicle for channelling and exercising aggressive and libidinous impulses within the safety of the therapeutic environment. Throughout the case material, vigorous physical and creative response activity demonstrates how impulses can be redirected or displaced, especially potentially harmful impulses. However, it is always the possibility that symbolization may exacerbate symptoms. Yet during the creative work, one hopes that some excess libido does get left on the page.

During creative work, drive impulses can achieve cathartic relief, as the hydraulic theory of drive discharge of 'building up and letting go' dictates (Lorenz, 1966). Built up libidinous and aggressive energy must find an avenue for safe yet gratifying discharge—whether through team play or creative outlet. With Hilda, our Latina deaf girl, latency still provided a refuge where the drives remained innocent, yet were subject to imminent typical development. Such ambivalence points to the id-inflected confusion that girls, both typical and spectrum, must navigate, as the media peddles the 'ideal' of desirability, which is out of reach for almost everybody. Hormonal surges can occur as adolescents of either sex fawn over images of unattainable teen idols. Processing the stimulus requires a shift from fantasy to some degree of reality, testing for these neurochemicals to subside and hopefully stopping short of acting out physically or destructively.

With Owen and Lee, id-derived imagery and their symbolic equivalents were given graphic form as unconscious contradictory impulses that impeded their functioning. The goal in therapy was for sex and aggression to be redirected and perhaps neutralized by having the creative response allow critical distance between the impulse and the act. Yet the power inherent in the drives is rarely so easily disarmed.

Magical Thinking

Around 1767, one ten-year-old William Blake was tormented by the death of his brother. Always a sensitive, free-spirited child, he reported seeing him levitate when lying in state. He also saw angels in the trees and the head of God in his window. As Davis writes (1977), the visionary eye and mind usually atrophy as we mature—yet for Blake they never did. As a visionary artist, he later wrote, 'Therefore I print; nor vain my types shall be: Heaven, Earth, & Hell henceforth, shall live in harmony'. Blake's propensity for magical thinking, which evolved into inspiration rather than delusion as an adult, reflects the powers of the primary process regardless of typicality—as children, most individuals have visions, fantasies and escapist moments, which then 'leak' into our normative thinking processes and even our actions. As a child perhaps on the spectrum, given Blake's propensity to fall into magical realms, it is a wonder how his psyche managed to mature and emerge intact. As a source of poetry, piety and search for truth, Blake is an exemplar of the sensitive child artist—one whose times rarely accommodated mental difference. It was fortunate that his understanding father spared his being publicly persecuted by homeschooling him to avoid the possibility that the child might invite derision or worse if caught hallucinating in school. A printer's apprentice by ten, Blake never abandoned his portal to transitional space, which became the source of a lifetime of creating fantastic works. Many children on the spectrum are not so fortunate.

Social Mores of Magical Thinking

Expressions of the magical id-derived instinctual drive are not confined to the delusional child on the spectrum. Such processes are again a psychic imperative and cannot be fully repressed—only redirected, as was the young Blake set up with an engraver to harness his talents. The downside of magical thinking is to hold one's personal thoughts and feelings as 'gospel'. Blake's were accommodated by illustrating poems from the Bible as a means of directing and camouflaging his errant visions, yet without becoming a proselytizer for his own cult. On the cultural front, delusion becomes complicated when masses of intact adults remain wedded to magical thoughts or beliefs which defy logic. As was Blake's case, belief systems may be codified into faith-based and culturally acceptable forms, such as the world's great religions. Like any other stimuli under pressure from the primary process, any of these can morph into radicalized, even bizarre, belief systems that may impact the lives of others. This state of affairs is amply illustrated by our current decades long war with religious radicals whose literal interpretations of mythological texts have led them to act out in the most heinous ways, imposing their beliefs of the fantastical.

Magical belief systems also persist among the United States citizenry. Millions still hold that certain religions, ethnicities, races and genders are innately inferior—or innately dangerous. Whole swaths of the national population question the validity of evolution, which is of course a scientific certainty. A significant segment denies the reality of global climate warming. Conspiracy theories abound bordering upon the delusional, ideas which recently have accessed the highest reaches of governance. Radicalized religious sects which still hold literal interpretations of the Bible are the norm in large, less sophisticated segments of the country. While many intelligent and psychologically healthy individuals have reconciled their faith as coexisting alongside of science, the spiritual and pragmatic realms can and do coexist—as Blake demonstrated by celebrating the Christian faith in many of his works (though many, in keeping with his spectrum mores, are over-the-top fantastical). It is the radicalization and proselytization of these beliefs which have become a form of mass madness, destructive enough to affect individual freedoms, national politics and even world affairs.

For children on the spectrum, this overlay of worldwide insanity is juxtaposed with their already at-risk predisposition for excitatory arousal and magical thinking. At the mildest level, there may be inattention, daydreaming or fantasizing. In more frequent or severe cases, there may be some 'disassociation', where self-absorption gives way to finding refuge in 'another world'. Everyone has experienced periodic bouts of dissociation, as anyone who has 'spaced out' while driving on the highway can attest—wondering where the last half hour went as they missed their freeway exit. Yet some children's attention deficits or autistic withdrawal can assume magical thought processes on a consistent basis. This goes well beyond believing in Easter bunnies or imaginary friends. Magical thinking becomes a psychopathology when the capacity for reality appraisal is arrested, becoming so delusional that it interferes with daily functioning. Art productions serve as both a refuge for their inner thoughts and a defence to fend off the demands of the outer world. Blake is one of the few individuals who could contain and transform the realm of the fantastic into a profitable and creative life. Others on the spectrum may not be as fortunate, with constant defending against intrusive thoughts and feelings which often translate into creative responses that are painfully distorted.

The Ego and Superego

The most adaptive defence to fend off or creatively utilize irrational beliefs remains the rational mind. Freud's construct of the ego, now referred to as 'executive function', modulates control over the more primitive and reactive neuro-id. The ego strains to keep the thought disorders already described somewhat in check. Healthy ego function indicates a mature brain, which can rationalize and reality test, even while being subjective—cognitive dissonance holds that there is no 'one' reality, but many. However, the sane mind still must distil its sensations and thoughts and delay gratification of the libidinal and aggressive urges. Kramer writes that as an organizing force the ego constitutes man's most indispensable organ of survival; to it are ascribed all the higher mental functions.

> To perceive reality as we know it, to postpone instinctual gratification and factor in behavioural consequences, ego functions especially when the drives are most aroused. Without the ego, mediating sexual and aggressive impulses would have a free reign, becoming a mortal danger. (1971, pg. 68)

Its higher cortical abilities include attention, reasoning, planning, inhibition of impulses and a functioning memory. The ego also includes the capacity to mitigate the effects of mindblindness, enabling one to read the intentions and body language of other functions of 'attunement'. Executive function also mediates self-awareness and self-monitoring stimuli to the extent that relatively accurate inferences can be made resulting in appropriate responses. This capacity requires what Kris termed the ego's 'conflict-free sphere' (Kris, 1952, 1999). The capacity to 'compartmentalize' is critical, as clear and rational thought processes may then coexist with id-derived thoughts or feelings. This capacity allows us to entertain thoughts of irrationality, while those of imagination must coincide with our capacity for decision making and reality testing. The creative individual routinely 'dips' into this primary process material for inspiration, imagery or melody, or even for solving a mathematical problem. Yet every time one creates, the key is to emerge from such transitional space intact. One cannot remain in an altered state, however creative, lest they go mad.

In children on the spectrum, succumbing to regression is an ongoing struggle. The capacity to compartmentalize is a difficult cognitive feat. Executive function may be mired in 'open mic' states, becoming irrational, obsession driven or lost in unworldly thoughts. As the cases bear out, primary process leakage can blur the boundaries of reality enough that one might be unreachable or make the poorest of choices. Therapy consists of bolstering the ego while capitalizing on the creative child's ability to give their inner world aesthetic form. In this way, the creative arts therapist acts as 'auxiliary ego', lending their own executive function whenever the child is in need. During any creative act, having a therapeutic or guiding presence assists in resisting the pull of destructive regression.

The Superego

As an extension of the ego, the 'superego' is another element of cognition that mediates the ethical and moral compass by which the ego is guided. Taboos may be hardwired as evolutionary imperatives which are almost universally prohibited. However, most variations are culturally defined. The culture's mores dictate moral beliefs and emotions which balance one's selfish needs with those accepted by intra-societal norms. The construct involves recognizing internalized borders of acceptable behaviour, which requires complex mental imaging. The processing of anticipated situations along with their evaluation of potential consequences is also essential to empathy. The degree of cultural subjectivity of the moral high ground is often extraordinary. Gang members kill and maim as a means of gaining status and authority. Note the public's insatiable appetite for books or movies about the psychopathic killers who rule organized crime, as children search more violent video games to vicariously exercise their insatiable appetites.

The superego is supposedly an antiquated Freudian construct, but its functions are now being brain mapped in the prefrontal cortex. All healthy individuals who are sufficiently mature experience regret, shame or other feelings that comprise a 'guilty conscience'. These emotions may operate in many different states of consciousness—whether in dreams, nightmares or repetitive conscious thoughts, which if they persistent can morph into clinical depression. From roughly age five, individuals are capable of empathy. I have observed young children greatly attuned to the feelings of friends and siblings and especially empathic to animals. Despite their early maturation, being sensitive to another's feelings can bring on distress if hypersensitive. Thus, the scope of the superego is vast; the function can be exemplified by a little boy's distress over hurting a friend's feelings, a parent's regret over disciplining a difficult child or a society's collective regret over invading countries whose governments we do not approve.

The developing child internalizes the behaviour modelled by their immediate caregivers and authorities, whether it is a parent, coach, mentor, celebrity or politician—these often form affiliations to cultures, all of which may contribute to 'ego ideals' of superheroes or other media figures. The superego then must help choose and mediate which individuals or subcultures to look up to—who or where are the role models who possess moral fibre and can instil it in their upbringing. As the spectrum child's capacity for self-reflection may be arrested, such that moral/ethical considerations are diminished, the therapist as auxiliary ego must be ready to step in, to guide and assist the moral/ethical aspect of executive function. My clinical practice case notations are full of references to a child's 'lack of remorse', 'oblivious to feelings of others', 'surprised that others are upset' or 'defended against consequences were given' and so on. Regardless of intact or even superior IQs, a version of empathy blindness that supersedes moral consideration routinely results in hurting the feelings of others. As maturation proceeds, it is hoped that empathy leads to greater moral-based decision making. Feelings of regret or guilt can be a healthy indication of developing ego strength, which in turn leads to more attuned interrelationships.

The role of the creative response activity is to explore the child's feelings of self and others, which include guilt, shame and regret. While therapy cannot be 'value driven'—as one person's ethics may not coincide with the parents or culture—the relative amorality of the creative response may help articulate contradictory positions. Assisted during this journey, the therapist elicits expressions which can bring to life where the child is in the process of being self-aware, which is the hallmark of growing maturation. This is a long and hard-fought journey, to evolve from aggressive or other drive reactivity to clear-headed and sensitive decision making and finding self-worth by one's treatment of others. All can be traced in the following detailed case example.

From Primary Process to Executive Control

For many spectrum children, the task of emerging from latency to early adolescent is to 'try out' life. It proceeds by trial and error—by making errors of judgement and learning from mistakes—to reach major developmental milestones. The process of 'synthesis', in which the elements of id, ego and superego are integrated, is the overarching goal of maturation, however incomplete or haltingly it occurs. For such an integration is not a linear process with children on the spectrum—it is more often a slow progression, characterized by peaks and valleys, of progress impeded by setbacks. It is our task as therapists, as many of the preceding cases have borne out, to help the process along through the creative process.

One eleven-year-old boy, Connor, fit the classic attention deficit hyperactivity profile on the spectrum in the latter stage of latency. In the beginning in creative arts therapy, his mother reported infantile self-serving behaviour. He was given over to fits of anger and frustration over anything which denied him immediate gratification. He resisted limits and was blind to the consequences of his actions. He was defensive in therapy—or with any adult—with an anti-authoritarian and contrary temperament which overwhelmed his single mother. He had few passions at the time, with isolative video gaming being the predominant medium, which both entertained and becalmed this otherwise hyperactive child. The mother reluctantly tolerated his obsession for this reason: while he was gaming, she was given a badly needed respite. Expressions elicited in therapy were invariably limited to the plots and characters from video games, from which meagre stereotypic metaphors could be gleaned. A breakthrough came when he established a relationship with a peer who taught him skateboarding. Like many in my practice who suffer hyperactivity, Connor was aversive to organized sport—with its rules and boredom of practice that were akin to school tasking. Skateboarding served as a means of leaving his shuttered room to exercise his energies.

Connor had returned from the summer break and was now entering puberty. His interest in skateboarding had now graduated in intensity, along with an overarching need to be accepted by its peer skate culture. Skateboarding then provided a 'high-reward' stimulus, engaging his need to rebel and demonstrate his growing physical and cultural prowess—all while being accepted within a peer group. A daredevil persona and an antisocial persona manifested, which may be manageable for the typical child but for Connor became problematic as boundaries were pushed. The 'intensity and frequency' of skateboarding incidents were, in the perspective of his mother, 'tipping over the edge' of acceptability.

Connor's impulsivity and difficulty taking responsibility are classic symptoms of ADHD, which are fuelled by developmental forces seemingly beyond our reach. During the onset of adolescence, adrenal and growth hormones and neurotransmitters such as serotonin are all in flux, which can then translate into persistent contrary behaviour (Romer, 2010). Because the pubescent brain is in transition, the maturing frontal lobes are at increased arousal levels and, with dysfunction, are given to more intense and frequent irrational acts. Baron-Cohen has written that puberty is the height of the hormonal surge—that of the 'extreme male brain' with its dopamine reward circuit, seeking out escalated rewards of risk-driven behaviour without regard for long-term consequence (2002). Thus, the adolescent cerebral cortex, or midbrain, contributes to elevate its hunt for 'optimal arousal' (Littman, 2014). Young adolescents with symptoms of ADHD have greater difficulty making conscious choices than typical conspecifics, but are driven on by behavioural impulses which are often misjudged.

In creative response therapy, Connor created interesting graphics for skate decks which were accompanied by cognitive behavioural work that addressed his various markers. The behavioural component would need to be somewhat camouflaged to not be perceived as the centrepiece of our gathering. Afterwards, we would offhandedly discuss scenarios of how to withstand daredevil peer pressure and to skate 'within himself' and accept instruction to skate with greater skill and more responsibly. Care was taken to offset any rule with an equal measure of positive reward.

Towards a Synthesis of Drives and Cognition

Controlling impulses while allowing their gratification through culturally con-structive means remains the ever-present challenge of spectrum child and adult alike. Connor's 'breakthrough' of synthesizing came perhaps with greater maturation. An indicator was when the drives of attachment, aggression and libidinous passions became more integrated. Evidence of this synthesis began outside therapy. By using his art in concert with his action sports, Connor's expressive outlets expanded, departing from bland stereotypes to creating more emotive images of himself. One piece that was brought to me from school was a doodled drawing torn from his workbook tablet. Connor offhandedly presented me with a self-portrait which encapsulated the strengths and weaknesses of the ADHD conundrum. It is realistically posed in a casual but aesthetic style with realistic contour-line work and subtle shadings which provide emotional nuance (Figure 7.6).

His elongated face reflects entry into early adolescence; he has longer hair, and his eyes seem unsure and searching. They are dramatically accentuated by deeper shading. The eyebrows point slightly upward, which reinforces a sense of insecu-rity—all expressive elements that were developmentally out of reach just the year before.

An alter ego and reference to the immature self also burst upon the scene. Charging into the composition is a cartoonish character Connor referred to as the 'it' (which incidentally Freud originally termed the 'id'). This wild-eyed cartoon leans in with flailing arms, screaming uncontrollably. Realism has given way to caricature, though it is carefully fitted within the 'fine line' of its border—a draw-ing within a drawing. Depicting both personas indicates an observing ego which now indicated self-awareness—differentiating between his impulsive, mindblind behaviour and that of a more mature self. There is now increased control with a stronger sense of boundaries. There is a clear intent to contain the 'it', indicating that sorting out these two alter egos is still very much a work in progress.

Reconciling these two selves indicated perhaps that behavioural strategies, with rewards and natural consequences, had been internalized, that our hours of role-play, scripting responses to slippery situations, now coexisted with more self-expressed, insightful creative responses. Each had complemented the multi-modal approach to therapy, with medication and psychodynamic work of neu-tralizing the drive energy while building self-awareness and executive control. There was now an awareness of the two competing selves and their turbulent self-defeating behaviours. He decided to show the piece to his mother, perhaps aware of the work's insight and symbolic value. By drawing upon his passions in the guise of skateboarding, issues of mindblindness, aggression and impulse control were transformed—in this instance. Whether such insights could be sustained and generalized and his art remain an agent of change is always the daunting question.

Figure 7.6 After a combination of time and treatment, Connor became more introspective—creating a sensitive self-portrait of both of his personas; an insightful teen and his disruptive alter-ego.

Eight
Functional Methodologies

Sitting Beside and Naturalistic Environment

In Britain, creative art therapists describe their method of 'assessing', from the word's etymology—that of a method of 'sitting beside'. In this mode, the therapist remains unobtrusive yet available to the client while the creative process unfolds (Gilroy, 2007). Being 'fully present' while remaining an integral part of the therapeutic or parenting process is a difficult balance to strike. It requires patient observation while in the client's own comfort zone or 'habitat'. In the last case, it was two years of sitting (and running) beside a boy who was actively skateboarding, and designing skate decks, which were finally transposed to self-referential portraiture. The 'naturalistic' method of observation begins by creating a 'facilitating environment' that nurtured the creative process along the hopes that insight can eventually be attained (Winnicott, 1971). The studio and skate park became for Connor one such facilitating environment, where in his element the freedom to make art and then skate outside during session was coupled with the tough negotiations of his behavioural program. Naturalistic behaviours were thus encouraged—that the permissible can coincide with natural consequence. Behaving naturally, without resorting to stultifying defences, attests that a therapeutic space has been achieved—where the potential for inner and outer worlds could be engaged through the creativity of transitional space.

The naturalistic method's appeal is that it is not limited to any one orthodoxy, but crosses professions and paradigms, working with a surprising range of clientele. Primatologist Jane Goodall is one such exemplar, whose renown was linked to her willingness to 'sit beside' her chimpanzees for long periods deep in the African jungle (1971). After the long days of observation Goodall would trek back to camp and take to her tent for long nights of typing up process notations. These detailed and voluminous notes provided her with empirically sound clinical impressions. It avoided the need for laboratory experiments, which are artificial environments, where data gathering is not factoring environmental and other variables. It has what is termed 'ecological validity' as the observer notes the ever-shifting variables which impact her subjects as they adjust and compensate for the changing environment. I have already alluded as to how fluid and protean our clients are, with changes in their neurochemistry, the environment and maturational growth. These and a myriad of other dynamic variables constantly change the clinical picture. Goodall's immersion allowed for the discoveries of primate behaviour in ways the world had never known—that chimpanzees can be depressed, have empathy, make tools and, most extraordinary, conduct war. By sitting beside my own clients for long periods, approximating their own environments, engaging and mirroring their interests, it was hoped that my own data collection would yield a modicum of insight by humbly echoing Goodall's method.

In the psychotherapeutic setting, again it was Margaret Mahler, Fred Pine and Anni Bergman who set the standard for naturalistic observation in their seven-year study of toddler/mother dyads (1975). What made their methodology revolutionary in the annals of child development was to create naturalistic settings. I took from Mahler and, later, Bergman the need for adapting the setting to wherever is conducive to therapeutic work. Like Mahler, I cohabitated the client in unusual settings, client soccer games, observing recess behaviour, peering through playground fences—even to working inside a family's car when the child refused to come to session. Mahler's research station was also not limited to the clinical consultation room but centred around a playroom where mothers and their babies interacted at ease. By filming the sessions, her collaborators could examine the nuances of each phase of development frame by frame. My own video initiatives echoed that of Mahler's example. Her playroom observations as well as my own could be 'cross-sectioned', meaning notations were compared between observers—whether they be supervisors, camp counsellors or graduate assistants. With their combined inferences, Mahler's multidisciplinary team established nothing less than devising the stages of child development, including those destined for the spectrum. Film and video documentation made for fascinating viewing—it anticipated this technological age, where every action is open to question or criticism.

Later, neurologist Oliver Sacks utilized a methodology based upon his insatiable curiosity and willingness to immerse himself in the lives of the people he observed and treated. He popularized the 'essay of the odd', seeking out and consulting to cases, some of which defied scientific explanation. He was often dismissed by those abiding by 'hard science' as being *literary*, a mere storyteller, full of feel-good anecdotes. He became a creature of fame, the subject of a movie, which did not dilute his devotion to laboratory experimentation and clinical practice. After Dr. Sack's passing, several obituaries indicated that he was hardly the model scientist. He famously proclaimed there was 'no prescribed path of recovery'—that only by becoming attuned to the patient's life can we gain the necessary empathy and insight into their behaviour. He was self-confessional, examining his own less than savoury proclivities, including his sexuality and substance-induced sufferings. He entered his own dark cave, working feverishly, while often speeding in altered states of consciousness. He took both hallucinogens and amphetamines, which both enlivened and eventually disturbed his work. He was hardly the lab-coat type, except when he was locked in on a problem. It was in the clinic when his powers came alive; his focus was formidable, almost autistic-like in its high-fidelity attention. His immersive techniques yielded many clinical insights, not as evidenced-based outcomes, but through incessant questioning and intuitive insight. Like Goodall and Mahler in the 1950s and 1960s, he was a taker of voluminous notes, almost to an obsessive degree. Armed with massive amounts of observational data, the footnotes in his books often outweigh the actual narrative. His role model was the great Russian neurologist, A. R. Luria, perhaps the father of humanistic scientists who spent hours carefully observing and then treating shell-shocked brain-damaged WWI veterans. As a methodological model, Sacks, like Luria, attempted to understand the fullness of the patient's life and illnesses.

The problem with the single observer model, even with supervision, is that the method has its limitations. The process then is subjective to the observer's bias. This is a weakness in any practitioner's work whose focus is upon helping children and working towards positive outcomes, rather than laboratory experimental research. It requires and assumes the clinician has not just accurately observed but has also mastered theory and practice, citing relevant and recent research literature. Once assimilated, one might venture an intervention that can impact the well-being of the client. As an antidote to observational bias, I welcomed having my own inaccuracies, biases, or unconscious projections 'checked' through supervision. My supervisors ranged from psychiatrists, principals, mentors and therapeutic/educational teams, who drew upon their 'collective' wisdom. The diversity of group opinion helped dispel professional, cultural or personal bias and helped arrive at more accurate assessments (Henley, 2012a). Supervisors are essential in counselling the therapist when my observations indicate that the clinician might have lost focus and strayed into tangents beyond the parameters of the case or project. Supervisors, colleagues and even interns were particularly integral to being 'checked'.

Being Checked

Like Mahler's team of interns, I benefitted by a constant stream of assistants and interns who were attracted to the work at The Hecht Group, as well as within the creative arts courses with special needs students in our university program. One such intern, Michele Amendolari, who is now an experienced therapist herself, has shared her journals and notated observations during her tenure as my assistant. Her observations were critical to my arriving at informed assessments about many of our at-risk college freshmen. Her reflective writings were a prime example of the naturalistic method, which included hours of observation of students and included notes on me, her supervisor, while teaching in the classroom studio. Reading her reflections and criticisms with me as the 'authority figure' was informative but also humbling. Transference and countertransference reactions to observations of self and others were critical to the naturalistic method of reflection and exploration. Within the studio, where creative behaviours could ebb and flow, observation of action and reaction could be duly recorded. These reactions were particularly challenging when outcomes were disturbing enough that they tapped both therapists' emotions. In some cases, it is not the intern who is lower on the hierarchical end of the process but the therapist, whose authority position requires some degree of supervisory support, criticism and, at times, even rescuing. These and other empirical observations formed another erudite master's thesis, where the stimulus, outcomes and interventions were analyzed within the university setting (Amendolari, 2003).

The Client at the Centre

The naturalistic method has at its roots in the humanities, as Carl Rogers (1951) recognized when he formulated the 'client-centred approach'. His practice attempted to meet the client or child at their level, with his taking up the position with a sense of humility, wonder, curiosity and unconditional regard. What is most relevant to my method is how the child is related to, with a sense of *transparency*—without the therapist's being seen as the sage, authority or 'answer' to their problems. With parents especially, I openly acknowledge my own limitations—that we all suffer sensitivities and neuroses on some level; thus we are all 'in it together'. Often, I was idealized as the perfect parent—a misconception I readily put to rest, that I had made many of the same miscalls or temper-headed decisions in my own children's upbringing. By not hiding behind an 'all-knowing' professional facade, it assisted in my forming a therapeutic alliance with those parents who felt guilt, shame or depression over what they perceived as failures on their part. I constantly emphasized that we all share the same goal together, meeting the challenges these children often present. I admitted how difficult or even impossible it is to truly imagine their way of being in the world—that it is a pretentious supposition. These empathic processes require a concerted team effort, with focus, discipline and hard work, rather than just a 'big heart'.

Stabilizing the Child Medically

The efficacy of creative response therapies with children on the spectrum is directly related to their medical stability. If a child is manifesting symptoms of hyperactivity, mood lability or anger issues, even the most effective interventions may be worthless. There is considerable debate, however, regarding prescribing psychotropic drugs to children especially at an early age. Dr. Hecht, our presiding psychiatrist, always grappled with the issue, trying as many therapeutic behavioural and environmental interventions possible before prescribing medication. His extensive workups involving genealogy, pathology, environment, sleep patterns and other variables all entered his medical recommendations. Many children came to me unnerved by these personal interviews; feeling interrogated, one boy created a creative response that cried out 'TOO MANY QUESTIONS ASKED!' (Figure 8.1).

While these intake interviews were critical for helping me demarcate my approach to the child's creative response therapy, intakes and testing were in no way intended to be *therapeutic* for the child; as the image attests, the fifteen-year-old left the doctor's office beside himself. It was fortuitous he could draw out his frustration directly after.

Figure 8.1 After an extensive intake and personal probing with his psychiatrist, this teen vented his frustration with a strong self-portrait that registers his exasperation.

The newly medicated child was often beset by a new set of problems—medications often did not ameliorate symptoms; other times they exacerbated them. Dr. Hecht and his nurse were constantly titrating. In witnessing this informed trial-and-error basis came a new respect for psychiatry as an art form. Rooted in hard science, it was often the doctor's intuition, an obscure reference or the child's behaviour that led to further trials. I became convinced that psychotropic drugs are an all-important, life quality saving option. It was often my long-term cases of four to six years where the discernible effects of the complete therapeutic package could be seen. My own therapeutic interventions, prior early interventions, behavioural strategies and some form of medical intervention all made up the working parts of treatment. Eventually, almost every child in the practice was prescribed some form of medication to knock down their symptoms—whether it be a Benadryl to help a hyperactive child get some rest to a complex regimen of psychotropic medications.

However, there is cause for caution when it comes to medicating the very young or unmanageable children. The literature bears out that those physicians over-prescribing stimulant medications are mostly family care practitioners and in clinics whose clinical interviews are inadequate. In the urban inner city, problem children have been over-prescribed stimulants as a means of dealing with spectrum or ill-behaved children. As we witnessed with one university student, stimulants can be abused, as the use of medication becomes less a *control* tool and more an *enhancement* of one's mental powers of focus. While the dopamine reward circuit certainly enhances performance, long-term use leads to addiction, exhaustion and even a loss of normative concentration (Biederman et al., 1997).

Overcoming the Stigma of Psychiatry

During my tenure with the Hecht psychotherapy practice, the clientele comprised mainly middle class, mostly college educated and professional parents, eager to address their child's issues. Interestingly, this group was the most resistant to putting their children on stimulants or other powerful psychotropic drugs than the tradesman or working class folk. Many of these professional parents (including several psychologists) came to our practice after trying natural remedies, neurofeedback and other novel brain-training programs. Parents of children on the autism end were often steered towards applied-behaviour analysis regimens. Eventually, most faced the fact that these children have medical problems. After finally medicating and witnessing the profound neurological behavioural changes in their children, parents often came back lamenting that because of their own prejudicial belief systems 'their children had suffered *needlessly*'.

If or when medication is prescribed, however, both parents and teachers must realize it is not a 'silver bullet' that magically eliminates the child's symptoms. Medical interventions are intended to temper the symptoms sufficiently to make a *marked* difference, allowing the child to function better at home or school. It is vital that the child to be taught to listen to their own body. One boy, William, who was on the autistic end of the continuum, learned how to self-regulate. His response picture requires no interpretation: that when he has reached his limit of handling his world he requested a Xanax (Figure 8.2).

Part of his ability to develop self-monitoring was linked to being taught to be attuned to his somatic signals that included acute anxiety and nausea. Knowing

Figure 8.2 Self-regulation and becoming attuned to one's body are critical as the child develops an awareness of his mental state and medication needs.

when one has reached their limit and requires medication becomes a part of self-regulation. To use medication as a pre-emptive measure rather than a reactive intervention is a sign of developmental maturation that the therapeutic team constantly strived for. Being medically stabilized allows the adjunctive psychotherapists an opportunity for their behavioural program training or therapeutic interventions to effectively *reach* the child. Experience has taught us that when parents take their children off their meds of their own volition, disaster ensues. Parents may have good intentions to improve their children's appetites so they can gain needed bulk or wanting to have a break to visit with their children unfettered by side effects as a kind of cost-benefit analysis. Withdrawing or changing medication often invites an infusion of new and even more malevolent symptoms. The treatment thus becomes incomplete, with time lost and increased drug and consultation costs, as well as the child suffering. Behavioural prompts may need increasing when medications have not reached therapeutic levels. One may require more punitive consequences and return to the cycle of negativity that is counter-therapeutic.

Behavioural Training

Several children arrived at The Hecht Group camp or in therapy after having had years of such behavioural-based programming. It was quite easy to spot them, as they were indeed *well trained*. Unlike many other children, eye contact was sustained, language was more formed and their knowledge-base was advanced compared to the other children. Socialized behaviours were superficially polite, with an emphasis upon pleasing their elders—all worthy goals suggested by Attwood's training (2008). But years of a token economy system of rewards and consequences had left them reliant on external rewards. Learning appropriate behaviours sometimes came with a price—of reward-addicted behaviours that were at odds with our creativity-based program.

One boy, eleven-year-old Sean, was a bright and well-trained child with impeccable manners. He was a quiet, unassuming boy on the autistic spectrum who was trained in Applied Behavioural Analysis for three years. During the initial group camp projects, he asked what he would earn for 'positive participation'—a term most certainly learned from his behavioural curriculum. My response was 'a nice time, Sean', 'perhaps a new friend' or 'something to show your parents'. His reaction seemed confounding. He was a child taught to constantly self-monitor to remain 'appropriate'. He would constantly 'scan' staff and myself for the 'appropriate response', then use these cues to assist in interpreting the situation at hand. Often, I felt all this 'vigilance' left him exhausted, anxious and even *distracted*. Eventually, he tried to habituate to our model and its child-initiated activity. During creative response therapy, Sean began to gradually loosen his rigid defences and the adult-scripted training. During one free-associative project, the goal was unclear. It encompassed relaxation, daydreaming and observing weather patterns often taken for granted, then included a post-response painting activity. One summer day, the children were invited to

lie on their backs on the lawn and simply look up at the cumulus cloud formations drifting in the sky.

Like enormous ships under sail, cloud formations floated past, creating shifting
forms and colours. After lazing in the grass, their counsellor, Shannon Pearce,
invited the group to describe what they 'saw'. Again, Sean was new at this process,
as perhaps it accessed areas of consciousness which perhaps his training had suppressed. He was thrown off-kilter, as he had not fully acclimated to projects that
were not craft or product oriented. Instead, this was as a veritable Rorschach test,
not part of a script that he could regurgitate to an adult. Observing him adjust, I
found it fascinating how even in a free-associative activity he 'complied'. As he laid
back awkwardly, intently listening, first to the instructions and then to the other
children's associations, he seemed to gauge which responses were acceptable.
When art therapist Shannon asked whether he saw something, he finally spoke
up. His voice, at first unsure, he tentatively described a 'pirate'. 'Oh, a pirate?'
she responded. 'What else?' 'With big muscles … and a sword' and 'the ocean
splashing all up'—as the clouds broke apart and seemed to become great waves
of roiling foam. We were all taken aback at his quick adaption and, indeed, positive participation—though it did not come easily. The project began to tap what
we termed the child's inner visions, memories and obsessions that could flow in
and out of consciousness—like that of the clouds. His associations of pirates
and swords were wholly within the lexicon of a latent-aged boy, full of characters that included pirates at sea. The pirate characterizations were totally within
the acceptable parameters of his developmental vernacular—adventuresome and
exciting. Despite the emphasis upon cognitive work, the primary process, with all
its aggressive associations and passionate swashbuckling, showed through and
enhanced the child's creative response.

The Downside of Behavioural Training

Given its evidence-bases data demonstrating improved listening and speaking,
Applied Behavioural Analysis makes it especially popular among certain schools
and insurance companies. Yet it is for this reason the technique has also been
discredited. One young adult writing in her blog, *Unstrange Mind,* described
her early years receiving Applied Behavioural Analysis as being spent having
every word and action analyzed, and then numerically tallied. She referred to
the forty hours per week of one-to-one behavioural analysis as being akin to
'puppy training'. She felt that one's behaviour should never be 'modified' but
'educated'—that the two are distinctly separable—that human communication
is more than forced eye contact. Yet one must acknowledge that no one can
tolerate an out-of-control child who cannot care for themselves and are aggressive to others. Yet for a child who had long undergone child behavioural training and then matured, her 'finished' self left her with an existential dilemma. It
was the ruling neurotypical 'majority' who decided which behaviours are acceptable and which rules are to be obeyed. She remains resentful that a part of herself
'was erased'.

This backlash from adults who endured strictly behavioural training has emerged as a new self-advocacy. One such group is the Autistic Self-Advocacy Network, whose advocates profiled referred to the operant conditioning model of Lovaas as demeaning, unethical and even abusive. One anonymous writer exclaims that years of coughing up the 'correct answer' for years on end left her psychologically damaged. It essentially buried the 'essence' of what it meant to be autistic, an existential identity that 'was left demeaned and unexplored'. They call for 'effective communication', which may be nonverbal, computer generated or in other alternative forms as a means for solidifying their identity. It is a natural outcome of having been oppressed that many self-advocacy movements sometimes become radicalized. Their strident opinions are also *reactions* themselves; in response to prejudices, they attempt to rattle the cage of the status quo. Once attention is drawn to the cause, however, one must then preach moderation. Sean's program perhaps demonstrated the most moderated approach, as his parents ensured the boy could self-care, communicate with neurotypicals and achieve academically. His camp experience taught both his parents and himself that it's now acceptable to be different—that the 'other world' is a source of untapped inspiration. Constraining it only leads to stifled defences and a loss of self-identity.

Current Early Intervention Model

There is a consensus among moderates in the field that a combination of modalities should be instituted to reach the whole child and their disparate needs. One common thread that unites all methodologies is the need for early intervention. A model program which embodies the multimodal approach is the progressive 'transactional' model of the Early Start Denver Model. Its curriculum is based upon an integrated approach which is embedded with the child's play activity (Rogers & Dawson, 2009). Naturalistic methods during typical play sessions emphasize a child-directed theme in conjunction with developing a trusting relationship with the therapist. Both participate as 'equals', elaborating ideas and engaging in interpersonal exchanges. Responsibility, civility and other social mores are ritualized at the end of the activity, with the child's assistance in the clean-up and transitioning to the next activity. Young children are socialized within their frame of reference without bringing out alien or 'appropriate' responses as much as building relationships through a curriculum that is relational. Lively, positive and dynamic interactions emphasize positive affective expression—everything evenly remotely positive is celebrated—a nod to the power of behaviour therapy. These positive responses are then mirrored by all those important to the child: the teacher, mother and therapist. It is a relational and object relations model as much as behavioural training, which reinforces the idea that learning and relating are inseparable. The Denver Model stresses the importance of data collection as evidence based to ensure outcomes are empirical enough to back up clinical notations and impressions.

Like almost every researcher in the scientific community, Rogers and Dawson have sought to validate their work through brain imaging. Their scans have suggested that the Denver Model has shown a neurological curative effect upon the child's social-communicative circuits, including developing the mirror neuron system. Interventions suggest an increase in IQ, language acquisition, and facial recognition and relational synchrony (Rogers & Dawson, 2009). This approach renders the strict behaviourism model antiquated unless the child is so severe as to be uncontrollable or aggressive. It permits a child to evolve along with their 'real self', while also practising becoming part of the typical world, with respect and compromise being the cornerstone. With such an early-intervention, play-oriented program, the child is then primed at a later age to succeed in other pro-creativity programs, such as Montessori or Waldorf schools. Brain plasticity and developmental milestones are still malleable, with libidinal and other drive energy still raw and energetically directed. By age five, the 'social brain' has already been formed, and without intervention, dysfunction becomes more intractable. Without relationally based early interventions, as the child grows into latency, primitive defences may take hold. Cognitive and behavioural limitations may be impossible due to the child's immature and reactive defensive behaviours. The environment plays an important role, in contextualizing the fit into any methodology.

Survival Mode

One critical caveat of early intervention is that these programs often require financial resources. Schools cannot afford such individualized, faculty-intensive special services. Seeking out support services also requires the wherewithal to navigate, then overcome, bureaucratic obstacles and other resistance. R. Miller (2015) has written a harrowing account of being a poverty-stricken mother while struggling to cope with her toddler's emerging symptoms of autism. As babies are most often born to those couples or single parents who are starting out their adult lives, resources for services may be in short supply. For others, poverty is a generational way of life with services woefully inadequate in perpetually impoverished socio-economic environments. Options for treatment may be minimal, rendering the discussion on whether to use this method or that a moot point, for some children and their families are not electing a program; they are in survival mode.

Returning to the case of Tonya (pg. 44), early intervention might have reduced reactive aggression and hypervigilance to tolerable levels. Later behavioural programs might have mitigated her impulsivity. Yet the consistency necessary for this method was an impossibility—she returned home to the same chaotic environment which exacerbated her problem to begin with. Considering where she lived—the projects on the near West Side of Chicago—aggression and reactivity were *adaptive* traits. If approached with a cognitive method, would a therapist consider someone's behaving wildly and aggressively in her war-zone neighbourhood over-vigilance or a 'thought distortion'? Would they dissuade the child that *faulty thinking* about her negative emotional states about herself and others was irrational, distorted or overly negative? Tonya was acting 'rationally', albeit with a damaged ego, according to the mores of her hostile environment. This child's multiple-spectrum involvement and vulnerability to the violence of street life rendered her in a reactionary 'fight' mode. Her behavioural/emotional state was not cognitive malfunction but symptomatic—the reason that contributes to negativity when engulfed in dangerous or hostile circumstances. Tonya was left with emotional scarring of a horrific reality—hers was not irrational but an accurate appraisal of reality. To attempt to cognitively reframe it any other way becomes absurd, discounting the child's contextual circumstances. Overlying these environmental challenges is the ubiquitous media, whose sprawling presence affects children in the poorest environs, with mixed outcomes.

Nine

Media and Technology: New Challenges

Evolving methodologies must now factor in new media and technology, which requires reevaluating the ways in which we approach the spectrum child and their psyche. This rapidly changing environment of digital media and portable devices impacts many of the fundamentals described in the earlier chapters. Methods must keep pace, adapt and even be reinvented if the therapist is to remain a relevant force of creative and mental growth. This may require entering into yet another alien world, where as yet unnamed forms of communication and expression have an impact upon the children we serve.

In 2010, I held an interview with a child on the spectrum and her mother, casually asking the child who her favourite pop star was. This eleven-year-old girl with mild autistic markers nonchalantly cited 'Hatsune Miku'. Feigning interest in hearing about yet another pop fad, my clinical ears perked up upon hearing her describe Hatsune as being 'not actually real'. She stated that the singer was her 'virtual idol' or a 'vocaloid'. This sent me running to Wikipedia, where I found Hatsune to be a humanoid pop star 'application' who appears on stage as a holographic projection. On YouTube, she dances as any pop star would but as a translucent body of light whose singing is done through a synthesizer. Despite being virtual, she interacts with her enthusiastic audience, even using 'call and response'. Hiroyuki Ito, her computer creator, programmed Hatsune as a prepubescent androgynous type of anime creature, with bizarre knee-length blue twin braids. Her song list includes an astounding 120,000 songs, which also exist in several software packages that are 'multimedia content creations'. Fans can create their own 2-D and 3-D animations and mix in their own soundtracks. Hatsune's concerts are as 'live' as any found in any arena, with enthusiastic fans waving light sticks, singing along and responding to the projection and her synthesized soundtrack as fully *real*.

The creative response has entered the realm of the virtual, without physical substance beyond a programmer's writing incomprehensible code. Who knows whether this virtual pop star will lay the foundation for this child's interest base for years to come, as was the case with my own experience with *Fantasia*. One never knows what formative experience will leave an indelible mark and lifelong influence. She could grow to see the art form reinvented many times over—such are the possibilities that await. What is certain is that within the past fifty years, technology has pervaded almost every child's life as never before—indeed it has become an extension of one's mind. Artificial intelligence can answer almost any question with a few finger swipes, from how to make a bomb to the theory of relativity. Meanwhile, information and fantasy have melded together, as the pop idol illustrates. 'She' is a lasered beam of light, a video game with user-guided digital effects, with an enormous, wildly devoted fan base that trends on social media. As a sheer spectacle, Hatsune and her software elevate the so-called 'real' to supernatural levels.

Violence, Play and Media

From time immemorial, children have play acted violence, whether parents approved or not. Progressive parents may ban gunplay, yet it will always be part of that particularly male play experience—for it takes only a pointed finger with a cocked thumb to serve as a six shooter, or for that matter, a stick for a spear, rifle or bow. However, in recent decades robust outdoor shoot'em-up play acting has given way to passive indoor activities, where virtual and interactive media have satisfied the appetite for play violence. Such passive exposure may translate into children's changed attitudes towards acting out violent behaviour. Bushman and Anderson (2009) define media violence as exposure 'to fearful stimuli in a positive emotional context' (pg. 275). Their studies indicate that violence in video gaming and other media is not so much a harmless, venting 'cathartic experience'. Instead, their findings indicate overexposure is linked to decreased empathy towards helping and other prosocial behaviours. The authors borrowed the phrase 'comfortably numb' from the Pink Floyd lyric to apply to the desensitization found in their subjects to the suffering of others (pg. 273). Violent media exposure, they assert, can instil beliefs that violence is normative, whether existing in fantasy or reality. For instance, when an anonymous CIA operative hovers over a video console, reads some code, then moves a joystick in such a way that a target some five thousand miles away is obliterated on screen, has this happened—or not? Who can tell? Clients, parents and therapists, even those in the military, increasingly struggle with this new reality.

These issues came to the fore with one twelve-year-old Asian adopted boy, Sung Li, as violent play was pleasurable but, more importantly, gained him entry to social acceptance. He was a mild-mannered boy who was an excellent artist, but presented with generalized adjustment and attentional issues at school, perhaps the result of moving into a new home and neighbourhood. In addition, at home he coped with adoptee and cultural identity challenges. Like Connor (pg. 136–39), he too had been an isolated gamer before being accepted into a peer group. He also played with almost addicted obsession, which precluded him from going out and making friends. However, gaming became a common denominator when he joined a group who acted out many of the violent video games he was familiar with—giving him a sense of social parity. These boys moved from staying intractably 'inside', to acting out all manner of killing and maiming while 'outside'—to the consternation of the parents. Alarmed that the boys were armed with the similar toy weaponry as the games, the play left little to the imagination. A simple stick had morphed into realistic grenades, guns and knives such that play began to escalate in intensity and frequency.

In session, I casually addressed the incidents of gunplay, remaining non-judgemental, yet as usual, benignly interested. Over several sessions of sitting beside him, he enthusiastically described their favourite games—'We like to play fight like survivalists after the apocalypse'. My job was to try to mirror back the exciting prospects of the coming apocalypse, while attempting to address the mother's agenda of toning down the violence. Our discussions led quickly to creating a picture, which over two sessions he worked on and was proud of, to the extent of wanting to share it with his mother. Again, the early developmental need to have one's passion mirrored back was alive and in play. The boy's enthusiasm blinded him to the fact that she might not just disapprove of the violent content—but she was also paying money for the privilege!

The triad discussion soon led to drawing a social scene of violence-themed play. The round robin of shootings, stabbings and lobbing bombs with word balloons vividly recounted the scenarios (Figure 9.1).

Figure 9.1 Violence is a fact of life, regardless of media influence. This boy re-enacted a video game, inventing ever-more violent means with his friends, shown playfully annihilating each other.

While his figures were all elaborately formed and animated, Sung curiously added little stick figures. These figures represented those who were of powerless status and marginalized. He remarked about the stick figures: 'these kids aren't anything—so they don't play'. Sung was differentiating between those who were an accepted part of the group and those who were pathetic outsiders unworthy of even being drawn. If this were the case, the image displays his own hard-won degree of self-esteem at being peer accepted. Identifying with their violent-themed play was a small price to pay for being part of a group with status. While this discharge and displacement of aggressive energy was age and socially appropriate, the issue of escalation as a parental concern needed to be addressed.

Entering the session, Sung's mother was coached about how to respond to his image. Shown the drawing, she began by applauding his *artistic* efforts, then gently expressed her concern over the non-stop level of violence. Her response addressed both the influence that video gaming had on the play and giving into social pressures with his new-found group of friends. She remarked to her son that 'while cool and fun, in this day and age, acting out scenarios with realistic guns and knives could be fatal'. Recent news accounts had shown how children have been shot by law enforcement while brandishing a fake realistic gun. The issue then became one of making 'better choices' as a means of allowing for vigorous play. At the same time, it was important to modify it enough to resist the peer pressure to escalate the violent content further. We then negotiated compromise. The deal permitted him the privilege of play fighting, but he would allow her to reach out to other parents to try to tone down the hyperrealism—to which he reluctantly agreed. Having his mother contacting his new friends' parents was a mortifying prospect—he fretted over its spelling the end of his first play crew. The mother explained the situation to her neighbours—that as a newly befriended and impressionable child, he would go along with intense levels of violence, putting him and perhaps the others at risk. The neighbours agreed and as a group vowed to contain the amount of time the boys spent glued to their screens and reached consensus as to which games would be played. They also provided the boys with Day-Glo coloured air-powered rifles or in summer 'super-soaker' water guns, which still allowed violent fantasy material to be exercised, but within a safer *form*.

The behavioural program and parental intervention recognized that it was beyond these boys' capacity to recognize such subtle distinctions of fantasy and realism, especially when it was so powerfully reinforced in their media play. Spurred on by their video games, they considered their play to be tame, having become numb to its hyperrealism. Yet eventually all the boys respected their parents' wishes and adjusted their play fights accordingly, with all new weaponry being harmless. In citing this case, however, we acknowledge that these boys hailed from a strong-knit community. Such cooperation and compliance would perhaps be unachievable in other demographic settings where parental and neighbouring supervision is lax or non-existent.

As with any tool, gaming technology can be used and abused, as it is the 'frequency and intensity' that tips the medium between advances in communication or a regressive, depersonalized medium that invites addiction. As a social binding agent, technology allows for equality and status, which is based not upon one's physical prowess but on skill and eye/hand coordination. Sung Li, a self-avowed nerd, had successfully become part of a new group of children who may not have otherwise acknowledged his existence. It opened his world to making social connections. Making sure he was cutting edge in the newest games brought him acceptance. With such tools at their disposal, technology has given children on the spectrum potentially a new and forceful voice.

Filtering and Imagination

Seemingly eons ago, art educators worried about how illustrated children's books or television were stealing away the children's imagination. Responding to advances in the technology of the 1950s, Lowenfeld denounced book illustrations and other media, which did the imagining *for* the child (1957). Meanwhile, Kramer (1958) referred to television as a child's 'ever-available slave'. Their complaint about the impact of the adult-conceived media and video now also seems quaint. Current imagery, information and news come raw and unfiltered for those who search its powerful engines. The emotional capacity for children on the spectrum to process this upsurge of barely censored material remains at odds with their fragility and impressionability. The crux of this discussion, then, is whether technology will exacerbate the spectrum child's hyper- or hypoaroused states. The question also arises whether its sheer volume and intensity may overwhelm the child's self-expression and imagination. While all children can now appropriate their culture through media as never before, its instant accessibility raises concerns about whether it helps or hinders their creative and therapeutic outcomes.

Digital Connectivity

Computer images, videos, games and the Internet can provide a relational connective medium. Noted writer Janet Malcolm considers devices so tethered to our personas that the medium can become anthropomorphized as the new transitional object (2016). As a substitutive entity, for a child on the spectrum digital devices can become objects of intense attachment—to the extent that they take on human attributes. For those especially on the autistic end of the continuum, their devices may be symbiotic relationships. Separating them perhaps mimics the separation struggles to separate from their mothers, though in this instance these are not sentient beings but inanimate (animated) devices. However regressive, many parents with children on the severe autistic continuum are glad to settle for *any* communication with their child. Whether by computer, smartphone or any other means of connectivity, the computer can be a bridge or precursor to actual relating. All means of communication must be considered, though the goal is always encouraging face-to-face communication. While texting from a bedroom may be the norm, as the saying goes, 'everything in moderation'. Tell that to parents in Asian countries who are often at the forefront of technological advances where over-dependence or addiction to devices can reach pathological proportions. In Japan, there is a word for this: 'hikikomori', or shut-ins, who may not leave the darkened cave of their rooms for weeks or months. Parents describe slipping meals under doors or peering into the darkened rooms, only to see their child reflected by the sickly bluish glow—the only indication the child was still conscious.

Greenfield (1999) describes how addictive gaming stimulates the brain with the same dopamine and other chemicals that condition the brain's reward centres to crave 'another fix'. As a neurobehavioural habit akin to gambling or porn, digital devices act as a 'digital drug', putting children on the spectrum incrementally more at risk for obsessional behaviours—especially those which involve avoidance of human interaction. Individuals on the spectrum may tend towards escapism and suffer time distortion while lost in the pleasures of their obsessive content. The ease of accessibility makes the medium difficult to exercise self-control. Video gaming may be especially addictive for those with ADD and ADHD features, where violence and crash-and-burn excitement can be exercised without real-world consequence (Rosen, 2012). Comfortable within this virtually violent realm, these children find built-in structure; clear, consistent rules; and extraordinary intensity. Their reward may be a positive sense of accomplishment, something that often eludes them in real life.

Gaming programs are conceived to encourage addictive behaviour. As a classic form of continual reinforcement, the games and their levels escalate, with no end in sight—hence, one is never 'done'. As the player advances level to level, rewards are meted out just enough to lure the player to reach the 'jackpot' of satisfaction, a cycle which may become self-perpetuating. To mediate, monitor and protect the spectrum child from all these travails, while permitting a degree of social parity and solidarity among peers, is a social imperative.

Social Media

Social media have also revolutionized interpersonal relationships, changing the way individuals communicate and network for sharing personal information. Assuming it is parentally controlled, children may have safety restrictions in place for posting personal info that would otherwise be private. Social networking expands the relational base, as described earlier—any means that enables a spectrum child to connect with like-minded peers, even on a worldwide scale. For those on the severe end of the spectrum, the computer allows them to interact with the world without the burden of being face-to-face. Rosen (2012) reports that technology can provide a sense of 'virtual empathy', where those who have been subjected to localized bullying or rejection can now find others who have shared those negative experiences. In a recent workshop one child's mother described posting his painting and text on social media and instantly receiving kudos from other spectrum children—described online as an 'empathy bomb'. Virtual media can transmit images, text and information instantly, and be responded to by anyone who has access to a device. Later in the case material, I consider how a child posted material about their spectrum challenges and was rewarded by an image and a letter from halfway around the world, all in a matter of minutes. Such affirmations for children on the spectrum are relatively rare, given how socially isolated and geographically widespread these populations are. To have a hundred kindred spirits all applaud and support a simple picture can have enormous personal impact.

Dangerous Connectivity

Rosen also warns, however, that if not controlled, postings open a child to greater vulnerability. Technology is now a medium where 'trending' information can be accessed with the click of an icon regardless of its content. This advancing freedom of information cuts many ways, as any tech-savvy child can conjure almost any images or videos. The medium seems barely under control, however, as servers strain to balance freedom of expression with search-engine censorship. Children may enter keywords such as the main economic export of Pakistan and inadvertently pull up the most recent torture, immolation or other hideous violence, which often eludes servers' or corporate control. No one can ignore how information technology is now untethered. It is freely shared or leaked, with the norms of privacy given over to almost total transparency. Institutions, religions, politicians and celebrities must now come to grips with being under scrutiny, where every morsel of information can be criticized and broadcast. As the spectrum child matures and eschews parental controls, revealing personal information poses a threat to those who are disinhibited and vulnerable from users who are frauds. The reverse of virtual empathy is founded upon the key element that the anonymity of the Internet can reduce impulse control. Unfiltered thoughts and feelings can be posted anonymously without consequence in preying, hacking and connecting with those who are vulnerable.

More distressingly, Sales (2016) points out recent research of the detrimental effects social media can have on girls—a point I raised earlier in the chapter on socialization (Chapter Four). She cites the increasing peer pressure to take and send explicit self-portraits to boys for their 'trophies', which may then be uncontrollably circulated. This and other forms of virtual abuse, even within the typical population, have been linked to soaring mental health issues and even suicide (Kowalski & Limber, 2013). The Centers for Disease Control and Prevention reports that in 2014, the population with whom I specialize—latency-age children between the ages of ten and fourteen—are now as likely to die of suicide as in automobile accidents. Rachel Simmons, author of *Odd Girl Out* (2002, 2011), states that mostly girls dominate social sites, especially those which enable them to receive instant feedback from their peers, whether it be validation or humiliation, leaving the most vulnerable at risk.

Advertisements fuel the peddling of a vast array of products and services which may leave children vulnerable to new consuming habits. Website 'hits' are tracked, targeting even young children, which may be counterproductive to the child's well-being. These issues are exacerbated for the child with spectrum disorders. Again, those on the vulnerable end may fall prey to being targeted or victimized.

Children with hyperactive or manic tendencies may be prone to consuming products impulsively or aggressively acting out with a sense of impunity that otherwise would be checked. As hormonal and neurochemical changes exacerbate impulse control during puberty, enormous forces are at play to disinhibit the child from seeking out the most taboo material available.

News, Media and Disturbing Content

On any given night, any child with sufficient awareness might become exposed to newscasts where raw violence, calamity, crime and sex may be the lead story. This is the nature of commercial media—to appeal to the morbid curiosity of the viewing audience. Cantor and Nathanson (1996) have done research on the fright reactions of children to online access, television and the news. They found that 37 percent of children from kindergarten, second-, fourth- and sixth-grade typical children had fright reactions to violent or disturbing news and online material. I have children come into session with distorted comprehension of news images, even those which might be studied in school as innocuous 'current events'. For children on the spectrum, processing becomes the salient issue explored in therapy. Yet I have found that these issues become the most difficult for which to find creative solutions, as the exposure is ongoing and escalating in their disturbing content.

One teen boy, Eric, often brought his interest in all things science fiction to session, especially if some media event, such as a new Star Wars or Trek movie, was being released—each was an age and a culturally appropriate topic to explore. Yet as he matured, his attention to media went beyond fantastical films, entering the realm of the 'new' real, or perhaps what I dub the 'surreal'. He began to obsess on government reports of how we are waging 'the war of the future'. Indeed, recent defence department memos reveal artificial intelligence will eventually become 'autonomous', meaning the drones and other robotics will be able to discern friend from foe. They can target enemies based upon facial recognition software. This teen also described enthusiastically how our military has created gaseous mediums that can temporarily anesthetize a populace, rendering them immobile while the aggressor seizes territory and assets. My own attempts to redirect Eric's 'facts' proved fruitless, as he created stick-figure storyboards of these 'thinking' drone-delivered killings, which I helplessly observed while they were being created. I offered weak comments, such as 'These technologies have many checks and balances' et cetera, with the hope of diffusing his excitement and anxiety. The fascination which this boy brought to the theme spoke to issues of paranoia and annihilation anxiety. They could not just be reframed or redirected through creative activity, lest he become over-stimulated. Several years later his rantings proved prescient.

Rosa Brooks (2016), after having served as an adjutant working within the Pentagon, wrote an essay that affirmed this boy's 'anaesthesia attack'. Her work at the defence department validated this teen's vision—that the cyber future of war is 'now', that warriors will still fight and die wretchedly in the desert or mud but they are increasingly eclipsed by the sterility of data sets and code. It is now common that cyber hackers, financiers, terrorists, drug cartels, private corporations and our own government all wage undeclared wars that are virtually invisible. Brooks writes that weapons of global destruction increasingly take the form of computer viruses. 'The battlefield will be everywhere', she writes, that the spatial boundaries between war and non-war have all but evaporated. Greater casualties may result, not by boots on the ground, but rather by biowarfare attacks on security agencies, power grids or financial institutions, which can bring our country to its knees. Eric had seemed excited by these prospects. As a defensive measure, we marvel how children on the spectrum can present as hyposensitive, with the same degree of pathology as those who occupy the hyper end of the continuum. It is probable that the fantastic has become so mind numbing, being blended with gaming, that spectrum children's reactions may not be so off-kilter after all. It is the new norm.

Whether to creatively engage or help repress this material is a critical therapeutic assessment. It is no easy task to implement cognitive and creative interventions which can tease apart these disturbing feelings of vulnerability. With such media exposure, allaying their paranoia, obsessions, anxieties and fears proves to be an overwhelming task. Our job, once again, is to preview, control and monitor all social media and news outlets. We assist the children to develop healthy defences that ward off these hideous occurrences on the other side of the world. Cognitive-based interventions, such as visualizing and creating a 'safe place', may offer some respite. Yet with the obsessionality of Eric's leakage of intrusive thoughts, only the defences of denial, repression or media avoidance could temper his escalating anxiety. Given real-world calamity framed by technological advances, children's anxiety should be considered within normative parameters and not be condescended to as paranoia.

In Cantor's research, a major defence employed by children was to align themselves with negative characters, which psychoanalysts term 'identification with the aggressor', a defence which is ubiquitous throughout the case material. By identifying oneself with those who are powerful comes protection, whether in real life or within the magical realm. Again, this is where video games and other interactive media may allow meek children, such as Connor and Sung Li, to overcome a feeling of powerlessness and instead become the all-powerful assailant. If one *becomes* the operative drone killer, then one is empowered to defend against such nightmarish possibilities. It is a weak means of reality testing, bolstering the ego through fantastical defences against unwanted stimuli, yet we work with what we have.

The Actual Sufferers

What is sometimes lost in the conversation is the reality that most of our clients cope with these horrors on a second-hand basis from the comfort of their homes or school computers. This almost overshadows the reality that millions of children are living through these horrors. Countless children, such as the beleaguered, kidnapped girls of Nigeria; those being bombed in Syria; or the refugees washing up on shore after dangerous voyages, are caught in insurgencies that require our awareness and empathy. They endure unspeakable horrors, with no end in sight, which defies my own and perhaps the readers' imagination.

With the spotlight on the misery in Nigeria, Syria or Iraq, or that created by some new insurrection, we may lose sight of those who are domestically dispossessed—children within our own country, such as Tonya (pg. 44), who wages her own war daily, dodging the drugs, promiscuity and parental negligence. While it may not be Syria, the spectre of gang warfare as a horrific everyday occurrence gets lost in the conversation. The reality of the Nigerian girls and life on Chicago's West Side is rendered in the abstract by the onslaught of media. This news coverage limits our capacity for empathy when we are constantly inundated by images of each new, unimaginable suffering. Most viewers are not moved to tears or rushing to the phone to contribute money for these causes. The reality is that in the face of unrelenting suffering, the novelty of it all eventually wears off. The media *distances* us from the plight of millions; regardless of how horrible, we become numb. To be mindful of these realities is to keep a perspective on the unimaginably traumatic sufferings of others—who may not be so distant after all.

Computerized Communication

Technology has unarguably revolutionized learning and communication for those with special needs. In educational and therapeutic programs, any children, those who are nonverbal, speak a foreign language or dyslexic, can have computer-assisted language programs and one-click image downloads. Many anecdotes cited on the Internet describe how siblings or parents interact with their spectrum children via the computer, to the exclusion to any other form of interaction. Adaptive software programs customize translations, take audio dictation and interact through online games or chat groups and thus further social discourse—from accent reduction to explanations of English idioms. Writing programs correct, give feedback suggestions and provide related references to speed up and enrich communication. While 'facilitated communication' has been largely discredited (Riggott, 2005), on par with the Ouija-board effect, the computer still constitutes a lifeline that can reach children who are walled off within their autistic orbits. Computer-word or picture-board devices may hold out the promise that non-verbal children might be able to convey something of their world. My experiences in session, however, have proved mixed; higher-functioning children have helped augment their monosyllabic responses using a keyboard—*if* writing has developed as their dominant mode of communication. For the children more severely involved, the results appear more limited.

During a recent workshop at the Denver Art Museum, I interacted with a severely autistic child who was scribble painting in the museum's art studio. Fitted with a communication device, a computerized 'word picture box', his aide was helping him express what he wanted to see and do next. His answer was 'See Baby Einstein'. What first struck me was how technology miraculously enabled this very severely involved child to communicate. But the questions that beg to be

Plate 1 Triangulation and splitting for anyone can be hurtful, and feelings are often further exacerbated for children with spectrum issues. This group drawing explored their complex, triangulated friendship.

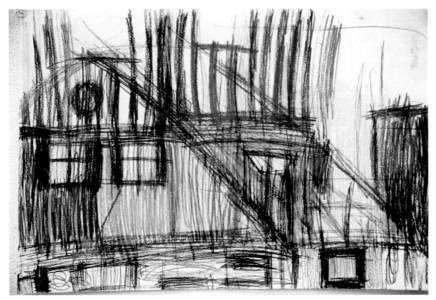

Plate 2 Despite legal blindness and autistic mannerisms, Jay was an accomplished and obsessive artist. His architectural renderings were always linear rather than solidly composed.

Plate 3 D.J.'s artistic passion was directed mainly towards rendering the colourful construction vehicles that surrounded his tiny bungalow on the fringes of Chicago's South Side.

Plate 4 A Russian adoptee who was particularly polite yet selectively mute chose this mandala as a means of containing unnamed fears within the form of a collaged Shaker box.

Plate 5 As a shut-in living in the projects in the Bronx, this teen records his isolation and limited vision of 'The Hallway', rendered with brilliant draftsmanship and dazzling colour.

Plate 6 Sometimes we forget about the 'real sufferers', the children left traumatized who are struggling to survive in war zones. Painting a cowering penguin is perhaps a fitting metaphor for her deep isolation and trauma.

Plate 7 A teen with multiple spectrum markers, Jeff possessed a photographic memory. Any stimulus could be faithfully recorded, as evidenced in his capturing the energy and spirit of this park.

Plate 8 Max presented with classic autistic symptoms but possessed unusual insight into his condition. In this powerful volcanic image, he breaks down colours into discrete feeling states.

Used with permission of Rebecca and Max Miller.

answered, now that we knew what he wanted (if that is indeed what he wanted), are how does that essentially change his bizarre perspective of our current reality? Do we go and find a baby Einstein, or do we try to re-wire both the technology and his mentation to unscramble what was perhaps a random response? These questions leave me unsettled, but also hopeful, that *some expression* via the vocabulary computer was voluntarily shared from a child who was otherwise locked within his own world.

Image Research

During creative response activities, what used to be hard-copy resource images now consist of instant downloads, which can access almost any image, subject, theme or idea. Today, photoshopping this image would be an effortless keystroke away. A thumb scroll and a few keystrokes would summon any model, spec or colour scheme. It is laughable that for years I maintained hulking filing cabinets filled with discarded ad agency stock photographs, which I would scavenge regularly. These high-fidelity images, sorted by theme, were a great resource for collaging or when drawing from copies was beneficial. During the years of my tenure as a therapist, our huge stock-photo books used for research were eventually replaced by our computer's downloads. The technology during the 1990s and 2000s, when I conducted most of my clinical work, remained weak compared to the stratospheric possibilities with current devices. One child recently remarked, 'it's my second brain'—for any idea, we just pull up the information or image. A child commented, 'I'll just ask my phone!' 'Then we can even post our session on social media—in real time!' It is a brave new world.

Visual Culture

Creative response activities have now been recast beyond the physicality of the visual or creative arts. Even the most severe child on the autistic continuum appropriates the 'visual culture' that surrounds him, from a child's obsession with luxury car ads to the echolalic singing of ad jingles. Artists in this text draw upon images of company dump truck logos as well as television ads for superglue; each is part of the cacophony that defines visual culture. Feature films have long been seamlessly integrated into commerce and culture—as many Batman and Star Wars fans queue up at shows clad in their cult costumes. These subcultures are now legion, comprising a vast amalgamation of modalities (Howells & Negreiros, 2012). Old and 'new media', many of its art forms yet unnamed, include every techno-creative material and yet-to-be devised technique. Visual culture is not limited to imagery but encompasses our environment at large as a vast multimedia experience. It may take the form of ephemeral art, non-art (leaving just the 'idea' of art) or more action-driven social protest art. Expressions are 'ready made', including advertisements, billboards, podcasts, bulk mailings and other personally generated or commercial broadcasts. Appropriating this culture has become more widespread in both therapy and education, as boundaries between the aesthetic and the informational/commercial paradigms are blurred. Everything is constantly newly blended or rebranded. Conceptual or formal references in creative responses expand accordingly—anything imaginable may become the outcome.

The emphasis on visual culture celebrates well-worn symbols that have been integrated as cultural icons and mated to those which are the most novel. The next innovative visual or multimedia art commodity may have an impact upon young, up-and-coming artists, including those with spectrum issues. Those who excel at digital technology and display multiple markers may not only succeed in many art forms but also excel as the 'next wave', from animation to game design—with only a minimum of human interaction necessary. The reverse of the hyperaroused individual may give way to hypoarousal, as those within the spectrum habituate to the avalanche of signs, symbols and neon text that proliferate in the physical environment. These stimuli may be dwarfed by the sheer volume and innovation of digital stimulation that can be experienced online. The layering of physical and digital dimensions creates a multifaceted canvas from which the spectrum individual may ponder the next image or creative response. Contextual meanings will increasingly be self-invented, whether as objects of self-stimulation or obsession or absorbed as an artistic medium. The barriers are so open and undefined that those of neurodifference may eventually have an *advantage* in the future. From possessing a radically unique world view and utilizing technology unfettered by typicality may come fresh, uninvented forms, which may become the requisite for the yet to be defined 'new norm'.

Discussion

The future of creative response activities will be irrevocably changed by access to ideas, images and media by the Internet. Assistive and connective technologies have become an intrinsic player, in both therapeutic and educational settings. As an integral part of their generation, computers are now an extension of the children themselves. Digital devices, with their images of billboards, architecture and digital displays, surround us in our daily lives and, with their seductive stimulation, may be highly motivating. Technological novelty might overcome people's avoidance reactions and thus invite engagement when there was none. Moving a joystick or mouse can become a novel and predictable process, which are two constants of motivation for any individual. To give children on the spectrum a sense of control, whether a virtual exploration of the world or to enhance their already experienced travels and interactions, may still prove its worth. Digital phones, cameras or videos permit children to interact with their surroundings at their pace, with their own aesthetic eye and on their terms. Rather than having to be lured into a creative response activity, they may now take the lead through a medium that has become second nature. Personal devices also provide children with a shield that can distance them from an object, a person or a stimulus, which may otherwise be overwhelming. Thus, we remain open to any art form, visual stimulation or technologies which facilitate any creative contributions for those on the spectrum.

The problem lies, however, in the unfettered advancement and accessibility of technology with its influence over fragile children who lack the controls which modulate such incoming material. As devices become more evolved, will designers factor in and build limitations to combat the potential for abuse? Or will all taboos be swept away from culture towards digital anarchy?

Will technological innovation come at the cost of moral guidance? How will id, ego and superego be reframed?

When appropriating technological culture, caution and close parental monitoring become essential to ensure that its reach is benign and safe. While the trappings of visual culture must be accommodated to tap any redeeming qualities in evidence, we must factor in the hyper- and hyporeactions of those on the spectrum. Each stimulus, whether it be a disturbing news report or image, will often be amplified and even distorted. Hyperreactions may reach traumatic or obsessive levels, with images or ideas becoming intrusive or even nightmarish.

Hyporeactions, as we saw with Eric's 'autonomous killing' obsession, which was formerly in the realm of science fiction, will lead to a blurring of realities. With unfettered access to media, therapists may be at a loss to control their session's content—inviting unanticipated and uncontrollable outcomes.

Social media and connectivity remain a revolution of relatedness—as untold thousands of individuals with neurodifference can find each other and commiserate. Yet again, as the technology expands further into the virtual realm, with social and individual games attracting countless anonymous players, including those on the spectrum, the potential for addiction remains a powerful stimulus. As the digital realm expands and becomes ever-more surreal, ethicists within the arts, humanities and sciences will be faced with new paradigms related to issues of 'free expression'. As benign and seemingly helpful technologies evolve, they will most assuredly be co-opted into the forces of evil and destruction. Research and development will remain as amoral as the id construct unless society bands together to set guidelines that ensure our security. My hope is that technology eventually self-evolves towards greater insight into its own powers—that its artificial intelligence begins to impose its own sense of curatorship and self-control. When technology evolves beyond 'information' into a means of enlightenment—one that deepens interrelatedness, insight and creativity—it might then finally prove its worth.

III

The Artists

Structuring the Arc

In finding a sensitive method with which to continue our exploration of these creative children, there is an inescapable dilemma. How to stay true to a vision of organizing case vignettes without pathologizing is daunting. To refrain from also establishing hierarchies of functioning or other judgemental means and still organize the succession of sub-headings is perhaps inescapable—that one's 'functioning level' by default is the most effective means of demonstrating the 'loose arc of the continuum'. Does one work backwards from a gifted college student with only subtle hints of a shadow syndrome? Or begin at 'another' end, with the child whose spectrum markers are severely impenetrable?

Whether we start with the greatest severity or the least, what is most important is that the level of functioning is not an indicator of the *quality* of outcomes. It has already been demonstrated that many of the most interesting and therapeutic outcomes come by way of severely involved children. The self-stimulatory child who may draw an infinite number of circles, star patterns or stick figures may be therapeutic and aesthetically compelling in their own way. This was illustrated in Figure 1.1 (pg. 20), when I placed a severely involved child's intricate line work next to that of Jean Dubuffet's, a master artist of raw art, or L'Art Brut, school. Several readers of this manuscript found the child's work far more fascinating and aesthetically challenging. Dubuffet was a pioneering aesthetician and artist. Yet the non-verbal, handicapped artist was perhaps conveying something more urgent—something of his own complex world which could not be described in words. Such is the reach of creative response activities: that in varying degrees, all children and young adults can be stimulated so they can express their creative strengths while increasing their comfort and relatedness to the world.

I have elected to begin the continuum by following a developmental course, introducing the artists and their outcomes by 'beginning at the beginning', to probe case material describing those who embody the earliest stirrings of the creative act—giving form to the original creative impulse. By marking the dawn of creative expression, one may then follow its meanderings as capacities evolve and move jaggedly forward and backward as we plot its course. It is the 'loose arc' configuration that forms the course of the continuum with its shifting constellation of markers. It is perhaps a most fitting structure, as it does not 'fix' the individual with one diagnostic identity. Since a major theme is that we all present with spectrum markers to some degree, there is no end point of the continuum, but only shades of 'being'.

Beginning with children on the spectrum of greater severity allows for a point of departure from which the reader may plot the course of creative responses as they are made special. Their development from playing around, self-stimulating and eventually culminating into products may progress and regress over different points on the curve. While those on the more autistic end begin the narrative, they are encountered once again, when the book shifts from artistic outcomes to those of 'action sports'. Structuring these by activity rather than involvement is another instance where severity is beside the point and the emphasis is instead shifted to a different kind of creative response. The book will end with those individuals who have mostly overcome their symptoms, despite their conditions being lifelong. Several are the rarest individuals—those who were treated successfully enough to overcome the debilitation of their conditions. Several could articulate with clarity how they experienced and took ownership of their conditions. This is rare territory indeed, to glimpse well into the darkness of the cave and gain insight to a journey one cannot really 'know', but only express.

Exploring the creative process through individual case vignettes brings theory and practice to life. By examining specific outcomes, one might gain a deeper understanding of how the therapist and the client function in whatever contextual setting and activity. Because the case material makes use of multiple paradigms that overlap, cross-referencing is unavoidable. Earlier case material may be referenced, brought back in greater detail, or used to further expand upon certain theoretical or intervention ideas. In this way, I hope to weave this narrative thread in a way that is organic, sequential and enlivening to the material.

Ten

On the Autistic Continuum

Introductory Children: Tad

Encountering so-called 'classic' children on the autistic continuum is a rarity. They display such a striking demeanour that Kanner described them as being particularly beautiful children (1943). The facial morphological studies by Aldridge and colleagues (2011) agreed that the classic autist's facial features are often finely featured, some with pale, translucent skin and luminescent eyes. Some are 'toe walkers' and carry themselves with a regal demeanour—like a fairy prince or princess. In my many years of practice, I encountered only a few of these most fascinating children. Once, for all of twenty minutes, I had the pleasure of working with one such eight-year-old child, Tad, while running a project station during an arts festival for children with special needs. I immediately noticed this child and could not take my eyes off him. He was circling around my project area, taking a furtive glance and then spinning away—classic approach-avoidance behaviour. He was also a toe walker, which gave his movements a ballet-like demeanour. I noticed too that he carried a sheaf of automobile brochures, references to visual culture; taking this cue, I turned my back to him and held up some glossy magazine cutouts. Speaking to 'no one', I implemented Goodall's ethological method. The luring process began as I waved the car-magazine collage cutout elements together, as a means of 'making first contact'. It entailed 'going to where the child was', of not being a demanding teacher but modelling instead Rogers's 'transparency' model—I tried to become invisible but beckoning. These interventions were sufficient to pique his interest, but not enough for him to overcome his avoidance. The luring method remained a benign proposition, with no pressure or expectation to participate—though that was the goal in mind. I was careful not to make direct eye contact, using only demonstrative communication, including sign in slow, repetitive phrases. I sought to convey that I was not dangerous—that I was a 'predictable' creature who had interesting 'stuff'. This was augmented by signed and verbal phrases, such as 'Good colours', 'Fun car', 'Mother help', et cetera.

Eventually, his mother ushered him over, where he cautiously began checking out the array of collage and mixed-media materials available. She explained that he did sign and had 'read' my intentions—which she found astonishing, given the brevity of time involved. His arm flapping and hand clapping was a positive response indicating excitement. He began to wave some of his own car pictures and even their specification diagrams. I mirrored this by leaving some silver metallic paper from other ads. He picked them up, an enormous accomplishment. Tad began sliding the material between his fingers in a self-stimulatory way—again, his mother questioned how I knew he might be drawn to acetates. In my experience, these textures provide a pleasant tactile sensation—sliding back and forth, the film of silver seemed an 'anchor' during his ten minutes of work. We were both 'making special', as a gateway to more manipulative activity.

I also cleared a portion of the project area for him, asking my interns to care for the other participants away from our work. He approached and darted, flitted away, then swung around for another visit, eventually pausing long enough to shuffle his papers along with ours, all with Mom's guidance. She facilitated the process by modelling the technique. He responded and began smacking down pre-glued elements to colourful cardboard. His mother seemed delighted if not relieved that Tad was finally in capable hands—giving her some respite from the day's excitement.

After creating some cursory appliques, Tad finally looked up with a frozen smile and a blank gaze that seemed to cut right through me, as though I did not exist. Only his favoured self-stimulatory materials and medium held his interest. I had experienced this 'autistic gaze' many times, but its chilling effects have never been diminished. It was as though he was only briefly visiting this world, dipping into a laboratory provided him that was tailored to his exacting needs. Later, his mother explained he had an encyclopaedic memory for luxury car models and could recite options and prices to whomever, in a sing-song, echolalic manner. There was barely any interaction, even as I worked my own collage in parallel—mirroring his movements. In unusually close proximity, she was amazed he tolerated my presence without fleeing. Perhaps this 'modelling behaviour' suggested that this like-minded person coveted shiny materials as well, someone who would also leave him to his own devices. Upon completing his collage, he tossed it aside and moved back to his protective orbit, spinning about, glancing at the other stations. His work seemed to hold little value beyond the process and the materials that created it. The mother, however, was visibly emotional and thankful. She exclaimed our station was the only hands-on experience he had engaged in during the whole day's arts fest. The mother then expressed that rarely in her son's life had a professional accepted so unconditionally Tad and his work *with* his autistic behaviours—without attempts to 'modify him'. I replied that the point of this Special Arts Fest was for the children to be themselves.

Pre-Creative Responses

This fleeting encounter with a fascinating child still begs the question whether his stereotyped expression was a 'creative' response activity. It was symptomatic of self-stimulatory and disconnected expression, the end product holding little meaning. My response to this question is a qualified yes; something was made special. The spectrum curve recognizes that stereotypical, echolalic or self-stimulatory expressions constitute part of the 'pre-art' response. Tad's obsessive attachment to car features constituted a libidinal, motivational stimulus. As with many children on the extreme end of the continuum, this was the first step in evolving creative responses. Tad had accomplished a series of creative responses; he had successfully separated from his mother—though she was emotionally available to him. He had approached an unfamiliar situation and permitted my presence. Tad had engaged and even briefly fabricated materials and was invested, in his own way, in the process. These steps form the formative building blocks of the creative response activity.

One must bear in mind that I was only briefly a visitor to *his world* as much as he was to mine. However, had I worked with him long term, the goal would have been to gradually *expand* his expressive and relational repertoire. This would entail introducing new interactions, environments, materials and processes which could creatively bridge his 'inner' world with that of the 'outer'. While he had worked within his own comfort zone without the expectation of interaction, long-term work involves cautiously adding demands—which almost always meet with resistance or reactivity, whether it be avoidance, withdrawal or fight-or-flight behaviour. Whether it would be possible for him to ever make an attachment with me as a therapist is open to question. In my years of experience, the smallest of increments of habituating and proto-creative exploration may lead to greater comfort and frequency of experimentation. Perhaps another introductory vignette may bear this out.

The Unresponsive Child

Deep autism remains a mystery, even for the most seasoned observer. Being with the children for extended periods of time, as an outsider looking in, can be fascinating, frustrating or even beguiling. One seven-year-old, Ahmed, with a partial vision impairment, posed a special challenge in that he rarely interacted. Neither did he acknowledge most incoming stimuli unless it came from his teacher or parent. However, over three years of sensory stimulation work in his classroom, he had sufficiently habituated to me to eventually take walks to my studio, where he felt around and was given many sensory objects to interact with. Eventually, we extended our walks to the hallways and even the administrative offices, where the copiers and their rumbling sounds drew his attention. After three years, Ahmed finally produced his first creative object.

First Contact

Slightest of boys, fine boned, with deep-set Arabian eyes
'Hello, Ahmed! Hello … in there …'
'See this, feel this, like this?' I sign to him hand in hand, but
Nothing.
Forget it, ya know what, I say to no one in particular,
I have some work today in the copy room …
You wanna come, I sign?
Follow if you like, now talking to myself.
Tailing behind, I never looked back, but felt him shadowing.
Tiny footfalls on the hallway terrazzo.
'Welcome to THE COPY ROOM!'
His head now lifts, touching around the room,
betraying the slightest flicker, a secret, imperceptible interest.
Spread before him are banks of copiers, the hulking beasts,
clunk thump, lights flash, papers spill out, thunks again, again.
He touches one as it comes alive.
Stacks of paper slide in thick collations,
the machines race, whirl, clunk again, oh, forever jammed!
Secretary afraid to come over … that's alright, we're working!
Unsure, she bends down ripping out the ragged goddamn stuck paper.
'Why is he here?'

WHY *IS* HE HERE? Oh, we're in therapy, folks! …
DON'T TOUCH! says the doudy one with the lapel pin.
I drop in a tray myself and Ahmed gently feels the cartridges riding their rails.
His head follows their glidings, such effortless beauty.
Reaching in again, I sign, No, no. He pushes me away.

Next, the bigger console machines, their refrigerator weight emitting
a strain of groans.
Their base tones from deep within … kachunk kachunk.

Ear to motor, eye to light, now chest to chest ... He's chest bumping
those machines!
Experiment: I place my keys under the mat ... Push this button, Ahmed!
Taking his hand, we press on ...

It's a *first*.
The keys print slides out,
Next a stapler, a plastic flower,
He grabs a secretary's *Pop Tart* off a desk,
Sorryeee! No, no, signed again,
Holding the mat open, I beckon him ...
Ahmed, enter the darkness deep in the copy cave.
I'll wait on you, Ahmed, waiting, waiting. Then,
he slips his own tiny hand underneath, smooths and pats down that mat.
...
NOW PUSH!
The copy button pressed draws a half smile.
The thing chugs to life, belts and glides and toner all collide.
He hops, hops, like pee-time jitters ... waiting, waiting, waiting still ...
Out spits the paper.
Now all business, he takes the leaf, eyes it closely, squinting.
Then cups it by both hands,
his back to me, this paper is secret.
'I'm not looking, Ahmed'.
He crumples it tight in his tiny fist, forming a wadded ball,
held in closed hands.
Now, even the nervous secretaries have all eyes on Ahmed.
He formally presents the ball of paper to me,
With a downward-slightest grin—his eyes beaded up.
I'm unwrapping now, almost there ... all eyes on that ball!
And then ...
I can only bow my head; the *room* bows its head ... as I receive his gift.
Secretaries, now unbearably curious, call out, 'What's it say?'

UP YOURS!

Figure 10.1 This deeply autistic child's first interaction and image—which was secretly composed. As described in the previous narrative poem, it was 'birthed' by the school's copier. Scrunched up, it was handed to the author as a secret 'present'.

So much for the great therapist and the creative response activity! Mixed outcomes, *any outcomes,* are often small treasures which must be honoured. Once the first image has been formed, it is the communique from a distant place, a gift as it were, even if the therapist is 'flipped off'.

The Exponential Figure

Another ten-year-old, Richard, with severe involvements, was a student of Ms. Dawn in her developmental sensory stimulation program. Richard would gladly come and draw for hours on end. He had two stereotyped formulas. The child was at times exclusively a 'tapper'—a self-stimulatory process whereby a felt-tipped marker would be tapped against the paper, making clicking sounds and resulting in thousands of random dots and dashes. Ms. Dawn often placed two pictures side by side. At other times, Richard would draw stick figures; their exacting schemas remained unchanged. His figurative forms multiplied exponentially across the horizon of the page, piling up against the paper's edge like a wall (Figure 10.2). If he had been permitted a roll of paper, he would have doubtlessly continued *ad infinitum*.

Ms. Dawn's goal of permitting him to self-stimulate and work figuratively also focused upon widening/extending his aesthetic reach. As the figure itself was intractable for *three years*, her response was to vary the art materials. With a variety of papers, colours and glitter, he could create special effects, backgrounds and scale, without disturbing his style or content. Eventually, she 'threw him a curve' by giving him her white sweatshirt, inviting him to draw upon something that he associated with his beloved teacher. With this novel, three-dimensional ground, Richard's figures abruptly changed from the endless, precisely horizontal replicates to a dynamically inventive, figurative composition (Figure 10.3).

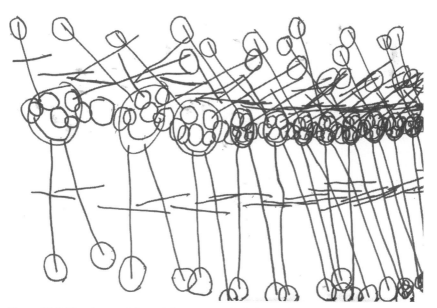

Figure 10.2 Developmental arrest does not preclude interesting, creative expression. Richard created a countless parade of schematic figures and marks made by self-stimulatory 'tapping'.

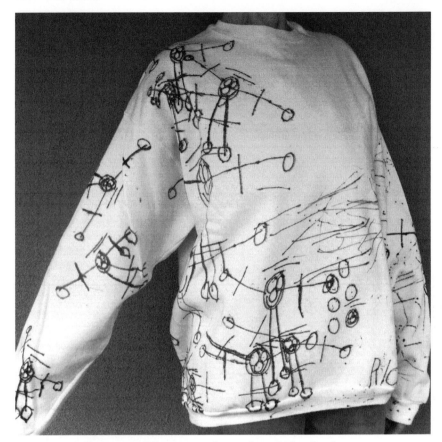

Figure 10.3 When given a different ground to work on, Richard's schemas were upended. The result is a brilliant composition of figures which seem to crawl about Ms. Dawn's sweatshirt.

It is perhaps a work worthy of *any* chic designer, though in the Outsider Art aesthetic, this was not his *intent*. Oblivious to the mores of design, his figures travel randomly around the garment. He sometimes reverted to tapped-out dots and dashes, which seem to punctuate the design. He would then return to his iconographic figures, which seem to explore the negative space. Compositionally, his art was never the same.

Training Grad Students in Artistic Empathy

To appreciate the complexity of these seemingly stereotyped figures, as an artistic 'empathy exercise' I had my graduate students try to copy these works. Accurately re-creating them proved exhausting and time consuming—if not impossible. By re-creating these figures, the students had gained insight into the complexity of 'personal' stereotypes, which are often dismissed as mere self-stimulation. These thousands of repetitions were a remarkable 'brand' of imagery, their exponential style now being appreciated technically and aesthetically. It offered the students an immersive yet confounding experience. They came to understand that extending Richard's frame of reference and diversity required that Ms. Dawn not pressure him for formal change. Her intuitive intervention—that only a sweatshirt might result in a 'breakout' style—was perhaps due to his symbiotic attachment to her. With his comfort level secure, he could then push along the developmental process. His capacities had been latent all along—yet he required just the right and improbable stimulus to unlock his graphic brilliance. The students came away with a lesson on empathy and an understanding of the issues of stereotyping, dealing with a strange form of graphic giftedness, and the role attachment plays as a potential conduit for change.

The Artist Obsessed

Every so often a child's object of obsession and self-stimulation *is* his creative expression—all that matters is the art. Seven-year-old Jay was a multiply handicapped child, with autistic features and suffering visual and hearing impairments (Henley, 2007). He was a mature and obsessed artist from the beginning and developed over a four-year span as any developing artist would.

During my first observation, he was nimbly climbing up a playground geodesic dome. Along the way, he came upon another child stalled ahead of him. Finding the child blocking the way, he nonchalantly tossed him off the bars as though he were a rag doll. Luckily, the child flew off unhurt into soft sand. Though shocking to witness, it was amazing that this small, wiry child possessed the strength to pick him up. To Jay, the toss-off represented more an inconvenience than an act of aggression. Interpersonal relations for this boy were inconsequential. Yet when this same boy was engaged in art material, his senses came alive. Working at home and in class he created hundreds of drawings, with portfolios bulging with stacks of pictures drawn on anything from paper bags to ruled paper. Beyond being a prolific artist, his work was intricately architectural. Buildings, houses and interiors consisted of a profusion of energetic lines of multiple colours in a distinctive linear style. In his many architectural renderings, colourful lines race up and down, diagonally slashing through solid objects of rooflines and walls in an almost perfect perspective, which is deserving of a colour plate (Plate 2).

Buildings are not so much solid spaces as much as energetic lines and pulses of colour that somehow combine to form the structure. While working, Jay's eyes remained inches from the paper in the style of Ahmed, the copier boy. Jay would trill in delight as he picked up and discarded coloured pencils, all at a breathless pace. Most of his works were completed in minutes and then tossed aside; he was ready to begin the next work.

My contribution in this process was to stand aside and keep the colours coming, as Prismacolor pencils are soft and points break after a few strokes. When Prismacolor art stix became available (coloured pencils without the wood), he worked with even greater ferocity. Houses and other architectural forms emerged from a cacophony of hastily scribbled line work. As a creative response, it was still stereotypical, idiosyncratic and self-stimulatory—yet the outcomes were always different, with new structures, exteriors and interiors, all fully formed artistic expressions. As with Tad, the process was everything—the product was often tossed aside, as Jay anxiously awaited to begin a new piece. I was tolerated only as a means to an end—as the 'keeper of the colours'. Once he had come to recognize me as the gatekeeper and realized we had mutual interests, I began to place greater demands on him. Upon arriving, he would sign frantically 'colours, colours, blue, yellow'.

As this was long-term work (unlike the half hour spent with Tad), I eventually paused before handing him the art stix. This was a request from the child study team members, who asked me to begin 'running interference', to hold back his precious colours until he would communicate interpersonally, even at a cursory level. I began each session signing 'Hello, Jay. How are you today?' 'How's Jay?' 'Can you say, hello, David?' Just these few simple greetings drew such violent tantrums that several times his aide and teacher ended up on the floor restraining him to minimize destruction and the danger of injury. After four months of this 'forced' taming ritual, he began to sign 'Hello, David. How are you?', to which he did not wait for an answer. Instead, came the signs 'Colours! Where colours?' These introductory routines were finally assimilated. Jay grew to expect that inter-relating dialogue would be required if he were ever going to be allowed to draw. Once he had satisfied these entry requirements, he was left unharassed during his coveted two three-hour studio marathons.

After six months of unrestrained drawing, an art therapy intern, Cindy Caprio-Orsini, began working with Jay; she initially underwent the same rituals as I had. She introduced painting on canvas to Jay, which I counselled would anger and overstimulate him. Yet a paradoxical effect occurred, as his handling the viscous material came with unexpectedly thoughtful, measured strokes. He still worked feverishly, however, and rarely would wait for the next canvas. Unless caught in time, he would quickly squeegee the entire canvas and scree off his picture with a yardstick or the brush handle or even smear it away with his hands. Again, the product was secondary to the kinetic process (Henley, 2007). Over the course of six combined years of work with Caprio-Orsini and me, Jay developed into an artist worthy of exhibition and formal recognition. Caprio-Orsini's master's thesis plotted his course, bearing witness that the promise of progression is a long-term proposition (1988).

A Trip to the Zoo

Saturdays at the Art Institute of Chicago were devoted to children's arts and museum programs for typical children. I approached the director and offered to adapt the Institute's programs to include those with special needs and to involve art therapy interns as aides. This new adaptive program had two distinct components; the first involved the children visiting the museum's vast collections or another local outing, prior to the second half, which was studio work. The stimulation posed by the Egyptian exhibit or medieval suits of armour always resulted in interesting outcomes filtered through these children. Our youngest participant was an undiagnosed six-year-old named Ike, who presented with limited language and mild autistic symptoms. He worked alone, in a self-stimulatory way, and was intensely focused on creating highly original stylistic drawings. His preferred subject matter was animals and other wildlife. After one visit to the Egyptian galleries, he drew mummified cats, which took on humanoid characteristics. In turn, when he interpreted the human mummies, he endowed them with zoomorphic attributes. All his renderings were fascinating creative responses, and our interns delighted in witnessing and working with this precocious yet autistic-like child.

It was no surprise that when Ike was taken to Lincoln Park Zoo, he could not contain his excitement. His viewing an animal exhibit was not a matter of breezing by like most other children, who excitedly moved on to the next exhibit. For Ike, experiencing an animal required a process of intense scrutiny—often to the chagrin of the aide who was trying to keep him with the group. Pairing with an art therapy intern allowed him to keep his own pace, and the intern could document how he stood mesmerized by many exhibits, particularly the reptile enclosure. While the others moved on, Ike had the good fortune of witnessing feeding time for the crocodiles, which were given whole fish to devour—a grisly business. Our intern recounted how, glued to the fence, he babbled in delight and seemed ecstatic during the feeding. This was nothing less than a primordial act, as this hulking dinosaur creature, unchanged since the Cretaceous period, opened its great jaws and swallowed large fish whole—it must have constituted a super-stimulus for this young child.

Upon coming back from the zoo in the afternoon, the group of children returned to their schedules, which included their drawing time. Without intervention or direction, my intern reported that Ike sat for the second hour drawing away. During the following class, the intern described his intense drawing process—carefully working in permanent felt marker without any preliminary marks. The outcomes were remarkable hybrid figures, most of which possessed both reptilian and hominid features. Figure 10.4, depicting the primitivistic humanoid/alligator, is stylistically akin to prehistoric petroglyphs.

The dominant element in the figure is the wide-open snout, which he would have witnessed during the crocodiles' feeding time, showing their bared rows of teeth. To witness the feeding must have had an overwhelming influence on his art and style.

This skilled, imaginative and well-behaved child worked within his own developmental level, yet the outcome is far beyond the normal schemas and stereotypes expected of even the most gifted. That he anthropomorphized the gator was both ingenious and whimsical. It points once again to Modernists such as Paul Klee, who proclaimed that children were free of preconceived notions— that even he would be hard pressed to re-create such imagery. Ike's figure is a fully formed piece which sublimated any number of presenting problems—being

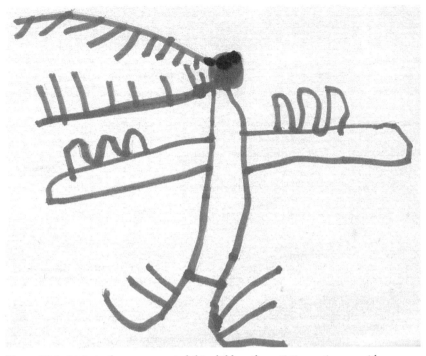

Figure 10.4 A trip to the zoo presented this child on the autistic continuum with a super-aroused experience. His special gift was to playfully translate animal imagery into humanoid forms.

away from his routines and class environs, being surrounded in a crowded public space and dealing with the stimulus of a real-life monster—up close. How could it not be a possibility to this autistic-like child that the croc could come crashing through its swamp enclosure to just snap him up! All his sensations were highly aroused, yet despite the excitement, he remained relatively calm and focused, both on the trip and while re-creating his adventure. Drawing upon this monumental experience resulted in whimsical figures whose unusual dance-like movements perhaps even referenced a touch of humour. Saturday enrichment contributed both behaviourally and aesthetically. Although his sensory apparatus and proximal distance were challenged during the feed, he maintained himself, sublimating via the passionate engagement of a favourite stimulus.

Holding Water: Idioms and Autistic Humour

Another boy on the autistic end of the spectrum, eleven-year-old Devin, has been described on pages 55–6 as having worked with the idiom 'fish out of water'. Because literal speech was an issue for all the children in his group, we chose an idiomwhich held metaphorical meaning—of being kids 'out of their element'. Aside from proclaiming that our dropped bass was now literally a fish out of water, he proceeded to create a drawn response—one that was no less ingenious—to this seemingly exciting stimulus. A gifted artist, he drew an odd Dickensonian-type figure, elongated and hunched over, who had haplessly dropped the fish bowl—or had he? In the image (Figure 10.5), Devin's creative solution was to acknowledge that, yes, the glass bowl had smashed to pieces. Yet again, what's to keep him from turning the idiom on its head? The picture displays the water's shape as being held intact; its solidity is somehow preserved,

Figure 10.5 Devin drops the fishbowl, yet the water and fish remain, 'held' as if by wizardry. It is an example of autistic wry humour that is a unique perspective on the laws of physics.

along with its capacity to contain and preserve the fish, which suspended in mid-air, seems unfazed.

The magical idea that the water will hold its shape without being materially contained is an autistic-like thought, but one that is rarely expressed in such an articulated, pictorial representation. It is perhaps a prime example of the spectrum child's odd take on Piaget's concept of object permanence but also Spitz's idea of the stimulus barrier. Both imply that after the glass bowl has shattered, the water inside can somehow hold its shape. It is a magic trick, or a visual pun. The 'fish out of water' concept is not necessarily of the literal or physical realm of the every day, but has been 'played with' by entering the space in between—that of solidity and the magical. Devin's playing around behaviour with our idiom of the day is perhaps more akin to a Zen koan than a psychological concept of transitional space. It poses the occurrence as an unanswerable riddle.

Receiving this creative response requires no analysis; it transcends any theoretical constructs, deserving nothing less than a gentle smile and a bowed head. Quirky outcomes aside, figurative language improves when activities such as this *demonstrate* how idioms or figures of speech can be malleable and interesting for the language-involved child. Parents were encouraged to work on idioms and other quirks of language at home to enhance comprehension through enjoyable means. Like the routines of reading nightly bedtime stories, it's necessary to reinforce these abstractions of language by cognitively *practising* them to become functional during times of social discourse.

Zoomorphs Redux

Children on the autistic end of the spectrum express their relatedness in unexpected and contradictory life forms, such as with humanoid creative expressions. Previously, Ebie's life-drawing endowed a wooden mannequin with human-like animation (Figure 2.2), while Devin created a pair of engaging dolphin friends (pg. 62) and Ike anthropomorphized an auspicious encounter with a crocodile. These are cases when once again, a social encounter became a moment of enchantment. It was Devin who assumed animal personas as self-identifications, which perhaps eased the stress of interpersonal relating given his tenuous self-identity. After a group camp social session, he was able to displace his social anxiety and the stress of interaction by transforming 'friends' into zoomorphic creatures, with whom he could better relate. One camp afternoon, it had begun to lightly rain, an unremarkable occurrence in summer. We often continued working in light rain, as it was an opportunity to feel like camping, with everyone gearing up and braving the elements. Curiously, I had noticed that he and another boy had remained on the porch outside the cabin, 'standing beside' each other, facing outward but seemingly enjoying the moisture after a heated morning. They exchanged few words but without pressure to speak or even relate. It was a rare, spontaneous social interaction between two partners, creating a more intimate setting.

Later, during free drawing, he re-created the scene in a narrative drawing. However, one of the boys had been transformed—one human figure stands casually under his rain hat while the other nonchalantly had become a reptilian animal (Figure 10.6).

Each character is rendered matter of factly, with an understated style. Devin manages to express social awkwardness with aplomb. In this case, the two share a relatively intimate moment, as the lizard creature comments dryly, 'Nice weather

Figure 10.6 When Devin and a friend are caught in a summer shower, they stand casually beside each other, laconically chatting in another humorous and zoomorphic visual pun.

we're having', while the boy, playing the 'straight man', responds laconically, 'Yeah'. Which character is self-identified as the self-portrait artist is up for discussion. As is often the case with those with developing egos, the characters might be a 'condensation'—a composite of both identities which are interchangeable. The boy's face is obscured by his rain hat and thus does not gaze out from the picture—which is indicative of spectrum shyness or inhibition. However, he seems at ease in every other respect—from his set but rosy lips, stylish V-neck, washed jeans and neatly tied sneakers. Meanwhile, it is the lizard that boldly stares ahead, looking forward with binocular vision. He is alien yet has a direct gaze, seemingly without any inhibition.

Observations of Devin indicated a certain pleasure while he was focused upon his work. As with many artists on the autism end, his interior world surfaces in the form of internally gratified passion, with giggles, intermittent smiles and the murmuring of dialogue as he drew the piece. Each of Kramer's aesthetics of formed expression are achieved—with Devin's evoking a wry humour, done with a minimalist touch, while being true to his eccentric, endearing self—all through ingenious means. Devin's 'conversation' may have been completely internal if it hadn't been for the drawing response image. As the ego of these children sometimes is less formed, self-identity assumes a more fluid, or 'Zelig'-like, persona. Yet such contradictions seem well tolerated. Each figure in the drawing stands alone within a relaxed proximity. The drawing calls to mind Winnicott's seminal construct of two individuals 'being alone in the presence of the other' (1965). Each character appears at peace with the other, sharing a quiet moment of their world together, but without an 'obligation' to interact. There is comfort in knowing one needs only a few words and mostly silences to just 'be' while still having a sense of relatedness. Perhaps, however, it is too far a leap for Devin to pose while fully human—one still needs to be a harmless yet affable creature for such comfort to exist. Most typical individuals *would require* such obligatory small talk—a situation many new couples endure as conversations are punctuated by long, awkward silences. As a creative compensation, Devin finds an ingenious solution, morphing into another life form whose droll sense of humour lessens the anxiety of relating while standing around idly during an afternoon summer shower.

Stasis and Emergence

Moving up the developmental ladder, we encounter other oddly 'gifted' artists whose drawings reflect the world through the lens of 'quiet aloneness'. One of Ms. Dawn's students, fourteen-year-old D.J., was at the time a middle school boy who was selectively mute, living in dire poverty on Chicago's South Side. This feeling of isolation was not bothersome, however, as his behaviour was mild mannered, even when pressed to participate in groups. When around his rambunctious peers, he simply quietly withdrew into drawing regardless of anyone else's agenda. One of the first images presented to me was a long cargo train seen from his home vantage point. Its boxcars plod on endlessly against the big midwestern sky in a matter-of-fact isolation, dryly and expertly rendered without distortion. There is an inherent loneliness about trains and their forlorn horns and click-clacking trucks amplified through great distances in the city. Another cityscape image of a Chicago expressway is almost perfectly rendered, but again, it is conspicuously sans any human activity, save a few trucks slipping through the composition (Figure 10.7).

The acuity of his subject matter was most certainly derived from his endless commutes on the expressway; the roadway has perfect perspective and foreshortening, as it diminishes with distance. The highway lamps, electrical transformers, abutments and especially the power lines are accentuated, rhythmically criss-crossing the composition. On the overpass is a train of unspecified vehicles, which conveys motion and relieves the work of a static sensibility. These vehicles are strong and convincingly rendered but still somewhat faceless and anonymous; they move away from the viewer, offering only a glimpse of them. There are few graphics or indications of human involvement that personalize the vehicles. While a sense of aloneness seems to be evoked, it is consistent with the artist's inner existential position; he lives in isolation, firmly within himself, yet selectively allowing stimuli into his world. Self-regulation is demonstrated in his treatment of the content, as D.J. deletes the bustle of traffic that is always on Chicago's highways. Ms. Dawn's bonding with this mild-mannered, but selectively mute, child led to four years of steady creative and mental growth in her adaptive art education setting (Henley, 2012b).

This African American boy lived in an almost forgotten corner of the city. His small bungalow was located within feet of the Department of Transportation's

Figure 10.7 When withdrawn, this talented artist, D.J., captured the normally hectic highways of Chicago with an emptiness that seems a symbolic equivalent for his isolated existential state.

truck and materials depot. On occasions when we took D.J. home after one of several exhibitions of his work, I found the area unnervingly isolated—even in *daytime*. Yet perhaps it was the constant comings and goings of giant excavators and salt loaders that served as his sentinels. Raised alone with his grandmother, these city-owned and operated depots with their trucks and piles of sand were perhaps a stimulus barrier par excellence for both—guardians acting as a buffering agent against the cacophony of the inner city. Thus D.J.'s isolated home spared him the rancour of the projects and their gang turf wars. Being sequestered with his kindly grandmother, I observed how D.J.'s bonds were strong with this maternal caregiver, with more voluble verbalizations. This and a caring school environment perhaps gave this child a solid attachment, which he manifested by a sense of being centred, self-assured. He was, however, selectively mute and like other artist children deep into the autistic end of the spectrum, buried himself in art.

As a day student bussed to a therapeutic school, D.J. was permitted, within reason, to draw almost ceaselessly, producing hundreds of pictures during a single week's time. Trucks were a favourite theme, as they perhaps seemed 'alive' to the boy, rumbling down the road, with the air horns blaring and the muffled chatter of jake brakes. However detailed and realistic they were drawn (from memory), they were rarely shown being driven by a driver. Though drawn in static profile, the colourfully designed cement mixer is rendered as a formidable presence (Plate 3).

When in action, its tremendous revolving drum spins away, keeping the concrete sufficiently moist to pour. He faithfully renders its hydraulics, chutes and driverless cab. He reproduces the graphic design of its brand by marking several zigzagged lines of the company logo, thus the reference for appropriating visual culture. Ms. Dawn's interventions were subtle—sitting beside him and facilitating materials, integrating his studio time in group contexts while gently welcoming outcomes.

D.J.'s art was remarkably 'fully formed', in the Kramerian sense. His drawings were visually economical, and being isolative as the child, he also was true to himself. Given his mild autistic features, however, these static compositions—a long boxcar train, empty highway and a mammoth but driverless truck—did not evoke 'feeling' in the relational sense, but he revelled in his passion. Here, again, there is autistic relating, as the endless varieties of trucks and their signage and graphics were to him almost sentient in their existence. He was also able to demonstrate an acute awareness of his environs with their vast scale and kinetic workings. He modulates his portrayals in line with his capacity for what activities he can handle. Despite his constant omissions of the human element in both schoolwork and artworks of this period, he eventually progressed under the skilful tutelage of his sensitive art teacher. D.J. displayed 'hints' of pictorial elements, which perhaps stood for his own variation of self-empowerment. In one single line, he depicts a tall spire that is either a radio or utility pole confidently towering over the lanes and overpass; its lithe, linear, vertical form pierces the sky, strengthening and 'holding' the scene with quietude and elegance.

The Reality of News

After D.J. had spent over a year in Ms. Dawn's studio and had participated in a summer enrichment program, he arrived at a new narrative, one that included human interaction. While some of his depictions were unremarkable figures of school and street life, many others included subject matter well outside his comfort zone of mechanics and vehicles, indicative of his year of developmental stasis. In one series of works, he became obsessed with the police and fire departments, an adventurous period when Professor Kramer had the occasion to visit the boy at his school and observe his drawing process first-hand. She was fascinated by the steady progression, from the countless expertly drawn, driverless vehicles to scenarios which now included human figures that created a new narrative—many of which were dramatically recounted instances of exposure to the news media.

One of the most memorable instances he lifted from either the media or another medium of visual culture. It was a scene which obviously disturbed the artist but also piqued his interest. This realistic action image recounts a chase scene in which a patrol car has broadsided another, smashing both vehicles in the process (Figure 10.8).

What is significant is the emotional expressivity of the officer shown crying out in pain, while the other is equally dramatic as he whiplashes forward into his airbag. Flurries of line work accentuate the violence of the collision and its aftermath commotion. The narrative is equally distributed between human suffering and fascination with the crumpled vehicles. D.J.'s image displays an awareness of both dangers and excitement posed by the inner city, with his reactions being ambivalently presented. For a male African American teen, he was possibly aware of the Chicago police force's deteriorating community relations. The minority community does not often view the police and sheriff departments as 'protectors' who serve their community, as much as 'predators' whose barely concealed racism and heavy-handedness are daily facts of life. That these officers were reckless in their pursuing both gang members and innocent bystanders on the South Side of Chicago is not a surprise. It is collateral damage, except now it is *they the citizens*

Figure 10.8 As D.J. matured, his compositions included appropriating visual culture into his narrative pieces. This action image is a response to a police chase gone terribly wrong.

who suffer the consequences of their actions—for all the community, including this reclusive child, to see. While Ms. Dawn reported no anxiety or emotional turmoil, internally, D.J. almost certainly was processing these harsh realities.

On Being Exhibited

D.J. was also becoming socialized sufficiently that he agreed to be included in exhibitions—not just teen arts festivals, but *galleries*. One major venue on the 'gold coast' of Chicago was the Richard Grey Gallery, whose namesake magnanimously took down his impressionist collection and handed the lavish gallery over to a group of artists with special needs. At the opening, D.J. enjoyed being the star of the show, with several of his works being purchased by eager Outsider Art collectors. Breaking with former taboos of confidentiality, D.J. was photographed by the press enjoying the spotlight, proud and jazzed by gallery-goers' attention. After such a Cinderella night, Ms. Dawn and I drove D.J. back to his humble home, where his grandmother could scarcely imagine the posh opening. When asked about the evening, he cast his eyes downward but bashfully smiled. When asked whether he was hungry, D.J. commented he had 'already et', but regardless, was served a piece of sweet-potato pie. He was home again, with his grandma, amongst the night-lit sleeping monsters parked in the yard, predictably to be awakened again, after this weekend of enchantment.

On Flying a Kite

In this next account, an eleven-year-old girl suffered terribly with autistic features. Emma struggled to overcome years of uncontrollable wildness, intensely deluded thoughts and hypersensitive sensations. These and other spectrum issues were addressed through years of weekly psychodynamically oriented therapy. Like D.J., Emma survived through her artistic work. The case was contributed by Professor Kramer, who on many occasions described and shared in detail the art and facts about this fascinating child. Kramer described how Emma was quite content to remain in a world of her own, drawing, playing piano by ear and working on grade level in school. While her art indicated her issues of loneliness, one would never know it judging by her behaviour. Kramer commented that when Emma entered puberty, her art expanded with new awareness of her surroundings. She commented that the image we studied together reminded her of Hesse's coming of age novel, *Demian* (1919, 1960). Kramer agreed that art allowed Emma to emerge from autistic isolation. However, when subject to the full force of the outside world and its visual and news media, Emma's new-found awareness led to greater anxiety and suffering. Her inner world was 'cracked open'. As Hesse wrote, 'those who would be born must first destroy a world'.

Emma was blessed with a supportive, secure environment with her biological mother as well as a therapeutic companion who also served as a caregiver—one who assisted Emma in translating the vagaries of the world. This high-level team accommodated the child's social isolation and peculiarities. In this case, the child was not placed in a special education setting but rather in a Waldorf School, where atypicality is the norm—everybody is an accepted eccentric in some way. Waldorf's focus on gentle hands-on sensory activity, with an emphasis on self-directed learning through the arts, embodies creative response activity at the institutional level. Because Emma went about her business without much need for affirmation from others and was academically at grade level, she was an equal except for inhibitions in social discourse. Students and teachers accepted this state of mind and did not attempt to 'fix' it, unless she transgressed inappropriately into the social sphere of others.

The drawing in Figure 10.9 is one of many done on miniature two-inch-by-two-inch paper. It was, Kramer described, a response to a trip to the park that included flying a kite—an innocuous activity, which we might take for granted as a gentle sensory experience. Yet in analyzing the activity, many practical and metaphorical issues come into play. In the drawing, the child must get the kite 'off the ground' and manage another force, 'the wind', which is not always an easy physical task. Kinaesthetically, she is required to run persistently enough to get the kite airborne. The metaphor seems fitting, whether it be an interaction, an idea or a kite. In this creative response, Emma successfully managed to get the kite airborne, and yet obstacles persist. Flying the kite (Figure 10.9) seems to pull the child towards the brink of a precipice.

Figure 10.9 Innocuous activities, such as flying a kite, are given emotional weight by a child whose sense of safety is tenuous and as fragile as the tiny plant that guards her from falling into oblivion.

The kite drifts away from the cliff edge as though it tugs the child towards the abyss. Unless the kite is forcefully controlled, Emma could be taken along with it. Undeterred and as diminutive as she was, Emma 'stood her ground', Professor Kramer proclaimed. Emma drew in some 'self-protections', as Kramer termed them, including a single, diminutive plant. It too is solidly rendered, but is barely rooted in the cliff face, forming a tenuous boundary between the child and oblivion. What an extraordinary pictorial idea, I recall Kramer saying, to provide a stimulus barrier of safety, yet allude to its tenuousness. One misstep and she could easily trip over the plant, or worse, it potentially could grab at her feet. In a cavalier gesture, Emma is shown unperturbed, holding the kite with one hand, indicating a degree of 'poise under fire' in the face of uncertainty. In an article examining 'annihilation anxiety' in children on the autistic end of the spectrum, I described multiple examples of these kinds of double entendres, wherein a perilous journey is undertaken or a robust challenge is met while the threat of annihilation looms over the narrative (Henley, 2001). For this child, sufficient ego was mustered to resist the pull and remain intact, as the next image bears out.

Emma resolved these feelings, Kramer explained, as therapy entered its second year. Still fascinated with a micro-felt tip and two-inch squares of paper, she drew yet another, more substantial cliff (Figure 10.10).

This drop-off is beautifully stepped down, without the bare slope of the kite picture. It has a weathered, old-growth tree anchored into the rock face over

Figure 10.10 This same child perhaps resolved some of her fears by creating a seaside cliff. The rounded and contoured version appears less harrowing than the other cliff face.

a strangely drawn field or sea. Below, on a levelled slope, is the suggestion of human presence. A finely drawn typewriter is shown next to an open book, each indicating that someone had roamed those weathered rocks. Otherwise, our 'writer' is conspicuously absent. The two works exemplify the 'package deal' of the spectrum. There is anxiety and danger along with stark beauty. Ego strength struggles, resolves and then again becomes vulnerable, all within the intrusions from the primary process. The outcomes possess a realistic yet lyrical quality— demonstrating interpersonal and aesthetic awareness in another astounding act of sublimation.

Attachment and the Post-Adoptee

In the 1980s and 1990s, families from Western countries searched throughout Eastern Europe for orphans for adoption, where over sixty thousand babies have been adopted. This figure is now in the hundreds of thousands. It became apparent that some of these couples had unwittingly adopted psychosocially disturbed children. In The Hecht Group, I was given nine post-adopted children from Eastern Europe over a ten-year period. Two of these children were the Romanian boys previously described in Chapter Seven (pg. 122). Both boys experienced attachment issues linked to previous maternal neglect while in orphanages. One family adopted four Russian siblings, most of whom displayed spectrum symptoms, including attention deficits and attachment issues. My client, whom I saw sporadically when in crisis, displayed more severely inhibited autistic features. Svetlana was adopted at age five and was a twelve-year-old at the time of treatment that lasted over a two-and-a-half-year period (Henley, 2005). She had luminous blue eyes, which were not at all autistically vacant; to the contrary, they were curious and seeking. With her white-blond hair, translucent skin and reed-thin frame she presented with a countenance of invisibility, a wallflower who seemed to disappear especially when observed amongst her more active siblings. She was a well-behaved child—almost too much so. The adoptive mother said with pride, 'from the moment she was picked up from the Russian orphanage, she was given love, structure, faith-training and a private special education'.

She was brought to creative arts therapy, given her ongoing, selective muteness and extreme shyness; she had shown little progress with two previous therapists. I was to draw upon her fastidious crafting and artistic gifts, which her mother hoped would 'bring her out of her shell'. As a young child, Svetlana was taught 'appropriate behaviour' through cognitive behavioural therapy. Through seven years of behavioural training, routines learned through unending practice and modelling by older siblings, she eventually adapted to school and family. However, when first attending therapy and put in unfamiliar circumstances where there was no 'correct answer', she, like others previously described, seemed lost. Peering at me with those eyes like liquid pools, searching my face for the needed cue, she seemed to fade to black.

During instances of withdrawal, I intervened by switching gears from open-ended outcomes to the familiar craftwork she had done at home. Her own version of mindblindness asserted itself most when the behavioural regimens that trained her to compensate were taken away. For a year, we avoided the fine arts, music and writing, as her inhibitions were too great for demonstrative media. Structure was provided so she could feel safe working on intricate beadwork, ceramic cups and batiked scarves. When she became interested in digital photography, her artistic freedom expanded with several monochrome landscapes being created during our many walks. These too were blandly attractive without any hint of discord.

One of our rituals was going shopping at the local art supply store which was conveniently around the corner from the practice. Sorting through media and craft projects was something she looked forward to—something we could do in tandem, utilizing the tantalizing media as a communication bridge. On occasion, she would gravitate to a medium or project and indicate her desire to purchase it. In this case, it was a small craft box made of papier mâché. Per our arrangement for shopping, I reminded her that she would need to place it on the counter, speak up audibly to the salesperson and take charge of the purchase on her own. Having Svetlana overcome her shyness enough to purchase her box was analogous to the luring method which gently forced her hand, much in the same way as Jay and others; to communicate, they will be rewarded with the things they covet most—a basic tenet of my form of carrot-oriented behavioural intervention.

The papier mâché box became a three-dimensional mandala. It was circular, of Shaker design, with a round lid, which was meant to be decoupaged. Designing within a circular form is not a simple proposition, as composing and demarcating areas require planning and decision making. Svetlana set about over four sessions cutting collage from my books of stock photographs. She addressed the object's four discrete segments: the inner and outer box and the two facets of the lid. Starting outside the box, she composed another neutral scene of purple mountains and other stereotypic elements. The lid also juxtaposed a mountainous scene with a howling wolf emblazoned across the top. The following session she sorted through old National Geographic magazines to begin work on the inside. To my surprise, she began to cut out elements taken from a story on the Roman catacombs. Departing from her usual saccharine images, she began fabricating and decoupaging these coloured plates of bones into the box's interior. Working carefully, she lined the walls and base with a frieze of skeletons. The finished work (shown sans lid) was shockingly powerful. Upon anticipating another decorative box, I was faced with wall-to-wall images of ancient dead Christians (Plate 4).

Despite this seismic shift, there was no behavioural change, let alone catharsis. There was no outward betrayal of the tumult which one might surmise that simmered beneath her autistic core. Those bones remained as well behaved as the child herself and were neatly capped off by the innocuous cover.

As a container for her repressed affects, the paper jar allowed Svetlana to safely express her feelings in the privacy of her own box. It became a metaphorical container of her feelings, which was shared with me without expression—the image did all the communicating. Her attachment habituated, she perhaps felt confident in expressing 'disturbed' content that was suppressed for seven years of post-trauma. While we shall never know whether this image refers to the trauma, it is consistent to the orphanage neglect and abandonment she experienced as a child. What was critical in over four years of work was allowing the child to progress at an almost glacial rate—to sit beside, wait out her defences and support her fragile psyche beyond what had already been reconstructed by this loving adoptee-blended family. While we remained in a slightly uneasy coexistence, our rituals of venturing into town, sometimes with camera in tow, shopping and interacting with the community, paved the way for an eventual creative response. The vessel perhaps held in tension the child's inner and outer worlds.

The container is a fitting example of the transitional 'space in between', from the box's sunshiny lid to the darkened cave of the box's interior, containing another condensation of primary and secondary processes. Morbidity stood alongside spirituality without contradiction. In keeping with her cognitive work, it was significant that the primary process material remained safely inside—where it would stay. For this young teen, her tenuous ego required protection from the traumas simmering within. The work exemplifies Kramer's criteria for a sublimation; as our relationship strengthened, Svetlana perhaps felt emotional and creative risks were worth taking. Despite being done by just this shadow of a child, the image formed a symbolic equivalent for critical trauma sustained so early in life.

Annihilation Anxiety at University

The container form as a metaphor for id-derived fantasies of annihilation was also used for a boy on the collegiate level. An undergraduate, named Ryan, with undisclosed Asperger's features was often around during my art therapy classes. When teaching as a ceramics professor, I sometimes had contact with students who were taking elective classes—who worked beside our class on their respective projects. This likable and bright young man was one such student. Since ceramics was an inclusive studio, there was a welcoming atmosphere of a creative community. Though visibly distracted and ill at ease during demonstrations, Ryan worked fastidiously on every project, in line with years of his own cognitive training. He too required considerable reassurance that there was no 'exact' way to be creative. With support, he hand built a range of vessels and sculptures according to the projects assigned. During times of uncertainty, he quickly gravitated to me, 'sensing' my understanding of his situation.

For the final project, an architectural form was assigned, which allowed for the simplest to the most complex forms, accommodating every skill level. It was still a rigorous theme particularly if clay was sculpted into hard-edged geometric forms. Clay prefers to retain natural, curvilinear shapes. Ryan, however, chose the box form, which required an external form to support its walls. He also laboured to choose an architectural style he could sculpt on his own. Together, we went through possible choices. To my surprise, he chose to sculpt his former high school. Obviously, sculpting a school building was overly ambitious if not impossible; thus, I suggested perhaps just the facade would be less daunting. This he initially resisted, not being able to 'let go' of what he insisted was a 'good choice'. Eventually, he understood that building a realistic facade from memory would be

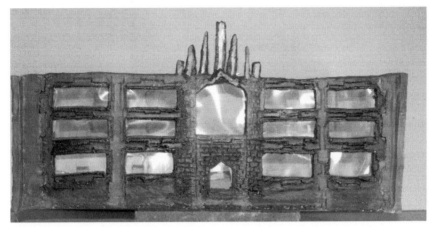

Figure 10.11 At university, this teen created a monumental ceramic facade. Little did the instructor realize that within the student's high school model, he had secretly referred to a cult film where the students were devoured by their own 'faculty'.

difficult enough—even with the technical assistance of the graduate assistants. He determinedly set to work developing the skills by trial and error along with the support resources for its execution.

Ryan carefully measured and cut his clay pieces with a steel rule fastidiously to the centimetre. He constructed a three-sided rectangular box that he felt satisfied an accurate representation of his school facade—complete with a crest of spires (Figure 10.11).

I observed his progress every few days and was surprised he did not give up in frustration. The graduate assistants made sure the piece was buttressed, strengthening the corners so it would not distort during the firing—an extension of Kramer's third-hand intervention (1986). As a young man with autistic obsessional rigidity, the stakes were high. Given his intense investment in getting his school 'right', his anxiety was palpable. This waiting period was especially critical during the weeks of the long drying-out process (when stress cracks occur). Add in the twenty-four-hour cycle of heating and cooling which all potters have to endure, and his fears were escalating. When the sculpture finally emerged from the kiln intact, Ryan and everyone else were greatly relieved.

Like all students, Ryan was expected to keep a personal journal of his work. Reflecting on theme, technique and the glazes used, as well as references to its content and meaning, the academic segment was laborious. The journal finally completed, he shared it with the class, commenting on the process, accentuating the help he had received and describing the finished product. When his professor asked whether he would share it with me, he agreed. Upon reading, I was aghast. As I read, it became clear he had shared only the 'appropriate' content, leaving out the segments that indicated the work's meaning was not limited to an ordinary architectural project. Creating his high school had triggered obsessional and thought processes of the 'other world'.

Like many young people dealing with spectrum issues, Ryan tried to fit in with the prevailing fads of current teen culture; in this case it was zombie films. Zombieism is currently a mainstream cultural phenomenon, a morbid part of our visual culture. However, Ryan's interest went well beyond the social craze. His interest was on the *real* zombie phenomenon. He wrote about how certain herbs and rituals in Afro-Caribbean cultures could induce near-death symptoms that mimicked death states. During much of his journaling he had melded the creation of his high school sculpture with zombieism—two disparate but soon-to-be understood relationships. Intellectualism was an important defence for this Asperger-linked young man, one that had been reinforced for years during cognitive therapy.

Sculpting his old high school, however, had inadvertently triggered vividly morbid disclosures that the high school was not just a 'fond memory' but was also a 'hall of horrors'. His writing made overt references to being 'swallowed up' during high school, enduring its alien environment and intensity for five years. His essay then referenced his favourite cult film, *The Faculty*, where he wrote, 'faculty chased down horrified students, infecting, dismembering and even consuming them'. While it represented age-appropriate cultural interests, his incapacity to maintain clear boundaries was obvious. The project had unwittingly allowed the uprush of previously repressed thoughts and feelings to be expressed. They oscillated between experiences during his school years, the absurd 'B' movie and his long and deep-seated fears of annihilation.

This was a solid sculpture, a bulwark to defend him against intrusive memories and fantasies. His sculpture indicates how his defences had remained intact; being a 'facade', it was a false face to the world, a strong, undistorted edifice behind which his fears were contained. He had created a challenging work that was admired by his classmates and praised by his instructor, yet its meaning remained a secret relegated to his journal—read only by his two professors. By engaging these entwined themes, Ryan was able to exercise id-derived thoughts while on the surface participating in the cultural mainstream zombie craze with other nineteen-year-olds.

To defend against this intrusion certainly took great fortitude. It required years of training, inner resources and the understanding of empathic professors. He had controlled the regression of his fearful and morbid fantasies, keeping them 'private' by compartmentalizing them. To the outward world, he had created a strong sculpture while, inwardly, memories, fears and fantasies were exercised and perhaps 'distanced' by the privacy of his writing. While not a sublimation, Ryan was able to create a compelling symbolic equivalent for his past and present. It was an amazing accomplishment by anyone's standards.

The Empty Hall

In some cases, fragility of thoughts and feelings become not so much a response to a strong stimulus—but what is *absent* and only barely suggested. The cliché 'so much is said in silence' applies to the next young man. Mildly autistic on the continuum and also handicapped with legal blindness, his case explores how a solitary environment may become the salient issue. Living in a high-rise in the Bronx, one of the outer boroughs of New York, his apartment complex, with its seemingly infinite hallways, was a place of shadowy presences and sounds—each potentially malevolent, yet also familiar and even comforting. These contradictory perceptions came where close-quarter habitation is not an invitation to intimacy; living next to neighbours for decades, they may often remain anonymous—especially for a handicapped boy. Yet for Saul (pronounced 'Saool' in Dominican), this was his home. He and his siblings managed to live their entire lives in the projects, though it took an emotional and perceptual toll.

A superb draftsman despite his visual impairment, he was one of two clients who, despite walking into doors, could draw from memory with almost savant ability. Mild mannered and cooperative, Saul came to art sessions at a school for the blind in New York City ostensibly for therapy—though his issues needed little attention. Saul came 'to work'. It was access to a therapeutic space and unfettered studio time which brought him in for double and triple periods. His teachers were relieved that he had a sanctuary once a week where he could sculpt and draw in his dedicated space without instruction or therapizing. On one occasion when Saul was drawing, he began speaking about 'The Lady Next Door'. 'She's crazy—she screams and bangs on the pipes. If she sees me in the hall, she says go back to Puerto Rico, but I'm Dominican'.

> 'Sometimes I hear her whispering through the walls,
> Then she talks nice'.

Saul would remark about 'the lady' casually while drawing, his eyes only inches from the paper. It turned out to be true—the horror of it all was that this assumedly psychotic woman and Saul shared a common bedroom wall, even radiators. This situation created a disturbed symbiotic relationship with this woman … an unfathomable alien relationship. The intimacy of 'talking nice' was enmeshed with being verbally abused and tortured by her banging on the radiator and screaming expletives.

The hallway for Saul became another case of the 'space in between'. Neither house nor apartment, the hallway was a nebulous common area where strange furnishings, disappearing staircases and long stretches of nothingness invited distorted reactions and stimulated imagination. The lack of elements mixed with these special effects invites free associations as well as experiences that in this case resulted in a remarkable creative response drawing. One drawing, saturated in colour (Plate 5), displays Saul's lively, creative response to an otherwise creepy hall.

His expert use of perspective and architectural prowess attests to the exactitude and vibrancy with which he perceived his world. 'The Hallway', as he titled it, is a stunning reconstruction of a space he had to traverse every day for years, except for summers, when, thankfully, he visited relatives in the Dominican Republic. Its line work makes use of complex geometric patterns of zigzagging walls, doorways and other elements of perspective that precisely recalled this space from memory. Stairways wind their way up and down, disappearing into the endless floors he probably never visited. It seems a haunted space, devoid of people or hints of human activity.

The two-tone institutional colour scheme is garish but obviously a strong stimulus for this visually handicapped teen. Saturated orange dominates the composition, which is divided by royal blue. Evergreen enamel has been chosen for the elevator doors while a darker blue was painted on the through doors. There is just the slightest suggestion of the next hallway—what lies beyond—he probably never knew for sure. The ceiling is intentionally coloured with a dried-up marker, which Saul kept in a separate 'special' basket. It allowed Saul to use markers which are rarely nuanced, but being worn, they can show the hand of the artist. The scribbly technique added contrast, texture and a more muted colour to this great expanse. This motif is repeated in the brown-coloured floor, which appears to be concrete or tile with a carefully inscribed white accent border.

As a creative response to an ongoing issue, Saul's drawing is beyond the pale. Despite being an impoverished shut-in, Saul manages to electrify this drab scene. As a transitional space, his is a familiar trail—one that promised safe passage and the final arrival to his secure comfort zone. Yet traversing its elevators and long expanses of emptiness, the space also had the potential for an encounter with madness—any day could come another insane rant from 'the lady'. And though his anxiety over this recurring theme was kept manageable, by giving the space visual form, Saul had created a therapeutic psychic proximal distance. Strengthened object permanence was perhaps bolstered keeping its disturbing variables in place and more safely at bay. This is the crux of having unfettered access to the studio, to work and explore issues without the need for verbally processing or interpretation. It is a potential space that leans towards the positive as the young man worked out his issues solely through the creative response activity. Satisfied with the afternoon's work, Saul presented this drawing to me—a gift before summer break. It is a work I treasure. There are few images which exemplify Winnicott's space full of possibility, combining both the magical and mundane. Saul's gift was matched by only one other teen who also suffered a visual and spectrum handicap, who is described in Chapter Nineteen.

Growth in the City

Another inner-city child, Marcus was a student at the day-treatment school in Chicago in Ms. Dawn's open-studio program. Within Ms. Dawn's adaptive art education program, this mild-mannered yet mildly autistic-like boy moved well between peer groups and adults. However, his smiles communicated to intrusive others that 'we're good as long as you don't bother me'. Inspiration for creative responses came from an unexpected source. He was an excellent draftsman, but was not concerned with aesthetics. His drawings were literal minded; he drew in concrete terms about his interests, often in a storyboard format. Again, Kramer terms this use of images as 'pictographic', in which the 'intent' is to drive the child's narrative rather than to elaborate or aesthetically formalize his style or content. Since his interests included other creative activities, drawing was a means of expressing the scope of his related therapeutic and pre-vocational work. For example, Marcus could usually be observed tending the outside shrub beds on the way into the studio, as he was part of the school's horticultural therapy program. Ms. Dawn inquired whether he could partner with the greenhouse and do some indoor gardening in concert with the visual arts. The instructor consented, and a nearby plant nursery graciously donated seeds and plants for the children to cultivate both indoors and in their own small sensory garden.

For this contentedly silent boy, growing plants from seed became an all-encompassing passion. To feed his interest and facilitate a connection between him and his peers, the vocational shop built a series of Plexiglas planters by bending and gluing side panels together to create a see-through container. Through the planters, the children could observe all the rhythms of nature. The plastic's transparency showed a world complete with worms and one pet newt, which tromped around the black earth eating fruit flies which crawled around the seedlings that would later become mature flowers. Though lesson plans on this case have since disappeared, the graphic evidence speaks for itself; this twelve-year-old non-verbal boy responded with countless pictures where he recorded his fascination with gardening (Figure 10.12).

Beginning with planting seeds, he follows the growth process of their germination, with the initial sprouts and seedlings. Eventually, they grew until he enjoyed the mature multicoloured variations of full-flowering coleus plants. Yellows and deep reds contrasted with variegated forms that combined all the colours until they flowered and in the last sequences, when the coleuses went to seed. The twelve equally divided sequences are meticulously recorded, being drawn from life, which was made possible by having five planters rotating plants in different phases of growth. For this boy, horticulture therapy became another means of mediating between people—as he, like so many others in the book, utilized a secondary intermediary medium to soften direct social interaction. There was no direct teaching involved—all activity was self-generated in line with Allen's model of open-studio programming. He and a few peers began cultivating an environment where annuals, geraniums and even large ficus trees occupied a large portion of the studio.

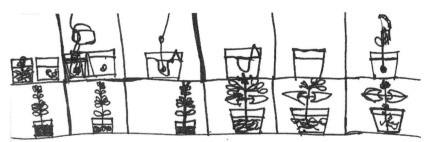

Figure 10.12 A boy living in the inner city records his impressions of planting a seed and following its growth through its life stages. It is more a narrative response than a formal aesthetic object.

As a postscript to this vignette, one day while changing classes, Marcus was found drawing with sidewalk chalk on the blacktop. His aides allowed him this pause; he spontaneously created a series of six-foot tall tulips (Figure 10.13). The scale of his drawings and horticultural passion were 'cultivated' on several fronts. In contrast to his realistic sequences, these large images were more fanciful and decorative in their form.

As an example of Winnicott's space in between, both examples reference Marcus's work *between* classes—that he was looser and more creative when transitioning between formal classroom environments. Working between perhaps signifies a more relaxed 'all-bets-off' sensibility, when the mind is more relaxed and creativity flows without direction. Marcus's tulips were created out of a sense of playfulness and pleasure.

The creative response remained on an ephemeral level, as Marcus displayed little interest in preserving his pictures. Like Jay and other children with autistic-like obsessions, it was the *process* that counted rather than the product. He concretely reported sequences of the life cycles of his coleus plantings, while the tulips in the parking lot were free to dissolve as they may. They served as a record of his personal expression meant exclusively for himself as well as a means of non-verbally interacting with his beloved teachers. He eventually dispensed with drawing altogether and entered a high school vocational program in horticulture. It was here that Ms. Dawn left him in the vibrant greenhouse, which remained his sanctuary within the urban Chicago setting.

Figure 10.13 This same young man saw flowers in the most unlikely places. He spontaneously chalked a series of person-sized tulips on the blacktop in the school parking lot.

Wrapping Large Scale

Marcus's passion for working outdoors is an important aspect of the creative response activity, inviting expressions and participation that would be impossible indoors. Taking creativity outside becomes yet another dimension and means of expanding the creative repertoire beyond the confines of indoor space. At the different venues where I practised, I often called upon artist-collaborator James Pruznick to act as the catalyst when contemplating a large-scale or environmental work. As visiting artist, he would be presented with the materials at hand, and he would then devise a creative activity that invited a range of interesting responses. Some became 'action as response' activities, as interaction and engagement invited vigorous, hands-on participation. In one project, the theme was creating a wrapped large-scale outdoor work.

There is something intrinsically satisfying in wrapping objects. Many children in various programs took satisfaction in wrapping. One deaf/blind young woman gift wrapped everything 'in sight'. For her, wrapping objects in whatever paper was on hand enveloped even known contents in mystery, adding an element of surprise and novelty. Smoothing something over with a clean, often colourful 'skin' securely contains the object while inviting attention, especially in children responsive to the luring method—few children can resist tearing through the paper to open a gift. It may also serve as a stimulus barrier—one that separates a person from the object's unpredictability of the inside, with something protective and potentially decorative.

Artists also wrap and contain on a monumental scale. Christo is a prime example, covering huge swaths of land, buildings and even islands in fabric. Photographs taken from the air show him wrapping fabric around a series of miniature islands, recontextualizing the land's form. Christo's work formalized almost anything as an aesthetic work, raising our awareness of the object by making it 'extra special'. Current examples are found in the work of French photographer 'JR', the nom de guerre of a former graffiti artist. Once an outlaw tagger working in the shadows, his work eventually became not just acceptable—it is now universally acclaimed with multinational commissions! JR's process entails taking street and portrait photographs, most of which are from ghettos around the world. Using ad billboard material, JR enlarges his subjects to massive proportions. They are then pasted onto walls of whole city blocks and buildings—and most recently he wrapped the Louvre. Overwhelming in scale, the beautifully expressive faces—people of colour, gender, young, old, homeless, handicapped—are often interfaced with whole buildings, especially those in the throes of demolition. Buildings whose interiors are gutted and exposed husks of broken concrete and rebar are then graced by portraits plastered amongst the rubble; they all come alive, bringing humour and pathos to the discarded and soon to be destroyed. Their ephemeral images offer a powerful commentary on the dispossessed. He argues for the basic rights of identity and respectful treatment for all.

JR's process and intent is perhaps not unlike the work of Pruznick, who specializes in creating conceptual environments for children with special needs. On one project, Arthur, a twelve-year-old boy, was paired with Pruznick to help create an outside environmental wrapping. Arthur was deaf and had other multiple involvements, some of which were autism related. Wary of his peers, he was most comfortable with adults with whom he could communicate about his many academic interests. The project began by introducing Arthur to the enormous quantity of the school's surplus military-grade silk, which somehow was stored and forgotten. Inexplicably, I was informed by the administration that the material was actually material from WWII-era parachutes. Having Arthur work with this material in a large-scale environment was meant to draw him out and have his self-expression become more vigorous and explorative.

Delving into the school's cavernous cellar, Pruznick began lugging out the masses of silk, inviting Arthur to help. Yet this was an unknown subterranean space, far from the predictable environs of the 'topside' school setting. This journey down to the school's cellar, confronting the massive crates of material, was somewhat overwhelming. I counselled Pruznick to scale down the operation, to begin the process by bringing samples to the studio and creating a maquette—a small model that first conceptualized the project. He bent wire which he fastened to a two-foot board—springing the arch to create 'ribs' not unlike a covered wagon—a familiar enough form for the warier children. Once the large masses of silk were brought up and laid out visibly on the school's yard, a degree of trust began to be established. The material's presence was no longer amorphous or overwhelming but now concrete and more predictable. Pruznick's approach brought a playful tone to the project—embarking upon an adventure into the unknown—which, heretofore, could not be emphasized.

The material was extraordinary to begin with. Its faded white, pearlescent colour and slippery fine texture made it alluring. Because it was military grade, it had enough 'tooth' to hold and manipulate, even on a large scale. Pruznick proceeded to translate indoor maquette to outside, where on the courtyard lawn he began erecting the series of metal hoop frames into the ground, over which the silk would be draped. During the process, Arthur playfully ran in and out of the billowing cloth, as he realized it was like the parachute play, which is a common group activity for young or special needs children. Once it was erected, however, its unfamiliar tubular shape was something new and somewhat intimidating (Figure 10.14).

Arthur became noticeably more reticent. We interpreted this shift as a change of context; as it assumed a formal shape, its morphing from process to object became unpredictably unsettling. To acclimate him, he and Pruznick just 'hung around' this sheer tunnel, having lunch in our sensory garden, as Arthur kept an eye on this enormous white cave.

By being in close proximity, Arthur was able to habituate to the silk's 'behaviour'. With object-permanence anxiety and being tentative in nature, he could mark its movements—breezes made it billowy as though it were breathing. Once erected, Pruznick set up a video camera to document the building and the finished result—of how the other children were shown running through the piece, excitedly signing their impressions along the way. Arthur was allowed to use the camera, his image simultaneously showing on the monitor. It gave him a power

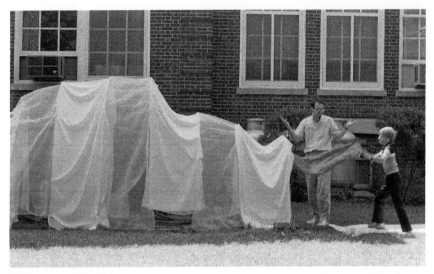

Figure 10.14 Working large scale sometimes requires quantities of free material and an expert to facilitate. The artist-in-residence, James Pruznick, assists this shy young man in his first visitation.
Used with permission of James Pruznick.

of observation from multiple fronts. The video footage still shows how Arthur helped transform this sheet on the ground into a seemingly living sculpture.

It was finally his turn for a run-through. The journey began, however, by requiring him to lift a coloured veil doorway to gain entry. This posed a problem for this most inhibited child, for it was a door to the unknown, one that he eventually overcame with Pruznick's lifting it for him. After entry, he resumed his enthusiasm for this simple yet magical new material, now transformed into an environment. Its translucency filtered the light, enabling him to make out the shadowy silhouettes of those inside and out. The piece fluttered in accordance with air pressure and the occasional breeze—animating the whole of the work. When inside, it allowed him both a low-stimulation environment and solitude, while encouraging him to sprint through it, which he and the boys eventually did at breakneck speed. At one point, the footage shows Arthur trying to sign to those outside, which was a playful 'peek-a-boo' behaviour. I had never witnessed this outgoing behaviour from this socially inhibited child. It was perhaps also important that Arthur could see Pruznick at the end of the structure, giving him a sense of object permanence—that the object would not somehow float away and there was indeed 'light at the end of the tunnel'. Perhaps this presence prompted him to linger longer than anticipated as he observed the world from within his personal 'cave'. Upon emerging, he responded with smiles as Pruznick and others applauded—he had entered the special space and emerged not just intact but energized, with a feeling of mastery and successful exploration.

Eleven
The Hyperactive Attentional Spectrum

From Autistic to Hyper

The spectrum has been envisioned as sliding along the curve—beyond the autistic spectrum, to include those with hyperactivity and attention issues. These children are differentiated in the previous vignettes by being more related than their autistic-like peers, with normative friendships, such as evidenced in the case of Connor (pg. 136), who befriended a group of skateboarders. While there are often social issues that this boy and others face, including mindblindness, they often blend in with typical peers. Boys are considered stereotypically as high energy and impulsive in their choice making, and so too are the girls, though their behaviours are considerably contrasting. Children and teens with ADD or ADHD are usually mainstreamed educationally, yet because of their hyperkinetic or attentional issues, they often function with pronounced 'peaks and valleys', meaning they require special education support services and social groups, such as Hecht's Camp Friendship, where they can practise their 'surplus' hyperkinetic levels while relating, at times, overbearingly with their more inhibited peers. In creative response therapy, these children may direct their drive energy in a constructive manner while they work on self-observing and -modulating their behaviour, whether it be on the hyper end of the spectrum or the attention deficited. Often, both conditions exist in tandem, which complicates the clinical picture and the interventions needed to address a range of complex symptoms.

Totally Off the Edge

Mixed types of children with attention deficit hyperactivity disorder are exemplified by the teenage artist Will (pg. 102). His involvement has already been described as highly volatile, with ADHD mixed with mood lability and perhaps early-onset bipolar. When his moods were bright, they bordered upon the euphoric and his flair for the dramatic, as his hyperactivity and mania dictated. Another of my teen 'skater' clients, Will preferred the snowboard to Connor's skateboarding. Also a risk taker to the point of recklessness, Will would come to the therapeutic school proudly showing off his latest cast or brace from activities such as skating to joyriding and being thrown around in a stolen car. As this attribute held social status, Will was held in high-esteem with his like-minded peers. At times his mood, activity level and social conflicts became unmanageable. Occasionally, when he posed a threat to himself or others, he needed to be restrained by the 'behavioural therapist', who was on constant call. Many factors came into play when Will became out of control, his strife at home, amount of sleep, substance use, or the unseen chemical forces at work within.

During free classroom time, Will would often draw, one of the few moments of the school day that his hyperactivity would gain an intense focus. In one instance, he reflected over a class trip to a local small-scale skiing facility—a trip earned by a month's worth of charting data that tracked his behaviour and academic productivity. Maintaining a semblance of compliance and productive schoolwork while not creating a classroom disturbance was a monumental task—especially for a monthlong duration. It was imperative to acknowledge (read, 'reward') even the most minimal behaviour gains, which both he and his peers had accomplished. A key goal was for *him* to acknowledge finally when he was in conflict, defiant or out of control.

To self-observe his negative behaviours was an ongoing long-term goal in which progress was measured in the smallest increments. Positive scores for every class member could be earned even with minimal progress—or no one would ever earn a privilege. Indeed, it was rare for him to accrue the needed numbers for a special trip outside the school, so it was a pleasure to be among the select few who could enjoy a day on the slopes. Upon the next day's return, he created a spontaneous response to his outing by drawing a caricature of himself during his day on the mountain. The picture shows a skilled draftsman at his 'peak'. He depicts himself snowboarding, not just carving up the hillside, but flying off the edge of a snow-covered cliff, turning flips and other tricks as he hurls through the air (Figure 11.1).

The sequence elegantly drawn *from memory* from multiple perspectives indicates a rare mastery over the imagined life-drawing form. Beyond his dazzling technique, he imbues the drawing with an ego-healthy dose of deprecating humour as he hurls himself, soaring in the air, only to fall head first into a snowdrift. It is a visual joke, one self-recognized as both his mastery and his folly. As a metaphor, it accurately reflected how this severely hyperactive and oftentimes manic teen navigated the twists and turns in his capacity to function. Again, the charts plotted his peaks and valleys of both behaviour and schoolwork. The drawing references this perhaps as a metaphor for the ever-present struggle to maintain self-control. Snowboarding, he remarked with all seriousness, was the most important 'thing in his life'. While this is age appropriate for a sixteen-year-old, it may be unrealistic. Yet it remained a goal, a passion and a productive means of engaging his hyperactivity. In a post-creative response, I am still in awe of how he balances intense action and metaphor, of his artistic gifts, his self-identity as an athlete and aspirations for the future. This behaviour was at odds with his volatile mood swings, non-compliance and sometimes bizarre behaviour. Yet again

Figure 11.1 Hyperactive teens may find an outlet in vigorous snowboarding, with recklessness being a prized attribute. Will demonstrates how a trick soared and then ended up a comedy of error.

we encounter the artist's persona of someone difficult to deal with daily while amongst an equally disruptive group of peers.

Yet on paper, Will communicated with inexplicable self-awareness, evoking a sophisticated humour and a sense of the absurd. In recounting the ups and downs of his trip, his image is starkly beautiful, drawn with an economy of means—almost as a sidebar after a day on the mountain. Self-awareness is again displayed in pointing out his failings as well as athletic competency—whether the image was actual or fanciful, I never asked. Again, it points out cognitive dissonance—the cognitive ability to hold competing or contrasting thoughts equally in mind and in art. It reminds the therapist or educator that symptomatology does not always diminish cognitive faculties. This and other of Will's work was well outside my own capabilities to draw figuratively from imagination. When presenting his signature single-line contour drawings in un-erasable felt tip marker, he reminded me that his artistic prowess far outstripped my own abilities. When instructing him on whatever project or admonishing him for some errant behaviour, it became a standing joke when Will would intone, in an exacting W. C. Fields voice:

'And so does the great artist sayeth ...'

Practising 'Mindfulness'

When teens partake in mindfulness and relaxation exercises, I have previously voiced a concern that mixed outcomes are the norm. Clearing the mind may elicit both positive and paradoxical effects. During the workshop held by our visiting guided imagery specialist, our snowboarder and star artist, Will, was one of the few students who thought it fun to try out the exercises. This was, of course, after joining in to shout down our visiting presenter and ridicule the idea along with his peers. During the sixth and last guided imagery/relaxation exercise, something must have struck a chord. Will actually focused on and followed the facilitator's directions. He had also generalized some of the teachings, enough that he could take a moment when beginning to feel agitated. I would remind him to use what he'd learned—to count to five, take deep breaths, and visualize the positive and other techniques taught by the workshop leader.

In this last session, the presenter began with the usual deep-breathing and 'mind-clearing' techniques. This warm-up was then followed by asking the participants to visualize themselves in a peaceful setting. I thought it a harmless enough stimulus. The workshop leader directed the few compliant students to 'find a pleasant setting—even if it starts out as a vague place. To let your thoughts bounce around until the vision of the space 'sticks''. This starting point allowed the mind to wander enough without undue demands and, in the process, set the stage for engaging imaginal or transitional space. The participants were then supposed to narrow their focus, adding a specific context, gradually increasing their details until a fully realized image was pictured and 'held' in their minds. Will dutifully closed his eyes and evidently envisioned his scene. He stayed focused, all the while breathing and with great effort trying hard to stay still and relaxed.

For this hyper and, at times, manic young man, it was a positive outcome to have managed each of these steps. I observed him for almost ten minutes where he remained still and breathing, despite the occasional ruckus that erupted around him. He then recounted to the presenter how he had pictured a bucolic setting, adding exacting details that took the presenter aback. During the creative response activity, he drew this image—a sketch of himself sitting in a pastoral field next to a stream babbling nearby—one that seems to encircle him (Figure 11.2).

Despite the positive relaxation and visualization phase, the drawing element prompted Will to depict himself in anguish. He is shown with elbows drawn to his cheeks, tears running down his face, obviously in distress. Will perhaps regressed to the extent that he includes his teddy, which sits nearby seeming to exhort him to 'chill'. Sitting somewhat menacingly nearby is a fallen tree, whose exposed roots seem to wriggle at the young man, a counterpoint to seeking its supposed peaceful shelter. Yet the gentle hills and meandering stream point to a relaxed sense of stillness. Several large trees, with the obligatory knot hole, stand as sentinels, perhaps providing cover for the exposed psyche. Nothing was said of the image besides sharing it with me in a moment of repose later that afternoon. I accepted the piece graciously without comment, but I found myself putting a rare hand upon his shoulder.

Few clients could so articulately remind the therapist that every stimulus and creative response activity possesses a double edge, that even well-meaning professionals, such as this experienced woman who facilitated guided relaxation as her job, can elicit outcomes that amplify rather than wash away negative thoughts. This points to the risk of regressing a young and unstable client, that when the client is intentionally put 'in touch' with their feelings, the outcome may be an

Figure 11.2 Will also practised 'mindfulness techniques' under a visiting professional's guided imagery exercise. Its unintended consequences, of visualizing a peaceful setting, also put him 'in touch' with feelings of despair.

overwhelming experience—one that is too fragile to 'handle'. Counter to the project's aims, the guided image and attempts at attaining mental stillness instead allowed a vacuum to be formed. Within this space came a negative scenario, which he pictured with exacting detail. The outcome then evolved from his hard-won capacity to visualize while in a contemplative state, while also loosening tenuous defences that invited the unpredictable. Caught in an uprush of affect, the transitional space might have assumed a negative connotation, wherein the teen's depression perhaps overshadowed his capacity for mindfulness.

How do we then analyze this series of outcomes which carried such peaks and valleys? Had this process been counter-therapeutic? After all, Will did not display any discomfort during the process or while drawing, and there were no deleterious behavioural after-effects. Hence, one might interpret the experience as the presenter did, as an emotional catharsis. Yet it was in her interest to pronounce it as such—thus muddying the interpretive waters further.

Gauging the stimulus and predicting possible outcomes once again remains the responsibility of the professional to anticipate. Once the stimulus is issued, the facilitator then may no longer be strictly 'in charge'—as the forces of the primary process take over. Yet the articulate nature of Will's graphic reportage, of depicting his peaceful scene while balancing paradoxical feeling states, speaks to a healthy conflict-free sphere. Will seemed to have developed what Franklin terms a more 'gentle relationship with one's thoughts, increasing the possibility of non-judgmental self-awareness' (2017). Will's evolving executive powers perhaps allowed for a distortion-free narrative, suggesting a mental compartment of healthy function. His existential and emotional pain is appropriately expressed, indicating a sublimation of exquisite proportions.

Charades and Non-Verbal Communication

What ideas and emotions are expressed through our hand gestures? Many individuals 'talk with their hands'—not just the deaf but also the hearing. From across diverse cultures, individuals use gestures consciously and unconsciously to accentuate their conversations. This was the question posed to a group of at-risk freshmen enrolled in the university's remedial program. The course was another edition of the elective, 'Art and Ideas'. Visual culture was explored through developing an 'aesthetic eye' and critically thinking through art experientials, reflective text and creative writing. As many in the group were minority and urban, their responses cited centred on hand gestures that were an integral part of sports, music and arts culture. In sports, elaborate handshakes, fist bumps, slaps and choreographed movements celebrate a fine play or score. Hip-hop lyrics and rhyme performances are noted for their distinctive body language, with hand movements that are decorative as well as communicative. Many are derived from gang symbols and gestures, but have been now generalized into the vernacular.

The lesson began with a discussion of imitative hand gestures which are an ancient form of communicating and probably precluded verbal language. Hand signalling evolved as a survival modality—pointing the way to fire, game or other tribes. Around the family and in other clans, it was perhaps a beginning form of empathy, as mirror neurons developed to be recruited to recognize and encode an expanding set of novel actions (Meltzoff & Brooks, 2007). Pre-verbal sharing probably included a range of facial and other expressive body movements, like the game of 'charades'. Working in groups, the students played the game, using just their bodies to guess a simple concept or expression. The students often used the shorthand of their culture; with much laughter there was also serious communication going on—from the humorous and exuberant to the profane or threatening. Many explored the hip-hop form, with its novel actions, which are further personalized by the artist. Students enthusiastically demonstrated different expressions: the 'back-off' and fist-pump gestures are exclamatory, the hands and arms spread in a semicircle indicate embracing the audience and the world, and the 'not-having-it' gesture is indicated by crossing the hands and then pushing the negativity and pretension away. One group explained how hand gestures are integral to the performer's persona. Several Caucasian, both urban and suburban, students discussed how they have appropriated the predominantly Afro-American hip hop aesthetic as well, adopting it as a vibrant part of their own culture. The 'cultural ownership' between groups—the idea of appropriating another's culture—led to what became a racially divided, heated discourse, which I stepped in to calm. Eventually, these adolescents restrained themselves (being on probation) and applied their research to a sculpting project.

I'll Show You

I reframed the debate as a postmodern construct—that eventually everything, including cultural iconography, gets 'borrowed' and then re-assimilated. It is a matter of historical cross-cultural influence that shapes our world. Along with these and many other references to gesture, the students would be exploring the range of meanings of hand signs through a sculpture project. We attempted to link these aspects of visual cultural communication with art expression to a personalized idea which could then act as a metaphor for one's life in general. One young man, Rodolfo, took this concept to the extreme.

The creative response assignment involved linking an emotional expression with a personalized hand gesture. Once chosen, the students were to freeze the gesture, enabling them to make an impression of their hands using a latex mould. While immersed in the latex mould and waiting five minutes, they would carefully slip their Vaseline-laden hands carefully out of this solidified, gelatinous material. The next step was to pour plaster into the negative mould, which created an exact replica, with every wrinkle and hair preserved. Once cast, the concept was to mount these hands with their varying gestures on the gallery wall as a group tableau. Writing a reflective critical essay about their intent and other decision-making processes was an adjunct to the project, which would then be orally presented during the critique.

Rodolpho was an intense and earnest young man who had suffered learning and attentional issues that plagued his every assignment. While he was vocal with interesting ideas, his poor reading comprehension and weak writing skills detracted from his outcomes. His learning disabilities required that I adapt my teaching strategy to include verbal and demonstrative directions. Oral presentation was accepted as an alternative to the standard written outcomes that compensated for his weaknesses.

Rodolfo approached me after class to discuss his project in private—which involved the previously described 'private expression rule'. This standard protocol allowed students to disclose all ideas with me without peer scrutiny. He tentatively described his chosen gesture realizing it would be considered profane. He began with the disclaimer acknowledging that it might be viewed as one of the 'taboos we discussed in class', *'that no viewer should feel threatened by a creative response'*.

Despite being a thoughtful and serious young man, Rodolfo admitted to becoming easily frustrated and angry about his handicap, citing instances when he 'lost it' at home and school and with his girlfriend. His frustrations often translated into altercations. Therefore, his choice expressed these feelings. He would cast a sculpture of 'giving the finger'. At first thought, I considered this idea an indicator of poor choice making and impulsivity linked with his ADHD. To help him think through his choice of a profane gesture, I asked him to recite back to me Kramer's three criteria of 'art in the truest sense'. Having studied the material, he was able to describe how art should evoke feeling and, thus, that it was OK to convey his frustrations. He described the importance of 'inner consistency' and that in this case he was being honest and true to himself and exhibiting economy, expressing a powerful message with obvious minimal elaboration. I applauded his understanding of the criteria and considered his argument was well informed and persuasive. But I also explained that it was the ultimate example of 'acting out'; yet he pressed his case.

He explained that all through school he had few academic role models; his family were labourers and his siblings dropouts. He experienced little encouragement in school, being a slow learner and reader, and was often prone to fighting. He was shelved in inner-city special education programs, which gave him little individual attention. 'Read enough so you can go carry cement', one teacher dismissively told him as a senior—a reference to working off his anger issues through 'constructive(ion)' means. This issue became a grudge match: he would prove to his teachers, peers and especially his laid-off father, who had said he was 'too slow' to make it through college.

The 'finger' would have them 'eat their words', he stated—it would not be aggressive or threatening, but a chip-on-his-shoulder expression of 'I'll show you'. Assessing his sincerity and the merit of his intent, I reluctantly gave permission knowing I myself could be accused of breaking the 'no threatening expression' rule. Assumedly, any number of students might object, or worse, complain to the administration. In any event, I relented, with the caveat that much trust and belief in him would be required on my part, that to transform 'the finger' without its lapsing into gratuitous obscenity or provocation was not so easy, but he assured me he was up to the challenge. I also made it clear that I would fail him if he didn't—thus, the stakes were high all around.

After the project was completed, the students mounted their works on the wall in the student gallery as a lovely collaborative installation (Figure 11.3). While this image is from another class, and thus does not include Rodolfo's 'finger', it is a tableau that is almost identical to his class's presentation. During the installation, a group discussion ensued amongst the students as to where this 'obscenity' should be placed. Several students, mostly girls, were outspoken in their condemnation of the piece, with one remarking it should be ostracized some distance away from the final composition. As part of the contrite attitude we agreed upon, Rodolfo immediately complied. Then the reverse occurred, that once alienated, the group's empathy emerged, calling him back into the fold. Then another student 'called me out', stating flatly that I had allowed the studio to become 'an unsafe space'—again, the tenet I had preached from the start of the semester. I accepted her criticism, but suggested that the work's story might mitigate her feelings after the artist explained his actions. As the students orally presented on their own intentions, Rodolfo's eagerly awaited statement finally came. He stood before the group. My notes from the time reflect how he had prepared his statement and how carefully he had chosen his words.

> 'All my life I was disrespected; I was called dumb cause
> I couldn't read aloud and got poor grades.
> I was angry at everybody.

Figure 11.3 In a university program for at-risk freshmen a young man created a casting in the form of an obscene gesture (not shown). Though accepted into a similar group tableau, it was seen as a provocation which some in the group resented.
Photograph by Michele Amendolari, used with permission.

So when Professor Henley trusted in me to do this piece,
I took it seriously and tried to do my best.
This is not a work meant to offend you.
It's a message to those in my past.
This finger is for my fifth-grade teacher who I heard call me 'retarded'.
It's for my high school basketball coach who benched me cause
I forgot what
the 'three fingers up' play meant.
It's for my school counsellor who said I'd never make it to college.
And finally it's for myself, cause it reminds me that if I fail,
The Finger will be aimed at *me,*
and that's not an easy thought to carry around.

Many in the group were moved by this artist's statement, though several still criticized the gesture as 'nasty'. Naturally, it received a lot of attention, which another student resented. She angrily called out, 'Can we move on—he's gotten enough attention already!'—a criticism which also had been part of our studies—that intent for the sake of self-attention weakens both the art and artist while also distressing the community. We had studied Richard Serra's *Tilted Arc* (1981, destroyed in 1989). Serra's piece was a ribbon of steel that divided a common space in New York, which long agitated and alienated the public who had to navigate it as part of their daily commute. Eventually, they pooled their indignation and had it removed from the plaza.

The group recalled this case study and applied it in this instance, some calling for its exile to a distant point in the tableau and some for its removal altogether. Rodolfo's piece remained a quandary, for while it resonated with several (mostly males), generating feelings of self-identification, several (mostly young women) felt it created a hostile environment. However, it was then pointed out that several other young men had displayed mixed/negative outcomes of their own, including one example of an only slightly modified gang sign—which posed the question whether to *call* that student out.

My graduate assistant at the time was afterwards asked for feedback, as this was our practice of 'being checked'. She bravely pointed out that she felt my permissiveness was off the mark, that Rodolfo's gesture compromised the group's unity and cohesiveness. I had not sufficiently anticipated the outcome, she said, perhaps because his argument at the time was so compelling. The finger incident called into question my own choice making, its degree of clarity and professionalism. Had I maintained the group's emotional safety? Encouraged inappropriate attention seeking? Tainted the entire tableau? As one young woman remarked, 'We've all flipped the bird, yet we didn't leave it plastered to the wall'. Indeed. Yet despite the controversy, Rodolfo's piece became a teachable moment, for each of us learned something—the artist, the students, the instructor and my graduate assistant—everyone could put into play the concepts we'd learned in the abstract. In this one creative response activity, our academic ideas came to life in the strongest terms.

Sexuality and Body Image

Sexualization of women is a universal norm—a phenomenon perhaps dating back to the Pleistocene age, when women and the fertility cults were the dominant forces of ancient cultures. In each epoch, women struggled to balance the procreative need for sexual desirability while resisting objectification as a sexual object, to be available simply for male pleasure. On the high school and university levels, these issues are constantly played out, as young women try out their sexuality through various means—both in acting out the dynamic and in symbolic expression. One university freshman in the remedial program was an attractive young woman named Belle, who presented with undisclosed attention deficits and learning differences. In many cases, girls who possess exceptional beauty (by Western norms) may result in a type of emotional insecurity. Beauty bias can be associated with a lack of intelligence or threatening in social and professional situations (Agthe et al., 2013). Nadeau, Littman and Quinn (1999) write that girls typically work harder to mask their symptoms especially regarding academics and social mores. They face social pressures to not 'act out' as boys often do, such as Rudolfo, with his emphatic 'Finger'.

Belle's beauty and figure came with above-average height, attractive features and prominent breasts. Through my female graduate assistant, I learned that there were issues I would not be privy to, which were held in confidence, as they were not relevant to the academic project. However, my own observations suggested that the other young women in the class perceived her as entitled, leading to an undercurrent of petty jealousies. It also became clear that male peers felt her 'unattainable'—a reasonable assertion. Again, one might surmise that beauty bias and unattainability also impacted her academic underachieving.

This issue found expression when the students were again body casting—which obviously would touch a nerve in this young woman. During this semester, focus was shifted away from hands to include faces or other parts that 'expressed their identity'—which tapped into Belle's ongoing body-image issues. The process again used latex moulds in the form of melted latex that was now to be brushed onto the body. Individual pieces would be mounted on sculpture stands. Once again, the private expression rule arose when Belle quietly approached me during class. Taking me aback, she stated, 'I would like to cast my breast'. Once I had recovered from this statement, I privately discussed with her the ramifications of such a raw and unadulterated self-expression. Covertly aware of her attention deficit issues, I queried her whether this was an ill-advised, impulsive decision. I urged her to wait until the next session to give the matter time and reflection. I also reminded her to re-read my lecture on aesthetic license and creative responses which might be considered private or gratuitous. She promised to reflect upon her choice until the following class.

A week later she again stated her intent, 'that for years boys have been dying to see her breasts and now I'm going to give them a taste, to shut them up, once and for all'. It was a strong statement, one that was emotionally charged but also rational, to desensitize the male obsession with large breasts by outing the mystery and to 'steal their thunder' by transforming the issue into an objet d'art. On the eventful day, she retired to the ladies room, where a friend painted the hot latex onto her breast, which, after cooling, was followed by a plaster shell to hold the rubber in shape. Since I would not witness the process, I harped on the plaster phase of the project, to cover the latex with reinforced plaster to keep the mould rigid. The last thing we needed was a large breast which was monstrously warped—its therapeutic, social and aesthetic ramifications were dire. It required two tries to accomplish an accurate and detailed mould. I inspected the first and was unsatisfied with the outcome—this piece, I insisted, had to be right.

I urged one more try, to be accomplished after class was adjourned when there would be fewer distractions surrounding the secret mould. 'Belle's breast', as it came to be known, became a bold and stately sculpture in white plaster (Figure 11.4).

It was mounted on a dowel and base without using coloured ink to accentuate its most sensual details, one among many other pieces, in a bid for it to fit into the exhibit and thus remain understated. By keeping the voluptuous features low key, Belle could address the issue of both economy and its relationship with gratuitousness, that with economy comes measuring 'too much information' while forcefully getting her concept across. In keeping with Kramer's criteria for a formed expression, this also included managing to stay true to her intentions, which she did. The piece also naturally evoked much feeling when displayed. The finished sculpture drew quiet 'ahhs' when unveiled. These achievements were underlined during the critique, as Belle alluded to her intention, stating 'for so long young men around me wondered how she was in the nude'.

'Now, here it is everybody. Any questions?'

This provocative statement was at first greeted with nervous laughter, but then, starting with the women, spontaneous applause erupted. The piece seemed to touch a sensitive nerve in men and women alike—as each was confronted by their own sexuality and perhaps regrettable behaviours. It also might have had the effect of de-cathecting the sexual association with the object. Posed standing on its strong, formal elements perhaps overtook its loaded content.

Following this artist's statement, the students themselves initiated a spirited conversation, which I allowed to flow without intervention. It is always a pleasure to disappear from the learning process, to be sidelined and transparent, allowing others to take the lead. By this metric alone can we measure a successful educational or therapeutic creative activity. They spoke about peer pressure in the university, where sex and alcohol, status and trophyism, and 'selfie' cell-phone madness was rampant. Belle's creative response to her own body, which perhaps had been a source of self-consciousness for her entire adolescence, was given a dose of closure. The libidinal energy attached to the object had been somewhat neutralized, achieving a sublimation which could be internalized and generalized in future behaviour. It perhaps helped fortify a conflict-free sphere, where the body image was no longer so emotionally charged. Building a stronger self-image

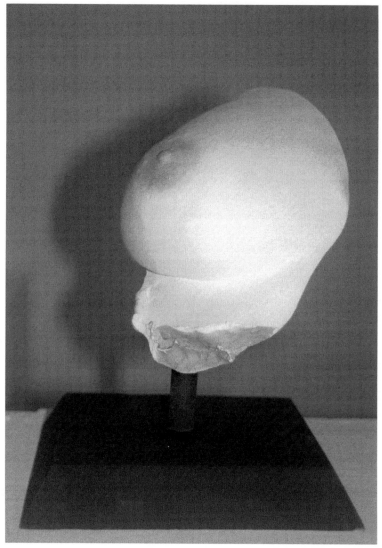

Figure 11.4 Another at-risk and attractive freshman prompted a provocative, creative response. After dealing for years with immature male peers, she gave them something to talk about—a cast of her own breast.

and self-concept towards greater maturation remains a crucial step for any co-ed, whether on the spectrum or not. Enhancing self-awareness for a freshman at risk is perhaps especially critical during these sexually troublesome times which have prompted a nationwide conversation on university campuses.

Twelve
Creative Action Responses

As a creative arts therapist, the therapeutic curriculum usually centres around eliciting an artistic expression to preserve impressions the child experiences as a form of documentation. Creating something acts as a 'diary', encouraging memory recall to fix the experience in time and space. Images help to re-articulate the experience especially when relating to others, which in turn assists with self-insight, enhanced cognition and socialization. Owen's football player image (Figure 7.3) and Connor's evocative skater portrait (Figure 7.6) are two examples of fruitful images which elaborate on their action activities. Will's superb action drawing in Figure 11.1 was intended to convey, in my absence, how his brilliant snowboarding trick ended, with his feet and board sticking up out of the snow. Since I was not on-site, he needed to convey that mix of mastery and sense of humorous failure that was vital if I were to vicariously enjoy the moment with him.

For others, the activity 'itself' may become the aesthetic outcome, making further elaboration either redundant or unnecessary. It is sufficient just to charge down a ski slope, play a contemplative game of chess or simply ride a bike. These and other creative actions may or may not warrant a culminating post-response activity. While there might be post-activity processing, often it is the action itself that invites self-evaluation. It may be complicated enough just to get up the nerve to try new skills, while keeping under control the anger and frustration when one falters. For many children, the goal is to experience action activities that will take them 'out of their heads' and into their bodies. Just introducing an action sport activity doesn't make problems disappear—they just change. The result, especially during training, may result in amplifying the constellation of spectrum issues. While the degree of novelty may be a prime motivator for trying new activities, these feelings are often combined with anticipatory anxiety—resulting in approach-avoidance reactions. But one must still trust the process, which if facilitated, a degree of personal success can be achieved and be inherently therapeutic as any creative art activity.

Making Activity 'Special'

To make activities special, the therapist, teacher or even coach must not only be able to break each skill down into manageable increments, but also make the experience an 'event'. One must announce, demonstrate and make the actions themselves greatly enthusiastic, which in turn may help motivate an inhibited child to mimic unfamiliar, potentially threatening body movements. Each activity is framed within the 'personal best paradigm', that participation and effort are the keys to a special and successful experience. For instance, at the Camp Friendship program, head counsellor Carrin Honeycutt initiated a new action program using novelty to convey how a new activity would be 'special'. She proclaimed with fanfare a new 'bike club'. This was to be a special program in which everyone was invited—but it required self-control and awareness. By framing this otherwise unremarkable, even humdrum activity, as especially challenging and special, the children's interest level became naturally elevated. From BMXers to those who could manage balancing only with training wheels—everyone's skill level was welcomed and accommodated. Those who could not bring a bike would have one made available. Booklets from the department of motor vehicles were handed out for the children to learn correct hand signals so they could physically communicate with the other riders and vehicular traffic around them. This means of communication was safety oriented but also a novel, sophisticated means of expression.

On the appointed day, almost all the children donned their helmets, decorated their bikes with streamers and numbers, flashed their safety lights and set upon the training course. Some activities involved weaving their way through cones, while older groups took off in a line keeping a safe proximal distance on an outing to the lake beach. Each child was given a small kit for repairs and basic 'maintenance', which increased the investment in their bicycle—to explore its mechanical workings rather than simply take it for granted as just a 'ride'. Being mindful of their bike's maintenance needs was a lesson in empathy itself. Each kit contained a set of wrenches, lubricating grease and other objects, which prompted some children to work on their bikes as often as riding them. With the multiple gears, cables and spinning wheels, even those on the autistic continuum delighted in seeing the bikes turned upside down. Their wheels freely spinning, they became objects to spin and reimagined into a something strange and special.

Thus, Honeycutt elicited the most colourful range of therapeutic outcomes imaginable—from the 'spinners' to a 'runner' who just took off into nowhere, leading counsellors on a frantic bike chase. One boy panicked when riding in a line, crying out to Honeycutt that he feared for his life. One little girl who had never ridden was fearful of being on something that launched her into such 'fast' motion. This kinetic hypersensitivity is also overlooked, as a walking pace is far different than gliding down a hillside. She was first taught to balance in situ, and then slowly, with the assistance of an aide, they walked around the grassy field. Eventually, she worked up to riding with the aide 'jogging beside' the child, holding her seat for balance. Her success was measured not only by how long she could peddle, but also by how she was able to safely control her falls onto the soft grass. As advanced participants weaved through an obstacle course, the other children, or 'teammates', spontaneously initiated an impromptu rally. Children cheered on their fellow cyclists in the spirit of good sportsmanship. The activity required nothing further beyond the action couched in novelty, which then took on a life of its own. Again, this counsellor, and now experienced special educator, became a transparent entity, setting the stage, quietly motivating everyone on, and transforming everything out of the ordinary.

On Catching the First Fish

For some individuals, particularly those on the autistic end of the spectrum, forays into new sensory experiences have been identified as possibly creating participatory anxiety. This was observed in a teen named Carl, a bright and verbal young man with autistic features who was one of eight group-home clients participating in a day's outing. This twenty-year-old young man was part of a field trip to a private pond where he was to have his first fishing expedition. He presented with two contradictory feelings: anxiously perseverating over wanting to finally catch a fish, while also obsessing over the fear of 'pulling an animal' out of its home. In an echolalic tone, he intoned repeatedly how fish are protected in the water and how some fishermen injure or even kill the animal when hooked. It took a few hours to work on desensitizing his feelings of ambivalence. Meanwhile the activity was demonstrated by a counsellor who showed Carl how the fish could be caught safely without causing injury, especially since we ground the barb of the hook. We also demonstrated how fish are hooked into a keratin-like material akin to fingernails, which are impervious to pain. By netting the animal and immediately returning it to the pond, he witnessed how, with a swish of the tail, the bass dove into the depths, unharmed. Once this concern had become tempered, Carl began the slow process toward facilitating a successful outing.

Preparing individuals unfamiliar with a rod and reel is rarely an easy task, especially to elicit a positive outcome. Casting a spinning reel for the first time—to coordinate the rod in a back-and-forward motion and cast and release the reel's trigger at the appointed time all required breaking down each increment with great patience. Then to send the lure in the right direction further complicates this deceptively simple activity. To prepare the clients, we made a game of casting, where a fun factor was built in to help endure the repetitions of practice. It was called 'casting the bobber' in which the individual aims a bobber tied to the line, which was cast towards a stationary target—a hula-hoop lying in the grass. Those who could coordinate the movements and get even remotely near were deemed ready to graduate to the fishing activity. After many attempts, it was clear Carl would not be able to master this coordinated movement. By using 'hand-over-hand' interventions we cast together. Since the fish in the pond were semi-tame, results came quickly. Once the fish was hooked, Carl excitedly reeled it in. Being finally able to land his first bass, we allowed him to hold it before release.

Fishing has long been associated with contemplative sport, with the repetitions of casting and angling reaching almost metaphysical levels. As a form of transitional space, the fisherman may lose himself in the process, to the extent that a fishless outing makes no difference. It is the ritual that becomes the locus of attention, wading in the rushing stream or pond-side setting, enjoying the camaraderie of peers, including a hearty lunch, all making the sport special. In this case, the young man eventually approached his own modest goals, as indicated by a reduction in perseveration and his elevated anxiety levels. Sensory pleasure was derived from simply standing still and waving the rod back and forth, reeling in, casting out—all became peaceful along the pond shore. Once comfortable with the routines and its repetitions, his vocalizing diminished to manageable levels. His awe-struck expression seems to capture the rasa of the fishing experience. The tactile experience increased his awareness of these magnificent creatures living invisibly under water. But now in its intimate proximity, handling the animal became an activity 'made special'. Cradling in his hands in apparent wonder, his tenderness and curiosity finally quieted his incessant questioning as he became immersed in the experience (Figure 12.1).

While not a cure for this young man's obsessionality, this action sport outcome demonstrated an eventual quieting and calming effect, from which other similar activities could be built upon.

Figure 12.1 Action-sport responses can be equally creative to those in the arts. This young man on the autistic continuum is mesmerized by the experience of landing his first fish.

Competitive Edge

Competitive skiing is a challenge for any child, requiring skill, endurance, long periods of practice and family support—of travel, expense and commitment. For a teen on the spectrum, making the transition between recreational skiing and competition was nothing less than momentous. It required a tenacious will and drive to adjust from recreation to *racing*—upping the skill levels and competitive spirit. Increasing the ante to competitive levels was accompanied by anticipatory anxiety and eventually obsessionality. As a compensatory mechanism, becoming obsessed both intensified focus as well as increased the child's anxiety levels. It is a natural outcome for those on the spectrum, of pushing beyond one's comfort zone.

I first encountered K.T. at an action sports facility called PROGRESH. Owned and operated by my son, Kyle Henley, its cavernous space features a forty-foot ramp which shoots airborne skiers, snowboarders or razor scooters into an enormous airbag. Others jump and flip on trampolines, and skateboarders practise tricks, then switch off to tackle the parkour obstacle course—all of which result in new skill sets and perhaps an adrenaline rush. Henley has adapted each activity to individuals of all levels, including many participants with mixed and even severe handicaps. Whether it be a Down syndrome child enjoying their first bounce on the trampoline or a professional snowboarder training on the massive ski launch for an upcoming competition, coach Kyle's facility prides itself on inclusiveness for everyone. In this environment, K.T. was fully accepted as an accomplished athlete.

Early intervention became a key to success. Kyle had begun working with K.T. as a four-year-old, first in gymnastics, where they worked on developing a sense of her body moving in space. Later, these individual lessons extended to her first snowboarding experiences, where once again, the coach would 'run beside' the child, up and down the small training hills, spotting her, adjusting form and urging her on. This work continued sporadically over an eight-year span—such is the time commitment necessary for many spectrum children to graduate to higher-level instruction. She remains one of the many action sport athletes who still train at PROGRESH while also entering the competitive phase of skiing during middle school.

K.T.'s competitive skiing was not a program for those with special needs, but a skilled group of *contenders*. Not many children on the spectrum, particularly those with noticeable symptoms, can manage racing down a slalom course against their typical peers—but K.T. has so far managed to do so with success. Slashing vertically down 200 metres of mountain and negotiating some thirty gates without barrelling into them require a high level of concentration. Race events were intense, on both a physical and an emotional level. But rather than being fearful, her anxiety was focused on 'missing a gate', which was equated to being 'disqualified'. The prospect of being disqualified could not only leave K.T. out of the competition, but also became a metaphor for wholesale rejection, accentuating her neurodifferences. In K.T.'s mind, disqualification is a finite state, where there are no 'do-overs'. She perceived that any mistake might render her participation permanently irredeemable. That she could always start afresh was, for an extended period, a difficult concept for her to retain. Each of these issues was addressed by her cognitive therapist, with the emphasis on emotional regulation that appealed to K.T.'s powers of intellect. These goals were then reinforced by coach Kyle's work, both indoors and on the slopes. Her mother, a leading advocate for autism awareness in Colorado, guided K.T.'s path with an eye towards assisting her daughter to self-monitor her decision making—whether to take a break from competition or continue onwards. Per recent strides with her cognitive therapist, K.T. is now able to articulate when she cannot 'handle' the pressure or temper her self-criticism. She now accepts her place finishes and missing a gate without being devastated—all high-level accomplishments.

Ancillary Problems

Yet with such competition, anxiety takes its toll. As with other cognitive and behavioural programming, symptom substitution becomes a possibility. K.T.'s obsessions beyond her place finishing also expanded to include her general physical fitness, weight and diet. These issues tied in with her athletics and were hypermonitored by the child. The dieting and odd food choices lent the girl a sense of 'purity of being'. This ancillary issue then expanded further, such as being a compulsive cleaner. K.T. kept her room perfectly, insisting at one point that her sheets be laundered daily—until her mother set appropriate limits. The stimulus behind this obsession began when K.T. became aware of the microscopic creatures which inhabit our bed linens, clothes and bodies. 'Dust mites' are other-worldly creatures which would unsettle any individual, but for K.T., they are monstrous and disgusting parasites that invisibly inhabit her world. Being hypervigilant, she struggles to filter out this intrusive and debilitating awareness. Thus, she displaces the idea of her bed crawling with bugs by having them be 'purified'. Laundering, as well as repetitive washing of her own body to shed 'skin cells' (on which the mites feed, another loathsome detail), takes up enormous emotional and behavioural energy.

Another extension of obsessionality involves her ski outfits, as she requires the same all-black suit and pink helmet, with no variation. Clothes were often felt as being abrasive, such as blue jeans, with their metal studs and long break-in time being desired but ultimately not handled. Outfits chosen for a first occasion must then be worn again to the same affair. To normalize these obsessive perceptions, one must bear in mind that our clothing becomes a kind of 'second skin'. It intimately envelops the individual at differing layers and puts one's appearance 'out there' for all to judge. It is normative for everyone to feel somewhat vulnerable about the fit and whether their outfits are appealing, particularly if new. These perceptions are amplified when there is hypersensitivity to visual and tactile sensation. Thus, K.T.'s skiing is almost overshadowed by the mental energy required to maintain her 'look' while remaining within her comfort zone. Laundered clothing and linens and ironing the same clothes over and over are not only hygienic actions, but as the mother wrote, they bring order to her world. They perhaps function as an antidote to the sensory messiness that comes with the controlled chaos of ski events as well as her own high school environment.

The Runner

The latest challenge for K.T. was making the transition from a private behavioural school to a community-oriented public school. After several months of the mainstream setting, she had balanced the inevitable frustration and stress with successful adaptation. K.T. has taken adventurous classes such as theatrical makeup design, where she can experiment with being creatively transformed into different personas and identities. Most importantly, she has joined the freshman cross-country team as a means of training for the skiing off-season. Although an inexperienced runner, K.T. works relentlessly at this new endurance sport. This additional competition—one that entails running until one is completely exhausted—has led K.T. to phone her mother daily from school. Calling Mom to monitor the laundering process may be analogous to the natural developmental milestone of 'checking-back' behaviour. During infant development, toddlers routinely scoot away from their mothers in a bid for separation, exploration and independence. Yet the little one inevitably will 'check back' with the mother to ensure her proximal distance allows for both physical and emotional availability (Mahler et al., 1975). This motivational ambivalence is rooted in Piaget's object permanence and Mahler's object constancy—a dynamic already described as an issue that is commonplace throughout the lifespan. Everyone checks back; we call, text and scroll through phones to the point of obsessionality. Typical individuals of any age or functioning level physically return to their support base, whatever that is, especially when managing the stressors of everyday life.

For the child on the spectrum, this construct carries greater emotional *weight,* with the need for reassurance being of a greater intensity and frequency. When K.T.'s object constancy is shaken, she reverts to her obsession of calling Mom to 'check' what phase the laundry is in: wash, spin, dry or sometimes folded. Making seemingly innocuous phone calls home, something millions of schoolchildren do via their ubiquitous mobile devices, is a displacement strategy—enabling K.T. to redirect and self-modulate the anxieties that accompany her increasingly hectic teen lifestyle. Tenuous object relationships are sure to ebb and flow as her regimen of therapy, academics and action sports becomes more routine. Yet she still can run a cross-country course or charge down a Colorado slope, which is an expression that defines this teen's self-image. There is no need for further elaboration. It is an artform all its own. With such an early and continuous support network and her fearless capacity to try almost anything taxing, K.T.'s creative responses are met by a ferocious resolve.

Wrestling on a Diet

As a sport, wrestling is demanding for any child; it is time intensive and punishing, requiring intelligence, diligence and conditioning. For a deaf wrestler, auditory input is completely absent. The necessary compensations are numerous. Trying to juggle the action—to watch the clock, keep track of the score, be aware of the mat boundaries, anticipate the opponent's moves while executing one's own—becomes overwhelming to manage, let alone excel in. To witness their sacrifices, operating as a minority culture with its travails and, yes, prejudices against their handicap, required summoning great inner strength to overcome. It was a privilege and a humbling experience as a new varsity coach to learn from these deaf athletes and support them in their bid for parity and a place in an alien world of sound.

One boy, Roy, experienced particular difficulties managing his impulses regarding the self-discipline required to maintain his competitive weight. As we saw with K.T., dieting can become obsessional. Skiing did not require dietary restrictions—though no one could convince her of that. Meanwhile in wrestling, it is often one of the centrepieces of their training regimen. It is routine to shed at least ten percent of body weight to be competitive with their opponent who *also* has cut down to his most essential musculature. Gaining the self-control to maintain a low-calorie, high-protein diet with healthy dietary choices of fruit and vegetables was alien to many teens who were accustomed to junk food and sweets. Hence, it became an issue when working with this challenging population with whom I spent two years being both coach and therapeutic facilitator.

A talented middleweight, Roy had difficulty managing his dietary regimen, even when it was in his competitive interests. Early on in my first season, he was often overweight to qualify for his weight class, resulting in his disqualification. By not possessing sufficient willpower, Roy ate calorie-laden junk, which affected his position on the team. Peers pressured him to comply, whereupon he would become upset and angry—often blaming me, as I was somehow responsible being 'the coach'. This dynamic is common with children with attentional or hyper-active behaviour, but this 'blaming' behaviour was immature at eighteen. We worked diligently with each boy to develop a slow weight descent, which was supervised and health conscious—but was useless when deviated from.

Dieting in wrestling is one of the few action sport activities besides dance that is required to enhance performance. It does not involve the use of drugs or artificial aids, just a healthy junk-free regimen. However, when taken overboard, wrestling increases the potential risk of developing eating disorders. Although monitored by the school nurse and given a special healthy diet at the residential school, Roy had bouts of binging on junk food, then using laxatives and avoiding water to compensate for his extra caloric intake. It was a situation setting himself up for failure, and as his coach, I counselled him that the team depended upon him to stay true to his dietary regimen if he wished us to stay competitive. This was a highly motivational stimulus, as Roy's strengths were that of a warrior. He wres-tled fiercely, never giving in, always wrestling to the last 'touch' (a necessary alter-native to the referee's whistle). It was competition that focused him, with an inner fire like that of K.T. to overcome the dietary obstacles to succeed. However, he would need supplemental support if he were to qualify for his weight class.

As an intervention, I often took the time to train and 'wrestle beside'. As we travelled the Eastern Seaboard for tourneys, I took care to monitor his meals, which were taken at the same table. I stressed burning calories as an antidote when he did lose control and binge. With several other wrestlers, we held extra workout sessions together after practice, where I matched them push-up for push-up, on through our entire callisthenics routine. Extending myself for him and other boys was an unusual therapeutic intervention. I was both exhorting him to self-sacrifice while also therapeutically training beside him by doing our sit-ups as equal partners. We held each other's ankles while doing the exercise, working the core abdominals, burning fat and toning muscle—together feeling the pain.

As we entered the second season, his relatedness and self-discipline had increased. Now more mature and committed, he became more open to my coaching, perhaps feeling at last he was in competent hands. I continued to work alongside him and the rest of the team, sustaining black eyes and hurt shoulders along with the rest, such that my influence carried more weight. Now in his senior year, I found a different Roy. He no longer went off his diet—to the contrary, he became highly disciplined. At first I was pleased, but then I noticed an obsessive quality to his weight-training program. The nurse reported that he constantly checked his weight during the school day. This did not endear myself to the school nurse, as perhaps she thought I was placing too much pressure on the teen, with diet being a sensitive topic. When he also reported a kind of 'purity of body' sensation like K.T. had, I understood the problem had become one of obsessionality—that his regimen of self-control was now an overcompensation and that he had 'gone overboard'. I was anxious he was perhaps even bordering on an eating disorder. When I was told that he was weighing out each meal on a portion scale, as well as calculating caloric content, my fears were realized.

It has been pointed out that individuals occupying the spectrum often do not 'come out' on the so-called normal behavioural hash mark. During the last of the season when weight control became most difficult as the months of dieting wore on, his anxieties were manifested by even more strenuous workouts. On several match days, I learned he had worn the dreaded 'rubber suit' to bed—which among wrestlers, is the last desperate straw at weight reduction. At night, while sleeping in the suit, much water content in his body evaporated, leaving him dehydrated.

Finally, the season tournament finale was held, the culmination of four years of competition. Roy earned runner-up medal honours in winning his four matches. He is shown in a photo taken for a feature story on our deaf wrestling team, the reporter fascinated by the requirement of my being a therapeutic-minded coach. Roy prepped before his finals match, which he eventually lost by a heart-breaking last-second point scored by the first-seeded opponent (Figure 12.2).

With everyone satisfied, we celebrated not just his exciting place finish, but also all those other teammates whose 'individual successes' were as deeply appreciated. Back from our journey to the tournament, we adjourned to the nearest pizzeria to celebrate the team's third-place finish out of fifteen schools. During the pizza party, I found Roy's dietary regimen was temporary—to my great relief. He was wolfing down his slices while I counselled him and the other 'weight cutters' to eat slowly, in moderation, lest they suffer stomach cramps—an admonition that was utterly disregarded. For once I was glad to see him cavorting with his teammates

Figure 12.2 Eating disorders are usually considered a female issue. This deaf wrestler became obsessed with dieting to make his weight, though the issue subsided after a successful season.

and revelling in their fast food and Cokes during a special moment, after four gruelling months.

One might consider Roy's case a mixed outcome. Although this athlete had struggled to develop dietary self-discipline, it eventually came at a cost of going overboard nearing the pathological—of which I was partly responsible. I had aided and abetted this handicapped boy's dietary regimen, which could have been gone out of control and been construed by others at the school as overly punitive and ethically questionable. Yet his figure and weight loss were to all eyes (including the principal's) not appreciably affecting his appearance—his cheeks were not too drawn, his muscle definition not overly defined. Luckily, the dieting obsession was a temporary one. The upside was that, moving on to spring baseball, he had developed a workout regimen that was more mindful—that competitive sports involves exercising the entire mind-body connection. The success he achieved in his weight class was generalized, which enhanced both self-esteem and, finally, perhaps also in his belief in me, that a lowly art teacher and 'hearing' coach, who doled out the pain, could in the end become an appreciated mentor.

Pitching and Tics

The mechanics of the baseball pitcher's art are one of the most intricate and aesthetically appreciated of all action activities. The overhead pitching motion is meant to deliver a high-velocity or erratically moving ball to an incredibly small strike zone—all in such a way that its movement confounds the hitter. Its coordination involves the whole body, with arm and shoulder movement, along with the lower pelvis and hips, which serve to transfer potential energy to the baseball. It is an art that takes years to perfect, with only a select few athletes able to master the mechanics to throw accurately and without undue risk of injury.

The intensity of pitching stems from shouldering much of the responsibility for the team's success. The pressure to maintain accuracy and velocity while keeping one's composure is immensely stressful. The pitcher's physical motion is strangely erratic; it begins slowly with fidgeting around, with many repetitive movements, from tugging at one's cap to walking in circles. Once settled, the pitcher stares in for the signs, which to many may seem like an eternity. But once the wind-up begins and the pitcher unleashes the pitch to the batter, it is among the most dramatic yet primitive acts of aggression dating from prehistory. To discover how to *throw* was perhaps what defined humans from our earliest ancestors. When in the hands of an artist-athlete, the ability to control this aggression, albeit barely, is one of the most dramatic elements in any game. As the pitch reaches the batter within seconds, there is either a loud crack of the bat as the hitter makes contact, or it whizzes blindly past. Whatever the result, this process requires replicating each pitching movement with exacting synchronicity, some sixty to seventy times during a single game. The pitcher is the executive on the field; all plays emanate from his performance. With such pressure comes the need for tension-relieving 'rites' (Anshel, 2012) in which pre-pitch, ritualized behaviours often reach obsessive-compulsive levels. In cases where the pitcher is coping with spectrum-related issues, these stressful situations complicate the situation exponentially.

Earlier, I alluded to a freshman baseball player-client who was gifted enough to make the freshman high school squad. Tom was almost six feet tall at fifteen, with a lanky, sinewy frame. His pitching velocity and accuracy proved him to be an already formidable opponent, having pitched with success throughout grade school. He was referred by his parents when his pre-pitch rituals became evermore complex and lengthened. When in high-pressure situations, his array of obsessive movements included stepping on and off the mound a certain number of times and then wagging his cap again, for an exacting number of repetitions. Most alarmingly, he would suddenly stretch out both arms and issue a loud barking sound, enough so that the umpires officiating the game would sometimes complain.

Tom was finally diagnosed by Dr. Hecht as having features of Tourette syndrome, which explained his ritualized actions as modified tics. The aetiology for his Tourette's was perhaps the rarest and most controversial of all spectrum disorders. His parents described how Tom had been infected with Lyme disease at age thirteen. In the 1990s, Lyme disease was mainly an East Coast deer tick-borne infection. Once a person has been bitten, the spirochete *Borrelia burgdorferi* enters the bloodstream and deposits itself mainly in connective tissue. An initial infection leads to an array of symptoms, including flu, arthritic pain and low energy levels. If the diagnosis is missed or left untreated, as was the case with Tom, the bug can infiltrate the cerebrospinal fluid, leading to neurological and psychiatric symptoms. In Tom's case, the delay in diagnosing the disease and not immediately treating his subtle symptoms with antibiotics led, inexplicably, to the emergence of the motoric and vocal tics. After being put on multiple courses of antibiotics, the efficacy was spotty—requiring rounds of multiple therapies, including further courses of intravenous antibiotics, hyperbaric oxygen therapy and eventually psychotropic medications. After two years, these combined therapies eventually drove the disorder into remission. Yet the tics persisted for another year, leaving the parents and child demoralized.

Tourette syndrome is treated medically for mixed-type spectrum symptoms, including tics, ADHD and mood disorders. At that time, the therapeutic team was shown video taken by the father displaying how his tics erupted after school hours. Upon returning home, he began ticing with almost unbelievable ferocity. They were 'let loose' with almost seizure-like, uncontrollable movements, probably since they were suppressed during the school day. Even when controlled, his symptoms were noticeable enough to affect both his social and athletic life. After a year of treatment, the tics subsided enough that he could pitch at a competitive level. However, with competition came a resurgence of tics, which began to escalate. He was then attending weekly creative arts therapeutic sessions as part of The Hecht Group's psychological team, who decided that Tom be referred to a specialized sports psychologist. After five consultations, he returned to me to work on his techniques for 'positive creative visualization'. The sports psychologist effectively utilized guided imagery as a means of 'image generation', meaning visualizing the pitching motion and its eventual release, with many repetitions.

The psychologist's letter to Dr. Hecht explained that he worked on generating a mental or kinaesthetic picture of the activity, including game scenarios which modulated the amount of stress produced. Once Tom could mentally reproduce his mechanics, it became a matter of 'image maintenance', which attempts to sustain the positive image. Again, with me in weekly session, he would explore situational stressors that crept into his mind during games, all while attempting to relax and control his breathing cycle. The main goal was for Tom to draw upon a state of mindfulness that utilized his intuitive faculties. Thinking too much, after the body has already long memorized an action, has a negative impact upon the mind-body connection. During the image transformation phase, the psychologist's process was modelled on the Anshel method of acting upon corrective or adaptive behaviours. After demonstrating his mentalization methods, we would return to therapy sessions where we practised techniques as an action-oriented activity. Tom would pitch to me using a foam ball that was given to him by the sports psychologist, which could be thrown indoors even with great velocity. Because of limited space, he would pitch at close range without the ball even generating a sound as it hit the wall. During practising his pre-pitch wind-up, he would focus upon mindfulness without over-thinking his sense of self-observation. With body memory doing most of the work, too much self-observation can have a negative paradoxical effect. However, there were cognitive-based exercises that we worked on part of his regimen.

These took the form of replicating his pre-pitch rituals—beginning with pacing on and off the mound. I asked, 'Could we reduce the 'walk-around' to twice instead of three times?' Then we addressed cap twirling exactly three times—again, could he manage reducing the 'tug' by one? Finally, his most telling symptom would be re-enacted, spread eagling both his lanky arms, which was accompanied by a startling barking sound. Could he lower the volume down one click? Stretching one's arms is a natural movement for a pitcher—yet it had become joined to the symptomatic tic vocalization. Could he yell into his mitt instead of after the out-stretching arm ritual? As we worked on reducing the frequency and intensity in slight increments, only then would I allow him to release the foam ball—which, in session, was a reward for both of us.

During training time, I discussed these measures with his coach. Adjusting the environment for a handicapped individual is critical for accommodation, beginning with enlisting the cooperation of his coach. We all agreed that Tom now needed to be used sparingly only in low-pressure situations—especially not in relief for a 'save'. The coach was to monitor the frequency and intensity of obsessive pre-pitch rituals and how they impacted his capacity to compete. These observations included keeping detailed process notes in the naturalized setting which were brought to session. This record keeping was critical to give both the coach and me a snapshot of Tom's performance.

After two months of early spring therapy, I drove to his high school field and surreptitiously watched Tom pitch a game. Again, it was not unusual for this therapist to go into the field as part of applying naturalistic observation. With adaptations in place by the coaching staff and the focus now being to protect the boy, his symptoms had become more tempered. His quirks remained visible, especially when the other players' failings led him to be visibly upset. He pitched well, however, keeping his composure for four innings and giving up just one run. The most evident advance was his ability to vocalize into his glove rather than with more obvious outstretched arms. Afterwards, I made myself known and greeted Tom and his parents. They were delighted that I had made the effort to attend a game—and thankful I had not let him see me. We both shared the hopes that the Lyme disease would remain dormant and most of his Tourette syndrome was in remission. As for his wind-up and delivery, it was an action creative response that was indeed something beautiful to behold.

Thirteen
Mood Involvements

Creativity of Mania

Issues of mood regulation in the art world reached crisis proportions when, in 1888, the artist Paul Gauguin arrived at The Yellow House in the south of France to join his comrade Vincent van Gogh on a painting holiday. Gauguin encountered an artist obsessed. Van Gogh appeared to him as an ascetic monk, devoted only to spreading the doctrine of a 'new' art (see the painting *Self-Portrait Dedicated to Paul Gauguin,* www.harvardartmuseums.org/art/299843). At other times, Gauguin would find him transformed, a raving drunk whose outrageous antics drove his friend from the house in Arles within only a few months. His unpredictable, exulted, frenzied behaviour became too much even for his equally eccentric best friend. Van Gogh ended up hospitalized—self-mutilated and unhinged—although his creative faculties remained spectacularly intact. Anyone who has gazed into the saffron field with crows in flight (*Wheat Field with Crows,* www.vangoghmuseum.nl/en/collection/s0149V1962) must have experienced the awe and mystery that van Gogh miraculously captured in his final months.

Dysregulation of moods and feeling states can also occur with equal drama in child artists on the manic spectrum. After years of focusing on adult bipolar, the paediatric form has now been given greater consideration. The arc of the spectrum includes those symptoms whose intensity and severity include volatile mood swings, euphoric or magical thinking, and depressive episodes severe enough to include suicidal ideation (Papolos & Papolos, 2006). The markers seen in the paediatric form may be as complex as van Gogh's—with prolonged periods of lucidity, piety, sophisticated cultural interests and hyperfocused behaviours, such as creative activity. Paediatric symptoms may be equally diverse and contradictory especially since they are still immaturely formed. Various markers may mask the condition, as children may be diagnosed with symptoms of ADHD or depression or have the condition dismissed as a matter of exuberant temperament. Many individuals on the manic end are highly productive, overcompensating with high-level performances that are desirable in school and social situations.

All these issues came into play with a bright fourth-grader named Shelly, whose intellectual prowess was matched by the intensity of her classroom conduct. She was well behaved but tended to exhaust every teacher with her hyperdiligence—asking and answering her own constant questions. A perfectionistic child, she often overworked her assignments, completed extra-credit projects and excelled at creative activity. She was undiagnosed and unmedicated, as the parents were reluctant to acknowledge there was a problem—after all, she was a straight-A student with relatively good conduct. But the school saw otherwise. In class and groups, she tended to be controlling and bossy; hence, her teachers convened a team meeting which I attended, where they urged a workup and counselling.

Shelly often required 'reining in', as in class situations with her peers and in groups she could be ridiculing or even a bully. Yet the child was not just bright but also an avid draftsman. She responded well to art therapy, which became a means of bypassing her highly evolved linguistic defences. Her drawings told the full story. Shelly drew on, chatting away, yet refused to acknowledge any unwarranted behaviours. Efforts to promote self-regulation and -observation were then designated the main goals. Shelly happily obliged to draw out her issues, elaborating and articulating each as though she was fully cognizant of their social implications. She required no stimulus. In one instance, she announced she would recount a moment when she was asked to solve a problem at the chalkboard—an innocent enough theme but was also an invitation to a mixed outcome (Figure 13.1). Well after her math problem was solved, Shelly proceeded to *take over* as the teacher, as the drawing matter of factly demonstrates.

In a frenzy of action, Shelly is shown pointing at the board, calling on students and complimenting her peers for getting the right answer. She is even shown

Figure 13.1 Differentiating between a high-energy child and early-onset bipolar is not easily diagnosed. This bright young artist was a 'force' when the teacher allowed her to take over the class!

dismissing a child to go to the restroom. The intensity of the narrative is achieved with well-crafted composition, word balloons and animating the participants. Momentarily overpowering even her teacher, she was resolutely told to take her seat and spoken to after the period. Yet Shelly's mother did not recognize any problem, as this was a gifted, articulate and handsome child whose performance was stellar—aside from going 'overboard'. 'Why mess with a good thing?' the mom quipped.

As Kay Redfield Jamison's story of her own mania attests, the bipolar condition fuelled her extraordinary accomplishments, a trait which was reinforced by her academic colleagues (1997). She drove herself relentlessly to reach ever-higher heights of productivity until her world came crashing down. Would Shelly's mania evolve into bipolar as Jamison's finally did, eventually plunging her into despair and suicidal depression? One never knows the course of the spectrum arc in such a young child, whether her moods would begin to swing, especially towards the depressive end. If this did constitute childhood mania, its course would be impossible to predict, as the paediatric form is unstable and still maturing alongside the child. In supervision, Dr. Hecht sought to raise the mother's awareness of Shelly's being predisposed for such a condition, as it ran in the family. It was important to monitor whether Shelly would begin to experience 'lows' along with seemingly everlasting highs. With only a consultation and five sessions of creative arts therapy, we shall never know whether the child's moods became polarized—or whether her social or school relationships became a debilitating issue. But the drawing remains a testament to the spectrum child who can be superior in almost every way, but remains at risk for future pathology.

Naming the Monster

Bipolar can be masked by these and other strengths, which can present as intensely creative and productive. However, high-level functioning often occurs according to the child's favoured areas of interest, to the exclusion of Barkley's 'low reward' activities (Barkley & Newcorn, 2009). Because of the extremes of self-regulation, bipolar may present functionally as ADD or ADHD, yet the two disorders distinctly differ, with the emphasis being that of mood lability and regulation.

One young man, Allan, a teen originally from Europe, was a gifted actor, debater and artist who was seen in expressive arts therapy from age twelve to twenty-one. He was intense in session, as his passionate storytelling knew no bounds, from discussing the injustices of law enforcement, to the character flaws of Hamlet, to wrapping himself in medieval lore and Arthurian legends. These subjects he would describe in exhaustive and vivid detail for the entire session, if permitted. For the first four years, we worked through a family trauma, by which time, at sixteen, he began to manifest markers of undisguised mania *and* depression.

Video gaming was a perfect fit for when his lethargy took over from his 'highs'. Sitting in the darkness for hours with the now-vintage and relatively tame 'Grand Theft Auto' thrumming, the video game would fill a crucial void for his diminished social and acting life. On occasion, Allan would 'draw out his demons', which was guaranteed to be a mixed outcome. In one session, he drew a violent scenario where a policeman's head is forced into a blender by an uncommented-upon, alien-type creature (Figure 13.2). It is a graphic image of aggression, mitigated only by the fantastical scenario.

When I questioned why the officer deserved such a fate, he murmured that the 'pig had it coming'. The policeman who had purportedly mistreated his suspect was a reference to his own family's misfortunes. His aggressive thoughts rendered him mindblind to any empathic understanding of how it constituted a graphic reaction. Adolescents with active spectrum issues are often vehemently anti-authoritarian in the manner of the 'extreme male brain', previously described by Baron-Cohen (2002). Allan was all about 'being in the right', that righteous indignation becomes necessary at times and thus expressing extreme violence is an appropriate reaction. Dr. Hecht considered the work a negative outcome, disturbing enough to adjust his medication levels.

Figure 13.2 Early-onset bipolar can be debilitating and is often masked by ADHD and other spectrum disorders. Anti-authority fantasies were explored, a backlash against law enforcement.

To address symptoms of mania, mood swings, distractibility and perseveration on hyperfocused topics, Dr. Hecht began to titrate medications. Comorbid issues included lack of focus, neglected academics and oscillations between ecstatic and darkened moods. Allan, however, resisted medication—describing life on lithium as feeling like a piece of 'dead wood'. Refusing medication for those with mania has a long tradition, as it dulls the creative 'high'. This is a popular notion among those with 'artistic temperaments' whose lifestyles provided cover or masked symptoms. Jamison describes in *Touched with Fire* (1993) how the great Romantic poets, particularly Lord Byron, wrote of his 'impassioned moods and fiery highs' as a 'fine madness' and his lows mixed with highs as 'to those who, by the dint of glass and vapour, discovers stars, and sail in the wind's eye' (cited in Jamison, 1993).

During art therapy, Allan continued creating monsters, which we attempted to 'name'. Being a verbal person, I attempted to have him narrate his works to clarify and give a sense of reality to his creations. I was vigilant that he not 'feed off' his associations to escalate his emotions further. Hence the verbal stimulus possessed a double edge. Now in high school, he created another 'all-powerful monster', whom he stated 'easily annihilates his enemies yet saves the righteous'. It is a superbly drawn yet fearful dog-faced creature with a long samurai braid, spiked elbow crests and dagger paws (Figure 13.3).

Allan was still exploring the dichotomies between good and evil, full of magical and realistic references, indicative of a tenuous ego that suffered lapses into primary process 'leakage'. He described the superhero's 'strengths of conviction', but when asked about the quality of its decision-making process, as to who is saved and who gets killed off, he was evasive … it was too pointed a question on my part. He disregarded my query and went on to describe how its bodily form could shape shift to an unassuming man, one who could blend in socially and become an actor or writer or even a member of the king's court. Here again, fantasy was linked to his wish fulfilment, with his alienating diatribes remaining barely contained. He then wrote on the creature's need to self-protect if it were to be effective, a clear reference to his own sensitivities to social insecurity.

Allan and I spent the last three years in therapy while he was at university, seeing him while on campus in New York City. Free to discontinue his medication altogether, his social life began to suffer, as few peers could withstand his unending rants. When in his lows, lethargy and again the 'dead wood' feeling would return. Allan struggled with the demands of these side effects while navigating his major and the fast-paced culture of the university. He oscillated between isolating himself and struggling through courses, which required high-level acting. In therapy, he had also now become consumed by 'avatars', characters chosen as his 'embodiment' as part of his gaming life. These were not childlike fantasies but had evolved, along with his intellect, as deeper, more sophisticated obsessions. It is a fascinating illustration of how maturing executive control still struggles to manage id-derived intrusions. In the heat of passion, he lectured me on the Sanskrit meaning of 'Vishnu', meaning 'descending from' as the destroyer of worlds, being incarnated into earthly form. He explained how after a visit to a

Figure 13.3 This same teen, Allan, was an avid gamer when depressed, whose characters were translated into evocative figure drawings. This samurai creature is rendered with control despite its aggression.

wolf sanctuary he had taken on the mythological 'werewolf', or more properly, the 'lycanthrope', as his avatar. It is a creature of almost universal folklore that could undergo a metamorphosis from man to wolf hybrid and embodied power, stealth and immortality. It also had 'vulnerabilities', Allan lamented—from the full moon to wolfsbane, every culture back to Roman antiquity had developed a remedy to combat the archetypal creature.

When he began drawing his avatar, he took the piece home, worked on it and then brought it back to the next week's session as a fully formed figure—another zoomorph which possessed an intensity that overcame any other predecessors (Figure 13.4).

It was a fully formed expression and sensitively rendered figure shown howling in emotional pain. The face is hidden, but its body language captures the essence

Figure 13.4 During Allan's freshman year at university, he took on the avatar of a werewolf as a protective totem. Fantasy was an outlet for his imagination when assuming manic proportions.

of his suffering. The sensitively drawn figure is powerful, but remained part of an active fantasy life with a magical sense of an ego ideal. While his mania could blur the boundaries between the fantastic and the real, he never fully regressed to delusional states. This line is often tenuous and in flux, staggering in frequency and intensity as the child attempts to reconcile the oncoming storm of volatile moods.

Manga and Raw Aggression

In another case, a fourteen-year-old girl struggled with bouts of mania with highly labile moods with almost constant aggressive ideation and conflict. Denise was an artistic young teen who was in conflict over everything: new friends, new clothes, new digital devices and increased personal freedoms. In many instances, she could not communicate her needs without resorting to profanity and threats. She could not handle her tantrum impulses especially within the demands of the social school setting. Wild and non-compliant at home, it was a glimpse of how a girl expresses unbridled aggression.

Denise's cartooning skills were meant as private creations, which usually went unshared, but became the focus of our work together for two years of art and bibliotherapy. They consisted of mostly violent-laced video game heroes laced with Japanese manga, with anime images of little doe-eyed 'school girls'—a disturbingly ubiquitous aesthetic among young and old in Japan. A favourite was the manga series *Gunslinger Girls*. The plot supposedly revolved around a mental health rehabilitation agency, when in actuality, it was a 'black op', a secret government military operation which employed young traumatized girls who were easy to brainwash. They were then fitted with cybernetic implants endowing them with super strengths and became trained ninja assassins at the behest of a rogue government agency, not exactly a prime stimulus for a child with hypermanic and aggressive temperament.

After one memorable occasion, Denise came to session directly after an altercation with another girl and began creating a storyboard drawing series. The series of images done in silence is self-explanatory. She handed the piece to me without comment, perhaps finding the drawing too disturbing and was perhaps more secure in my possession. Given its wildly aggressive expressions with broken yet deft line work and screamed-out word balloons of threats of violence, it was a positive outcome to articulate her feelings and fantasized powers (Figure 13.5).

Though Denise was not personally violent, the images point to a conundrum in the creative response. Did allowing a personal stimulus reinforce the twisted Japanese manga culture driven by adult male fantasies? Do the images precipitate actual violence? In creating her own version, does such image making absorb, deflect and perhaps neutralize some of these intensely antisocial and aggressive feelings? Or does it stimulate them enough that the fragile and labile child actuates them in real life?

These questions must be left to the researchers who measure the incidents of media-induced violence, whose conclusions vary. Miller (2017) reports that Japan's long-standing tradition and subculture includes sexualizing pubescent girls and figures prominently in manga—it has been an adult iconic cultural form for several generations. It also may act as a supernormal stimulus. Its appeal fits Tinbergen's definitions for this phenomenon, which has since been revised by Deirdre Barrett (2010) to include video and other cultural icons whose exaggerated features unconsciously act as powerful stimuli. These may elicit id-derived responses which defy individual and cultural rationality. Barrett was one of the first in the field of human ethology to examine the effects of the supernormal stimulus and apply it to video game addiction, pornography and visual imagery—which certainly qualifies the exaggerated facial traits of anime.

As a creative response activity, it required the input of the therapeutic team. Would these images and fantasies of revenge be allowed to continue to be expressed if they began to be acted out? The team would have to implement the

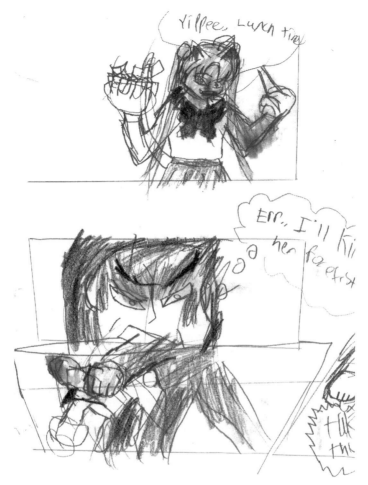

Figure 13.5 Manga and anime content can be particularly violence-toned. Shelley's manic and anger issues were expressed using a storyboard format, based upon anime video gaming.

'cannot handle policy rule', explaining to the child that, at this time, the situation has become too much to handle. Proclaiming that the child can't handle a situation does not imply they are somehow 'bad', but just for the time being, requires limit setting or assistance from others. The team considered whether her expressions were cathartic and healthy displacement until her behaviours proved otherwise. While little headway was made in neutralizing the intensity of her reactivity and obsession with anime, the goals nonetheless were attained, as she never became overtly violent to peers or others. It remained to be seen that once more stressful demands were placed upon her, more violent-prone behaviours might begin to escalate.

Fourteen
Delusions and the 'Other World'

Private Worlds

Hallucinatory delusions may accompany children on the autistic continuum which become ego-syntonic, becoming integral to the child's thinking and feeling states. For children with developed self-awareness, they may also be kept a guarded secret lest others find that they are 'harbouring' bizarre delusions. One young teen, A.J., finally confided, after four years of art therapy, that he was often accompanied by what he referred to as the 'presence'. He described it initially as a hazy, transparent figure, a being from another world, which hovered over his shoulder, whispering to him. He occasionally responded, arguing back to leave him alone—which to others was seen as strangely talking to himself. At other times while being tormented, his behaviour became almost identical to a Tourette's tic, as A.J. would jerk his head and murmur something inaudible over his shoulder. Unbeknownst to anyone, this tic was an adaptive measure to ward off that which invaded his mental space. After almost a year of art therapy, A.J. finally gave graphic form to the 'presence' (Figure 14.1).

It is an amorphous, eye-like apparition, which appeared hovering in the periphery and dissipated especially when attempts at 'eye contact' were made. It whispered things into his ear and basically tormented him for years, coming and going with seeming randomness. By his externalizing the 'presence' through the creative response, it was hoped the presence would be 'robbed of its thunder', yet the child later indicated that this was not the case. It seemed to aggravate the presence to the extent that it warned the child 'never to draw him again'.

Such is the power of the primary process on the autistic continuum; it can exert its id-derived pressures with tremendous longevity, like a recurring, sometimes lifelong, nightmare. To combat these disturbances, medication regimens were revisited, schoolwork was no longer mandatory, and in session we reverted to craftwork. Concrete and predictable, craftwork was intended to keep the child grounded, not allowing the imagination to wander—but to keep imagery out of the child's otherwise tormented consciousness. As the boy moved through four years of individual therapy and summer camp, the presence began to wane as he readied for adaptive college. Perhaps it had run its developmental course, or the

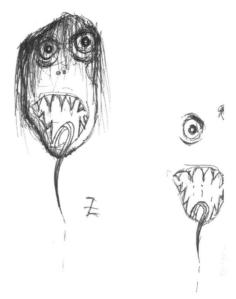

Figure 14.1 Apparitions, delusional companions and other distortions of perception can be part of the autistic spectrum arc. This boy felt a 'presence' whenever he became lost in his own world.

cumulative effects of long-term therapeutic intervention eventually contributed to neutralizing this horrific apparition.

Filtering the Intrusive Thought

Filtering has been cited as a challenge to individuals on the spectrum, as was observed in the last vignette—as a child's delusions were persecutory and perceived as incredibly real. One boy, Lonnie, also experienced invasive thoughts so vividly that they were an actual movie. These disturbed sensations were freely pictorialized throughout his art as a means of expunging them from *inside* his head—another example of creating proximity distancing. Lonnie's drawing was a kind of sympathetic magic—that if he drew his persecutors being chased off and defeated, it might well come true. It is yet another interesting parallel to the shaman's work. If drawing could help drive the bad spirits away, the sufferer might be left in peace.

His narrative drawing concretely addresses the torture of being plagued by his constant invasive thoughts. In this piece, Lonnie's memories seemed to take on a life of their own (Figure 14.2).

Its compartments perhaps provide a tentative measure of protection. Harking back to Grandin's memories of her mind being an 'open microphone', this intrusive 'presence' is given a full measure of form on the page. It exists as a faceless shadow figure who is being chased angrily by the boy, who yields a hatchet to drive it away. The concept of 'time' perhaps intends to ground the proceedings,

Figure 14.2 Amongst some children on the autistic continuum, persecutory delusions may be secretly held in confidence. This piece is a psychic road-map of the child's thought processes and problem solving.

but is completely ambiguous. With a weak and vulnerable ego and tenuous filter, the creative response perhaps serves to bolster the weak stimulus barrier. By creation of something substantive, Lonnie's elements formed a distancing stimulus, including several physical barriers. The creative response activity enlisted the ego, attempting to rid the disturbance, like those dreamers who attempt to control their nightmares. In this case, I assisted the child in fending off the delusions and helped decipher the inner from the outer world. Building ego by cognitively scripting 'happy endings' assisted in grounding him as a form of sympathetic magic—if I said they were gone and pointed to his picture, he would take my word at face value. What is again interesting is that such delusional images do not loosen or overly distort the proceedings. Their fidelity remains at a high level despite the id-derived forces that brought them into being. The narrative of both form and content was remarkably intact. There was little regression in behaviour or the image, which is an astounding feat. It is a testament to the therapeutic emphasis upon building ego or executive function to compensate for these intrusions from the 'other world' as this next case also demonstrates.

Delusions during Lacrosse

Fantasy worlds may operate in parallel to relatively normal functioning—it happens all the time, as we may fantasize during the long workday, in transit or during downtime. It is perhaps an effective example of the 'default made network' inaction. With Kris's 'conflict-free sphere' in operation, even certain spectrum children possess sufficient ego to maintain fantasy-based thought processes. In one unique case, normative functioning continued even while the child suffered debilitating delusions. 'Kevin' was seen for two years in individual therapy for attention deficits, impulsivity and social awkwardness, though he was fully mainstreamed, had friends and was athletic. Despite his handicaps, he had made the freshman lacrosse team—a rare feat for a spectrum child, as the case material has already pointed out how rough contact sports present significant attentional and impulse-control challenges. In this case, Kevin's teachers and coach noticed moments when Kevin was not fully 'there', when he seemed to lose touch and become unresponsive—whether during math, on the playing field or walking home from school.

Unlike the children who secreted away their hallucinations, Kevin was quite candid when describing how he was seeing and hearing a 'devil dragon', among other creatures who were trying to influence his behaviour. He reported a pharaoh who stopped him right in his tracks in school, telling him to do 'bad things'. These became frequent enough that they began interfering with his schoolwork and especially his lacrosse game. After experiencing these 'messages' on the playing field, he was relieved to be benched by his coach and left alone to cope with these various 'beings'. During follow-up sessions, he drew elaborate images as a response to these delusional thought processes. In one complex image, we are confronted with the boy trapped in a maze of suffering (Figure 14.3).

After drawing this intricate maze with himself caught as though in a spider's web, he wrote a lucid, but roughly composed text which he incorporated into the image.

'I recently experienced visions. I come to see Dr. H. if I see evil things for instance

Once I saw a friend that had spiral horns with a pointed snout and sharp teeth on its head

And had fiery red flames around its body, giant dragon wings with a sharp spike tail.

Can I manage living with these images?
Can I live a normal life with them?
Right now, can I handle them without becoming a weirdo?'

This stunning admission involved a helpless boy who could articulate both visually and in writing the depths of his suffering. His articulation attested to his ego strength and capacity to compensate. He could depict himself caught in a labyrinth but was able to reach out to me, his therapist, and share his frightful experiences with raw honesty and insight, including his fears for the future. After this alarming piece was completed, the team was mobilized, for this was a sweeping regression. He was seen by Dr. Hecht for a psychiatric evaluation to determine

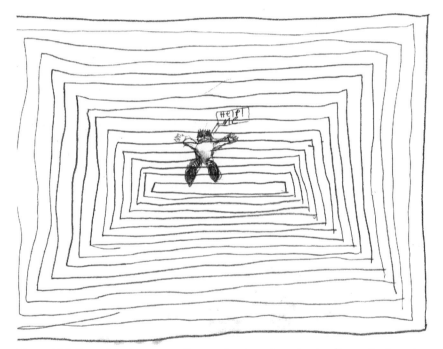

I Recently Experienced, visions. I
come to Dr. Henley if I see evil things
for instance once I saw a fiend that had redern
spiral rams horns, with a pointed snout and sharp teeth
on its head, and it had fiery red flames around its
body, giant Dragon like wings with a sharp one spike
tail.
can I manage living with these images?
can I live a normal life with them,
right now can I handle them without be coming
a wierdo?

Figure 14.3 Some delusions are undiagnosed and require extensive diagnostics to sort out. This boy with attention deficits revealed hallucinations both pictured and described in writing.

whether a low dose of an anti-psychotic would have some efficacy. It proved to do so, but its side effects deadened his motivation and coordination for competitive sport. His sympathetic and insightful teacher was in phone contact throughout the crisis. In the spirit of a 'least restrictive' educational accommodation, she agreed to scale back academic assignments to concentrate solely on tasks that focused upon his clarity of thinking.

He was sent for an fMRI to ascertain the existence of any brain lesions, seizure activity or other neurological hard signs. Since Kevin was on speaking terms with his delusionary figures, we began having him 'vocally answer back', admonishing it to 'stay away', to even be rude and tell it sternly to 'shut up'. I helped him visualize 'slamming a big freezer door on the image, to keep it locked inside, frozen so it couldn't speak'. Yet even this cognitive intervention proved too strong, as envisioning being trapped in a freezer became 'stuck' in his mind, rendering it a negative outcome. Adjustments in medication and cognitive-behavioural interventions had mixed results in tempering the frequency of auditory and visual hallucinations. There came the expected 'symptom substitution' as he began to indiscriminately have 'yelling' arguments directed not just at the apparition, but also to his parents and siblings. Amazingly at the same time, Kevin discussed his burgeoning crush on a neighbourhood girl, expressing with a dark humour how it was the 'worst time for this to happen'. We then worked for weeks on keeping his thoughts and dialogue 'inside' and 'quieted', to not betray his torments in this critical first-crush relationship. He befriended this girl, taking walks in the park, and did well to manage his delusions, which gradually went into remission. His medication regimen was monitored, while the teacher and I remained in close phone contact, alerting each other to any new behaviours to the clinical team and his parents. For the following four months, process notes indicate sporadic symptoms, severe enough to keep him out of competitive sport. Only time would tell whether these delusions were a precursor to dreaded diseases such as schizophrenia. Yet for the time being, this young man's struggles remained a positive and productive process—one that attests to the benefits of long-term, team coordinated, therapeutic support and creative expression.

Fifteen
The Written Word

Breaking the Negative Cycle

For many children on the spectrum, any form of writing is torturous. In academic writing, they deal with deficits of receptive and expressive language, from simple spelling, to engaging figures of speech, auditory recall, organization and even vestibular involvements of balancing the pen. The ability to imagine what other characters are feeling or thinking brings back the mindblindness issue. Characters' feelings may not be accessible to the child on the autistic end of the spectrum. Contemporary culture does not help the cause, as written communication has become so truncated and cursory through rapid text messaging that formal expression has become expendable. Even phoning someone to tell a story is too time consuming—or expressions are saved for social media. As most children associate writing as part of the educational curriculum, they have already experienced a repeated cycle of failures and negative feelings towards this as an expressive medium. In creative response activities, therapeutic writing tries to distance itself from school chores and reframe it as an enjoyable means of reaching out to another. Witness Kevin's eloquent statement (pg. 241) about suffering his demonic visions. Despite this debilitation, he was still articulate and emotionally communicative. Writing is perhaps at its most powerful while its author is under such duress. Kevin found that combining writing with images is in line with Grandin's observations that many children are visual thinkers.

In creative response therapy, penning a letter is still seen as possessing therapeutic, social and evocative power. However, it often requires an engaging and novel stimulus to jump-start the process. In the alternative therapeutic school, I began one creative writing assignment by reading the emotion-laden yet formal letters of the near-illiterate Civil War soldiers. These young men were the same age as the students, which for them was a difficult concept to grasp. In eloquent terms, they expressed their loneliness, fear of impending violence, camaraderie of fellow soldiers and hopes for the future—all issues which still resonated. I explained how many of these writers possessed the most meagre education, much of it coming from reading the Bible. This great work of literature enabled them to become literate enough to compose letters with a formal grammar, with a dignity that has been lost in the curtness of contemporary culture. The art of letter writing has all but vanished in contemporary society—such that many of the children in our private practice had never written one, except on the computer. Computer-facilitated writing helps overcome the dysgraphia and other issues associated with writing by hand. However, I remain resolute that to totally *abandon* handwriting just because it is a struggle, gives in to the handicapping condition. It is an important means of expression—as a stimulus for self-expression and long a benchmark of what it means to be civilized!

During therapy, I made it a point as a creative activity to mark occasions in the children's lives by having them create a card on blank stock, decorate and inscribe it, to send to loved ones, friends, even Santa. To send and receive a card or letter I believe is still a great pleasure. The responses were almost always positive. Parents, friends and families of the children all expressed delight at receiving a note of thanks, acknowledging one's loss or grieving of a pet, a note from one's summer vacation, even a letter to the North Pole. Even for the youngest or severe child, a scribbly figure captured a moment of their feeling that, when mailed, conveyed personal feeling. We often sent our cards off with an activity, by walking to the local post office, choosing interesting stamps and slipping them through the send slots—which often created excitement and even appreciation by the postal workers. They came to expect our little troopers, with bundles of cards at the ready, and played along in being sensitive and helpful.

In the therapeutic school, we made a point of sending letters to the newspaper editor when in our spirited classroom debates it was decided their opinions should become part of a wider public discussion. In one instance, the students discussed and then protested the state's first impending 'bear hunt'. To their amazement, the class's letter was published—such is the excitement and power of the written word. It began as a class discussion and then expanded to the afternoon's activity—such was the 'organic' nature of the curriculum. If something was 'hot' we stayed with it. During the group discussion, our most literate student became the 'scribe', condensing differing opinions, editing the document and then in group work helping articulate the class's consensus on the position taken.

The medium need not be focused on 'doing' the writing. One teen on the autistic end enjoyed combing antique stores for old sepia-toned postcards of strangers, which are full of endearments and stories from across time and across the world. An idiosyncratic hobby, I often wondered if these remote writers from the past somehow taught this bright young man the 'language of the other', leading to greater insight into their mind-sets and emotions. Such is the circuitous route teaching may take.

The Light

I have also cited an example where social media presented an opportunity for two children to be brought together as pen pals, despite being separated by

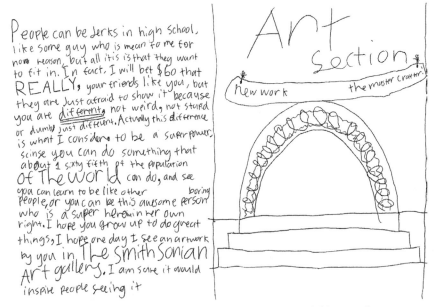

People can be Jerks in high school, like some guy who is mean to me for no reason, but all it is is that they want to fit in. In fact, I will bet $60 that REALLY, your friends like you, but they are just afraid to show it because you are different, not weird, not stupid or dumb, just different. Actually this difference is what I consider to be a superpower, scinse you can do something that about 1 sixty fifth of the population of the world can do, and see you can learn to be like other boring people, or you can be this awesome person who is a super hero in her own right. I hope you grow up to do great things, I hope one day I see an artwork by you in The Smithsonian Art gallery. I am sure it would inspire people seeing it

Art Section
new work   the master crafter

Figure 15.1 Social media has allowed for connectivity amongst children on the spectrum. This boy sent a handwritten letter and drawing from a half a world away in response to a child's posting. His new found pen-pal answered electronically within a matter of seconds.

three continents. When a seventh-grade girl with undisclosed spectrum markers reached out to others online about her social issues, a ten-year-old boy named Austin didn't respond via computer. Instead, he wrote and illustrated his best wishes all the way from *New Zealand*. His message is one of optimism and hope, expressing 'everybody should be like her' (Figure 15.1).

Reverting to his autistic mechanized sensibilities that have been illustrated throughout the text, he develops a machine for cloning the girl (not shown). He deems her so special that 'difference is really a superpower'. Accompanied by a card from the parents, who also wished the girl well, it was the exotic postage stamps that also thrilled the girl most. His letter, a mix of literary, pictorial and conceptual work, overflowed with empathy for the girl, but also blended his own challenges of being on the spectrum. Many on the autistic continuum have a directness and unblinking honesty that embraces the postmodern ideal of mixed outcomes. The idea of 'I', 'you', 'we' and 'others' worked simultaneously together, a rhetorical device enabling Austin to convey a truth involving several dimensions. Such is the nature of these children, mixing raw sincerity, an autistic form of empathy and some creative high jinks—all can work together, becoming in this case a piece of mail art. Separated by thousands of miles, kick-started by a posting on social technology, a cry from down under was heard, and a kindred spirit was inexplicably found. His message was not to give up, using a form of creative response which was expressed in the most eloquent written and endearing illustrated form.

Light Leads to Dark

Expressive writing may motivate children and teens to also express negative feelings with candour and honesty, that captures their struggles 'in the raw'. At the alternative school where we had penned the letter to the local newspaper, I also attempted to have them write poems. Poetry therapy was conceived as a combined sensory, academic and therapeutic activity. For brevity's sake, I introduced the haiku as a therapeutic form of writing, in which they tried to capture the 'rasa' of something personal in just a few lines. Using the haiku model of a 5/7/5 syllable count, I recited aloud, not just for the beauty of these poetic images, but also emphasized to dramatic effect—'how short they were!' For those who would participate, we took turns reading the seventeenth-century Japanese master, Basho, who wrote:

> With every gust of wind
> The butterfly changes its place
> on the willow.

The Zen sensibility engages sensory experienced nature themes, which may be so fleeting and instantaneous that they are ordinarily overlooked. Appreciating them requires a degree of observation, mindfulness, even a stillness of thinking, all faculties in short supply with these students (and many typical others). The poems also sometimes embrace suffering and expressions which honestly express feelings passionately. With brevity on its side, several of the students created short but sometimes illuminating images, such as giving a desirous glance, punching a fist in the air, or seeing new-fallen snow on an evergreen. While many were derogatory or gave little effort, others could pen a few simple lines using this structure, which helped the students capture the simplest thought or sensory impression.

The haiku project was planned as a multisensory project. Beginning with mindfulness for the sensitive observation of nature, next came a few attempts at writing. Once some jottings were created, we added a visual component of photocopying something of personal value. Next to the blackened page were a bracelet, a car fob or a torn collage element. The poems were then written next to their images. In this way, I hoped to increase personal investment, using several art forms to combine several projects into one. After the students copied their poems next to their images, these were videotaped, with either the students or me overdubbing the reading of their verse. The added element of the video helped animate the poem, giving it a personalized image and stronger voice. Against the black copy paper and contrasting white oil crayon, the poems became more 'special'—feeling alive and artful. It was also a video broadcast, which formalized the recital—especially if others wished to view their work.

One bright young man who lived in the backwoods of rural New Jersey and rarely spoke created an image I almost confiscated but then intuitively allowed, a silhouette of a rifle. Next to the image, he contextualized this reference:

With the squirrel shot
We licked our lips, into the pot,
In went the tomato and game.

By not reacting to the gun image and biding my time to see what developed, I was rewarded with an appropriate use of an otherwise forbidden symbol. Out came a poem from a boy usually hidden away in hoodie and silence. Another young man, Jacob, was a seventeen-year-old on convict parole. When asked about his contribution, he handed me a paper consisting of a single profanity: the word 'fuck'. While not consumable for the other students, for this hyperactive and barely literate teen, it constituted a start. Again, I tried not to 'react' by not rejecting the 'piece' outright and tried to accept it seriously. Jacob responded with mixed emotions, first ridiculing me for accepting his 'nonsense' but also piquing his interest enough that he remained awake for the rest of the activity. However, he was disappointed that I would not permit it to be filmed or have the one-word obscenity recited. While I acknowledged that everyone from popes to presidents uses the 'F' word in *certain situations*—it should be used sparingly to amplify or accentuate the meaning of a phrase. I suggested to revisit this word later in the week to see whether we could rework it enough to pass the class's behavioural 'private expression rule'. Deprived of a profanity-laced opportunity to act out, he responded with indifference. I then proposed that we watch a film where *fuck* is used with greater strength and is not 'gratuitous'. This was a critical buzzword. It was used almost daily, with the idea that any violent or sexual profanity can be expressively useful, but such expressions become gratuitous when they are markedly unnecessary. We spent months debating and working on that distinction.

On Friday media day, I announced we'd screen some scenes from John Boorman's coming of age film *Hope and Glory* (1987). This 'creative film therapy' segment involved a story of children who lived through the Battle of Britain. When the Luftwaffe left London's East end in flaming ruins, British children often were left to fend alone with their mates. They played amongst the rubble of their neighbourhood with hardly any supervision—Dad might be away at the front or fighting fires, while Mom might be working in the munitions factory or out scrounging for food. While their adventures seemed quaint to the students by today's standards, one element caught the class's attention. The children decided amongst themselves that only 'one word' was sacred to their 'tribe'. It was forbidden to use unless the direst circumstances *demanded* its use. It was a 'call to arms', an emergency red alert used as a *last resort*. At the appointed time during the film's most dramatic life-and-death scene, a boy cried 'FUCK!', at which time the children sprang into action and convened together to deal with the present crisis.

While writing in response to the film, I approached Jacob yet again and asked, 'How would *you* use the word if "made special"'? Jacob responded, barely audibly murmuring, 'how bout "fuck this or that"'. Again, it was a start. By the end of the project, he was at last able to articulate 'why' it was fuck 'this' in this haiku-like poem in what I assume was about facing his dreary school days … a condition of his parole:

> Fuck the morning, sleep still in eyes.
> Pillow Head …
> What the Fucks—Fuck the whys.

This ex-convict had written his first verse to dramatic effect, using the profanity as an intensifier. While still not ready for prime time, it was accepted and even graded. I began reflecting about the poem. I was reminded how serious literature, even the storied *The New Yorker* magazine, has begun including the word in their magazines, both in reportage and fiction. As the standard bearer of great journalism, the current editors could take a lesson from Boorman's film, as well this young man's poem. Aroused by this thought, I began some informal research, making note of the word's use in each issue over sixteen weeks. I found that the word was used *weekly*, often to almost no dramatic effect—in other words, *gratuitously*. The word appeared in different forms on average three times per issue—from politics, to fiction, to personality profiles. While not so nihilistically used as was the case with Jacob, to my sensibility it was even worse; its intent seemed *trendy*. Who am I, then, to be calling my students 'out' for being profanely inappropriate? What is this magazine's intellectual intent? Attention seeking? Has *The New Yorker* become so irrelevant that a new generation of editors finds its use profanely hip—re-branding it to avoid its being stodgy? Such hypocrisy goes unnoticed by these disenfranchised teens. Such is the world in which we live.

Rhymes Straight from the Hospital

On rare occurrences, children on the spectrum display such serious mental illness after a traumatic episode that hospitalization may become a necessity. Mixed-type hyperactivity and mania exist on the spectrum and touch many points on the curve: intense emotional dysregulation, attention deficits, social awkwardness and any number of other psychiatric symptoms. One thirteen-year-old boy named Tim was hospitalized after a psychotic manic episode when his mother was diagnosed with terminal cancer and could no longer care for her boys. After his inpatient stay, his symptoms were ameliorated, and he was mainstreamed back to public school. I was called upon to act as his therapeutic companion in school. Three times each week, we engaged in creative projects while I helped establish whether it was safe enough to keep him in the mainstream setting. With little experience in being an outside consultant and with such a fragile child with suicidal ideation, the stakes were never more serious.

During the month's period of gaining trust, he began to bring in his 'secret' shoe boxes. They contained wadded up papers with fragments of 'slant' rhymes, which in the hip-hop form were pieced together for rapping. Most had free-associative verbiage with rude rhymes, such as:

'George Bush, more and more the mush,
kiss my tush, just smoke some kush,
… check out that bush!'

There were perhaps a thousand rhymes in three boxes, which he seemed to have catalogued by heart. I asked whether he had put together a full rap, and he replied he had but that he was not satisfied with the results and perhaps we could 'get something together'. Seeing him three times a week afforded me the time to observe this eighth-grader closely and learn to handle his labile moods, allowing me to gauge his mental health or creativity on any given day. It enabled me to check in with the supervisor of the child study team to mark his stability and suitability for mainstream middle school.

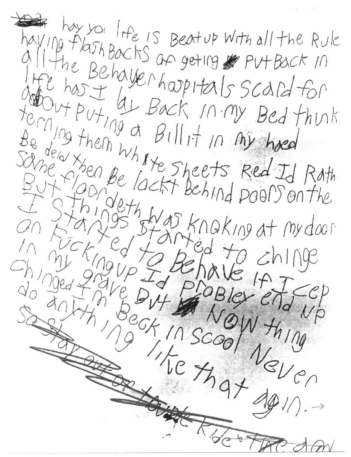

Figure 15.2 Writing rhymes or rapping has become a major cultural and expressive force, especially for children who find conventional writing a taxing and uninspiring process.

As he progressed, I suggested to him that formalizing his work might yield results. Everyone has unfinished projects, I told him, which they 'just can't get together'. This boy's case was no different—except for frequency and intensity of fragmented and fearful thoughts. He became stable enough to increase the demands on our project other than my just sitting beside and passively listening. In the third month, he brought in a short rap with a beat which we had set up for him to record over. Tim had begun a series of rhymes which directly addressed his hospital stay. This was surprising given our relatively brief relationship and budding therapeutic alliance. Illustrated in Figure 15.2, Tim's words are written verbatim.

It was a powerful moment when he rapped it:

> Hey yo, life is beat up with all the rule
> Having flashbacks of getting put back in
> all the behavioural hospitals—scared for
> life as I lay back in my bed think'n
> about putting a bullet in my head
> turning the white sheets red
> I'd rather be dead than be back locked behind doors
> on the same floor
> Death was knocking at my door
> But things started to change
> On fucking up
> I'd probly end up in my grave
> But now things changed
> I'm back in school
> Never do anything like that again!
> So stay outa trouble kid
> Stay outa trouble
> Stay in school!

After the rap and making revisions from his first draft, he expressed a desire to be included in the school's talent show. I was taken aback, wondering if he could be serious: 'Putting a bullet in my head turning the white sheets red'? This moment of being 'taken aback' is one that has been a long thread running throughout the case material, conveying my continued fascination for these children.

In any event, his suggestion left me running to the child study team and principal. They conferred and expressed the hope that I could help Tim make the piece more palatable for a grade school audience. Tim agreed, toned down the 'white sheets red' imagery, deleted 'fuck' and then at my suggestion added an ending which involved some audience participation—to get the kids worked up, get the auditorium *moving*. The last three lines were amended:

So stay outta trouble kids
Don't be a fool
Stay in school
(Assembly to roar in unison)

Hey Yous! Who likes this school?
Can't hear you!!
Who likes our school?
Who likes our school?
We all do!
We all do!
(then recited alone)

'See that? That's why *I'm cool* ...'

Because I was teaching at university at the time, I could not attend the show to support or coach Tim. The principal who felt resistant to the idea (he was not happy having the boy in his *school*) eventually rose and helped Tim through his performance. He went a step further by prompting the children in the auditorium to join in on the chorus of 'We all do!, We all do, like our school'. He rallied the children, who were at first reserved and polite as was requisite for any school assembly in this rural, upper middle class school. But eventually the show caught fire, and their collective voices rose. Some were reported to have rapped along with Tim with all the hand-jiving and bad-assed attitude. The video taken indicates that the principal's facilitation was impeccable—not too patronizing for Tim, but standing nearby and being vigilant if he began to falter. He exemplified proper personal distance—close enough for emotional availability, yet far enough away to encourage Tim's individuation.

In the end, the creative response checked all the boxes of Kramerian-formed expression. Tim's use of the hip-hop form was economical to the point of monosyllabic. His self-confessional lyrics evoked a gamut of feeling, straight from the heart, communicated to an entire student body—to the point of their cheering on the last lines. Despite deleting some of the more graphic references, the artist remained true to himself—indeed, that he assented to having the work edited for student consumption indicated increased self-observation and regulation. Again, if the emotional and social payoff is significant enough, 'approach' may overcome 'avoidance'.

Sixteen

Shadow Syndromes and Religiosity

In searching my materials on individuals with subthreshold shadow syndromes, I found three examples with informed consent *and* strong imagery; each touched upon religion as a loose theme. Why, it is difficult to speculate. Perhaps there is a continual search for these individuals to decipher life's magicality—where faith and religion are barely separate from the realm of the 'real'. In the first example, reality testing was not so much an issue of magicality but of ethics and hypocrisy involved in culture and religious life.

The stimulus was to explore different cultural, political and spiritual topics within an elite charter school in Chicago with a well-informed, hand-chosen group of high school students. The medium of collage was employed, using images and text and photocopiers, which reflected the workshop's location in the school's library. It was part of a citywide 'conversation' about culture, beliefs and acceptance in high schools across Chicago. In this first case, the collage-based project became a creative response that pitted political and ethical reason against a test of faith.

Felipe was a gifted boy of Latino birth and a scholarship student who was pointed out to me as being introverted, with language deficits and other special needs. My immediate impression was that these issues were almost certainly linked to being raised as a child in a Latin American 'favela', where childhood traumas, impoverishment and limited English were the norm. He was another example of children whose environments had arrested their growth but who had retained the latent potential to compensate and achieve later developmental gains. Indeed, how does one pay attention without fully comprehending the culture and language? Felipe had compensated for his distractions by being, among other things, an excellent artist. I made a point to give him some individual attention, explaining in my limited Spanish the concept of how to choose the themes, as well as compositional possibilities of using background, midground and foreground as collage elements. Being considered gifted despite his language deficits, he grasped the concept and began a strongly opinionated piece, which given his introvertedness, surprised most of those in the small group. After much experimentation and reshuffling of themes and elements, he settled on elements which explored his feelings about his faith—which he later indicated he was devoted to—yet in conflict with.

Despite being pious within the liberal atmosphere of his elite private school, Felipe had developed enough self-awareness to exercise strong opinions of both his culture and religion. He expressed the historical and contemporary hypocrisy within the Roman Catholic Church. He explained to the group that he would collage a work exploring both his faith and the issues which led to a crisis of faith. He began with an image of the pope then, Pope John, in a news clipping of his visit to Latin America. As a Latin American himself, Pope John's visit was both an act of humanity but also an affront. During his visit, there were no apologies given for the treatment of his culture and the indigenous peoples, which the Church plundered for gold and then mercilessly 'consiguio borrado'—or 'rubbed out'. His theme also centred on the Church's backward views on birth control, which directly resulted in his country's dire overpopulation, poverty and crime in urban areas. He began to find images that would try to express his feelings, which were cut and pasted to appear as sufferers. Their contorted bodies would convey the impoverishment of the 'converts', while the Vatican functioned more as a corporate business, more interested in spreading doctrine and gathering riches than bringing parishioners closer to God.

In his three hours of work, he assembled a powerful composition—one that positions the pope 'at the top of the heap'. Felipe showed the pope in his immaculate finery, waving a dispassionate hand, and he announced the title would be taken from Genesis 1:28: 'Go Forth and Multiply'. The image of the pope was given added emphasis, as he is perched atop an entangled pile of emaciated bodies. Imagery flowed off the page, the only collage to do so within the group, again attesting to this boy's untapped giftedness. Text is shrewdly obscured with the words 'Help stop' … then a crafty suggestion of the word 'abuse'. The photocopies appeared intentionally grainy. When assembled they created an abstraction of human elements, each of which was overtly miserable. Only one figure was left intact; a young child is shown curled up like a foetus and is emphatically positioned closest to the pope (Figure 16.1).

After a lunch break, the group assembled for critiquing and journaling. When Felipe took his turn, he continued to express his intention, now firmed up through the collage. He felt enmity especially for the proselytizing missionaries and their charities who prey on the ignorance of the vulnerable and impressionable. In contrast is the greatest story ever told, that of Jesus, who became Christ and the symbol of sacrifice and redemption. His faith was unshakable, Felipe stated, and he had no plans to renounce it. Both ideas were held without being contradictory—again, cognitive or spiritual dissonance remains the hallmark of the postmodern ethos of the creative response mixed outcome.

All were awed by this creative response—enough that I immediately photocopied it—for this young man was so articulate and thoughtful but also desperately *trying* to remain a devout believer. He calmly delivered his argument, spoken in halting English. The well-crafted work was well received by the group, including several other Catholic students who voiced that he had the nerve to expose his true feelings. It was evocative without becoming overly gratuitous. The text was ingeniously obscured enough to not be insulting. Because this was a gifted, liberal

Figure 16.1 Immigrant children often present with attentional issues suggestive of the spectrum. Collage work allowed this teen to bypass language and express his feelings about his faith.

and empathic group, their support celebrated his boldness. One Latina girl helped him finish his sentences, asking, 'Is that what you mean?' and thus facilitating the processing. This allowed both the teacher and me to cement the group's autonomy, as we were left to observe from the sidelines. This sensitive group of gifted students served as a 'collective therapist'. Their unified voice not only validated the work, but also helped form a group bond where criticism was taken in as the maternal 'good object'—one that was unconditional, comforting and encouraging of further exploration.

Religiosity Obsession

While most people in the shadow syndromes are characterized by eccentricity and temperament, at times they may assume more obsessional proportions. Individuals with 'loose' thoughts and proclivities for magical thinking, such as my earlier example of van Gogh (pg. 229), often gravitate to religious themes which are culturally, even universally, sanctioned. By having obsessions become religious, the individual can tread the fine line between faith-based thinking and the demons that need to be kept at bay. They might resist becoming consumed or too literal in their beliefs, appropriately camouflaging their fervour, devotion or obsessions.

One intelligent sixteen-year-old, E.C., displayed all the hallmarks of Asperger's syndrome. He presented with religious obsessions that somehow did not interfere with his functioning. He eschewed most social interaction and instead spent almost all his free time writing illustrated books while alone in his room, but was otherwise working above grade level. According to his concerned parents, most of his themes dealt with calamities from the Old Testament. E.C.'s work in creative response therapy consisted of a brief course of six sessions, during which he freely shared his religious interests. His obsession had become a closed-off system, with his powers of rationalization being a formidable defence, leaving little room for therapeutic intervention. The therapeutic team discussed the case at length to ascertain what course of treatment might be developed. Dr. Hecht discussed with the parents that if his 'interest' began to debilitate his ability to function, they'd consider prescribing antipsychotic medication. He noted, however, that those on the autistic spectrum do not always have their obsessions or delusions neutralized but, instead, the medications may lead to side effects and 'symptom substitution', meaning that other, more pronounced side effects replace what was for now an otherwise intact and functioning yet introverted teen. All agreed that now his preoccupations did not impact anyone outside his inner world.

In one example, the theme was the Book of Exodus, where he illustrated the 'Plagues of Egypt'. This is a powerful story of rebuke from 'Yahweh' to the Egyptian oppressors, damning them for holding the Israelites in slavery. He illustrated these and other Old Testament stories in volumes, without proselytizing to others. His drawing collections were voluminous. Figure 16.2 is page 299 out of some *five hundred* pages. In this section, E.C. was exploring the biblical seven plagues, featuring the 'frogs', in which the Lord pronounced 'If you don't let my people go I will plague your people with frogs' (Exodus 7:25-8:15).

The pagan Egyptians are depicted being smothered by millions of the amphibians, which hop onto the women, an infant and a man. Each was rendered without undue distortion beyond the gospel's description. Even the clothing and belongings of the period are accurately portrayed. The next leaf (unshown) was even more disturbing: the fourth plague of 'flies', where people are swarmed by the buzzing insects. In the 'Flies', the biblical-era Egyptians were of an elevated social status but were not immune to God's wrath. In this leaf, a soldier and aristocratic lady are being attended to by her slaves, and both are being swarmed by the insects. E.C. uses dashes and dots to depict the whizzing pests as they swarm the couple, while word captions, such as 'bzzzz', ensure that the viewer is following its dramatic theme. As a storyboard, the drawings are at the service of the narrative are not intended to be stand-alone works of art. One horrendous Old Testament story would be hurried into the next, almost inexhaustibly. As a creative response, their therapeutic value, while compelling, remained limited. Therapeutic efficacy was also negative, as he had no intentions of departing from his 'project', certainly not by any therapist's interventions.

In consultation, Dr. Hecht discouraged anything more than having me listen to E.C. recite these stories. Any elaboration was viewed as stimulating further or 'feeding into' the pathology. This is the danger that any self-motivated stimulus may morph into a close-ended obsession—again accentuating how any stimulus can be double edged. Unless there is room for expansiveness, a new direction that

Figure 16.2 Faith-driven belief systems may become a magnet for children suffering magical thought processes. This boy's skilled artwork focused exclusively upon Old Testament stories.

demonstrates the child can *move through* the obsessional narrative, it remains stagnated to any intervention. All I could do was sit beside and on occasion attempt to link the narrative to a real-world metaphor, keeping the sessions completely 'cognitive'. Even when appealing to his beliefs and intellect, he became suspicious that I was reframing his narrative as a mythology—one that came uncomfortably close to questioning his faith. Attempts at grounding him during his endless flights into myth and fantasy proved fruitless.

In the end, creative response therapy was terminated, as the boy's preoccupations were so deeply entrenched that therapy seemed to infringe upon his religious beliefs. This was taboo; his religiosity was inviolate. One could only hope that the preoccupation would be tempered through the natural progression of maturation. Peer influence and cultural factors also might 'normalize' his obsessions. His worried and discouraged parents reluctantly discontinued creative arts therapy. Meanwhile, his preoccupation continued unabated, with volume upon volume of illustrated books being produced as his only outlet for creative expression. E.C. aspired to be a religious scholar. Ensconced in this world, he was left to his devices. My hope was that he would make it to seminary school or another suitable placement. Perhaps in more cloistered environs, his scholarly work would mature and become productive while remaining out of the public eye.

Spectrum Issues on the University Level: Bibliotherapy

During my work with university students who came with undisclosed spectrum issues, it was fascinating to observe those individuals who had developed compensatory mechanisms to help filter out disturbing course material that tapped unresolved issues. One bright college student was April, a sophomore enrolled in the honours program—which is an amazing feat unto itself given her autistic features. She was a pale, fine-featured and fastidious individual whose quiet demeanour was offset by dressing in unusual outfits, lending an artistic flair to her unusual countenance. Despite markers suggestive of mild Asperger's syndrome, I was surprised at her choosing drama as a major, until she explained her specialty was costume and set design. In this area of the field, she could balance being near others during a group production with having extensive alone time with her patterns, fabrics and sewing machine. When shown her portfolio (how the students introduced themselves), her work displayed not only the skills of costume design but also a facility for figurative drawing. When asked by a classmate whether she would consider fashion design, she shyly expressed that the field was 'too competitive'. Having taught at an art school where stressed-out fashion majors were the norm, I understood how April could never tolerate such a cut-throat culture and business.

April had enrolled in my interdisciplinary class entitled 'Arts and Ideas: The Psychology of Creativity'. This course explored several modalities of creative expression and was group learning process oriented, which April managed, albeit with discernible discomfort. It was also obvious to this therapist/instructor that her excellent coping skills were indicative of long-term cognitive behavioural therapy. The coping strategies learned were most apparent when she utilized self-initiated 'cues', catching herself when becoming agitated or withdrawn or displaying odd affects during social interaction. Most probably, as April developed her capacity for self-awareness of her idiosyncratic behaviour, she could be mainstreamed into a challenging academic and arts program. However, she was almost certainly strained at times to temper her residual symptoms. Especially when the social aspect of the course became stressful, autistic-like behaviours subtly surfaced, such as 'self-dialoguing'.

Thinking out loud is not specifically pathological—many typicals routinely talk to themselves. In his book, *The Voices Within* (2016), Fernyhough discusses how inner dialoguing among the normative population may assist in creative problem solving and give self-encouragement and perseverance. Negative emotions may also be rebuked. Self-talk may contribute to weakened object constancy, such as when speaking to those loved ones who have departed. In April's case, self-talking 'leaked' enough to become audible to her peers, which became obviously awkward. Her 'talking back' was perhaps in response to intrusive thoughts or feelings about the project and peer work. In the group, she was 'out of step' with her peers, often discussing irrelevant and idiosyncratic material, which seemed largely dismissed, as she was, after all, an 'arts major'. While she was adept at disguising her feelings, her issues became more transparent when working on provocative material, such as the eighteenth-century novel *Frankenstein*. For this honour student, reading and writing on this novel became more akin to a bibliotherapy experience rather than being merely an academic exercise. It encompassed the great theme of the enlightenment—of 'man playing God', along with a myriad of other monumental issues.

On *Frankenstein*

For this segment of the course, April and her cohorts would discuss the novel and then write up their own impressions, including emotional and metaphorical insights. The classic Gothic novel *Frankenstein* was written by Mary Wollstonecraft Shelley while virtually still in her teens—the same age as most of the students in the class. One summer, when Shelley wandered the continent, her eccentric group holed up in an ancient villa in Geneva. She and her notoriously bohemian friends, which included the outlandish Lord Byron and her future husband Percy Bysshe Shelley, the group encountered summer lightning and thunderstorms on the shores of Lake Como. Together, they passed the long nights by telling horror stories in the flickering candlelight. Shelley's story would later develop into the novel, but during that momentous evening, it was still just a tale spun from her imagination for the amusement of others.

Shelley's tale explored the disturbing theme of technology and mankind overcoming death and playing god; it entailed also the power of superstition versus the scientific, the moral ethical dilemmas of medical research, and especially her crisis of empathy for those of 'differentness'—issues still as relevant today as in eighteenth-century Europe. Her character, Dr. Frankenstein, was endowed with great intellectual prowess but also terribly suffered from anxieties, struggling with the ethical and moral considerations of his brilliant yet deviant research, that of the 'monster'—an experiment which proved to be his undoing.

During group discussion, April displayed what I surmised was her thorough and hard-won cognitive behavioural training. She listened generously, waiting for others to speak without talking through them or responding out of turn. She could make informed comments that demonstrated she had read the material and had attempted to take in the views of others. However, as a stimulus, *Frankenstein* left her at her most vulnerable, as its theme and otherworldly character perhaps struck a deep emotional chord. In one group discussion, she became tangential, obsessing over Elizabeth, Frankenstein's angelic yet tormented fiancé. Elizabeth, she stated, suffered from the doctor's obsessions and dark research, which kept them apart for over six long years! When the wedding was finally announced, April began detailing the possible eighteenth-century wedding gown styles—her speciality, but secondary to the plot. She discussed and later wrote at length about how Elizabeth's gown should have been 'embroidered guipure lace with an underlayer of silk shantung'. In perusing my tattered copy of her essay, I revisited my comments, urging her to move on from Elizabeth's wedding or 'black mourning attire' and try to engage the 'great themes'.

To help move her beyond costumery, I provided her with subtle 'hints' about the metaphors at play. I asked her how the dramatic location and its abundant nature and wild weather could play as metaphors for the different characters' sense of mood or conduct. She seized on the suggestion, citing the contrasts in landscape between the beautiful Alps and the frightening glacier. Weather also perhaps reflected oscillations of feeling states—from the sun shining on the sublime Mont Blanc to the frightening storms over the lake, with their 'brawling waves'.

April had most studiously avoided joining a discussion on Frankenstein's 'Creation', perhaps the most extreme 'neuroatypical' character in history—the parallels were just too close to home. I dared not intervene to ask her directly about the character's feeling states. The class's discussion about the depth of its despair and rejection were allowed to 'wash' over her. In keeping with my use of Kramer's third-hand intervention, I did not expect or require her to contribute or to absorb this loaded material or include it in her final essay. When the group did address Frankenstein's Creation directly, April began again to 'think aloud', murmuring odd sounds and inaudible words while her cohorts spun a rapid stream of descriptors: the Creation being Rousseau's pure 'native child', then having been cast from his Eden, lashed out and became murderous and unmerciful. In the end, it considered itself an 'abortion'—forbidden by its creator to even exist! During this animated discussion, there were 'competing sensations', meaning the volume and intensity of group exchange seemed to leave April agitated. Yet in the end, she survived with her compensatory defences intact despite the obstacles surmounted. Upon submitting her essay, it seemed my coaching and the tolerance of her peers enabled April to write a distinguished paper. It was full of her idiosyncratic digressions on lace and wedding gown styles, but also forcefully addressed the themes we had discussed—the powerful forces of nature as metaphors that evoked so many moods and emotions. The paper was a bit confusing because of these competing sensations; all the characters' betrayals, sufferings, shame and torment were overwhelmingly *unrelenting*. In a veiled way, April did finally address the issue of the creature's neurodiversity. As a remarkable outcome, I quote from the most telling passage:

> Humankind's creations will always be imperfect, some experiments will even end in disaster. But the reader needs to appreciate where there are good intentions and struggles. By attacking those who are different, whether it be the scientist or his creation, one shows ignorance of its complexity, rather than understanding. Victor's suffering was self-inflicted and showed a lack of sympathy and he paid terribly with the lives of his loved ones. This theme happens in life and literature whether the work is in the twenty-first century or the Romantic era.

This excerpt has many facets that perhaps personally resonated; it alludes to Dr. Frankenstein's good intent but ultimate 'poor choices'. It may have referred to her peers and others in her life who perhaps were not fully grasping her own creations, that her own obsessing over creations might have extended to that of

Elizabeth and the finery she should have worn. At times, I expected her to merge with this melancholic figure—that she herself might float into class, dressed in the finery of the part—for that was her art form.

The quote addresses the creature's alienation. Her wording is exceedingly careful as she skirts the issue that was perhaps closest to her—that of her own 'complexity' and perhaps, ultimately, her own life's sufferings. April's creative responses reflected this turmoil, which seemed to mirror that of Shelley herself— whose persona perhaps merged with Elizabeth. In the end, identification was a powerful force, with both young, creative woman being surrounded by theatrical characters, each of great sensitivity, struggling through life's great dramas.

Trigger Warnings

Two of the last three case vignettes covered potentially disturbing material— Felipe confronting contradictions in his faith and April coping with a monster that raised her stress levels. In university experientials, invited regressions during assignments tap thematic content that is emotionally loaded. For those of a delicate sensitivity there comes a necessary disclaimer, now termed 'trigger warning'. An indiscriminate use of such warnings is to censor certain inflammatory content in coursework. This movement is most prevalent in elite liberal schools where strident political correctness has attempted to displace academic freedom. However, there is an appropriate need for disclaimers. I included a moderate version within the project or coursework, even when I was training creative art therapists. When working with material that is disturbing, one can assume that stimulus barrier issues may be engaged, both unconsciously and consciously. While not written as a matter of school or university policy, my own disclaimer and alert was posted in every syllabus to indicate that certain themes would be studied:

> The subject matter and experientials engaged in this course may be perceived as being disturbing or objectionable to certain students with special sensitivities. In such a case, a suitable alternative project with relevant themes and equal rigor is to be researched. It is the responsibility of each student to devise, discuss the project and gain the approval by the instructor when working on an alternative project.

This disclaimer was meant for those who indeed had been traumatized to the extent that material which dealt graphically with themes such as domestic abuse, rape and other potential trigger topics might lead to serious decompensation. This being a community school setting, the students were expected to be responsible enough to handle appropriate content and to ensure that it was not 'over the top'. While the novel *Frankenstein* might have engaged many issues which tapped into April's inner conflicts, we worked together to navigate those which I realized could be loaded. By directly avoiding the 'Creation' and his feelings of betrayal, rejection and neurodifference, I awaited the time when she demonstrated her capacity to engage—which turned out to be her final paper. Again, the act of writing appeared to give the proximal distance needed for April to be able to address sensitive topics. Being attuned to students and their sensitivities, especially in a remedial, interdisciplinary or honours program where learning differences are more atypical, remains a part of the therapeutic professional task of *anticipating* potential issues before they become disruptive or otherwise problematic.

Seventeen

Domestic Violence

Almost two thousand adults are killed by family members or intimate partners annually in the United States. These unspeakable acts of violence may leave a psychological scar upon the children, to the extent that even citing incidents in references became unbearable for me during this writing. Though becoming increasingly rare (despite the proliferation of firearms), cases of uxoricide do surface. Working with a child who has lost both parents is a mixed blessing—one draws upon compassionate efforts to assist the child to restore a degree of trust and security in the world, while witnessing the effects of the ultimate in child abuse. For children on the spectrum, we can expect the trauma to exacerbate their symptoms, predisposing them to even more severe markers on the continuum. Here again, sitting beside in a naturalistic setting becomes the dominant methodology as the therapist tries to gain the trust of children who have been betrayed by their own parent(s). No attempts to desensitize or debrief the child result in a positive therapeutic outcome. In my experience, rarely will something be volunteered to process. It is the epitome of honouring sitting beside and 'come what may'.

In one of the three domestic shooting cases I have seen, a twelve-year-old boy we'll name Jon suffered his traumatic loss at age seven. He was seen in creative arts therapy for four years, from age eleven to age fourteen. He was referred by his family, after having 'gone silent'—the words used by his kindly but overtaxed grandmother and now the de facto mother. He had already been identified in school as a child with attention deficits with 'overly quiet, immature, silly and impulsive behaviour' and was fitted with an individualized education plan. The child study team also reported that he was selectively mute with certain teachers or especially those well-meaning but incompetent personnel who attempted to directly address the effects of post-trauma. The result was an unsurprising retreat deeper into the child's inner self. Interactions with peers tended to be solitary, though Jon would ride bikes and was a master fisherman and participated in family activities with his siblings and neighbours. He preferred remaining in his comfort zone, in the company of his large, extended family. Two uncles had become male role models and father figures, while his cousins and three siblings served as playmates in preference to his peers.

In therapy, Jon responded well to the non-verbal atmosphere. He rarely uttered a word and usually presented with a far-off look of being disengaged. However, having been exposed to building forts and other construction projects with his uncles, Jon was skilled with his hands. He enjoyed working in media which especially offered 'resistance'. Resistance is a term used by Uhlin and de Chiara (1984), which refers to materials and techniques that require a tactile toughness—a sense of physicality, whether it be driving a nail, fixing a train track or disentangling a spinning reel. He enjoyed the resistant malleability of wax and clay as sculptural media. Each of these activities 'pushed back', adding an element of struggle to the activity and serving as an outlet for this mild-mannered child's potentially deeply repressed anger.

Many children with attention deficits are often 'selectively' focused—with high-reward activities given almost infinite attention. Jon proved himself a master fisherman who for hours of days on end could pass the time solitarily along a pond or riverbank. He had accompanied his uncles to fish at their mountain cabin. In his rural surroundings, he had also been taught to shoot shotguns and compound bows. He began to deer hunt soon after the domestic event—the effects of which I can only speculate. Perhaps it was the cultural norm to join his aunts and uncles in their tree stands during deer season. His uncle taught Jon firearm safety, and he became an accomplished shooter, such that he was often successful at taking a deer, even when the adults had not let off a shot. Jon was an excellent tracker as well. It was fortuitous that there was a river and field that abutted our clinical offices. During our field sessions, he led me on tracking expeditions where deer, raccoon and other animals inhabited the sodden floodplain; he often spotted animal life I had not noticed. In the woods, he seemed to become invisible, holding still, camouflaged, rarely spooking a sunning turtle off a log. During our therapeutic activities, we were two individuals essentially coexisting in parallel. Tracking consisted of following him, pausing to listen, then quietly proceeding for half the hour's session. We would then return and either make some art or discuss our outing—with my doing most of the talking. While it seemed that my walking beside was a solitary endeavour, it references Winnicott's concept of 'being alone in the presence of the other'—when two trusting individuals can fully be at peace together without the obligation to converse or even interact (1965).

One of Jon's most enthusiastic creative response activities was to depict his taking a deer during the first day of hunting season—a time when this semi-rural community barely held school, so many children were out in the fields. The drawing rendered is a carefully detailed portrait of the event; he is shown posing with his kill, proudly holding up the buck's rack (Figure 17.1).

The work is normatively within the developmental stage of dawning realism, with the felt marker work being well elaborated and rich with detail and narrative. The picture is counterintuitive, however, in that it celebrates a killing. He smiles, awkwardly holding up his prize, yet there is no overt aggression or signs of 'blood lust'. It is matter of fact, in keeping with his understated demeanour. It is also a fully formed aesthetic piece, carefully re-imagined from memory, with a complex array of emotions at play. Given Jon's autistic markers, his affect in this

Figure 17.1 For this child already on the spectrum, overcoming an additional traumatic domestic episode rendered him withdrawn, although his graphic narrative was richly elaborated.

piece is difficult to decipher. He is shown with a pasted-on smile which seems overworked—more of a black moustache. This key affective feature is perhaps a sign of emotional ambivalence, but we shall never know. He is superbly decked in full hunting camo, his field glasses dangling, the brand name on his insulated hunting boots proudly labelled. The telescopic high-powered rifle—an advanced weapon—is given meticulous treatment. It is depicted as awesomely powerful, with its camouflaged shoulder strap. These details point to a healthy narcissistic sense of self-empowerment that is appropriate for a twelve-year-old hunter—one who is coming of age and entering the young adulthood of his culture.

The work also points again to the selectivity of the artist's intentionality. In the hunting field, he is not labouring over low-reward activities like math or doing his chores. He was somehow able to stand silently during long hours in the damp and cold December dawn, patiently waiting with intense focus. When his quarry appeared, his aim was spot on. His only comment was the laconic 'it was clean shot'—which perhaps is an allusion not only to his marksmanship but also that the animal did not suffer. He had successfully harvested a large and elusive prey when others had failed. In this instance, he became *the* 'provider' to his family, loading a freezer full of venison for the winter to come. The rendering of the deer is most interesting. The animal is shown without any visible wound, blood or even indications that the animal is dead. The deer kneels in repose, almost relaxed, its bent legs and black-coloured hooves grounding it to the forest floor. Its eye looks strangely back towards Jon. It is an ambiguous expression that, like the child, is difficult to read. The buck is drawn transparently, the rifle showing through. It is as though the animal is no longer of this world, the gun now taking up its life space. Above the forest, trees loom tall with branches that create an interesting overarching canopy. Their scratchy bark gives them strength and substance. A single black and abrasive looking shrub is the only agitated element in the composition.

As is often the case, the analyst can provide only a form and content reading on the work, as deeper interpretation into its symbolic representation would be speculative. It is a complex image considering the child's minimal commentary. Given this deep-seated trauma, the piece was left alone. Jon was firmly 'held' within his image and therapeutic environment that was trusting—resulting in a sense of quiescence. Therefore, no questions were posed about the work, and no answers would be forthcoming. This was part of our unspoken pact.

I must confess that during the time I worked with this boy, both in session and camp, even at both our homes, my own professional boundaries began to blur. During the ensuing years, his terrible circumstance and beguiling nature had prompted every rescue fantasy imaginable—that I would eventually bring this child out of his autism. His case required perhaps the most intense clinical supervision from Dr. Hecht, with continual transferences, boundary confusion and questions over methodological efficacy. As his therapeutic companion, we had shared many muddy treks and spent hours of casting and fishing off a dock, wading waist-deep in streams seining for minnows—all in virtual silence but still sharing moments. During our four years together, many wonderful activities and images were created. I tried my best to hold true to the pact—that I would wordlessly accept the present and the past without question.

Eighteen
War and Trauma

Humanity is so violence prone that Freud's theory of instinctual aggression and the primordial death instinct seems so obvious as to be an inarguable, forgone conclusion. I have already pointed out in the strongest of terms how mankind's individual and collective aggression has remained a constant since time immemorial. In modern times, we might think its continuance to be inexplicable, given the extent to which we consider ourselves to be 'civilized'. Freud and countless followers have cast humans as being capable of unbridled savagery. We are saddled with a never-ending death cycle, with millions of war dead and countless others being collateral damage. Bruce Perry writes that violence fascinates *and* repulses us (2001). Yet going to war is still considered ennobling—a matter of national and personal pride, often with blind allegiance to the state. Violence is a means to an end—to a thirst for power and oppression over others, domination over the world's shrinking resources and cultural/religious pride. School shootings are themselves a kind of war, in that the perpetrators are often linked to a self-invented cult of nihilistic anarchy, which is played out in video-enhanced killings. These are such all-powerful stimuli; the death drive supplants all civil rationalization or reconciliation. War has and will continue unabated with ferocious ideologies and governments of the insane.

The tragedy of often-displaced, orphaned, uneducated and injured children leaves deep psychic and physical scars. At the time of this writing, there are child orphans and refugees from war-torn Africa, the Middle East and Eastern Europe. Some children have been forced or drugged into killing the enemy themselves. Others have been sold into slavery and raped and have reverted to feral states, with many accounts of how children live a shadow existence, some within their city's sewers. As I write these words, many of the kidnapped Nigerian schoolgirls still hide terror stricken in jungles and forests. Some captives are war brides, and others are passed around to different soldiers. Many children have endured war their entire *lives* and know nothing else. These child survivors carry with them the trauma present with spectrum issues in many guises, from the overtly aggressive to the shutdown autistic. They require the gentlest of therapeutic treatment. Violence activates threat responses in children's developing brains. Excess activation of the neural systems creates a 'hyperarousal continuum' of threat responses that can alter brain chemistry, which is observed in emotional, behavioural and cognitive behaviour (Perry, 2001). Jon (pg. 263) is a case in point; dissociative reactions induced by trauma left him disengaged from those aspects of the external world that were threatening or held minimal rewards. Unless tracking or hunting, Jon's otherworldliness and dreamy continence rendered him within the default mode's 'different place' (Perry, 2001)

As with this child, the children referred to our practice were not just trauma victims per se, but also had a spectrum condition that predated their diagnosis of post-traumatic stress. Those who were regarded as purely trauma victims were referred to other creative arts therapists who specialized in this population. Some art therapists have gone directly to the children in war-torn countries, such as Julia Byers, who wrote the compelling *Children of the Stones,* a harrowing journey into war-weary Gaza and the West Bank (1996). This brave work is the naturalistic method at its purest. However, some spectrum children who were already being treated at The Hecht Group were referred to me, especially those who were now nonverbal. Others, such as the children who endured the events of September 11, 2001, were typical grade school children, seen by Ms. Dawn, their art specialist.

On September 11, 2001

In the opening vignettes of this book, I stated that the spectrum in its various shades might be best understood by exploring the most severe of cases. However, in addressing the effects of war and trauma, it is the neurotypical child who might yield the most insight. It is the creative responses of these schoolchildren that perhaps most compellingly illustrate how they coped with war conducted on our soil. The vicious pre-emptive strike against the World Trade Center is unparalleled in U.S. history since Japan's bombing of Pearl Harbor. The effects of this attack rippled through my caseload of spectrum children with predictably disturbed feelings of annihilation anxiety and other drastic post-traumatic expressions. Their creative responses were so severely pathological that it would be gratuitous to share these works even in a book on the spectrum disorders. However, it might be helpful to explore the art of Ms. Dawn's public grade school students who were in the New York City/New Jersey area, close enough to have suffered losses and surviving family members within her regular art classes.

On that fateful day, Ms. Dawn immediately cancelled her lesson plans and offered empathetic art activities for all the children school wide. The response was immediate and graphic. Most children wished to draw, the most direct medium available to record their feelings of urgency and loss. There were no clinical notations recorded on these children or their art, as research was obviously not a priority. Nor do we know whether these children had pre-existing special needs, were in gifted programs or otherwise—whatever the case, their art speaks for all. The productions created depicted scenes that were accurately and appropriately rife with violence and fear. However, it is the distinct *lack* of distortion which distinguishes their creative responses from pathological art. While the content is *terrible* to imagine, the formal elements (depictions of people, places and things)

Figure 18.1 September 11, 2001, rocked our world. Here a mainstreamed third-grader expresses the event with stunning precision and intensity without pictorial distortion of thought or feeling.

are expressed in relatively straightforward terms. And, whatever the form, each of these expressions captured the overwhelming feelings of that fateful day.

Without psychologizing we might first consider the art drawn by a third-grader we'll refer to as L.T. (Figure 18.1). This nine-year-old boy gives an appropriately harrowing image recounting the suicide attack, with the planes' explosive impact generating first the smoke, then the flames, and eventually disintegration, all in one image.

There is an emotionally frantic rhythm to the work, which according to Ms. Dawn, was regressive compared to this boy's 'regular' art style. Given his sense of urgency, the intent is pictographic, with elements which included scribbled-style flames and debris. Included also are the ill-fated 'jumpers', whose word balloons accentuate their desperate cry for help. No child should have seen these images. Almost certainly he watched the day-long televised coverage, yet almost all major networks did not show those jumping to escape the inferno. The power of the media coverage might have aggravated his response further—especially if seen multiple times. Like all the others, Ms. Dawn accepted this piece without any intervention beyond being a sympathetic presence. In my work on-site with the survivors, the clinical supervisor expressly warned that there be no attempts at debriefing—even by the most experienced trauma specialists. The creative response was left alone to be intrinsically cathartic. What the children required was an environment where predictability and the rhythms of daily life continued to minimize their alarm, by providing some leniency and extra care.

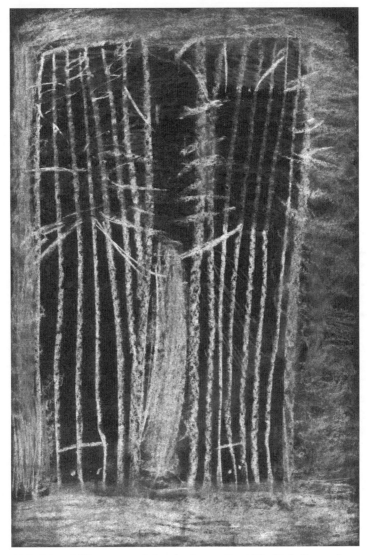

Figure 18.2 Other children responded to the destruction of the Twin Towers by aesthetically expressing the event. This fourth-grader abstracted the towers through colour and form.

Another image by a fourth-grader, Jack, appears more abstract and formally executed (Figure 18.2). His choice of white- and grey-coloured chalks contrasting over the black ground is more an aesthetic response, with the event not expressed as a narrative or pictograph.

While this image does not graphically depict the conflagration and impending death of thousands, it nevertheless conveys the gravity of the situation. The two towers seem more like figurative twins, which they were, symbiotic siblings mirroring each other's fate. The energetic use of interwoven line work treats the impending doom of the towers as being wobbly and tenuous. But its agitated piercings and slashing movements are a kinaesthetic record of the child's movements during the process. Though he avoids direct reference to the carnage, his energetic line work and figurative composition still convey the horror of the event. The choice of black paper might also have held meaning. Perhaps it reflected the frightful blackness of the day, or he had watched the scene televised at night. He might be referencing one of our darkest hours in history, as one moment the enormous Twin Towers were solid and present, and the next second there was just the empty September sky—the concrete and steel now left transparent in dust and debris.

To me, a first-hand observer who witnessed the event from ten blocks away, the columns of debris particles did seem to stand motionlessly 'after the smoke cleared', well after the buildings came down—a sight that was strangely mesmerizing if it weren't so terrible. One woman standing next to me screamed out 'they're gone!' only after the sun shone through the twin clouds. Perhaps as the impact of the illusion was finally stripped away, it was driven home by the shocking reality of it all. Regardless, we shall never know the latter artist's conscious or unconscious intent. By witnessing the creation of this image Ms. Dawn recounted, he was quiet and focused in his movements, without displays of outward emotion. It is enough that this Jack had captured the moment of compelling repose—teetering on the edge. Both works are a testament to the resiliency of intact children who are not burdened by deficits and mind damage. We shall never know their clinical histories, though their mental health and emotional strength shine through this darkest of days.

Post-Traumatic Veteran Returns to His Child

Despite being a child therapist, it sometimes becomes apparent that it is not the child who is the 'identified patient'—but in reality, it is the parent. These parents were routinely referred to the psychologist or therapist 'upstairs' who worked with adults. However, in one case, Dr. Hecht referred a boy and his father for dyadic creative response therapy. The bright and active three-and-a-half-year-old boy was brought to session initially by his mother, who explained the unusual circumstances. His father, a veteran of the war in Iraq, was one of the 'invisibly wounded'. He was one of countless drivers of convoys in shamefully under-armoured vehicles. Unbeknownst at the time, this reservist, who anticipated just playing a support role, had sustained blast-induced brain damage from an improvised explosive device (IED). This insidious injury left no immediate or visible lasting damage (McKee & Robinson, 2014). However, during his deployment in 2005, the armed forces were still entrenched in the outdated paradigm which considered 'battle fatigue' and after-Vietnam 'post-traumatic stress' emotional—even characterological disorders—implying the soldier was somehow too fatigued or stressed out or didn't 'measure up'. For hundreds of years, concussed or traumatized soldiers were given medical leave after being blasted and then were returned to the battle line, but invisibly damaged. Now, these men and women were returning home in droves, with too many untreated, often left to their own devices to assimilate back into civilian life. Though the blast had clearly left him impaired, I was unaware, as were most others, of the neurological component to his injury. Thus, I treated the problem as an emotional/mental trauma. His wife insisted he had 'returned a different man'. At the time, he had not been identified as mTBI (mild traumatic brain injury), given the lack of noticeable physical damage (McKee & Robinson, 2014). Thus, he had yet to even receive adequate treatment from the Veterans Administration due to the syndrome's lack of manifestation.

Depressed, yet kindly, with a flat, pasted-on smile, Johnson, as they called him, was distanced from both his wife and child. He was as yet jobless and was self-medicating with alcohol. His relationship with his child had suffered arrested development—he rarely played alone with his son, which the mother addressed by having the family play games together. He attended six dyad sessions, wherein I facilitated shared activities in which I hoped to engage both the father and son. As the boy enjoyed scribbling, we began by creating figures known as 'tadpoles'— big-headed face circles, some with emerging limbs which he had begun to name 'Mommy' with any identification of Daddy being conspicuously missing. While the boy was drawing, I tried to mirror the child's enthusiastic but unintelligible story. By modelling these behaviours, I was basically 'teaching' the father how to show enthusiasm and increase his investment in the process, without needing to understand its infantile content. I explained and demonstrated how facial, body and voice components most effectively connect with the child. I encouraged him to move in closer proximity, to kneel at the child's level. To have him become animated without feeling pressured or be competitive with my own performance was another challenge, requiring close supervision. I carefully scripted my comments, narrating in a rhetorical way, 'Oh, what a big head with yellow hair!' or 'what is that big boy doing?' et cetera.

I attempted to gently cue the father when to engage, when to mimic baby talk or sound effects. We worked on shared drawings, handing him a crayon and showing him how to mirror the drawing style of a three-year-old character on his own. In using this developmental approach, the father's own drawing deficits would not be put on display. His attempts after three crayon sessions were not encouraging, with the father losing interest, once again lapsing into the passive observer.

During session three, I switched to playing dinosaurs using the models on our eight-foot-long realistic prehistoric diorama—a project that had replaced our miniature train set (refreshing the novelty of the studio in the process). Perhaps the father's own boyhood memories of dinosaurs could awaken an interest in assisting his child in animating these creatures. The dad was encouraged to move around the lifelike sauropods amidst the jungle of the Cretaceous. Again, I demonstrated how to have the models play around and interact on the diorama, climbing the miniature volcano, velociraptors crashing through the trees, splashing in the water of the pond I designed, all to hopefully share this narrative with his son. When the child's own playful dinosaur enactment began to have one dinosaur devour another, I was curious whether this aggressive play might 'trigger' some post-traumatic or other response. I carefully scanned the father for any disturbed affect. This play during our last two sessions began to show promise, when the mother abruptly ceased therapy. After months of frustration and endless waiting, she had finally found an expense-free therapist through the Veterans Administration, where treatment of an unknown sort was provided free of charge.

Within this brief course of dyad therapy, few discernible gains had been made in moving toward a bond between father and son and was thus counted as a negative outcome. The object relationship was unchanged with discernible movement in paternal relating. He remained distant both emotionally and proximally, but remained compliant and well meaning. Yet I believe Johnson did recognize that these sessions were about 'how' to be part of his son's life. In the termination session, I encouraged him to use what he learned, how to play in a manner that was therapeutically attuned to the child, such as taking a splash in the family pool or playing dump trucks in a pile of dirt—each required little skill or time and would perhaps kick-start some relating. Yet these goals were perhaps premature. For someone who had just a few months earlier been blown out of a truck while facing a fanatical and invisible enemy, the scars of war rendered even child's play an insurmountable obstacle. I pointed out to the mother that there would be no 'quick fix'. There would be required long-term physical and mental healing on the part of the father and perhaps further maturation on the part of the son. Relating to a three-year-old is not so easy for many men, with the play repertoire being so limited in form and content. With so many calls for increased and timely services from the very same government which sent them into battle—all for dubious reasons—hopefully further attention will be more actively paid to those who suffer blast-induced trauma.

Terror and Its Toll

Post-traumatic stress was also evident in a child named Eva, who came to therapy two years after having been rescued four years earlier from a Latin American insurgency, where civilian and child collateral damage had long become the norm. After her rescue, she had been adopted by a loving and professional American family who tried in vain to address this child's most delicate nature. Selectively mute, but bright and gifted, she took refuge in playing musical instruments. Exposed to American culture at age eleven, she was now almost obsessed with being taken to the Broadway theatres, which was the only topic she ever discussed. She came to me with the parents' caveat that *any* queries about her life or trauma, or even about attending the shows, were verboten. In fact, no issues at all could be directly addressed on any account, as was evidenced by the failures of two preceding therapists. The earning of trust was almost an impossibility, the mother counselled, and only the most non-threatening parallel interactions described earlier could be used as the luring method. Anything more actively therapeutic than sitting beside, wordlessly facilitating creative activity, and the child would immediately depart and never return. Those were the terms.

Eva was reserved and regal in bearing, tall and thin with high Amerindian cheekbones and long jet-black hair. Though pathologically shy, she loved animals, as those with a delicate nature often do, finding comfort in their therapeutic company. In one breakthrough session, she departed from Broadway and began discussing the newly released documentary film *March of the Penguins* (Jacquet, 2005). I feared it to be a mixed if not dangerous stimulus, given the hardships and even horrors those birds endured. These extraordinary Antarctic birds migrated *en masse* across hundreds of miles of the barren frozen wastes—a compelling story for any viewer. It had obviously affected her deeply. Taking up a palette of vibrantly painted acrylic, she carefully depicted a landscape with one immature bird huddling in a far-off corner (Plate 6). Its metaphors of isolation and threat of survival should be obvious to any reader.

The lone penguin is carefully placed at the far extreme of the pictorial field facing away from the barren yet colourful landscape. Its bleakness is offset by its pastel blue body and big yellow feet, which brightly contrast with the thick band of horizontal yellow. It is a paradoxical work—displaying the figure's fragility and sensitivity with a brightly sun-lit scene. It is this dissonance that gives it its formal and narrative power. The work echoes Anna Freud's contention that a child with a strong constitution, who had formerly been given familial love and care by her family, could survive post-trauma, that she could still find passions in life—of theatre and to play music and paint heart-rending little paintings that did not deny or repress. That despite these terrible circumstances, whether it be witnessing a terrifying fire fight or watching waddling birds brave the inhospitable wastes of the bottom of the world, a lone figure could still *survive.*

As her work evolved, I grew slightly bolder in my interventions. During one session, she had sculpted four petite penguin chicks in polymer compound, which she announced were floating on an ice pack ... a verbalization hitherto not expressed. She was at a loss as to choosing a medium which could convey how they might drift in the sea. As a third-hand intervention, I silently offered some Styrofoam to form the ice, which I was relieved that she accepted. She ingeniously broke the Styrofoam in four pieces and glued the chunks to a dark blue paper (which I also wordlessly provided). She placed a chick on each piece, indicating they were now being dangerously separated. It was at this juncture that I made a fatal miscalculation. I made some slight allusion to the metaphor 'they seem hopeful despite being on separate ice packs'. Eva looked up, and betraying no emotion, calmly left the studio. She quietly greeted her mother in the waiting room, and they both left without a word—though her mother phoned later, and we said our 'good-byes'. After six months of weekly sessions, I made a single reference that slightly brushed against her trauma, and she was gone.

Although Eva walked out on our individual work, with her mother's insistence, she reluctantly attended our summer camp—with the cardinal rule that I would make myself scarce. The challenge in overcoming her approach-avoidance was to lure her into participation. This would be left to an unlikely source—another spectrum child. An insightful intern intuitively decided to pair her with a boy we'll named Rex, who was among the most hyperactive and loquacious children in the camp—though with a friendly, endearing manner. During activities along the lakeshore, they were to research and build stone 'cairns', the practice of stacking rocks as trail markers, burials, even in primitive astronomy. Tapping into childhood into block building, it was among the earliest balancing experiences whose creative response comprised both play *and* work. After surveying the scene and examining the works of Andy Goldsworthy and the ancient Stonehenge, the stimulus was self-motivating.

Counterintuitively, Eva somehow did not resist their pairing. All were fascinated as Eva stood near this boy while he carried on, happily chatting away and lugging stones. They were a world of opposites, with this boy giving a running narrative on the process of selecting, sizing and stacking. All the while she ignored his ramblings and moved silently through the rocks. The video still of the two of them clearly shows her approaching and fully engaged in the process (Figure 18.3). Interestingly, Eva sometimes took the lead, by *correcting* his impulsively ill-balanced rocks—inadvertently becoming one of the more fully functioning teams.

This unlikely duo—balancing his incessant noise with her statuesque repose—created a therapeutic alliance *and* a lovely monument.

One of the few verbal expressions she initiated with her counsellor was for permission to go down to the lake and 'check' on her cairn days after its creation.

Figure 18.3 Eventually partnering with a child of opposite temperament, this video stills shows this same statuesque, mute child taking the lead in creating stone cairns along the lake shore.

Accompanied by the intern, she repaired the work, which was one of the few to survive the ebbing tides, storm surges and other elements. It seemed an exercise in both object permanence and object constancy, as she displayed a sense of self-investment that resonated beyond anyone's expectation. While my own bumbling individual work had threatened the child, her own therapeutic visitations pointed to how the therapist is sometimes unnecessary or even a hindrance, except as a holding environment. For this to be formed, it first took archetypal materials of stone and a seaside environment that stimulated complete artistic absorption and investment. Then the relational element became vital—a whole team of unobtrusive players, an inventive intern, a supportive mother, my covert supervision and a therapeutic companion, who despite being oblivious, slapdash and hyperkinetic, could keep this otherworldly child tethered to the camp experience.

Edith Kramer as Child: Surviving through Her Art

As a child, art therapy pioneer Edith Kramer dealt with two world wars, in which Austria was on the losing side in both, and several economic depressions. She was born after the fall of the Austrian/Hungarian empire and fled the Third Reich at the last possible instant, but these were topics which were not discussed until well into her eighties—a common 'life review' practice. As a child, much of her family was dispersed, with some perishing during WWII. Her childhood was a mixed affair, with a colourful yet unstable cast of characters which collectively formed the 'good-enough mother'. After reaching young adulthood, she emigrated to the United States in 1939 after Austria's annexation to the Reich. Landing in New York City, she began to teach woodworking at the progressive Little Red School House in Greenwich Village and then eventually worked with disadvantaged youth, which became the standard for working therapeutically with children. After seven years of practice as an art therapy pioneer, yet still working in relative isolation, she helped co-found the field which still bears her indelible stamp.

As my mentor and friend, we used to spend breaks in the studio having tea, during which time she reminisced about the past. It was as though she thought out loud, as there was no expectation of including me in the dialogue. Ideas would pour out as chain associations, jumping from Darwin's ideas on the evolutionary roots of aggression to reciting the poems of Goethe. On one of our many forays to the Metropolitan Museum of Art, she became completely self-absorbed yet inadvertently 'held court' in the gallery. Once, she began describing the secret powers of dwarves that often inhabited the paintings of Velazquez (Henley, as cited in Gerity & Anand, in press). As though speaking to herself, she described why they were so prominent in their gilded finery, valued as sexual playthings, and how their secret inside information about those in King Philip's court gave them special powers—all while ignoring the small crowd of bystanders who leaned in to listen to her 'lecture'. It was often an endurance test to stand for an hour while she 'entered' each painting—such was her ability to enter and emerge from transitional space.

Although a magical presence with children, Edith was famously intolerant of most adults. Many who crossed her ideas incurred her intellectual wrath. In retrospect, I consider Edith's self-absorptions as subthreshold symptoms of the spectrum. Unless at the podium presenting to a large and appreciative audience, she was content to work day after day in the solitary environs of her studio. She perhaps recognized this and sought adult interaction through teachings. Starting the program at New York University, for over thirty years she taught and mentored graduate students in the therapeutic uses of art.

In 2007, she was nearing ninety years of age and announced she was ready to retire to her ancestral Austria. One evening she brought out something unforeseen. It was a portfolio of drawings she had done at age fourteen or fifteen, the likes of which I never knew existed. They dealt with the French Revolution, a volatile period when another dictator was deposed and the New Republic was founded, while ushering in yet another Reign of Terror. She was, at the time, living in poverty in a depleted and defeated Germany, during worldwide depression, anarchy in the streets and the communists battling Hitler's rise to power. As an impressionable young teen, she read avidly on the revolution, in French, and began a series of pen-and-ink works which chronicled the many lively players of this historic time: Robespierre, Voltaire, Marat, Marie Antoinette and others. As is the case with many elders, she had inexplicably reached back and reminisced to me about her formative years, which now included sharing these astonishing illustrations.

In one scenario (Figure 18.4), she portrayed the famous 'Storming the Bastille', a turning point in the rebellion leading to the French Revolution.

This political prison, armoury and fortress represented all that epitomized the tyranny of the royal monarchy. In sketching out a few of the thousand partisans, or *vainqueurs,* Kramer's agitated, abbreviated strokes register the excitement of the moment. Men rushed the drawbridge wielding axes and pitchforks, their vengeful faces distorted in rage and determination. Her rendition is sparse and on point—in keeping with the storyboard or illustrative nature of the series. In subsequent illustrations, Kramer worked with greater care and even in colour, one of which shows Queen Antoinette and King Louis attempting to flee Paris only to be recognized by an innkeeper from the monarchs' faces on a coin. Kramer's depiction displays the queen's agitated and frightful state while the king appears more collected and demonstrably affectionate to his wife. Both would eventually face the dreaded guillotine (Henley, as cited in Gerity & Anand, in press). Both images reflect Kramer's romantic fascination with this historic moment, yet beneath were perhaps simmering feelings of deeper gravity.

To analyze one's teacher and the founder of an entire field is not a task to be taken lightly, especially given the artist's scant commentary. Edith sat in repose as she gazed at the only surviving drawings from her childhood (Bobst Library Archives, New York University). But one may conjecture that chronicling the revolution was no accident. Not coincidentally was the work done during the anarchy that reigned prior to the Nazi's rise to power. Drawn for her own needs, the work's informality and disregard for formal stylistic realism indicates that the twenty

Figure 18.4 Professor Edith Kramer's child drawings were long kept in private storage. Her teen interest in chronicling 'Storming the Bastille' represents one of twenty loose and sensitive sketches.

or so drawings were not meant for general viewing; they were a personal visual diary—perhaps the reason they remained hidden for over seventy-five years.

This was a child who already lived completely through her art. Amongst this tumult, she was often left to her own devices by her family. Edith was an intensely serious child, with her artistic gifts and imagination a matter of emotional survival. The choice of the French Revolution perhaps became the conduit to transitional space, where the imaginal and romantic of a dreamy adolescent were offset by the treacherous times through which she lived. Her art was an act of sublimation where the characters and narrative stood as symbolic equivalents for this young artist—one who continued to imagine and create despite the tumult around her.

Nineteen
Hope and Advocacy

As an antidote to the cases of war and violence, it is fitting to end this text on a more hopeful note. Throughout the case material, I have endeavoured to paint these special children in the light of their resilience by illustrating their positive creative strategies for addressing life's challenges. Creative response activities formed just one of the building blocks for furthering their adaptation to the world and its demands. The promise of their success is based upon society's ever-expanding inclusiveness, among families, public and increased educational and mental health services. It is hoped that social gains will continue amongst schoolmates and neighbourhood kids, who are the most developmentally ill equipped to be empathic minded, yet can do some of the most emotional damage. I was fortunate to assist in this process of socialization, which was part of The Hecht Group's 'wrap-around services'. Here, the children had at their disposal the collective wisdom of creative outlets, surrounded by a skilled and diverse therapeutic team. As part of our initiatives, we enlisted parental and family support, educational coordination and community-outreach programs that still serve as a model for the future. The outcomes of the creative response process showed these children to be up to the task of dealing with sometimes unimaginable conditions. Over the decades, I found their often single-minded creativity indicative of an inner strength. I often marvelled at how ingeniously they overcame adversity and through their creative productions, illuminated their many struggles. One of Kramer's hallmark sayings is that it is the artist's responsibility to *confront* through self-expression—to paint, to write, to portray all the horrors of the world in balance with its boundless beauty. It is dissonant yet sage advice, for without *both* opposing forces, she intoned, there can be no *hope*. It is the construct of hope that drives self-worth, passion and the inspiration, to *will* the individual to survive. Snyder (2002) has investigated this abstract construct after having been inspired by the great analyst Karl Menninger's lectures and, as a result, established the 'hope theory'. His studies find that when the ego is enriched and supported, the individual naturally attempts to find pathways towards positive thinking, positive associations and elaborated ideas. The many outcomes of creative response activities bear out the theory that our children constantly explored expressions that assisted them to press onwards.

While the world that surrounds these children remains an unpredictable and even a hostile place, the immediate outlook for those on the spectrum is increasingly bright. Advocacy for spectrum conditions, such as autism, attention deficit hyperactivity, bipolar and others, is widespread and growing. Grassroots programs and national and international consortiums of professionals, educators, politicians and especially the parents have come together. Conferences, research and clinical efficacy are now active in assuring special needs will be accommodated. It is perhaps the mothers who deserve the most credit. Fresh from the newfound activism for progressive ideas of the 1960s feminist movement, mothers of children with autism formed the Children's Defense Fund, which funded research that among other accomplishments helped to discredit Bettelheim's misguided 'blame the mother' theory. Their support enabled researchers to find alternative aetiologies, such as genetic pre-dispositions, infectious diseases and immunological problems, beyond those of neglectful mothering. At the forefront are technology and social media, which have offered instant access to all individuals who can now tell their own stories, share their experiences and provide links to services and forums. The Internet service YouTube has hundreds of videos of individuals with every imaginable disorder, with first-person accounts that now include their creative response outcomes.

In searching for positive anecdotes with which to inspire the ending of this book, I recently reviewed Donna Williams's compelling recollections of her autistic life experiences. I have previously cited how she survived her feral upbringing (pg. 30). As an adult, she depends upon creative activities to sustain her—from art to music to therapeutic writing. Having recovered from her classic autism is almost unprecedented. Through her sheer force of will and the support of her relationships and community, as an adult she became articulate and personable. In one video, Williams described the themes of her figurative sculptures as a correlate to different emotional states, of feeling 'transparent', of being 'face-blind', of feeling like 'retaliating' against those who hurt and disavowed her. Yet in her magically spiritual paintings is a sense of the transformative that both transcends and embraces the traces of her autism. Hope, then, is the doorway to transitional space—that to enter, create and then emerge from the cave of darkness may move one from despair, as Churchill was once famously quoted, towards 'sunlit uplands'.

Advocacy

Most of the cases in this book maintain the confidentiality of the artists and required extensive informed consent from parents and young adults to be published. Some case accounts go further and require fictionalization, as the details of their involvements are such that their identities must be changed. No children would want to read about themselves twenty years later as a 'case study' with pathologies and personal details exposing what may be a difficult or unbearable memory. Confidentiality and fictionalization have remained the bedrock of clinical reports from the time of Freud, with his use of first or nicknames to label his cases. However, there is a new movement afoot in which individuals, such as Polly Samuels whose nom de plume was once Donna Williams, have 'come out' to share their stories, proudly showing their work in galleries, on websites and via other social forums. Some parents are not only giving consent but are permitting real names and photographs of their children to be published. While these young people are undoubtedly the highest of success stories, a badge of courage is still required to be included in a project such as this, where symptoms inevitably become part of the narrative. While every effort has been made to provide a balanced analysis of their positives, even when weighing the negatives, the result is a weaving of 'mixed outcomes'. Then again, any book written on random individuals would undoubtedly be beset by their own issues—with only the shades of 'frequency and intensity' separating them from the children occupying our loose arc.

Overcoming

Unlike many children whose symptoms reflect hyper-vigilance, alienation and struggle, our cover-artist Jeff Gross flourished as a creative, well-adjusted person. Despite his own difficulties with Rubella-based deafness and legal blindness, he adapted almost miraculously given years of familial and therapeutic support. During his eight-year tenure within the school for the deaf, he became a celebrated artist, eventually exhibiting and becoming widely known for his monumental imagery, as seen in his extraordinary rendering from memory of the hi-rise projects that dotted his urban environment. According to his case file, Jeff's 'blindisms' slowly tempered as he matured, sufficiently to render his autistic-like rituals, benign and 'ego-syntonic'. This term refers to an individual who has integrated and thus 'normalized' his condition, becoming comfortable and at peace within himself. He became a school role-model, one who demonstrated that the most severe multiple handicaps can be successfully overcome, becoming an exemplar of hope and advocacy.

The few spectrum-related symptoms that persisted during our four years of studio work were related mainly to severe sensory deprivation. For instance, he suffered object permanence issues, such that he felt his work could somehow disappear when not in his line of sight. Thus, all his work was held under lock and key—initially, he wore the key around his neck. One of the rarest of artistic savants, his gift separated him from almost every other client in my career. He was legally blind in his right eye and wore thick corrective lenses; the left eye was a prosthetic. Somehow, Jeff was able to visualize and memorize his environment despite being blind enough to walk into closed doors. When I first met him at the school for the deaf, he was almost exclusively drawing subway maps. One large-scale piece, still in my possession, required taping six tagboards together to make a seven-foot-tall colour-coded map. He relished this process, separating the different lines, marking their connections and stations, and indicating 'express' or 'local'. This vibrant subject matter was well within Jeff's comfort zone. From his home in New Jersey, he and his father rode the trains and subways and experienced the bustling city life during his many visits to New York. He was thus encouraged to pursue these themes as part of his creative response activity.

During art therapy, in an 'open studio' format, described by Allen (2008), Jeff was allowed undisturbed studio time, where he could dialogue with his images—often signing to them in his own 'inner voice' in an animated manner. Few interventions were forthcoming, as he was highly self-motivated and explorative. I did encourage Jeff to depart from his schematic maps and draw *about* the subway, not strictly its routes. Getting this concept across through sign language was not easy. Aside from the logistics, it abstracted what was an already stereotypic schema. When I showed him visual resources of subway trains and other imagery, Jeff's latent gifts came alive. He began to draw a profusion of subways, platforms and escalators, as well as elevated trains that featured graffiti. He drew about the buses of the New Jersey Transit on their way through the tunnels and bridges to New York City. The ability to take in a scene, memorize it and then put the image faithfully to paper drew the interest of Dr. Sacks, who was sent a sample of Jeff's drawing for his consideration. He pronounced Jeff's drawing— an elevated highway teaming with trains, buildings and multilevel buildings— 'unprecedented' (personal communication with Sacks in 1989). He wrote about how Jeff's creations called for 'new theories not only for art making but also for definitions of vision'.

This sense of incomprehension is linked to the paradox of being able to draw what one cannot visually see. Citing the multimodality of human perception, the problem is framed as to how visual pictorial expression can belong to more than one sense. According to the theory of eidetic memory, Jeff's drawings suggest that the image is somehow assimilated and remains an unshakable and literal 'picture' in the mind's eye. Ebie (pg. 30) too perhaps possessed eidetic perception, as his vast repertoire of electrical components were often sketched in the air with his eyes closed before putting them to paper. In the case of Tracy Carcione, a blind artist whose drawings were exhibited at the Museum of Modern Art in 2002, she was able to draw geometric forms, such as cubes, from five different vantage points, including from 'above', and became a sensation. Carcione's foreshortening and convergence of lines were 'touch generated conversions', meaning she used her compensatory haptic, or touch, sensations as a means of relaying form without the need for sight. Kennedy's theory attributes the ability of the blind or visually impaired to reconstruct an image to haptic or tactile sensation (1993). However, in the case of Jeff, haptic theory does not hold, as he does not rely upon 'sensory substitution', but rather is visually minded. Lowenfeld's work with the partially blind points out that many of his clients were visual in their creative approach (1957). The cover image of the high-rise demonstrates how Jeff could work in complex geometrics, with perfect perspective—not so easy a task when one is working out of their imagination or memory without the benefit of a ruler or other visual aids. Somehow, he could draw objects without the benefit of touch, but from far range with multiple perspectives of extraordinary accuracy. Obviously, the residual vision in his right eye concentrated a laser-like fidelity of objects that were somehow memorized and stored for later art sessions.

Another exemplar of one of his mature works is 'Amusement Park' (Plate 7), created in the fourth year of art therapy. By this time, Jeff had expanded his scope from close-ups of trains and stereotypical subway maps to creating lively large-scale panoramas. This highly detailed work also utilized the coloured felt tip marker preferred by his contemporary, Saul, and many other clients. Drawn after a family excursion, it explores his sensory impressions of the day— which for this multiply involved young man must have been extraordinarily stimulating.

The work includes two complexly formed roller coasters, several twirling rides, an aerial gondola and various others, which according to his parents were almost identical to those depicted in the drawn scene ('almost', since his parents could not themselves recall or verify so many details). Jeff's improvising indicates that his perception was not eidetic, which would call for an exact 'mind picture', but is suggestive of artistic license. As a stimulus, an amusement ride for a young man must have had 'supernormal' qualities, with each ride's kinetic action becoming a controlled onrush of sensory overload. Yet Jeff also presented with one conspicuous spectrum-related issue, his avoidance of humans in his compositions. It has already been established that this omission among those on the spectrum is common and almost certainly linked to their quality of relatedness. Though Jeff was well attached with a supportive family, I attributed his seeming autistic features to blindisms. In contrast to this suggestion of an autistic omission, Jeff's work is pathology free. As a handicapped individual, he experienced the world in an atypical manner and brought these sensations to his work with an authentic and graphically fascinating style. In the open studio, I suggested that perhaps there might be people in the trains, subways and parks. It seemed that figurative content had never occurred to him—after all, they are such minute elements compared to his monumental high-rises or amusement parks. Figures arrived in a naive yet mature style, yet are seen bustling about. In 'Amusement Park', people are drawn in a normative everyday manner. Individuals line up for their turn on the rides or for tickets or refreshments, or they loiter around, watching others on the rides from the sidelines. Jeff depicted the participants on the zero-gravity ride in a circular configuration, convincingly showing how they are pinned against the walls by centrifugal force. He discriminates between a distant roller coaster, with its extensive framing, and the oval-shaped, loop-the-loop G-force roller coaster, a 'clothoid' curve ride on which participants drop a hundred feet at sixty miles an hour—surely a breathless-looking contraption for a deaf/blind boy to take in.

After four years of making art in the open-studio format, his creative responses expanded precipitously with amusement rides, such as roller coasters, as well as parades and other large-scale activities which involved people. From stereotypical subway maps, Jeff's oeuvre expanded with his immersion into independent and intensive studio work. One large-scale piece was an eight-foot mural of the skyline of Trenton, New Jersey, drawn after having taken a single car ride passing by the city. After his work was shown to Ethel Kennedy's aides, Jeff was invited to the Kennedy Center for the Performing Arts to demonstrate his process, alongside other more well-known special artists, such as the late Richard Wawro—another autistic savant made famous in a film by Laurence Becker (1983).

After graduation, he entered vocational training and gained employment in a shipping and receiving facility. There, I would guess, objects again took on a life of their own as parcels made loops through an array of chutes and conveyors, which kept him sensory satisfied. In follow-up communications with his mother, she described how the day-to-day work schedule depleted Jeff's creative energies and that he has since returned to his formative years of making intricate maps of subway and train lines—as a welcome form of occupational or leisure-time creative response activity—after a hard day's work.

Animal Whistler

The celebratory, symptom-free art of Jeff Gross stands in contrast to those gifted individuals whose art evolved while they suffered terribly with their spectrum symptoms. Another young man, Jake Dion also used his creativity as an expression of joy and love, despite a deeply troubled childhood where many obstacles were overcome. Throughout his autistic childhood, he could establish and maintain an intimate relational bond to his mother despite his severe involvement. As a toddler, Jake progressed normally through his developmental milestones and language development, and then regression ensued. At age three, he was hospitalized with a roseola infection. His mother, Jenni, reports that after the infection had run its course, Jake's developmental progress was inexplicably halted overnight. A happy, well-bonded baby had spontaneously lost the capacity for language and had taken on many other autistic symptoms. To compensate, Jake began drawing to communicate with his mother, which proved to be a life-changing event. Art as communication, as well as other creative activities, became the lifeblood of this child.

During his childhood, Jake also became remarkably attached to animals. Jenni began early stimulation activities at age three, when they began to visit zoos, where animals were readily observable. Jenni's homegrown methodology was naturalistic in nature. She intuitively provided her son with as many enrichment activities in his own comfort setting as she could to pursue his passions. She has shared many fascinating childhood photographs of Jake's interacting with enormous zoo animals, such as hugging an elephant while barely out of toddlerhood. His mother has stated that Jake displayed a preternatural gift, one that might be characterized as an 'animal whistler'. Impossibly large and intelligent animals, such as elephants and dolphins, seem to trust, communicate and spontaneously 'come to him', without any trainer or other behavioural trickery. Since this early age, Jake's fascination and mutual attachment to all animals have become a form of 'animal therapy'. His extensive journals are full of drawings and notes about a range of creatures. They also contain unusually insightful and informed information on the plight of nature and threat of animal extinction. Especially regarding his favoured elephants, he is highly aware and disturbed that they are being systematically wiped out across Africa. At a recent art opening, he whispered to me as we viewed a drawing of a matriarchal elephant and its young that 'gangs shoot down the matriarchs who possess all the knowledge'. Later, he again sidled up to me again and almost covertly whispered 'they now use automatic weapons which feed the craft market in China!' Such is his awareness and capacity to somehow filter, assumably with marked hyposensitivity, this accurate, horrific reality. Because of Jake's growing celebrity and his capacity to articulate his position on animal rights, he has met with politicians and dignitaries to raise their awareness of his passionate advocacy—for others.

Beyond his animal whistling and political activism, Jake is a superb draftsman. His art began as a vital form of communication with his mother, and it remained his primary language until he began to speak at age six and a half. As a long-term modality, Jake's giftedness has since evolved to savant levels. He now exhibits and sells his work through his website and is in several important collections. His drawings are almost photorealistic, which led me to believe that Jake traced his images using an opaque projector. But upon closer inspection, one can make out his process—of outlining his figures, shading in and adding other nuances which show the hand of the artist. As further 'proof', Jenni sent me photographs of his works in progress, with Jake at his drawing table, working on his favoured subjects, all *from memory*. His process is to draw for a few hours each day and then work in his garden. At his home farm, flower and vegetable gardens are vast and bountiful. He obsessively weeds beds and plants, working with the same fervour he brings to his art.

Jake's art is unusual in that it lacks the purely perceptual realism we found in the art of Nadia (pg. 33), who had limited conceptual awareness of her subjects. Far from eidetic mind tracing, Jake's art is inextricably linked to a heightened awareness of the relationship between himself, his mother and the animals he has long visited as an extended family. His animal rights activism is one based upon positivism and hope—a legacy left by the great Jane Goodall. Jake's lobbying is also quiet yet insistent and tireless. He uses his art as a vehicle for communication—as a creative response to a grim reality while persevering at every opportunity to ensure his efforts make a difference.

One of his photorealistic works in graphite is a drawing of a mother giraffe nuzzling her calf (Figure 19.1). The sense of mutual attachment is overpowering. Jake portrays both mother and child as having entered a transitional space where bonding is not limited to the 'mutual gaze' but is tactile and kinaesthetic. The sense of maternal smell is another important bonding sense. Their intermingling provides the needed contact comfort that is so critical to the object relationship of maternally providing sustenance and love. It can only be described as a combination of maternal-child bliss and struggle—his mother, Jenni, parenting alone, courageously dealing with a child in trouble, survived the experience through intensifying their emotional attachment. Projecting the sense of maternal caregiving through such intimacy also allows Jake to expand his interrelationships—to be linked beyond the maternal orbit, to that of the outside, in dynamic and

Figure 19.1 Jake is a photorealistic artist whose works often portray the tenderness between animal mothers and their babies. Despite being diagnosed with severe autism as a child, he is now verbal and an avid animal rights activist who articulates the plight of endangered species in speeches to groups and politicians.
Used with permission of Jenni and Jake Dion.

productive ways. Yet this exclusive relational-based content perhaps hints at the developmental insult that traumatized him after the infection—attachment has become an imperative. With mother at his side, he has sublimated early trauma with a miraculousness and an indefatigable hope he freely shares.

Renaissance Man and the Warrior Mom

I was introduced to the next young man after having seen one of his illustrations in response to his 'action activities' at the sports facility 'PROGRESH'. At the facility, which Kyle Henley operates, a young spectrum teen named Max works out on the trampolines and skateboards and then records his activities through creative work. Max is a prolific artist, musician and budding athlete who, with the help of his mother, Rebecca, published his own autobiography, *Hello, My Name Is Max and I Have Autism* (Miller, 2014). Remarkably self-aware, Max illustrated his story with many telling images, including a picture that recounts his early frustrations with learning new skills while appealing 'weird' to others. With his mother as chief advocate, Max has not just overcome his condition, but has become a spokesman for the spectrum, articulating how he struggled to overcome its most debilitating and frightful effects.

In his visual art, Max equates many colours to feeling states, a type of emotion-mapping skill learned without the services of an art therapist. In one drawing, he evokes an underworld beneath earth's crust, filled with black rock and oceans of magma with sunny skies peeking through (Plate 8).

About the image, Max writes:

> Red waves are coming for me while at my desk. My anger bubbles up—this is the blue—my frustration in the classroom. Black is my brain core—it is really dark. When I am in a good mood it's white and green, but when I get upset, it returns back to black.

As an art therapist, I would never break down an image or its elements into concrete symbols—such a practice is reductive and formulaic. However, one cannot emphasize enough that to have the child spontaneously work out the meaning behind his colours can be highly therapeutic. Cognitive and unconscious sources seem to operate in synchronicity, with primary and secondary processes effecting a sublimation. Kramer's criteria is again fulfilled, as the child evoked literally volcanic levels of feeling, with sure-handed economy, resulting in fully formed expression.

Max acknowledges that on occasion he needs to self-stimulate, though he has accepted this as part of his bodily expression, that the condition is an integral part of his persona. In my accompanying him around the Denver Art Museum, he remains amazingly 'typical'. Like any other bored teenager, he eventually becomes antsy if the adults blab on for too long. Only then will he display tic-like movements—which he camouflages very well. On these symptoms, he writes:

> I realize that autism is just a part of who I am. It is me, but it doesn't bother me. I just need some help in life. I'm lucky, my family has my back.

It was not always this way. Max's Mom wrote her own book (Miller, 2015), which describes the harrowing struggles. Her early years bringing up Max was still a time when advocacy and education for children suffering spectrum disorders were less enlightened. Rebecca recounts her numerous challenges almost matter of factly, giving birth to Max while barely out of her teens and then being abandoned by her first husband. She was caught short without a degree and earned a living waiting tables late at night, all the while scrambling to care for a difficult child. His complicated toileting, screaming 'meltdowns' in public and rejections by schools at every turn constantly tested Rebecca. Nevertheless, this indefatigable mom persevered. When teachers deemed him an 'institutional case', she recounts in her book, in a pull-no-punches style of poetic prose, that the indignation she suffered only strengthened her resolve:

> I watched as the professional sat straight up as she authoritatively declared that Max was 'unteachable' and 'unreachable'. She pronounced that he would never thrive, Max would never learn to dress himself, feed himself, use the toilet, let alone read or write.

> Max smiled at me and pulled on my necklace, burying himself in my arm. I held him and rocked him. I saw a spark in his eyes and I knew he was there: I could reach him. I could teach him.
>
> (Miller, 2015, pg. 41)

After that epiphany, Rebecca realized that the only course was to become a *warrior mom* (Miller, 2015). She began by mounting a campaign to question each physician, research medical literature, and investigate different medications and alternative therapies, such as supplements and oils. Questioning the authorities, she took over as case manager and chief advocate. She was indignant at the many professions who were often diagnostically rigid, ill informed or even indifferent—perhaps tired of everyone's child supposedly being a 'special case'. Schools sometimes balk at accepting a child with intense needs because they require tremendous financial and personal resources. So to negotiate from a point of strength and stability, Rebecca went to night school and graduated as a registered nurse, all the while tirelessly case managing and networking. She worked with Max, stimulating his communication senses, and struggled with his self-help skills all while seizing upon and building his every interest. She became arbiter of which strategies showed promise and abandoned those which didn't.

At the time of this writing, Max and Rebecca form a dynamic duo—speaking publically to parents, agencies, educators and politicians. In their spare time, they run a non-profit clearinghouse for information and cultural events for others on the spectrum, called the Blue Ribbon Arts Initiative. During my last meeting with them, they had both collaborated and convened an art exhibition at the Denver Art Museum. Among other individuals on the spectrum, he was exhibiting drawings, photographs and a large Plexiglas cube sculpture, with urethane foam that had expanded and jutted out of pierced cutout shapes in the plastic, giving it a wild, unruly presence. As part of the opening celebration, children read poems, and some sang pop tunes. Max displayed his cultivated side when he closed out the evening performing an improvised piece on the guitar (Figure 19.2).

After the show, he decamped to a local jazz club with Rebecca to catch a late set. I later asked what he had heard, and he remarked nonchalantly, 'some guy blowing a baritone', which he said would be his next instrument. His influences range from Coltrane to the Ramones. Max is matter of fact about all his gifts, counting both his creativity *and* his autistic self-stimulation as the completed self. He wears his public persona just as well—whether skateboarding at PROGRESH or working the room schmoozing with officials from the museum. Max and Mom are a fully integrated team, whose creative responses seem to have few bounds.

Figure 19.2 Max and Rebecca, his 'warrior mom', struggled for years with his autistic condition. With her intensive sensory stimulation, Max has become an artist, musician and self-advocate.

Used with permission of Rebecca and Max Miller.

Twenty
Resonance

Rosie

The final case and parting image is a wondrous drawing created by Rosie, who, as a fifteen-year-old, captures the essence of both the challenging and creative sides of the spectrum condition (Figure 20.1). Swinging for many children on the spectrum is a primal act that affords the airy freedom of unfettered movement and satisfying self-stimulation. Dangling off a trapeze is a riff from this pastime, one that is familiar to anyone acquainted with children on the autistic side of the spectrum. Like many others, this child was lulled by such kinetic movement, and her joy requires no analysis. Now a grown woman who was cured from her autism by almost a lifetime of analysis and self-determination, Rosie became a mother, a grandmother and a New York–based professional artist. In consenting to be the book's finale, she preferred that in conveying the vagaries of her childhood, her art should stand on its own and speak for itself. I have honoured that request by keeping my comments brief. The epilogue is meant to transition from this long and perhaps academic read to an evanescent moment, one fixed in time and space that will hopefully resonate beyond the book's ending. Rosie's only remark about the drawing was the comment 'I just couldn't get the hands right in those days'— ever the self-critical artist.

The sketch is among the most magical life drawings from *any* child's case in my forty-year collection, including those of savants and the gifted. This miniature three-inch-square sketch speaks of her harrowing childhood journey, one that was both a fearful and an exhilarating ride. Her drawing captures for me a moment of bliss that leaves me lost for any more words.

Rosie
Swinging trapeze by barely a knee
gathers in a halo of hearts.
Never mind the abyss below.
The trust of being held
softens the fall and raises the spirit.

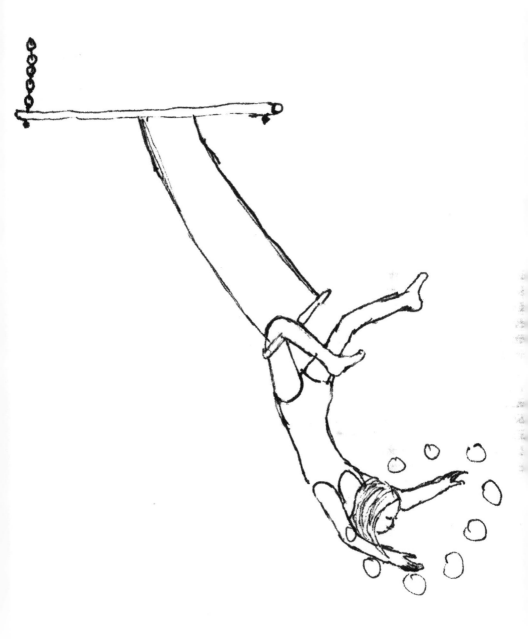

Figure 20.1 Rosie swings on a trapeze with wild abandon—dangling precariously and blissfully. She recently recounted over fifty years of struggle, overcoming what had long been an unwelcoming and incomprehensible world.

References

Agthe, M., Spörrle, M., Frey, D., Walper, S., & Maner, J. K. (2013). When romance and rivalry awaken: Attractiveness-based social judgment biases emerge at adolescence. *Human Nature, 24*(2), 182–195. doi:10.1007/s12110-013-9166-z

Aldridge, K., George, I. D., Cole, K. K., Austin, J. R., Takahashi, T. N., Duan, Y., & Miles, J. H. (2011). Facial phenotypes in subgroups of prepubertal boys with autism spectrum disorders are correlated with clinical phenotypes. *Molecular Autism 2*(15). doi:10.1186/2040-2392-2-15 Retrieved from https://molecularautism.biomedcentral.com/articles/10.1186/2040-2392-2-15

Allen, P. B. (2008). Commentary on community-based studios: Underlying principles. *Art Therapy: Journal of the American Art Therapy Association, 25*(1), 11–12. http://dx.doi.org/10.1080/07421656.2008.10129350

Altman, I. (1975). *The environment and social behavior: Privacy, personal space, territory, and crowding.* Monterey, CA: Brooks/Cole.

Amendolari, M. (2003). *Art education as an adaptive protocol: Engaging the process and product of art in a three-dimensional design college classroom with at-risk adolescents.* (Unpublished master's thesis). Long Island University, Brookville, NY.

American Psychiatric Association. (2013). *Diagnostic and statistical manual of mental disorders* (5th ed.). Arlington, VA: American Psychiatric Publishing.

Anshel, M. H. (2012). *Sport psychology: From theory to practice* (5th ed.). New York: Pearson.

Arbus, D. (1972). Exhibition catalogue. New York: Museum of Modern Art.

Attwood, T. (2008). *The complete guide to Asperger's syndrome.* London: Jessica Kingsley Publishers.

Baker, D. L., & Steuernagel, T. (2016). Comparative Canadian and United States autism: A narrative analysis. *Review of Disability Studies: An International Journal, 8*(4). Retrieved December 12, 2016, from www.rds.hawaii.edu/ojs/index.php/journal/article/view/78

Barkley, R. A., & Newcorn, J. H. (2009). Assessing adults with ADHD and comorbidities. *The Primary Care Companion to the Journal of Clinical Psychiatry, 11*(1), 9–25. PMC2660162

Barkow, J. H., Cosmides, L., & Tooby, J. (1995). *The adapted mind: Evolutionary psychology and the generation of culture.* New York: Oxford University Press.

Baron-Cohen, S. (1995). *Mindblindness: An essay on autism and theory of mind.* Cambridge, MA: MIT Press.

Baron-Cohen, S. (2002). The extreme male brain theory of autism. *Trends in Cognitive Science, 6*(6), 248–254.

Barrett, D. (2010). *Supernormal stimuli: How primal urges overran their evolutionary purpose.* New York: W.W. Norton & Co.

Bartels, A., & Zeki, S. (2004). The neural correlates of maternal and romantic love. *Neuroimage, 21*(3), 1155–1166.

Becker, L. A. (Producer), & Zimmermann, R. (Director). (1983). *With eyes wide open: The life and art of Richard Wawro.* [Documentary]. United States: Independent Productions.

Bergman, A. (1999). *Ours, yours, mine: Mutuality and the emergence of the separate self.* Northdale, NJ: Jason Aronson.

Bettelheim, B. (1959). Joey: A 'mechanical boy.' *Scientific American,* March.

Betts, D. J. (2003). Developing a projective drawing test: Experiences with the Face Stimulus Assessment (FSA). *Art Therapy: Journal of the American Art Therapy Association, 20*(2), 77–82. http://dx.doi.org/10.1080/07421656.2003.10129393

Biederman, J., Wilens, T., Mick, E., Faraone, S. V., Weber, W., Curtis, S., ... Soriano J. (1997). Is ADHD a risk factor for psychoactive substance use disorders? Findings from a four-year prospective follow-up study. *Journal of the American Academy of Child and Adolescent Psychiatry, 36*(1), 21–29.

Boorman, J. (Producer & Director). (1987). *Hope and glory.* [Motion picture]. London: Columbia Pictures.

Bowlby, J. (1960). Grief and mourning in infancy and early childhood. *Psychoanalytic Study of the Child, 15,* 9–52.

Bowlby, J. (1969). *Attachment* (Attachment and Loss series, Vol. 1). New York: Basic Books.

Brooks, R. (2016). *How everything became war and the military became everything: Tales from the Pentagon.* New York: Simon & Schuster.

Buck, J. (1992). *The house-tree-person projective test drawing technique.* Los Angeles: Western Psychological Services.

Burton, T. (1992). *Batman Returns* [Motion picture]. United States: Warner Bros.

Bushman, B. J., & Anderson, C. A. (2009). Comfortably numb: Densensitizing effects of violent media on helping others. *Psychological Science, 20*(3), 273–277.

Byers, J. G. (1996). Children of the stones: Art therapy interventions in the West Bank. *Art Therapy: Journal of the American Art Therapy Association, 13*(4), 238–243.

Cantor, J., & Nathanson, A. I. (1996). Children's fright reactions to television news. *Journal of Communication, 46*(4), 139–152.

Cardinal, C. (1972). *Outsider art.* New York: Praeger.

Cardinal, R. (1989). The primitive scratch. In A. Gilroy & T. Dalley (Eds.), *Pictures at an exhibition: Selected essays on art and art therapy* (pp. 113–126). London and New York: Routledge.

Cardinal, R. (2004). Marginalia. In J. T. Berge (Ed.), *Marginalia: Perspectives on outsider art* (pp. 77–101). The Netherlands: De Stadshof.

Carhart-Harris, R. L., & Friston, K. J. (2010). The default-mode, ego-functions, and free-energy: A neurobiological account of Freudian ideas. *Brain, 133*(4), 1265–1283.

Castaneda, C. (1968). *Teachings of Don Juan: A Yaqui way of knowledge.* Berkeley, CA: University of California Press.

Connelly, C. (2015). Who am I now? Art therapy, identity and adjustment after acquired brain injury. In M. Liebmann & S. Weston (Eds)., *Art therapy with neurological conditions* (pp. 99–115). London: Jessica Kingsley Publishers.

Damasio, A. (2010). *Self comes to mind: Constructing the conscious brain.* New York: Pantheon Books.

Davis, M. E. (1977). *William Blake: A new kind of man.* Berkeley, CA: University of California Press.

Delicato, C. (1974). *The ultimate stranger.* Novato, CA: Arena Press.

Dewey, J. (1934). *Art as experience.* New York: Minton Books.

Disney, W. (Producer). (1940). *Fantasia.* [Motion picture]. United States: Walt Disney Productions.

Dissanayake, E. (1988). *What is art for?* Seattle, WA: University of Washington Press.

Dumke, M. (2012). The shot that brought the projects down. *The Chicago Reader,* October 12.

Edwards, D. (2014). *Art therapy.* Los Angeles and London: Sage Publications.

Eibl-Eibesfeldt, I. (1989). *Human ethology.* Hawthorne, NY: Aldine de Gruyer.

Environmental Factors in Autism Initiative. Retrieved from www.autismspeaks.org/science/research-initiatives/environmental-factors-autism-initiative

Evans, K., & Dubowski, J. (2001). *Art therapy with children on the autistic spectrum: Beyond words.* London: Jessica Kingsley Publishers.

Fernyhough, C. (2016). *The voices within.* New York: Basic Books.

Flax, J. (1990). *Thinking in fragments.* Berkeley, CA: University of California Press.

Franklin, M. A. (2017). Art as contemplative practice: Expressive pathways to the self. Albany, NY: SUNY Press.

Freud, A., & Dann, S. (1951). An experiment in group upbringing. *Psychoanalytic Study of the Child, 6,* 127–168.

Freud, S. (1923). *The ego and the id.* New York: W.W. Norton.

Frith, U. (2001). Mind blindness and the brain in autism. *Neuron, 32*(6), 969–979. http://dx.doi.org/10.1016/S0896-6273(01)00552-9

Gaskill, R. L., & Perry, B. D. (2014). The neurobiological power of play: Using the neurosequential model of therapeutics to guide play in the healing process. In C. A. Malchiodi & D. A. Crenshaw (Eds.), *Creative arts and play therapy for attachment problems* (pp. 178–194). New York: Guilford Press.

Gerity, L., & Anand, S. (In press). *The Edith Kramer legacy: A multifaceted view.* New York and London: Routledge.

Gilroy, A. (2007). *Art therapy, research and evidence-based practice.* London: Sage Publications.

Goldberg, E. (2002). *The executive brain: Frontal lobes and the civilized mind.* New York: Oxford University Press.

Gombrich, E. H. (1963). *Meditations on a hobby horse and other essays on the theory of art.* London: Phaidon Press.

Goodall, J. (1971). *In the shadow of man.* Boston: Houghton Mifflin.

Gnaulati, E. (2008). *Emotion-regulating play therapy with ADHD children: Staying with playing.* Lanham, MD: Jason Aronson.

Grandin, T. (1986). *Emergence: Labeled autistic.* Novato, CA: Arena Press.

Grandin, T., & Panek, R. (2013). *The autistic brain: Helping different kinds of minds succeed.* Boston: Houghton Mifflin.

Graner, J., Oakes, T. R., French, L. M., & Riedy, G. (2013). Functional MRI in the investigation of blast-related traumatic brain injury. *Frontiers in Neurology, 4,* 16. doi:10.3389/fneur.2013.00016

Green, S. A., & Ben-Sasson, A. (2010). Anxiety disorders and sensory over-responsivity in children with autism spectrum disorders: Is there a causal relationship? *Journal of Autism Developmental Disorders, 40*(12), 1495–1504.

Greenfield, D. N. (1999). Psychological characteristics of compulsive internet use: Preliminary analysis. *Cyberpsychology and Behavior, 2*(5), 403–412. doi:10.1089/cpb.1999.2.403

Hammer, E. F. (1968). *Use of interpretation in treatment: Technique and art.* New York and London: Grune & Stratton.

Henley, D. (1983). *Self-injurious behavior: Art educational and art therapeutic interventions.* (Unpublished master's thesis). New York University, New York.

Henley, D. (1989a). Artistic giftedness in the multiply handicapped child. In H. Wadeson, J. Durkin, & D. Perach (Eds.), *Advances in art therapy* (pp. 262–272). New York: Wiley.

Henley, D. (1989b). Nadia revisited: A study into the nature of regression in the autistic savant syndrome. *Art Therapy: Journal of the American Art Therapy Association, 6*(2), 43–56. http://dx.doi.org/10.1080/07421656.1989.10758866h

Henley, D. (1992). *Exceptional children exceptional art.* Worcester, MA: Davis Publications.

Henley, D. (1998). Art therapy in a socialization program for children with attention deficit hyperactivity disorder. *American Journal of Art Therapy, 37*(1), 2–13.

Henley, D. (1999). Facilitating socialization with a therapeutic camp setting for children with attention deficits utilizing the expressive therapies. *American Journal of Art Therapy, 38*(2), 40–50.

Henley, D. (2001). Annihilation anxiety and fantasy in the art of children with Asperger's Syndrome and others on the autistic spectrum. *American Journal of Art Therapy, 39*(11), 13–21.

Henley, D. (2002). *Clayworks in art therapy: Plying the sacred circle.* London: Jessica Kingsley Publishers.

Henley, D. (2005). Attachment disorders in post-institutionalized adopted children: Art therapy approaches to reactivity and detachment. *The Arts in Psychotherapy, 32*(1), 29–46.

Henley, D. (2007). Art therapy and the multiply handicapped child. In E. G. Horovitz (Ed.), *Visually speaking: Art therapy and the deaf* (pp. 110–130). Springfield, IL: Charles C Thomas.

Henley, D. (2012a). Knowing the unknowable: A multidisciplinary approach to postmodern assessment in child art therapy. In A. Gilroy, R. Tipple, & C. Brown (Eds.), *Assessment in art therapy* (pp. 40–54). London: Routledge.

Henley, D. (2012b). Working with the young outsider artist: Appropriation, elaboration, and building self-narrative. In A. Wexler (Ed.), *Art education beyond the classroom: Pondering the outsider and other sites of learning* (pp. 7–30). New York: Palgrave Macmillan.

Henley, D. (2016). Lessons in the images: Art therapy in creative education. In J. A. Rubin (Ed.), *Approaches to art therapy: Theory and technique* (3rd ed., pp. 452–467). New York and London: Routledge.

Hesse, H. (1919, 1960). *Demian.* New York: Bantam Books.

Howells, R., & Negreiros, J. (2012). *Visual culture* (2nd ed.). Malden, MA: Polity Press.

Itard, J. (1962). *The wild boy of Aveyron.* New York: Prentice Hall.

Jaarsma, P., & Wellin, S. (2012). Autism as a natural human variation: Reflections on the claims of the neurodiversity movement. *Health Care Annals, 20*(1), 20–30. doi:10.1007/s10728-011-0169-9

Jacquet, L. (Director). (2005). *March of the penguins.* [Motion picture]. France: National Geographic Films.

Jamison, K. R. (1993). *Touched with fire: Manic-depressive illness and the artistic temperament.* New York: Free Press.

Jamison, K. R. (1997). *An unquiet mind: A memoir of moods and madness.* New York: Vintage Press.

Jones, E. J. H., Gliga, T., Bedford, R., Charman, T., & Johnson, M. H. (2014). Developmental pathways to autism: A review of prospective studies of infants at risk. *Neuroscience & Biobehavioral Reviews, 39,* 1–33. http://dx.doi.org/10.1016/j.neubiorev.2013.12.001

Jung, C. G. (1989). *Memories, dreams, reflections.* New York: Vintage Books.

Jung, C. G. (2009). *Red book: Liber novus.* New York: W.W. Norton & Co.

Kaiser, D. H., & Deaver, S. (2009). Assessing attachment with the bird's nest drawing: A review of the research. *Art Therapy: Journal of the American Art Therapy Association, 26*(1), 26–33. http://dx.doi.org/10.1080/07421656.2009.10129312

Kanner, L. (1943). Autistic disturbances of affective contact. *Nervous Child, 2,* 217–250.

Kennedy, J. M. (1993). *Drawing and the blind.* New Haven, CT: Yale University Press.

Kerley, K. R., Copes, H., & Griffin, O. H. (2015). Middle-class motives for non-medical prescription stimulant use among college students. *Deviant Behavior, 36*(7), 589–603. http://dx.doi.org/10.1080/01639625.2014.9515734.9

Knill, P. J. (1994). Multiplicity as a tradition: Theories for interdisciplinary arts therapies. *The Arts in Psychotherapy, 21*(5), 319–328. http://dx.doi.org/10.1016/0197-4556(94)90059-0

Kowalski, R. M., & Limber, S. P. (2013). Psychological, physical, and academic correlates of cyberbullying and traditional bullying. *Journal of Adolescent Health, 53*(1), S13–S20. http://dx.doi.org/10.1016/j.jadohealth.2012.09.018h

Kramer, E. (1958). *Art therapy in a children's community: A study of the function of art therapy in the treatment program of Wiltwyck School for Boys.* Springfield, IL: Charles C Thomas.

Kramer, E. (1971). *Art as therapy with children.* New York: Schocken Press.

Kramer, E. (1986). The art therapist's third hand: Reflections on art, art therapy and society at large. *American Journal of Art Therapy, 24*(3), 71–86.

Kramer, E. (2000). *Art as therapy: Collected papers.* L. A. Gerity (Ed.). London: Jessica Kingsley Publishers.

Kramer, E. (2006). Art as therapy. In H. Wadeson & M. Junge (Eds.), *Architects of art therapy: Memoirs and life stories* (pp. 11–30). Springfield, IL: Charles C Thomas.

Kris, E. (1952, 1999). *Psychoanalytic explorations in art.* New York: Schocken Press.

Laing, R. D. (1965). *The divided self: An existential study in sanity and madness.* New York: Penguin Books.

Lewis-Williams, D. (2002). *The mind in the cave: Consciousness and the origins of art.* London: Thames and Hudson.

Littman, E. (2014). What the ADHD brain wants—and why. Retrieved from http://drellen littman.com/WHAT THE ADHD BRAIN WANTS 2016 FINAL.pdf

Lorenz, K. (1966). *On aggression.* New York: Psychology Press.

Lowenfeld, V. (1957). *Creative and mental growth.* New York: Macmillan.

Macdonald, K. & Macdonald, T. M. (2010). The peptide that binds: A systematic review of oxytocin and its prosocial effects in humans. *Harvard Review of Psychiatry, 18*(1), 1–21. doi:10.3109/10673220903523615

MacGregor, J. M. (1992). *The discovery of the art of the insane.* Princeton, NJ: Princeton University Press.

Mahler, M. (1969). *On human symbiosis and the vicissitudes of individuation.* Los Angeles and London: Sage Publications.

Mahler, M. S., Pine, F., & Bergman, A. (1975). *Psychological birth of the human infant.* New York: Basic Books.

Makarova, E. (2000). *Friedl Dicker-Brandeis.* Vienna and Munich: Christian Brandstetter Verlag.

Malcolm, J. (2016). Yuja Wang and the art of performance. *The New Yorker,* September 5. Retrieved from www.newyorker.com/magazine/2016/09/05/yuja-wang-and-the-art-of-performance

Maslow, A. (1954). *Motivation and personality.* New York: Harper.

McKee, A. C., & Robinson, M. E. (2014). Military-related traumatic brain injury and neurodegeneration. *Alzheimer's & Dementia, 10*(3 Suppl), S242–S253.

Meltzoff, A. N., & Brooks, R. (2007). Intersubjectivity before language: Three windows on preverbal sharing. In A. Braten (Ed.), *On being moved: From mirror neurons to empathy* (pp. 149–174). Philadelphia, PA: John Benjamins Publishing Company.

Midgley, N. (2013). *Reading Anna Freud.* New York and London: Routledge.

Miller, L. (2017). Scholar girl meets manga maniac, media specialist, and cultural gatekeeper. In M. McLelland (Ed.), *The end of cool Japan: Ethical, legal, and cultural challenges to Japanese popular culture* (pp. 51–69). New York and London: Routledge.

Miller, M. (2014). *Hello, my name is Max and I have autism: An insight into the autistic mind.* J. Bonadonna (Ed.). Bloomington, IN: AuthorHouse.

Miller, R. (2015). *Being Max's mom.* Denver, CO: CreateSpace.

Moore, M. J., Hickson, M., & Stacks, D. W. (2009). *Nonverbal communication: Studies and applications* (5th ed.). New York: Oxford University Press.

Morris, D. (1967). *The naked ape.* New York: Vintage.

Moustakas, C. (1953). *Children in play therapy.* New York: McGraw Hill.

Nachmias, M., Gunnar, M., Mangelsdorf, S., Parritz, R., & Buss, K. (1996). Behavioral inhibition and stress reactivity: The moderating role of attachment security. *Child Development, 67*(2), 508–522.

Nadeau, K. G., Littman, E. B., & Quinn, P. O. (1999). *Understanding girls with ADHD.* Silver Spring, MD: Advantage Books.

Naumburg, M. (1947, 1973). *An introduction to art therapy: Studies of the 'free' art expression of behavior problem children and adolescents as a means of diagnosis and therapy.* New York: Teachers College Press.

Neihardt, J. G. (1932, 2008). *Black Elk speaks.* Albany, NY: SUNY Press.

Orsini, C. (1988). *An art therapy/art educational approach with a gifted multiple handicapped rubella child.* (Unpublished master's thesis). New York University, New York.

Papolos, D., & Papolos, J. (2006). *The bipolar child: The definitive and reassuring guide to childhood's most misunderstood disorder.* New York: Broadway Books.

Perry, B. D. (2001). The neurodevelopmental impact of violence in childhood. In D. Schetky & E. P. Benedek (Eds.), *Textbook of child and adolescent forensic psychiatry* (pp. 221–238). Washington, DC: American Psychiatric Press.

Peterson, B. S. (2005). Clinical neuroscience and imaging studies of core psychoanalytic constructs. *Clinical Neuroscience Research, 4*(5–6), 349–365. http://dx.doi.org/10.1016/j.cnr.2005.03.011

Premack, D., & Woodruff, G. (1978). Does the chimpanzee have a theory of mind? *The Behavioral and Brain Sciences, 1*(4), 515–526. https://doi.org/10.1017/S0140525X00076512

Raichle, M. E., MacLeod, A. M., Snyder, A. Z., Powers, W. J., Gusnard, D. A., & Shulman, G. L. (2001). A default mode of brain function. *Proceedings of the National Academy of Sciences, 98*(2), 676–682. doi:10.1073/pnas.98.2.676

Ramachandran, V. S., & Blakeslee, S. (1999). *Phantoms in the brain: Probing the mysteries of the human mind.* New York: William Morrow Paperbacks.

Rappaport, L. (Ed.). (2013). *Mindfulness and the arts therapies: Theory and practice.* London: Jessica Kingsley Publishers.

Ratey, J. J., & Johnson, C. (1997). *Shadow syndromes: The mild forms of major mental disorders that sabotage us.* New York: Bantam Books.

Richard, D. A., More, W., & Joy, S. P. (2015). Recognizing emotions: Testing an intervention for children with autism spectrum disorders. *Art Therapy: Journal of the American Art Therapy Association, 32*(1), 13–19. http://dx.doi.org/10.1080/07421656.2014.994163

Richards, M. C. (1964). *Centering in pottery, poetry, and the person.* Middletown, CT: Wesleyan University Press.

Riggott, J. (2005). Pseudoscience in autism treatment: Are the news and entertainment media helping or hurting? *Scientific Review of Mental Health, 4*(1), 55–58.

Robertson, S. M. (1963). *Rosegarden and labyrinth: A study in art education.* New York: Routledge.

Rogers, C. R. (1951). *Client-centered therapy: Its current practice, implications, and theory.* London: Constable.

Rogers, S. J., & Dawson, G. (2009). *Early Start Denver Model for young children with autism: Promoting language, learning, and engagement.* New York: The Guilford Press.

Romer, D. (2010). Adolescent risk taking, impulsivity, and brain development: Implications for prevention. *Developmental Psychobiology, 52*(3), 263–276. doi:10.1002/dev.20442

Rosen, L. D. (2012). *iDisorder: Understanding our obsession with technology and overcoming its hold on us.* New York: St. Martin's Press.

Rubin, J. A. (1978). *Child art therapy.* (2nd ed.). New York: Van Nostrand Press.

Rutter, M., Kreppner, J., Croft, C., Murin, M., Colvert, E., Beckett, C., Castle, J., & Sonuga-Barke, E. (2007). Early adolescent outcomes of institutionally deprived and non-deprived adoptees. *Journal of Child Psychology and Psychiatry, 48*(12), 1200–1207. doi:10.1111/j.1469-7610.2007.01792.x

Sacks, O. (1995). *An anthropologist on Mars: Seven paradoxical tales.* New York: Vintage Books.

Sacks, O. (2012). *Hallucinations.* New York: Alfred A. Knopf.

Safran, D. (2002). *Art therapy and ADHD: Diagnostic and therapeutic approaches.* London: Jessica Kingsley.

Sales, N. J. (2016). *American girls: Social media and the secret lives of teenagers.* New York: Alfred A. Knopf.

Samuel, P. (aka Donna Williams). (2016). About me. Retrieved November 15, 2016, from http://www.donnawilliams.net/about.0.html

Schore, J. R., & Schore, A. N. (2008). Modern attachment theory: The central role of affect regulation in development and treatment. *Clinical Social Work Journal, 36*(1), 9–20.

Schwartz, C. (2016). Generation Adderall. *New York Times Magazine*, October 12. Retrieved from www.nytimes.com/2016/10/16/magazine/generation-adderall-addiction.html

Selfe, L. (1977). *Nadia: A case of extraordinary drawing ability in an autistic child.* London: Academic Press.

Selfe, L. (2011). *Nadia revisited: A longitudinal study of an autistic savant.* New York: Psychology Press.

Silberman, S. (2015). *NeuroTribes: The legacy of autism and the future of neurodiversity.* New York: Penguin Random House.

Simmons, R. (2002, 2011). *Odd girl out: The hidden culture of aggression in girls.* New York: Houghton Mifflin Harcourt.

Simon, G. (2008). Understanding 'splitting' as a psychological term. Retrived from http://counsellingresource.com/features/2008/10/28/splitting-as-psychological-term/

Smokowski, F. (1993). *Drawing, a language of connection: Therapy through drawing with an autistic adolescent.* (Unpublished master's thesis). School of the Art Institute of Chicago, Chicago, IL.

Snyder, C. R. (2002). Hope theory: Rainbows in the mind. *Psychological Inquiry, 13*(4), 249–275.

Solms, M., & Panksepp, J. (2012). The 'id' knows more than the 'ego' admits: Neuropsychoanalytic and primal consciousness perspectives on the interface between affective and cognitive neuroscience. *Brain Science, 2*(2), 147–175.

Spitz, R. A. (1961). Some early prototypes of ego defenses. *Journal of the American Psychoanalytic Association, 9*(4), 626–651.

Spitz, R. A., & Cobliner, W. G. (1966). *The first year of life: A psychoanalytic study of normal and deviant development of object relations.* New York: International Universities Press.

Tinbergen, N., & Tinbergen, E. A. (1983). *Autistic children: New hope for a cure.* London: Allen and Unwin.

Truffaut, F. (1970). *The wild child.* [Motion picture]. France: United Artists.

Uhlin, D., & de Chiara, E. (1984). *Art for exceptional children (trends in art education).* New York: William C. Brown.

Varnedoe, K. (1990). *High and low: Modern art and popular culture.* New York: Museum of Modern Art.

Watts, A. (1961). *Psychotherapy: East and west.* New York: Pantheon Books.

White, R. (1993). Technological and social dimensions of 'Aurignacian-age' body ornaments across Europe. In H. Knecht, A. Pike-Tay, & R. White (Eds.), *Before Lascaux: The complex record of the early Upper Paleolithic* (pp. 277–299). Boca Raton, FL: CRC Press.

Williams, D. (1992). *Nobody nowhere: The remarkable autobiography of an autistic girl.* London: Jessica Kingsley Publishers.

Wing, L. (1964). *Autistic children: A guide for parents.* London: Constable.

Wing, L. (1988). The continuum of autistic characteristics. In E. Schopler & G. B. Mesibov (Eds.), *Diagnosis and assessment in autism* (pp. 91–110). New York: Springer.

Winnicott, D. (1965). *The maturational processes and the facilitating environment.* New York: International Universities Press.

Winnicott, D. W. (1971). *Playing and reality.* London: Tavistock.

Wiseman, F. (Producer & Director). (1967). *Titicut follies* [Motion picture]. United States: Zipporah Films, Inc.

Wordsworth, W. (1901). My heart leaps up. In A. Quiller-Couch (Ed.), *The Oxford Book of English Verse, 1250-1900.* New York: Bartleby Press.

Index